One of the   to
determine a   ric
people think   ....ge is to develop the
theory, methodology and tools to understand human
cognition. Cognitive archaeology as a subject is still in its
infancy, and archaeologists are adopting a variety of
approaches. One direction has been to develop an 'interpretationist', anti-scientific, literary approach. Another has been
to use a linguistic framework and develop a hermeneutic,
semiotic approach. A third approach develops a new
direction in prehistoric cognitive research which is rooted in
the scientific tradition and in an empirical methodology. It
draws upon the cognitive, the mathematical and the
computer sciences in an attempt to understand what techniques can be used appropriately on archaeological data, and
how to implement them efficiently. This is the approach
adopted by the contributors of *The ancient mind*. Together,
they begin to develop a science of cognitive archaeology.

The ancient mind

NEW DIRECTIONS IN ARCHAEOLOGY

The ancient mind

Elements of cognitive archaeology

Edited by
COLIN RENFREW
and
EZRA B. W. ZUBROW

CAMBRIDGE
UNIVERSITY PRESS

Published by the Press Syndicate of the University of Cambridge
The Pitt Building, Trumpington Street, Cambridge CB2 1RP
40 West 20th Street, New York, NY 10011–4211, USA
10 Stamford Road, Oakleigh, Melbourne 3166, Australia

First published 1994

Printed in Great Britain at the University Press, Cambridge

*A catalogue record for this book is available from the British
Library*

Library of Congress cataloguing in publication data

The ancient mind: elements of cognitive archaeology /
edited by Colin Renfrew and Ezra B. W. Zubrow.
     p.   cm. – (New directions in archaeology)
Includes index.
ISBN 0 521 43488 2
1. Archaeology. 2. Cognition and culture. I. Renfrew, Colin,
1937– . II. Zubrow, Ezra B. W. III. Series.
CC175.A53 1994
930.1'01–dc20   93–25033   CIP

ISBN 0 521 43488 2 hardback
ISBN 0 521 45620 7 paperback

Contents

Figures

Tables

Contributors

JAMES A. BELL
Department of Philosophy
University of South Florida

RICHARD BRADLEY
Department of Archaeology
University of Reading

KENT V. FLANNERY
Museum of Anthropology
University of Michigan

CHARLES O. FRAKE
Department of Anthropology
State University of New York at Buffalo

JAMES N. HILL
Department of Anthropology
University of California at Los Angeles

M. JULIEN
Laboratoire d'Ethnologie Préhistorique
Université de Paris I

JOHN S. JUSTESON
Department of Anthropology
State University of New York, Albany

C. KARLIN
Laboratoire d'Ethnologie Préhistorique
Université de Paris I

S. E. VAN DER LEEUW
Department of Archaeology
University of Cambridge

JOYCE MARCUS
Museum of Anthropology
University of Michigan

STEVEN MITHEN
Department of Archaeology
University of Reading

J. N. POSTGATE
Faculty of Oriental Studies
University of Cambridge

COLIN RENFREW
Department of Archaeology
University of Cambridge

CHRIS SCARRE
McDonald Institute for Archaeological Research
University of Cambridge

NATHAN SCHLANGER
Department of Archaeology
University of Cambridge

ALAIN SCHNAPP
UFR d'Histoire de l'Art et Archéologie
Université de Paris I

ERWIN M. SEGAL
Department of Psychology
State University of New York at Buffalo

LAURENCE D. STEPHENS
Department of Classics
University of North Carolina

EZRA B. W. ZUBROW
Department of Anthropology
State University of New York at Buffalo

Preface

One of the most taxing problems in archaeology is to determine about what and in what manner did prehistoric people think. Is it possible to make the 'mute stones speak', and will they tell us how (if not what) our predecessors were thinking? A fundamental challenge in archaeology is to develop the theory, methodology and tools to understand prehistoric cognition. It appears that as processual archaeology revolutionized archaeology in the 1960s and 1970s, cognitive archaeology will revolutionize the 1990s and even the early part of the twenty-first century. Cognitive science is still in its childhood and cognitive archaeology is in its infancy. One direction (already followed by some) has been to develop an 'interpretationist', anti-scientific literary approach. This view, allied to the relativist philosophy of 'post-modernism', has been associated with Hodder, Shanks and Tilley, and Leone. A second, recent approach has been to use a linguistic framework and develop a hermeneutic, semiotic approach. This direction has been espoused by Gardin and Peebles.

However, some workers have sought a rather different direction in prehistoric cognitive research. It is rooted in the scientific tradition and in an empirical methodology. This scientific view of the ancient mind seeks to draw upon the cognitive, and the mathematical and computer sciences. These researchers are beginning to understand which techniques may appropriately be used on archaeological data and how to implement them efficiently. *The ancient mind* is a collection of chapters written in this spirit which seeks to make effective use of cognition in prehistoric research. Together, they begin to lay some of the foundations for a science of cognitive archaeology.

The book is the product of a conference, generously sponsored by the McDonald Institute for Archaeological Research, which was held at Lucy Cavendish College, Cambridge in April 1990. An attempt was made to delineate:

(1) what are the trends in artificial intelligence, cognitive psychology and cognitive anthropology that are applicable to cognitive archaeology;
(2) what is the present level of theory in cognitive archaeology;
(3) what tools and scientific methodology are necessary for cognitive archaeology;
(4) what problems are amenable to solutions given the present state of cognitive archaeology;
(5) how do different scholars in different cognitive fields examine archaeological data in order to make cognitive inferences.

The book is divided into seven sections. To introduce the book Renfrew examines the general issues of cognitive archaeology and outlines some of the philosophical, archaeological and scientific background for this new direction.

In the section entitled 'The interdisciplinary underpinning', Bell examines philosophical issues, Segal the relevance of the cognitive sciences, and Mithen considers some basic issues in the emergence of the cognitive abilities of *Homo sapiens*. Schnapp uses written as well as material evidence to illuminate a specific question: the place of image making in ancient Greek society and religion.

In four chapters concerning 'Approaches to cult practice and transcendental belief systems', some new directions are indicated towards the elucidation of the ideologies of prehistoric communities. Renfrew considers the role of religion in early societies and the manner in which cult practice may be identified. Flannery and Marcus show how ceremonial space can be determined and how it changes over time in the New World. Scarre and Hill provide examples of value in the symbolic dimensions of death and burials in the Old and New Worlds respectively.

The section entitled 'Prehistoric conceptions of space and time' offers three papers. Bradley investigates how prehistoric inhabitants of Britain perceived boundaries and used symbolic means to demarcate space. Zubrow determined what are some of the prehistorically determined definitions of a village distribution in parts of the New World. He uses the concepts of knowledge representation and 'figure and ground' in conjunction with a testing methodology based upon Geographical Information Systems. Frake explores the relationship between space and time and its material representation in early historic populations.

The next two sections of the book, 'The material basis of cognitive inference: technology' and 'The material basis of cognitive inference: writing systems', are closely related. In the former, the two major areas of prehistoric technology are explored. Van der Leeuw examines prehistoric decision making in pottery production, while the cognitive aspects of stone technology, drawing upon the useful concept of the 'chaîne opératoire', are discussed in two papers by Schlanger and by Karlin and Julien. Similarly, concrete cognitive aspects of writing systems from the Old World are analysed in papers by Justeson and Stephens and by Postgate. In conclusion Zubrow re-examines cognitive archaeology, placing the entire subject in a broader context for the profession, as well as delineating some areas of future research.

In organizing the seminar which gave rise to this volume we owe much to the energetic administration of Dr Chris Scarre. The very substantial task of putting into publishable form the papers subsequently submitted has been undertaken by Dr Christine Morris, to whom we are most grateful. Our thanks also to Dr Jessica Kuper at Cambridge University Press for her encouragement and support.

PART I

Introduction

1
Towards a cognitive archaeology

COLIN RENFREW

Cognitive archaeology – the study of past ways of thought as inferred from material remains – still presents so many challenges to the practitioner that it seems if not a novel, at any rate, an uncertain endeavour. That this should be so is perhaps rather odd, for generations of archaeologists have written with considerable freedom about the thoughts and beliefs of ancient peoples, about the religions of early civilizations and about the art of prehistoric communities. With the New Archaeology of the 1960s and 1970s, however, came an acute awareness that much earlier work was in some respects not well founded, or at least that the frameworks of inference by which statements were made about past symbolic systems were rarely made explicit and were frequently defective.

This realization about the potential scope of the discipline, within the context of the optimism of processual archaeology (as the New Archaeology came to be called), should ideally have led to an upsurge of well-argued papers dealing with various aspects of what we have, in the title of this volume, termed 'The ancient mind'. But despite that early optimism, that was not the outcome, and the preoccupations of processual archaeologists were very rarely, in the early days, with human reasoning, or with symbolic structures, but rather with the more immediately material aspects of life. Culture was often defined, following Leslie White and Lewis Binford, as 'man's extra-somatic means of adaptation'. Arguing from a standpoint which has subsequently, and not unreasonably, been characterized as 'functionalist', workers often placed more emphasis on economic aspects and sometimes social aspects of the past, and tended to ignore the belief systems and indeed often the communication systems of early societies. These were the days of what may be termed functional-processual archaeology,

with an emphasis upon productive efficiency considered against a background of Darwinian selection.

During the 1980s the scientific aspirations of processual archaeology came under attack. The first critics were philosophers of science who noted that the philosophy of science (if not necessarily science itself) had moved on from what was regarded as the positivism of the 1950s into a 'post-positivist' era, and who clearly felt that processual archaeology should do the same. Hard upon their heels, and drawing encouragement from these critiques of scientific method, came workers who first termed themselves 'structuralist' archaeologists, and more recently 'post-processual' archaeologists. Proclaiming the death, or at least the imminent demise, of processual archaeology, these workers advocated an interpretive or hermeneutic approach. Their thinking was influenced by the advocates of Critical Theory in literary studies and in history, and by the so-called 'post-modern' approach (adopting a term first applied in the field of architecture and then very much more widely; see Bintliff 1991). But although the polemic was vociferous, more meta-archaeology has emerged from these debates than effective applied archaeology, and the advocates of 'post-processual' archaeology have still rather few case studies to their name.

The conference from which the present work emerged was held in the belief that reports of the death of processual archaeology have been much exaggerated. Indeed, workers in the processual tradition, including several represented here, are increasingly focusing upon symbolic and cognitive issues, and in doing so are seeking to develop frameworks of inference to take the place of (or in some cases to sustain) the sometimes rather intuitive and hasty conclusions of four or five decades ago. From this perspective it may be permissible to claim that processual archaeology, far from expiring, has entered a new phase which one might term 'cognitive-processual' archaeology (Renfrew and Bahn 1991: 431–4), acknowledging by that term both the principal field of study and the intention of working within a tradition which is broadly scientific, like that of the functional-processual archaeology of twenty years ago, although no longer so readily open to dismissal as mainly positivist in its philosophical stance.

For these reasons we would vigorously rebut what we regard as the somewhat arrogant self-denomination of the so-called 'post-processualist' archaeologists. The adverbial prefix 'post-' displays a modish preoccupation with current intellectual fashions. Yet it is hardly appropriate for the hermeneutic and interpretive exponents of this recent trend of thought themselves to offer adjudication as to whether or not it has entirely displaced the well-established scientific aspirations of the processual school. In reality, these are not 'post-processual' archaeologists but 'anti-processual' archaeologists, who advocate an idealist and indeed a relativist standpoint which has much in common with the thinking of the historiographic writers of the 1930s and subsequently (Trigger 1978), from Croce to Collingwood and beyond. They are, of course, perfectly entitled to return to those patterns of thought which the early processual archaeologists criticized, and they certainly do so with the much greater critical self-awareness which the 'loss of innocence' (Clarke 1973) of the New Archaeology encouraged. And certainly they do so armed with refreshing and often provocative insights from the critical theorists and the deconstructionists who have been so influential in other fields. But they are once again joining in what is in some respects little more than a re-run of an old debate between conflicting schools of philosophy, or at least between philosophical outlooks, where they situate themselves alongside Hegel and Croce, Collingwood and Lévi-Strauss, Geertz and Ricoeur and those idealists whose primary business is the understanding of 'meaning' located within the minds of specifically identifiable historical personages, and for whom historical explanations are to be found in the intentions of individual (or even sometimes collective) actors – to know (to choose an example favoured by Collingwood) why Caesar crossed the Rubicon.

On the other side of this philosophical divide are those thinkers who, with Darwin and Marx, or with Popper and Gellner, or in the archaeological field with Binford and Clarke, are concerned to situate human individuals and societies within the material world. In this way they avoid the rigid division between nature and history, so firmly asserted by the idealist, and to use the principles of scientific enquiry to explain, and hence understand, the behaviours of human beings and human societies. That there should be such a divide is perhaps to be regretted, and one of the purposes of the present work is to help to bridge the chasm, at least within our own field. But it should be clearly understood that those who assert this dichotomy, by proclaiming themselves to be 'post-processual', must take some share of the responsibility for its continuing existence. For this reason, while we acknowledge the validity of some of the insights of the anti-processual school in archaeology, and while we value the role that some of these may play in developing an effective cognitive-processual archaeology, we are sceptical of the utility of the proclamation that a new 'school' of thought is born, especially when it defines itself essentially by asserting its identity through opposition or contradistinction to an existing and productive tradition of thought and work. Even Hegel favoured synthesis above antithesis.

It is not the purpose here systematically to refute the claims of the anti-processual tendency in archaeology (e.g.

Hodder 1986; Shanks and Tilley 1987a, 1987b). Indeed there is little doubt that it contains many insights which, when winnowed out from the accompanying polemic, will prove not only productive but deeply instructive in developing our discipline. The observation may be sufficient that the dichotomy between processual and anti-processual is not in itself helpful, and that the 'debate' upon this polarity, for instance between Hodder and Binford (Hodder 1982; Binford 1987, 1988) has served to obfuscate as much as to clarify. That the early functional-processual archaeology (Binford and Binford 1968; Clarke 1968) did not lead rapidly to many innovative explorations in the cognitive field can hardly be denied. This may have been due in large part to Binford's own robustly materialist position, where any consideration of ideas in the minds of the ancient actors who formed the archaeological record tended to be dismissed as 'palaeopsychology'. It has for some time seemed an irony that the initial claim that the New Archaeology need not be fettered by the restrictive assumptions of the old, culture-historical tradition, in reality led to so little concrete progress in the cognitive or symbolic field, and this despite Binford's own early definition (Binford 1962, 1964) of the ideotechnic dimension or subsystem in culture alongside the sociotechnic and the technomic ones. The charge here against the more vigorous exponents of anti-processual archaeology is not that the issues they raise are inappropriate or unimportant, nor that some of their insights are unfruitful, but that their polemic is confused and ultimately unhelpful. In rejecting the scientific traditions of processual archaeology they are throwing out the realist baby with the positivist bathwater. Here we are instead concerned further to develop an approach, a cognitive-processual approach, which will, so far as is possible, use the existing methods of archaeological enquiry to investigate the early use of symbols and the development of cognitive processes.

Our understanding of what is appropriately meant or entailed by the methods of scientific enquiry is itself continually evolving, as developments in the philosophy of science clearly reflect (Wylie 1982). It is, perhaps, an irony that some of the most promising attempts at applying the philosophy of science towards the understanding of archaeological method (e.g. Watson, LeBlanc and Redman 1971; Salmon 1982) have been so deeply flawed or in some cases so superficial in their understanding of the nature and ways of archaeology itself that they have, in my opinion, confused more than they have clarified. I have, for some time, held the view (Renfrew 1982a) that for valid insights into the theoretical positions of archaeologists we would do better to look at their working papers, that is to say to the application of their thinking to specific cases, than to their more programmatic statements or to their attempts to write philosophy. With few exceptions the archaeologist's knowledge of archaeology is only marginally more extensive than the knowledge of archaeology among those philosophers who seek to write in our field. For that reason the chapters in this volume avoid, so far as possible, grandiose or polemical statements on the current state of archaeological thought. They focus instead on the urgent task of developing ways of forming structures of inference, in an explicit (and in some sense scientific) manner which will allow us to understand better how people used their minds, and formulated and utilized useful concepts, in early societies. That is the task of cognitive-processual archaeology. The validity of the initiative, or of the philosophical/methodological positions adopted, will not be judged by *a priori* epistemological arguments, but by what can be discovered, constructed, reconstructed or otherwise informatively asserted about the past.

The scope of cognitive archaeology: the 'ancient mind'

The term 'ancient mind' is shorthand, perhaps rather misleading shorthand, for the subject matter of cognitive archaeology. It is not meant to imply that there is necessarily something inherently different between the thought processes of yesterday and those of today. No distinction is implied between the ancient mind and the modern mind. It is important at once to assert that no *a priori* argument is entertained about some notional series of evolutionary stages in human cognition, and no such assumption is made here. In the same way we are uneasy about the title of Lévi-Strauss's work *The savage mind* (Lévi-Strauss 1966) – *La pensée sauvage* in the original French. We make no assumptions about different kinds or categories of thought.

In saying this, however, one cannot escape two problems, both of which lie below the surface when one uses a vague, all-encompassing term like 'the ancient mind' to indicate an area of interest. The first and most obvious is the whole question of the evolution of cognitive abilities from earlier life forms and through the fossil apes to *Australopithecus*, *Homo habilis*, *Homo erectus* and *Homo sapiens*. Even if we make the assumption that there is little physical difference between ourselves and our sapient ancestors of 40,000 years ago, we cannot escape the obligation of considering the minds of those more remote, pre-sapiens ancestors. It may be assumed that their thinking was, in many ways, different from our own. The preserved material culture may offer us some way of considering this issue, offering, for instance, opportunities for considering the reasoning and planning abilities involved in the production of stone tools. The recent work by Merlin Donald (1991), *Origins of the modern mind*, opens a number of useful avenues of speculation, as indeed

does Peter Wilson's (1983) *Man, the promising primate*. The task for the cognitive archaeologist is to devise methods of study and frameworks of inference which will, in practice, allow the archaeological evidence to be used to make contributions to the discussion which go beyond more general speculation.

If the first problem relates to the evolution of cognitive abilities and cognitive processes leading to the emergence of *Homo sapiens*, the second is the extent to which we may speak about 'pre-modern' forms of thought operating in our own species, in earlier societies. Henri Frankfort, in his stimulating work *Before philosophy* (Frankfort *et al.* 1949) emphasized the role of what he termed 'mythic thought' in many early societies. Whether or not this is an entirely appropriate notion of a mode of thought to contrast with our own, it cannot be excluded that concepts and modes of thought may have been employed in earlier times which may not feature prominently in the processes of thought and argumentation of modern societies. Even if we dislike the generalizations implied in the term 'the savage mind', this possibility cannot be overlooked. So that while, with our use of the term 'the ancient mind' in our title, we are not asserting any specific and fundamental distinctions between ancient and modern minds, nor are we denying that there might be useful distinctions to be drawn. The term is used for its convenient concision, and not for any supposed associations which it may carry with it.

The approach followed here, however, is not to set out different cognitive categories in some *a priori* way, to posit special 'ancient' or 'pre-modern' modes of thought, but to seek to study the way in which cognitive processes operated in specific contexts, and to investigate the interrelationship between those processes and the social contexts which harboured and promoted them. It will perhaps be appropriate, before considering further the nature of the insights which may be available, to look more specifically and concretely at the various fields of study which at once present themselves for consideration.

The scope of cognitive archaeology could be outlined in several ways (see Renfrew and Bahn 1991: 339–70). Perhaps the most concise approach is to focus explicitly upon the specially human ability to construct and use symbols. A symbol is something which stands for or represents something else: 'a visible sign of an idea or quality or of another object' (*Webster's Collegiate Dictionary* 1925: 974 'symbol'). The word derives from the Greek 'to place together', and the notion of juxtaposition (of X against Y), of representation (of X by Y) and of metaphor (where X is equated with Y) are closely related. Leslie White (1949: 11) defined humanity in terms of 'the use of symbols . . . All human behaviour is symbolic behaviour: symbolic behaviour is human behaviour. The symbol is the universe of humanity.' Similarly Ernst Cassirer (1944: 26) suggested that the human individual should be defined as an *animal symbolicum*.

> Man has, as it were, discovered a new method of adapting himself to his environment. Between the receptor system and the effector system, which are to be found in all animal species, we find in man a third link which we may describe as the *symbolic system*. This new acquisition transforms the whole of human life. As compared with the other animals man lives not merely in a broader reality: he lives, so to speak, in a new *dimension* of reality. (Cassirer 1944: 24)

An important component of the cognitive-processual approach is to set out to examine the ways in which symbols were used. This may be contrasted with the attempt to seek rather to ascertain their 'meaning', which would generally be the object of the anti-processual or interpretive approach. The distinction is an important one. As we shall see, both approaches must inevitably rely upon the insights and intuitions of the modern investigator. The creative, and in that sense perhaps subjective aspects of scientific inquiry are not in doubt and it is a common misconception of the scientific method deriving largely from the polemic of Bourdieu, that it is, in its inspiration, inhuman, mechanistic or lacking in creativity. But for the cognitive-processual archaeologist, it is enough to gain insights into *how* the minds of the ancient communities in question worked and into the manner in which that working shaped their actions. For the interpretive archaeologist, working in the grand tradition of idealists like Collingwood, this is not enough. One seeks, instead, to 'enter the mind' of the early individuals involved through some effort of active empathy. This total experience of 'being' that other, long-dead person, or at least undergoing an experience to be compared with theirs, is what characterizes the subjective, idealist and interpretationist approach of the anti-processual and 'post-modern' archaeologist. The cognitive-processual archaeologist is sceptical of the validity of this empathetic experience, and sceptical too of the privileged status which must inevitably be claimed by the idealist who is advancing an interpretation on the basis of this intuitive, 'I-was-there' experience. As in the conduct of all scientific inquiry, it is not the source of the insight which validates the claim, but the explicit nature of the reasoning which sustains it and the means by which the available data can be brought into relationship with it. As Popper long ago emphasized, validation rests not upon authority but on testability and on the explicitness of the argumentation – even if testing is not always, in practice, an easy undertaking.

When we come to consider in more detail the ways in which symbols have been used, we can, perhaps, think in terms of a series of categories of human behaviour. Symbols are used to cope with several aspects of existence:

(1) design, in the sense of coherently structured, purposive behaviour;
(2) planning, involving time scheduling and sometimes the production of a schema prior to carrying out the planned work;
(3) measurement, involving devices for measuring, and units of measure;
(4) social relations, with the use of symbols to structure and regulate inter-personal behaviour;
(5) the supernatural, with the use of symbols to communicate with the other world, and to mediate between the human and the world beyond;
(6) representation, with the production and use of depictions or other iconic embodiments of reality.

No doubt one may define other ways in which symbols are used to structure human life and human affairs, but these certainly cover some of the main headings.

The distinction between planning and design is not always a clear one, since so much human behaviour involves both. For instance, the temple-builders of Malta in the third millennium BC produced small models in limestone of the structures which they had built or were to build (Fig. 1.1). It is difficult now to know whether the model preceded or succeeded the construction of the building itself. But if the former were the case, this is a good example of both planning and design.

In some cases, however, it is useful to emphasize the distinction between the two. For instance, in the production of stone tools (Gowlett 1984; Davidson and Noble 1989; Wynn 1991), it has often been found necessary to acquire the raw material from some suitable source located at a considerable distance from the locations where the tool is to be used. There is no doubt that the use of the material in some cases entails a deliberate journey undertaken at least in part to secure its acquisition. That implies planning. Trade and exchange in later times likewise entail planning, in the sense of time-structuring, of a more complex kind.

The cognitive issues involved in tool production are of a related kind, subsumed under the term 'design'. The assumption is a long standing one (see Clarke 1968: fig. 39) that the production of most artefacts, for instance of such stone tools as Acheulean handaxes, involves the use of a mental template, which serves to guide the craftsperson producing the artefact. But the production of an artefact type need not depend upon any sophisticated conceptualizing, nor need it pre-assume the use of language (Bloch 1991). Yet unless the production process is an instinctive one which is genetically determined (as it may be in the case of termite hills or the nest of bower birds), then the term design is appropriate.

Measurement has a special place in the development of cognitive archaeology for several reasons. The most obvious is that measurement requires actions in the material world in which artefacts of a special type are often involved: weights, measuring rods, vessels of specified capacity and so on. Moreover the measurement of time involved many repeated, sequential actions. These, when recorded, often display periodicities related to those of the sun and moon, notably the number of days in the lunar month and solar year. These activities are of particular interest to the archaeologist since the artefacts themselves often survive and are available for study. One good example is the major series of palaeolithic bone and ivory objects with incised notations which have been so informatively studied by Alexander Marshack (Marshack 1991). Another is the series of stone cubes from the Indus valley civilization which may plausibly be identified as weights, and from which other aspects of

Harappan measuring practices and quantitative thought may be inferred (Renfrew 1982b: 17).

Symbols are used in various ways to structure inter-personal behaviour. One of the most pervasive in the modern era is money. Of course in earlier times the use of money might involve measurement, when cumulative value was ascribed by number (for instance in the case of cowrie shells) or by weight (where quantities of gold coins might be involved). But most coinages have a token aspect. The value of the coin is symbolic in two senses. First the very notion of 'intrinsic value' for a precious metal is conventional and symbolic (see Renfrew 1986: 160). But secondly the coin, or in the modern world the banknote, is itself a symbolic entity which makes, or implies, reference to goods in the real world. Today, when money is transferred from financial centre to financial centre by electronic means, the symbolic nature of the transaction is even more clearly apparent.

Another field of considerable interest, within the whole area of the symbolic structuring of human relations, is the representation of rank by symbolic means (nor should it be

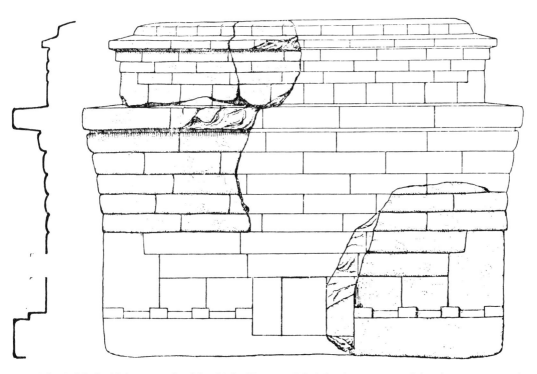

Fig. 1.1. Model of a Maltese temple of the third millennium BC. It has been suggested that these representations served as architects' models, for use in design and planning, as blueprints are today. Height 31.6 cm (after J. D. Evans, 1959. Malta. London, Thames and Hudson, Fig. 19).

noted that this is inseparable from the actual creation and establishing of social ranking) (Fig. 1.2).

To attempt to subdivide, in this manner, the different ways in which symbols are used may well be a somewhat artificial exercise. But it at least offers some glimpse into the scope of cognitive archaeology. And it shows how many of the aspects to be investigated are certainly not out of the reach of systematic research. The functioning of material symbols at a superficial level is often plain enough, although to analyse, more completely, precisely how they functioned can be more difficult.

In the same way, the use of symbols in relation to the supernatural is often perfectly clear. It is the more complete analysis of their functioning which can be difficult. No-one who has seen the pyramids, near Cairo, could doubt that the

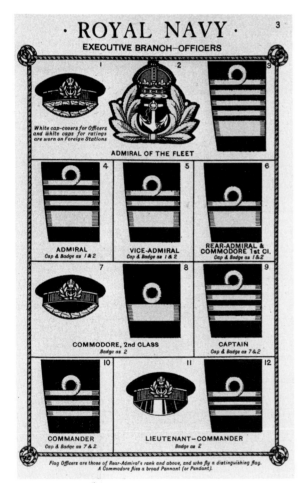

Fig. 1.2. Ranking expressed symbolically: the use of insignia in the Royal Navy.

pyramidal form had a special place in the Egyptian belief system. But to establish the different ways in which this symbol functioned is a much more complex undertaking.

The definition of the supernatural is not an easy matter, and the recognition of human activities directed towards the supernatural presents difficulties. Human play, for instance, particularly in its more elaborate and ambitious forms, often uses artefacts in a manner which, in a different context and with a more serious purpose, could be confused with religious ritual. Perhaps the earliest documented interactions with the supernatural arise in the context of burial, already in the Upper Palaeolithic period (Mellars 1991). The well-documented treatment of the body with red ochre, in a number of cases, is certainly noteworthy, as are other aspects of formalized behaviour associated with burial.

Now of course, in a formal sense, the evidence before one in the case of burial may be considered as relating to 'the disposal of the dead' rather than the supernatural. But very frequently the dead are accorded more attention than other categories of organic refuse, and in some cases it is reasonable to suggest, as a working hypothesis, that the living contemporaries of the deceased were acting in a manner consistent with a belief in an after-life for him or her. The activities constituting the ritual would, in that case, have a number of symbolic functions difficult for us to determine today, but the operation of the complex ritual as a whole may in part be understood.

The final symbolic category to be mentioned here, representation, comes very close to the literal meaning of the term 'symbol', as defined above. Of course not all symbols are visible or material – spoken words may reasonably be regarded as symbols – but no-one could doubt that all representations are symbols. The term 'depiction' is perhaps more tightly focused, with the implication that the representation is indeed a visual one, which in some senses resembles or looks like the thing depicted. Now it may be that several species of animals employ mimetic behaviour, where the behaviour of one individual looks like that of another to the extent that the human observer concludes that it does so deliberately. And of course mimesis occurs in nature through the agency of natural selection, where harmless species of insects take on the colouring of more dangerous species and in so doing lessen the danger of predation by birds. But it can be argued that only the human species creates shapes which look like other things (depiction) and which have a role or purpose other than that of being confused with, or taken for, the original form. The camouflage behaviour of insects is one thing, but to produce a representation of the human form, for instance, whether in two dimensions or in three, at a different scale from the original, is quite another. To my mind we have not yet sufficiently considered the momentous nature of the step taken when clay was first modelled, for instance, to produce a small representation of the human form, or when a sharp implement was first used to carve the outline of an animal on a piece of bone. The creation and subsequent preservation of representations, in this sense, offers us great potential for considering a number of important cognitive steps, from the first application of pigment in some ice age cave to the great fresco cycles of the Italian Renaissance.

I have the feeling, too, that the whole process of tool production, briefly discussed earlier, can productively be subjected to much more careful examination. The notion of the *chaîne opératoire* is a helpful one, and there must be other conceptual devices which we can employ to scrutinize, more closely, the cognitive steps implicit in the production of so complex an artefact as a handaxe.

These are some of the fields of investigation contained within the broader rubric of cognitive archaeology. It is the argument here that while their consideration cannot and should not seek to avoid the concepts of 'meaning' and 'interpretation' in the subjective and relativist sense in which they are used by the anti-processualists, it is more productive to seek, as far as possible, to use the well-established techniques of rational scientific inquiry, and to aim to develop these, where appropriate, by explicit theoretical formulations.

Towards a cognitive-processual archaeology

It has been suggested above that the early New Archaeology was, in general, optimistic about the potentialities of developing valid and explicit frameworks of inference for the whole range of human activities, including the technical, the economic, the social and the ideological (Binford 1962, 1964). Early studies favoured the first two of these, however, and explicit consideration of the cognitive aspects were sometimes avoided as bordering upon 'palaeopsychology' (see Binford 1987). In this way the preoccupations of the early years of processual archaeology were primarily with subsistence, with the human adaptation to the natural environment, and to some extent with economic factors. It is for that reason that this may be characterized as a functional-processual emphasis.

The essentially materialist preoccupations of this new functional-processual tendency led to reactions, notably on the European side of the Atlantic. Hodder, in a number of interesting papers, stressed the active role of material culture in shaping the social world in which we live, and along with a number of philosophers of science (see Wylie 1982), was critical of what was seen as the 'positivist' cast of the theoretical stance of the early New Archaeologists.

These observations, to my mind well-justified, were accompanied, however, by a reaction against science of any kind (see Earle and Preucel 1987).

Following the arguments of some of the more vociferous neo-Marxist thinkers, science was seen as a powerful instrument of domination, and those advocating a broadly scientific approach to archaeology (or indeed to anything else) were seen as the agents of imperialist hegemony (Miller and Tilley 1984). There was also a tendency, not restricted to avowed neo-Marxists, to see all intellectual developments as a predictable product of the contemporary *Zeitgeist* (Trigger 1981). The shadow of the atom bomb, of economic prosperity, or (in the light of subsequent events) of some alleged *crise de confiance* in the capitalist world system, were seen to have had a significant and (in retrospect) predictable impact upon the development of our subject. But while each of us is no doubt in some sense the product of our time, and while none of us can avoid the economic, social and ideological context in which we work, I have to say that I find most comments of this kind that have hitherto been formulated in relation to the post-war development of archaeology to be decidedly facile. They are facile, above all, because the climate of opinion, the contemporary actuality, the *Zeitgeist* has, for any given span of years, been delineated by these writers with a sloppiness and an absence of critical self-awareness which, on examination, I find remarkable. It is one of the implications of the work of these writers that to characterize any past period and culture in a few convenient words, in terms of a couple of rather ill-defined concepts, is irresponsible in the extreme. Yet this is precisely their own approach towards the characterization of the present and to their own 'contextual analysis' of the theoretical developments in our subject over recent decades.

The outcome of the 'critique' offered by the anti-processualist school, exemplified in some writings by Hodder (1982, 1986) and perhaps quintessentially in those of Shanks and Tilley (1987a, 1987b) has been a proposed rejection of the methods of scientific inquiry, and a move towards the relativism associated with the desire that modern archaeological writing should fulfil the objective of 'relevance' towards the social or other issues advocated by the researcher (see Bintliff 1991; Thomas and Tilley 1992). I have characterized this (Renfrew 1989: 36) as 'archaeology as wished for', and have pointed out that, employing these criteria for valid argumentation, there is nothing to distinguish the research which they would produce from the most fantastical assertions of the lunatic fringe about flying saucers, earth magic and corn circles.

It is not the aim here, however, to enter into full-scale polemic against the epistemological position of the anti-processualists, defective though some may find it to be. It will be more constructive to indicate some of the elements of the epistemological position of the cognitive-processual archaeology which, as I have suggested, has developed directly and without hiatus from the functional-processual archaeology of earlier decades. There is an unbroken processual tradition here, but along with it a change of emphasis towards the cognitive issues which, as I have suggested, were somewhat neglected after a few initial and programmatic statements in the first writings of the New Archaeology. It should at once be acknowledged that it is, in the main, those writers in what we may term the anti-processual tendency who have sought to focus on cognitive and symbolic issues, and much of their work has been of very great interest. The aim here is not in any way to belittle what they have achieved, but to indicate that, from the standpoint advocated here, they have achieved it in spite of rather than because of their polarized and polemical philosophically relativist standpoint.

The philosophical position, which many cognitive-processual archaeologists might advocate, may be described as a realist one. That is to say that one conceives of the past as really existing in a physical world, much like the present, with human individuals living their lives, and interacting with each other and with their environment very much as we do today. In other words, the past really happened. This clearly differs from an extreme positivist or empiricist position which might restrict our conception of the past exclusively to that which we can empirically learn about it. But this notion of a past which really happened is to be distinguished from our own knowledge of the past, which has to be based upon our own observations and inferences, and is thus constructed by us using those observations. We may set about this task in different ways, and there may, in that sense, be different constructions of the past. To speak of 'reconstructing' the past, if it implies that one is coming close to a unified view of the past 'as it was' is therefore misleading. And it is misleading not only because our reconstructions are hampered by lacunae in the available evidence, the data. It is misleading too, because even when the data are unlimited (as is perhaps the case if we seek to describe, or characterize, or sum up the present) the account which we shall give will be dependent upon our own view of what is significant, or what is worth reporting or considering. That we can view the past, like the present, from different standpoints does not prevent our asserting, however, that some constructions of the past may be in error in failing to use existing data appropriately or in employing erroneous data.

In the light of recent developments in the philosophy of science, moreover, it can no longer be asserted that 'facts' have an objective existence independent of theory. Facts modify theory, while theory is used in the determination of facts, and the relationship is a cyclic (but not a circular) one.

In the tradition of processual archaeology, a cognitive-processual archaeology will seek to be as 'objective' as possible, while not laying claim to objectivity in any ultimate sense. The aim of producing valid generalizations remains an important goal, although to frame these as universal 'laws of culture process' is now seen as impracticable. But at the same time, the claims of privileged access to other (especially past) minds, which sometimes seem implicit in the writings of the anti-processual school, are rejected. We all start off on an equal footing, with the opportunity of framing hypotheses about the past, and of pursuing these in relation to available data or to newly acquired data, in order to examine their validity.

Where cognitive-processual archaeology goes beyond its functional-processual successor is in the attempt to apply these approaches to the cognitive sphere. This undertaking certainly recognizes that ideology is an active force within societies, and must be given a role in explanations (as Marxist and neo-Marxist thinkers have long argued). It acknowledges too that material culture is to be seen as an active force in constituting the world in which we live. As Hodder (1986) has argued, individuals and societies construct their own realities, and material culture has an integral place within that construction.

One way of making the cognitive approach more concrete is to imagine each individual as possessing a cognitive map of the world, built up in the light of one's own experience and activities, so that this map or world-view serves as the referent used by the individual in determining his or her future activities. In setting out this argument (Renfrew 1987) I have used the term *mappa* to designate this notional internalized cognitive map. The suggestion corresponds with my own personal experience and I make what seems a necessary assumption that this does not differ radically from that of other humans. Indeed I take the existence of such a *mappa* to be the concomitant of the self-awareness and self-consciousness which we believe to be part of the shared human condition. It is a defining feature of self-consciousness that the self is separately identified and that 'I', 'thou' and 'the world' emerge as distinct entities. The individual thus distinguishes an external world, with a past, a present and a future existence. An important part of one's accumulating personal experience is the acquisition of knowledge about this world and the formulation of some projected constructs or models about its nature by the process of cognition which is sometimes called 'mapping'.

Once one has accepted this notion as a reasonable one, the systematic consideration of the cognitive map or *mappa* is no longer dismissed as 'palaeopsychology', although the danger still remains of the circular thinking which that term implies. To infer from the actions of an individual that his or her cognitive map possesses certain features, and then to explain those actions by the existence of those same inferred features risks a complete circularity of precisely the same kind which Marxist thinkers often employ when speaking of contradictions underlying social change. But when we have other evidence for the nature of that *mappa*, for instance in the form of depictions of aspects of the world, that circularity may be avoided. From this viewpoint, the project of undertaking cognitive archaeology is equivalent to the study of those preserved aspects of past material culture and of such of the activities of early societies as may allow us to make valid inferences about the cognitive maps of their inhabitants.

To tackle this task in a systematic and self-critical way is, in some respects, a new undertaking. Of course much work carried out by earlier generations, in the field of art history, for instance, or in the early history of religions, shares some objectives in common. But rarely does it have a very acute awareness of the difficulties and the implicit assumptions which accompany this task. Very much the same criticism may be made, as noted above, of the anti-processual school, whose exponents often display a comparable methodological naiveté, and who are sometimes equally willing to make that great conceptual leap towards the proclamation of 'meaning' which their approach requires and which their interpretations sometimes lead them to feel they have discerned. The defining characteristic of cognitive-processual archaeology, as understood here, should be the more careful and often the more painstaking delineation of arguments which can proceed more through the construction of frameworks of inference than by interpretive leaps. But often, it must be admitted, there are gaps in the chain of reasoning, and then the two approaches may become all too similar. The crux of the matter is to make explicit the assumptions and the inferences which sustain the argument. To do this for archaeological reasoning in general was the principal goal of the New Archaeology. It remains that of processual archaeology, of which cognitive-processual archaeology is the logical and natural development and extension into the symbol-using fields of thought and of communication.

References

Binford, L. R. 1962. Archaeology as anthropology. *American Antiquity* 28: 217–25
    1964. A consideration of archaeological research design. *American Antiquity* 29: 425–41

1987. Data, relativism and archaeological science. *Man* 22: 391–404
1988. Review of Hodder, I., Reading the past, *American Antiquity* 53: 875–6
Binford, L. R. and S. R. Binford (eds.) 1968. *New perspectives in archaeology*. Chicago, Aldine
Bintliff, J. 1991. Post-modernism, rhetoric and scholasticism at TAG: the current state of British archaeological theory. *Antiquity* 65: 274–8
Bloch, M. 1991. Language, anthropology and cognitive science. *Man* 26: 183–98
Cassirer, E. 1944. *An essay on man*. New Haven, Conn., Yale University Press
Clarke, D. L. 1968. *Analytical archaeology*. London, Methuen
    1973. Archaeology, the loss of innocence. *Antiquity* 47: 6–18
Davidson, I. and W. Noble 1989. The archaeology of perception: traces of depiction and language. *Current Anthropology* 30: 125–56.
Donald, M. 1991. *Origins of the modern mind*. Cambridge, Mass., Harvard University Press
Earle, T. and R. Preucel 1987. Archaeology and the radical critique. *Current Anthropology* 28: 501–38
Frankfort, H. and H. A. Frankfort 1949. Myth and reality. In *Before Philosophy*, ed. H. Frankfort, H. A. Frankfort, J. A. Wilson and T. Jacobsen, pp. 11–38. Harmondsworth, Penguin. (First published in 1946 as *The intellectual adventure of ancient man*. Chicago, University of Chicago Press)
Gowlett, J. A. 1984. Mental abilities in early man: a look at some hard evidence. In *Hominid evolution and community ecology*, ed. R. A. Foley, pp. 167–92. London, Academic Press
Hodder, I. 1982. Theoretical archaeology – a reactionary view. In *Symbolic and structural archaeology*, ed. I. Hodder, pp. 1–17. Cambridge, Cambridge University Press
    1986. *Reading the past*. Cambridge, Cambridge University Press
Lévi-Strauss, C. 1966. *The savage mind*. Chicago, University of Chicago Press
Marshack, A. 1991. The Taï plaque and calendrical notation in the Upper Palaeolithic. *Cambridge Archaeological Journal* 1: 25–61
Mellars, P. 1991. Cognitive changes and the emergence of modern humans. *Cambridge Archaeological Journal* 1: 63–76
Miller, D. and C. Tilley 1984. Ideology, power and prehistory: an introduction. In *Ideology, power and prehistory*, ed. D. Miller and C. Tilley, pp. 1–16. Cambridge, Cambridge University Press

Renfrew, C. 1982a. Explanation revisited. In *Theory and explanation in archaeology*, ed. C. Renfrew, M. J. Rowlands and B. A. Segraves, pp. 5–24. New York, Academic Press

  1982b. *Towards an archaeology of mind*. Cambridge, Cambridge University Press

  1986. Varna and the emergence of wealth in prehistoric Europe. In *The social life of things*, ed. A. Appadurai, pp. 141–68. Cambridge, Cambridge University Press

  1987. Problems in the modelling of socio-cultural systems. *European Journal of Operational Research* 30: 179–92

  1989. Comments on archaeology into the 1990s. *Norwegian Archaeological Review* 22: 33–41

Renfrew, C. and P. Bahn 1991. *Archaeology, theories, methods and practice*. London, Thames & Hudson

Salmon, M. H. 1982. *Philosophy and archaeology*. New York, Academic Press

Shanks, M. and C. Tilley 1987a. *Re-constructing archaeology*. Cambridge, Cambridge University Press

  1987b. *Social theory and archaeology*. Cambridge, Cambridge Polity Press

Thomas, J. and C. Tilley 1992. TAG and 'post-modernism': a reply to John Bintliff. *Antiquity* 66: 106–11

Trigger, B. 1978. *Time and tradition*. Edinburgh, Edinburgh University Press

  1981. Anglo-American archaeology. *World Archaeology* 13: 149–50

Watson, P. J., S. A. LeBlanc and C. L. Redman 1971. *Explanation in archaeology: an explicitly scientific approach*. New York, Columbia University Press

White, L. A. 1940. The symbol: the origin and basis of human behaviour. *Philosophy of Science* 7: 461–3. [Reprinted in L. A. White, 1949. *The science of culture*, pp. 22–39. New York, Grove Press]

Wilson, P. 1983. *Man, the promising primate*. New Haven, Yale University Press

Wylie, A. 1982. Epistemological issues raised by a structural archaeology. In *Symbolic and structural archaeology*, ed. I. Hodder, pp. 39–46. Cambridge, Cambridge University Press

Wynn, T. 1991. Tools, grammar and the archaeology of cognition. *Cambridge Archaeological Journal* 1: 191–206

PART II

The interdisciplinary underpinning

2

Interpretation and testability in theories about prehistoric thinking

JAMES A. BELL

Exploration of the prehistoric mind has moved to the forefront of archaeological interest. The question is not whether there is a cognitive revolution but how empirical investigations should proceed and what method(s), if any, should guide theory structure. This paper concentrates on the latter: on guidelines for building and assessing theories about prehistoric thinking. The central point is that archaeologists should aim at constructing testable theories of prehistoric cognition. Theories about prehistoric thinking should not simply be interpretations.

Interpretations can yield understanding; that is, they explain phenomena. Since interpretations are not testable however, there are no reliable criteria for deciding between them, or for moving beyond them. Only testable theories can deliver insight and further understanding. Insight is the product of finding a theory correct at a point where it might have failed. Further understanding can be gained when a failed theory is replaced by modified theories or other theories (Lakatos 1970; Bell 1994). In brief, if theories of the prehistoric mind are to be rooted in the artefactual data, and if they are to exploit artefactual data to yield even better theories, then they must be testable.

Interpretation vs. testability

An applied philosopher quickly learns that examples can drive home a methodological point better than an entire manuscript of philosophical argument. I will not avoid argument, but I think it will be helpful to begin by introducing a few examples to illustrate the difference between interpretation and testability. The introductory examples come from biographical and legal theory, but they will serve to make points pertinent to archaeological theory.

Thomas Jefferson is normally interpreted as a child of the Enlightenment. Jefferson, the author of the Declaration of Independence and an early president of the United States, did not doubt that man could improve his lot and that of his fellows by relying on inspiration, hard work and, above all, by clear thinking.

Jefferson's optimism is hardly mysterious. His ancestors had uprooted themselves from Wales, near Mount Snowdon. In a few generations they had established themselves financially, socially and politically in the American colony of Virginia. Furthermore, Jefferson had seen the power of ideas to move people. The Declaration of Independence provided an historic example. Many in the American colony risked their lives before and during the Revolutionary War for such abstract notions as freedom and a better sense of justice.

It is not then surprising that most biographers of Jefferson have been intellectual biographers; that is, they have focused on his ideas and how they influenced the founding of the United States. The intellectual tradition in Jefferson biography was evident in the first annual Jefferson lecture, delivered by Lionel Trilling in 1972. The lecture was on Jefferson as a thinker and it concentrated on the life of Jefferson's mind (Brodie 1985: xi).

A quite different interpretation of Jefferson is offered by Fawn Brodie in her biography *Thomas Jefferson: an intimate history* (Brodie 1985). Brodie brings into focus the personal and sensual sides of Jefferson, especially as they may have influenced his public life. 'Despite hundreds of volumes about Jefferson', says Brodie, 'there remain unexpected reserves of unmined ore, particularly in relation to the *connections* between his public life and his inner life, as well as his intimate life' (Brodie 1985: 7). Brodie develops a biography of nearly 700 pages, all informed by the assumption that Jefferson's inner emotional and personal life had a major impact on his more public ideas and actions. The upshot is an intimate interpretation of the man and his actions that diverges significantly from the standard intellectual interpretation.

A reader of Brodie's biography is left to ponder which is more accurate: the traditional intellectual interpretation of Jefferson's life or Brodie's new intimate interpretation. Ideas important to Jefferson, and Jefferson's actions, can be broadly explained in either way. Furthermore, despite Brodie's claim that the intellectual interpretations belittle important material, and dismiss abundant psychological material as 'unhistorical' or disregard it entirely, she readily admits that the psychological data underlying her own biography are not always easy to grasp, much less interpret (Brodie 1985: 7).

In brief, we are left with two contrasting interpretations of Jefferson's life. Each is reasonably consistent although contrary to the other, and each accounts for much of the historical data. Our understanding of Jefferson's life is clearly enhanced by two interpretations rather than just one. Each provides a different perspective, including alternative explanations for Jefferson's ideas and actions. Furthermore, there is a plethora of data to confirm either perspective. What is bothersome, however, is that neither interpretation is subject to serious challenge from the data. Without tests which could lead to potential refutation it is unlikely that insight or unanticipated new understanding could spring forth. The upshot is a tandem of interesting interpretations but no reliable way to move beyond either one or both.

The biographical reconstructions of Thomas Jefferson's life are typical of interpretations. They do increase understanding. More is known about Thomas Jefferson because of the multiple and conflicting interpretations than would be the case with only one interpretation or none at all. Since interpretations are not testable, however, they cannot deliver the type of insight that comes from passing risky tests, nor can they lead to unanticipated new understanding if they fail tests.

I will now turn to a second example, this one from legal theory. The strength of this example is that it incorporates both a testable and an interpretative approach. The contrast makes the difference all the more clear.

In 1987 Robert Bork was nominated by President Ronald Reagan to sit on the Supreme Court of the United States. After controversial and widely publicized confirmation hearings, however, the United States Senate did not uphold Bork's nomination. Despite many different opinions on what led to the rejection of the nomination, one major legal issue undergirded the entire debate: whether the Constitution of the United States should be read strictly, or whether it should not. The two viewpoints are reviewed below.

Robert Bork maintains that the Supreme Court should read the Constitution strictly; that is, according to the 'original intent' of its founders. Reading the Constitution strictly means the following: if a case appealed to the Supreme Court contains no definitive constitutional question, with the Constitution interpreted as originally intended by its founders, then the Supreme Court should let its issues be decided in the political arena or in state and other lower courts.

What concerns Bork and his supporters are the consequences of not reading the Constitution strictly. First, without original intent to provide discipline, Supreme Court Justices have and will allow themselves to rummage unchecked through the Constitution looking for 'emanations and penumbras' with which to justify social and political policies, and even personal preferences. The result is attempts to justify, constitutionally, that which should be fought out in the political arena or dealt with by lower courts interpreting legislated law. In brief, justices will legislate rather than adjudicate. Second, the Supreme Court has and will legislate judicially without accountability to the people. Supreme Court Justices are not elected, and an appointment to the Supreme Court is for life or until a justice resigns. Barring a very rare recall, the only systematic check on the power of the Supreme Court is a strict reading of the Constitution. Third, this check on the judiciary is critical in the American system of checks and balances between the legislative, executive and judicial branches. Without strict reading there is danger of domination by the judiciary. Judicial domination is all the more disconcerting because it is subtly cloaked as 'rule by law' and is perpetrated by a group of unusually bright and well-intended people (Bork 1990).

Critics of a strict reading of the Constitution contend it is not possible to determine original intent confidently. Perhaps more importantly, critics view the Constitution as a 'living document' which requires reinterpretation in light of conditions which have and will change in ways unforeseen by the framers of the Constitution. Instead of investigating or trying to accommodate original intent, critics of strict reading prefer *stare decisis*: the doctrine that procedures and principles laid down in previous judicial decisions should be followed unless they contravene the ordinary principles of justice.

The strict-reading view of constitutional law assumes that the Constitution itself provides the data for the Supreme Court to decide whether or not to hear a case, and to guide decisions when a case is heard. It does not provide leeway for the manufacture of constitutional justification on issues not elicited by the original intent of the Constitution. In other words, original-intent theorists insist that constitutional claims be strictly testable and that the Constitution be the testing device. Critics of original intent do not believe that the Constitution should provide such a strict test of constitutional claims. They endorse adding assumptions to and drawing loose implications from the Constitution, the effect of which is to pull more issues in under the constitutional umbrella. In other words, critics of original intent want the Constitution to be an interpretative device.

It is my contention that archaeologists of the mind would do well to model their theory construction and assessment after the strict-reading theorists of constitutional law rather than their critics. Advocates of original intent in constitutional law are, methodologically speaking, advocates of testability. Their critics operate quite differently. They, like the biographers of Thomas Jefferson, embrace such a large range of assumptions that they can offer interpretations but not testable explanations. The similarities and differences between interpretation and testability will be drawn out more explicitly in the next section.

The contrast between interpretation and testability

Formal presentations can be a curse in academic philosophy, at least in the eyes of some. While I normally try to avoid formality, a rather abstract exposition of interpretation and testability is an effective way to pinpoint the similarities and differences.

An interpretation requires (1) data to be explained. The interpretation itself consists of (2) other assumptions and/or entailments which enable the data in (1) to be explained. Furthermore, an interpretation should be (3) internally consistent: the contents of (1) and (2) should not contain contradictory elements. Finally, (4) when making interpretations the assumptions and/or entailments of (2) can be altered, deleted, replaced, or ramified in almost any way to explain (or ignore) the data, even anomalous data, in (1).

A testable theory shares the first three characteristics with an interpretation. A testable theory requires (1) data or information to be explained, and the theory itself consists of (2) statements to explain the data. A testable theory should also be (3) internally consistent. Characteristic (4) is not allowed when generating testable theories, however. The explanatory statements of testable theories cannot be so loosely altered, deleted, replaced, or ramified to account for data, especially anomalous data. In methodological idiom, testable theories cannot undergo *ad hoc* changes to explain away refuting data. Explanatory statements of testable theories can be changed, to be sure, but they can only be changed in ways that allow them to remain testable.

The upshot is that testable theories, unlike interpretations, will be subject to refutation by at least some data. In practice this means that testable theories cannot be modified in a way that simply explains away uncomfortable data. Like interpretations, testable theories can include speculative elements beyond the available data. Unlike interpretations, however, such speculative elements should allow for testing against other potential data.

Over the past few decades archaeologists have become familiar with methodological literature, whether from the philosophy of science or from archaeological sources. Many also realize by now that testable theories ('scientific' theories) are *not* ends in themselves. Testability is a tool, albeit an essential tool, for deciding whether theories merit empirical confidence (if they pass tests) or whether to

modify them or search for other theories (if they fail tests).

While many theoretical archaeologists are familiar with testability and its heuristic role in theory development, I am convinced that there cannot be too much discussion of the application of testability in archaeological theorizing. The upcoming section provides a detailed analysis of one example of testability applied to prehistoric cognition. If space allowed, similar analyses could be made of other case studies included in this volume, as well as some in *Representations in archaeology* (Peebles and Gardin 1992).

Testability in theories about prehistoric cognition

The discussion will be built around the reconstruction of cognitive elements found in the analysis of the Indus valley stones. This example is well known, especially since Colin Renfrew employed it in his inaugural lecture as Disney Professor of Archaeology at Cambridge University (Renfrew 1982: 16–19). A brief synopsis of the artefactual data will set the stage for further discussion.

The stones come from the four thousand year old civilization of the Indus valley, from the site of Mohenjo-daro. They are cubical, and coloured, and apparently had to be imported from a considerable distance. Most interestingly, the stones are multiples of a constant unit of weight, the weight equivalent to 0.836 grams of mass. The weights are multiples of integers such as 1, 4, 8, continuing to 64, and then 320 and 1,600. Scale pans were also found.

From the archaeological data above, Renfrew formulated a number of statements. The relationship of these statements (the 'theory') to artefactual data is of paramount importance in testable approaches to prehistoric cognition. For that reason the statements formulated by Renfrew will be reproduced *verbatim* below:

(1) That the society in question had developed a concept equivalent to our own notion of weight or mass.
(2) That the use of this concept involved the operation of units, and hence the concept of modular measure.
(3) That there was a system of numeration, involving hierarchical numerical categories (like tens and units), in this case apparently based on the fixed ratio of 16.
(4) That this weight system was used for practical purposes (as the finding of scale pans corroborates), constituting a measuring device for mapping the world quantitatively as well as qualitatively.
(5) That there existed a notion of equivalence, on the basis of weight among different materials (unless we postulate the weighing of objects of one material

against others of the same material), and hence, it may follow, a ratio of value between them.

(6) That this inferred concept of value entailed some constant rate of exchange between commodities. (Renfrew 1982: 17)

The set of statements above is sizeable. Despite that, additional statements were asserted in a later paper (Renfrew 1987a), and in an unpublished lecture even more were added (Renfrew 1987b). In any case, is there justification for associating the six statements above with the artefactual data? Or are these statements so loosely connected that they are merely speculative? In other words, is Renfrew generating a testable set of statements or is he just weaving an interpretation?

First, the statements are *about* the thinking of prehistoric people; they are emphatically *not* attempts to restructure their exact thoughts. For example, Renfrew does not claim that those ancient inhabitants of the Indus valley had an idea of weight or mass that was precisely the same as ours today. In other words, Renfrew's broad goal is to unveil some elements of the thinking of prehistoric people. In his own terminology, he aims to create a 'cognitive map', or *mappa*. A map is not to be confused with that which is mapped, but a map can indicate some features of that which is mapped.

Incidentally, Renfrew's wording in (1) is not entirely clear. He states that the inhabitants of the Indus valley ' . . . had developed a concept equivalent to our notion of weight of mass' (Renfrew 1982: 17). Particularly bothersome is the word 'equivalent'. What does it mean in this context? Renfrew's claim has been clarified in other papers and lectures, as well as in personal communications: that one feature of cognition in the Indus valley was a notion of comparative weight (Renfrew 1987a).

Second, it should be noted that some of the statements arise directly from the artefactual data, and that other statements are connected to those by logical relationship. The notion of weight (1) stems from the fact that the stones are calibrated against each other, and that calibration in units leads to (2). That the units are themselves arranged in a hierarchy suggests a system of numeration (3). The fact that scale pans were found indicates that there was a quantitative weighing purpose for the stones (2), and that there was a notion of (weight) equivalence (5). The use of the scale for weighing implies that there was value associated with weight, and that weight may then have been used as a measure to determine exchange value (6).

Third, the logical connections between statements are not just 'logical' from the perspective of a particular archaeologist. Similar if not precisely the same statements would likely be made by archaeologists whether British, French,

Greek, or Chinese; female or male; young or old; liberal or conservative; or characterized in any other way. In other words, the logical connections are more like those in mathematics, which hold regardless of the background, inclinations, or prejudices of the person using the mathematics.

The three features identified above – restricting statements to claims about cognition, linking statements closely to artefactual data and/or with each other by logic, and taking care that the logical connections are not subjective projections of a theoretician – all dovetail to render the set of statements testable. Below is further comment on these features.

The first feature is that statements are restricted to assertions about thinking; they are not attempts to restructure exact thoughts. One can understand this point by tracing the consequences of attempting to restructure exact thoughts. Claims about what prehistoric peoples were 'actually thinking' cannot be tested, because a potential refutation of such a claim would be another contrary claim about what prehistoric people were actually thinking. No test would be possible because the latter could not be found in prehistoric artefacts any more than the former. Remember that 'prehistory' means before the written word, but the precise thoughts of prehistoric peoples could only be found in written documentation.

Although claims about exact thoughts are not testable, statements about some features of the thinking of prehistoric peoples are considerably more amenable to testing. For example, if similar stones had been found which did not demonstrate weight ratios, then Renfrew's theory (his statements) would be refuted. Or, if there were evidence of trade in weighable items of reasonable value, then one would anticipate discovering similar weighing systems in the trade area of the Indus valley civilization. Admittedly, failure to discover such would not refute Renfrew's claim; weighing might have been controlled centrally, and hence might only have been done when objects were brought to Mohenjo-daro. Nevertheless, the discovery of similar weighing systems in the Indus valley trade area would provide further support for the assertion that the weighing system had a practical function in exchange. Indeed, there is evidence of such in Bahrain, and the stones are the weights typical of the cities in the Indus civilization (Bibby 1969: 354–5; also see 358–9).

The second feature is that some statements are linked closely to the artefactual data, and other statements are tied to the former by appropriate logic. The importance of linking at least some assertions in a cognitive map very closely to the artefactual data seems so obvious it hardly need be discussed. Nevertheless, the methodological reason cannot be overemphasized: to maintain testability. If Renfrew had leaped from the existence of the proportional stones to the inference that weights were central to the religious outlook of the Indus valley civilization, his assertion would have been virtually 'non-testable'. What could possibly put such an assertion to a potential refutation? One might say that *not* finding the stones in the usual religious areas would refute it. However, perhaps the location in which the stones were found was the central religious area even if archaeologists did not recognize it as such. It is crucial to avoid such 'non-testable' speculation if one hopes to distinguish what is empirically plausible from what might be a phantom of the imagination.

Statements not directly linked to artefactual data must be tied to others which are directly testable by artefactual data. The reason is that assertions not arising directly from data can only be vulnerable to empirical refutation if they are associated in a tight logical relationship with assertions that can be put to a direct test. For example, Renfrew's statement (3) that there was a system of numeration, involving hierarchical numerical categories, is tied logically to his statements (2) and (1). Statement (3) could not be directly tested by artefactual data; direct evidence of numeration would have to be written. However, discovery of similar stones but without weight relations would not only refute (1) directly, but would also refute (2) and (3) as well because of the logical connection of (2) and (3) to (1).

The third feature is that the logical connections which bind statements together must not be just subjective projections of a theoretician. The way to assure that they are not is captured in the above paragraph: the logical relationships between statements in a cognitive map must be close enough so that all statements are at least indirectly subject to testing. What makes such logical relationships adequate? Two properties stand out: entailment and consistency.

Entailment

Entailment, or implication, is one of the most controversial concepts in logical theory. There is a vast amount of literature in mathematical logic devoted to explicating and interpreting entailment, not to mention the literature devoted to entailment in the sciences. Fortunately, for methodological purposes an adequate understanding can be grasped quite readily: if X entails Y then a mistake in Y indicates that there is a mistake in X. This point is illustrated in the next paragraph.

Suppose that a system of numeration entails a concept of units. It would follow that if there were no units, then there would be no system of numeration. This example might seem rather simple, but the methodological point is indeed quite simple. If a set of statements (a theory) is to be testable,

then statements not directly testable themselves must entail statements which are directly testable.

It was noted in the previous section that interpretations and testable theories can both be modified to account for anomalous data, but that a testable theory can only be so modified if it remains testable. From a logical perspective the difference can now be understood as follows. When an interpretation is altered to account for anomalous data, additional assumption(s) are introduced which do *not* entail statements which are potentially refutable. In methodological idiom, *ad hoc* hypotheses are added to an interpretation. In everyday terms, an interpretation is modified to 'explain away' anomalous data. When a testable theory is modified to account for anomalous data, the additional assumption(s) must still entail statements which are potentially refutable. In methodological idiom, auxiliary hypotheses are added to the theory. Hypotheses auxiliary to a theory maintain or even increase its testability.

Incidentally, there is little if any harm in using less arcane terminology to characterize the relationship between statements in a testable theory. For example, suppose an archaeologist formulates statements about prehistoric cognition and asserts that the statements 'must be close to the data', or that 'the statements cannot speculate far from the data'. Such terminology seems quite appropriate so long as the meaning is understood; i.e., that statements which are not directly testable must entail statements which are.

Universal statements

A few comments on universal statements will end the discussion of entailment. Generalized statements, often called 'universal statements', are perfectly appropriate and even desirable *so long as they entail testable statements*. As a matter of fact, generalization can *increase* testability because a more sweeping claim can entail a greater number of testable implications. As counter-intuitive as it may seem, that is why universalization can actually bring theoretical statements 'closer' to the data. For example, Karl Wittfogel's research into the relationship between irrigation and state formation was done in the relatively arid Far East, but he universalized his claim: in all localities, including damp regions like Hawaii, state structure formed because of the need to develop and manage irrigation (Wittfogel 1957). Wittfogel's universalized claim inspired research into the relationship between irrigation and the formation of state societies in many other archaeological contexts, including Hawaii. The upshot of the generalization of Wittfogel's claim was more testing of his theory, not to mention the considerable insight into many other societies gained in the process (Earle 1978).

Now consider the consequences of generalization which

does not increase the number of testable implications. Such universalization may expand the range of an explanation but at the expense of turning it into an interpretation. Without test points there is no confident way to assess an expanded explanation. As argued earlier, without the possibility of testing it is difficult if not impossible to know whether an explanation is plausible or whether it is just speculation or even fantasy (Hodder 1986; for a critical review see Bell 1987). Generalized statements that do not entail testable implications should thus be avoided.

To summarize, explanations should be 'close' to the data: they should be directly testable themselves or they should entail other statement(s) that are directly testable. Explanations can be generalized, and indeed should be generalized, if such will increase the number of testable implications. On the other hand, explanations should be avoided which are not themselves directly testable or which do not entail testable implications. Finally, one should avoid generalization if such does not increase the number of testable implications.

Incidentally, the fewer data available for testing the more care should be taken when universalizing. The reason is that the fewer the available data, the less likely that generalizing will increase the number of implications that can be directly tested. To illustrate, consider the difference between theories which entail a relative cornucopia of artefactual data and theories which do not. Many theories about prehistoric economic and social organization can and have been beneficially universalized because of the relative abundance of artefactual data against which they can be tested. Even though the artefactual data appropriate for testing theories about prehistoric cognition may be more than is now realized, and even though further research will almost certainly increase the amount, there may never be an abundance of such data appropriate for testing theories about prehistoric thinking. If so, cognitive archaeologists should be all the more careful about generalizing their theories.

I do hope the cautionary note above will not be used to discourage generalization of cognitive theories when there is enough potential data for testing. I do hope it will discourage generalization when there is little or no potential data for testing.

Consistency

Entailment is a critical property of the logical relationship between statements in a testable theory. It can also be subtle, especially when a theory is generalized. Consistency is the other important property of the logical relationship between statements in a testable theory. It is not so subtle; indeed, to most it is self-evident that the statements constituting a theory should be consistent. The methodological reason for consistency is not so obvious, however. A brief discussion is in order.

Consistent statements are statements that can all be true in at least one interpretation. Why is consistency important, however? If statements are inconsistent – that is, if they cannot all be true in any interpretation – they validly imply any statement whatsoever. This has been an accepted principle of logic ever since it was established by Aristotle in the fourth century BC. If there is inconsistency in the set of assertions constituting a theory, then the theory will validly imply any statement including any potential refuting statements. The upshot is that no empirical information can possibly refute inconsistent statements. In other words, *an inconsistent theory cannot be testable*.

Few thinkers have endorsed inconsistency. One who did, however, has had an enormous influence on western intellectual currents since the middle of the nineteenth century. Georg W. F. Hegel reasoned that contradiction was more likely than consistency in the cosmos, and hence that theories can reflect those contradictions (Hegel 1977). Perhaps that is why the Hegelian intellectual tradition is so replete with vagueness, ambiguity, and outright contradiction, all dressed up in a writing style that is as confusing as its ideas. The most recent outbreak of the Hegelian tradition is the post-modernist movement, the irrational flavour of which has infected some well-known post-processual archaeologists (Hodder 1986; for a critical review see Bell 1987. Also see Shanks and Tilley 1987).

Fortunately, aside from Hegel and his followers few would argue that contradictions should be tolerated. Most insist that consistency is important even if unaware of the methodological reason. Interpretations are not testable, but even they should be consistent.

Conclusion

This has been a paper on how cognitive archaeology ought to be done rather than on criticism of alternative approaches. That is why the discussion of interpretation was not pursued in further detail, and why only passing comment was made on the consequences of ignoring the guidelines that make testability possible. I have had opportunity to level criticism in other papers (Bell 1987, 1991, 1994). Also, the arguments in this paper were tied as closely as possible with an actual example from cognitive archaeology. Finally, the appropriate philosophical framework for archaeology of the mind – methodological individualism – has been explored in other works and in a manuscript (Bell 1992, 1994).

The principal methodological points in this paper are summarized below. They are intended as a checklist for those working in archaeology of the mind. The checklist is not likely to be useful unless one is familiar with the underlying concepts, but it should help one recall methodological points without having to reread the entire paper.

(1) Testable theories are vulnerable to empirical error; that is, they can potentially be shown to be mistaken by at least some data.

(2) Testable theories are valuable because they merit empirical confidence when they pass tests at vulnerable points, and can be modified or lead to other theories when they fail tests at vulnerable points.

(3) Statements in testable theories cannot be arbitrarily altered, deleted, replaced or ramified to account for anomalous data. If the explanatory statements of a testable theory are changed, it must be done in such a way that the theory remains testable.

(4) Testable theories in cognitive archaeology consist of statements *about* prehistoric thinking; that is, the statements can highlight some features of prehistoric thinking but cannot reveal the precise thoughts.

(5) As with any testable theory, theories about prehistoric cognition must be structured so that they are close to the data. That means that the statements must either be directly testable or must entail other statements that are directly testable.

(6) The relationship between a statement that is not directly testable to one that is directly testable is characterized by two logical properties: entailment and consistency.

(7) A statement entails another statement if an error in the latter indicates an error in the former. Consistent statements are statements which contain no contradictions; that is, statements which can all be true under some interpretation.

(8) Generalized statements, or universal statements, can increase testability if they entail more testable implications. Theories should be generalized if such is the case.

(9) Generalization should be avoided if there is no increase in testability. In cognitive archaeology there may not always be artefactual data available, or discoverable, that is appropriate for testing generalized statements.

References

Bell, J. A. 1987. Reason vs. relativism: review of Ian Hodder's *Reading the past*. *Archaeological Review from Cambridge* 6 (1): 75–86

1991. Anarchy and archaeology. In *Processual and postprocessual archaeologies: multiple ways of knowing the past*, ed. R. W. Preucel, pp. 71–80. Carbondale, Southern Illinois University Press

1992. On capturing agency in theories about prehistory. In *Representations in archaeology*, ed. J.-C. Gardin and C. Peebles, pp. 30–55. Bloomington, University of Indiana Press

1994. *Reconstructing prehistory: scientific method and archaeology*. Temple University Press

Bibby, G. 1969. *Looking for Dilmun*. New York, Alfred A. Knopf

Bork, R. H. 1990. *The tempting of America: the political seduction of the law*. New York, Macmillan (Free Press)

Brodie, F. M. 1985. *Thomas Jefferson: an intimate history*. New York, Bantam Books

Earle, T. K. 1978. *Economic and social organization of a complex chiefdom: the Halelea District, Kauai, Hawaii*. Ann Arbor, Anthropological Papers, No. 63, Museum of Anthropology, University of Michigan

Hegel, G. W. F. 1977. *Phenomenology of spirit*. Translated by A. U. Miller, New York, Clarendon Press

Hodder, I. 1986. *Reading the past: current approaches to interpretation in archaeology*. Cambridge, Cambridge University Press

Lakatos, I. 1970. Falsification and the methodology of scientific research programmes. In *Criticism and the growth of knowledge*, ed. I. Lakatos and A. Musgrave, pp. 91–195. Cambridge, Cambridge University Press

Peebles, C. S. and J.-C. Gardin 1992. *Representations in archaeology*. Bloomington and Indianapolis, Indiana University Press

Renfrew, A. C. 1982. *Towards an archaeology of mind*. Cambridge, Cambridge University Press

1987a. Problems in the modelling of sociocultural systems. *European Journal of Operational Research*, 30: 179–92

1987b. Seminar lecture in the Department of Archaeology, Cambridge, Cambridge University

Shanks, M. and C. Tilley 1987. *Social theory and archaeology*. Cambridge, Polity Press

Wittfogel, K. 1957. *Oriental despotism*. New Haven, Yale University Press

3
Archaeology and cognitive science

ERWIN M. SEGAL

Introduction

Cognitive science is an interdisciplinary approach to studying mind and, in particular, intelligent thought and behaviour. It is a relatively new academic discipline which is developing from a merger of interests among certain linguists, psychologists, philosophers, computer scientists, anthropologists, neuroscientists and others (Norman 1981). Historically, however, cognitive science has not generally been extended to include archaeology or its issues. From the perspective of this cognitive scientist, however, it is obvious that archaeology could become a core cognitive science. The study of material culture is an important domain with unique data and methods which can contribute to the general understanding of intelligence. Also, archaeology can (and does) profit from data and methods developed in the other cognitive sciences.

In archaeology, a primary concern is what material culture tells us about the *living* culture that produced it. The artefacts and structures found at archaeological sites represent varying amounts of skill, knowledge and social organisation. By analysing these objects in the context of their appearance, one may be able to infer a great deal about their role in society and the intelligence that was necessary to create them and to use them. Research in cognitive science has shown that there are many constraints on how people solve problems and achieve other goals (Newell and Simon 1972; Newell 1981). Thus a cognitive archaeologist can study the objects and structures found at archaeological sites with an eye towards answering questions about the knowledge, purposes, practices and skills of the people who produced them. Such research can broaden the database and theoretical insights of cognitive science as well as add to the knowledge of the peoples who inhabited the archaeological sites.

To take a cognitive scientist's perspective on archaeology, one has to think about the cognitive processes involved in producing material culture. An archaeologist who is a cognitive scientist would use the tools and concepts of cognitive science to help implement Lewis Binford's programme to link 'human activities (i.e. dynamics) to the consequences of those activities that may be apparent in material things (i.e. statics)' (Binford 1983: 19). A cognitive scientist would consider, in some detail, what it is about the people and the society that accounts for the components of the material culture. This would include both the goals and purposes of the members of the community which motivated the organization and the sequence of behaviours that created the material culture, and the concomitant intelligence, knowledge and skill necessary to produce it.

Archaeology is fundamentally a discipline rooted in cognition. Material objects or relations among material objects become archaeological data only if they can be shown to exist in their current form or location as a direct or indirect consequence of intelligent behaviour. If an object's appearance can be entirely explained by natural (for which read non-intellectual) processes, it is of no direct interest to an archaeologist. For example, some primitively shaped stone tools found in the Olduvai Gorge 'might have been dismissed as natural were it not for the numbers that have been found' (Cottrell 1960). An object, however, could be of interest to archaeology even if its structure were entirely shaped by natural processes if it were believed to have been selected for use by humans for some intentional goal. J. Marcus (1990, personal communication) found some smooth coloured stones which were naturally carved which have archaeological significance. They were found in Olmec burial sites together with other burial objects many miles from where they originated. Although not created by intelligence they were acted upon by intelligence. This fact gives them their archaeological significance.

Concepts in cognitive science

The cognitive sciences have not yet coalesced into a single discipline with a unitary perspective on intelligence, but there has been much cross-fertilization of ideas within the special sciences and a growing number of research teams containing members from several disciplines. One methodological principle, which is close to universal among researchers who call themselves cognitive scientists, is the detailed consideration of the underpinning of any demonstrated knowledge of behaviour. This differs fundamentally from the positivistic and behaviouristic approaches that many of the sciences previously accepted. Researchers in cognitive science consider the structures, knowledges and processes, which underlie the observed behaviours, as well as the behaviours themselves. Cognitive scientists often use these mental concepts in their explanation of these behaviours. The power of a cognitive-science approach comes from the idea that intelligent beings have goals and intentions which are implemented by a complex hierarchical system of information transmission. Newell and Simon (1976; Newell 1981) claim that research through the years gives empirical and theoretical support to the importance of an information processing analysis. They argue that all intelligent beings are physical symbol systems, and being a PSS is necessary and sufficient for producing intelligent behaviour.

Newell (1981) identifies a hierarchy of at least five descriptive levels within all PSSs: (a) the device level, (b) the circuit level, (c) the logic level, (d) the programme level and (e) the PMS (processor, memory, switch) level. Each of the levels has its own principles and characteristics which are only partially constrained at the other levels.

(a) The device level identifies the set of physical units which must be duplicated and interconnected for a PSS. In a computer this used to be tubes and wires; now it tends to consist of semiconductive impurities on silicon chips. In organisms it consists primarily of neurons and synapses.

(b) The circuit level consists of the flow of matter or energy with particular voltages and resistances, or potentials and neurotransmitters. In a PSS something has to move through the system.

(c) The logic level refers to structural and functional patterns. Registers being on or off, the passing of bits occurs according to patterns of their combination; for example some units may turn on only if all connecting units are on (AND gate), or a unit may turn on only if only one of several connecting units is on (XOR (exclusive or) gate).

(d) The program level contains data structures, symbols, addresses and programs. Symbols (structured patterns) are stored in accessible locations, and there are programs to retrieve information (identify and possibly duplicate subpatterns) and operate on it according to some principle. The result of that operation may be the addition of new data to the data structure or some external output, or both.

(e) The PMS level is the functional level at which intentions, plans and purposes are realized. 'Here there is simply a medium, called data or information, which flows along channels called links and switches and is held and processed by units called memories, processors, controls, and transducers.' (Newell 1981: 75)

Since each of these levels is partially independent of the others, they must each be studied independently, and the interrelationships drawn, to have an integrated understanding of the whole system.

Researchers, including many psychologists, computer scientists, and linguists, who study information processing, spend much of their time abstractly characterizing the information flow in the highest two levels of a PSS. The study of information processing systems, i.e. systems that receive, store, modify, produce, send and act upon information (Anderson 1990), predates the identification of PSSs by a number of years. The mathematical concept of information was first proposed by R. V. L. Hartley in 1928 (Dretske 1981). Studying information transmission, and systems which deal with it, gradually developed during the Second World War and became well known not long afterwards (Wiener 1948; Shannon and Weaver 1949; Broadbent 1958). It is only after working with different information processing systems (IPSs) that Newell and Simon (1972) attempted to formalize a PSS. The representation of information in terms of structural relations among symbols, the changes in knowledge as computations upon those symbols, and actions as behaviours under the control of symbols is now a long standing tradition (see Fodor 1975; Pylyshyn 1984; Rapaport 1990).

An IPS has several components including receptors, memories, processors and effectors (Newell and Simon 1972). Such systems receive information from the environment through their receptors. They then go through processes of transforming, storing, comparing and evaluating this information. For example, assume that you see a duck. What happens informationally? In order for you to know that you see a duck, or to be aware that it is a duck you see, you have to compare part of the visual input with some representation of a duck in memory. Processors must parse the visual stimulus into meaningful components in order to isolate the duck from its visual context, and to compare the resultant duck information to a memorial representation. The representation must include not only information concerning the visual appearance of a duck, but also information identifying the visual information to be that of a duck. In order to behave appropriately, therefore intelligently, such as to say 'Oh, there's a duck', there has to be a link between your representation of the visual appearance and a representation of the verbal form 'duck'. In addition, this information has been tied to devices which control the effectors in your vocal apparatus.

The example above informally and globally identifies some of the processes that are involved in doing what is subjectively a simple task. Information processing is involved with describing the processes that are involved in solving problems, telling stories, perceiving objects, understanding sentences, and doing other cognitive things. It is also involved with the goal of understanding the cognitive events that occur. Describing the processes ultimately means specifying an effective procedure (and when truly successful, the effective procedure) which does the task. It should be noted that in many intelligent behaviours stating a procedure which is truly effective is an incredibly difficult task. Not only have many of the computational problems not been solved, but it is not often known what the problems are that need to be solved. Marr (1982) argues persuasively that clearly specifying the computational problems which underlie the intelligent behaviour is an important level of analysis. After a computational problem is known one can identify a procedure to solve it.

The concept of 'effective procedure' is one of the more important concepts in the symbolic sciences, and one which is needed at least on an informal basis in order to work within any cognitive science. 'An *effective procedure* is a finite, unambiguous description of a finite set of operations. The operations must be effective in the sense that there is a strictly mechanical procedure for completing them' (Brainerd and Landweber 1974: 1–2). One task for cognitive scientists is to identify intelligent behaviours, and to try to describe effective procedures which produce them. However, it is often not possible to identify exact detailed procedures which will produce the behaviour. In these cases the cognitive scientist can try to identify a set of conceptual and behavioural components which, when combined, could account for the global intelligent behaviours. Careful analyses of intelligent acts point to whether they are complex or not, and identify the knowledge and skill necessary to perform these acts. These analyses can be supported by several methods including careful study of the details found in the data, the evaluation of similar phenomena, computer simulation and the attempt to duplicate the phenomena under experimental control and analysis. The more detailed and varied the information cognitive scientists have about intelligent acts, the greater the confidence in their explanation.

Topics in cognitive science

Cognitive science often has a goal of specifying how different cognitive tasks are achieved. In order to do this one needs a clear description both of the end-product and of the conditions under which the task occurs. Unless one considers the conditions under which the task occurs the task cannot be accurately evaluated. To make this point, in his *Sciences of the artificial* (1969), Herbert Simon points out that the path of an ant over a somewhat rough surface is quite complicated. If, however, the ant's movement is evaluated in conjunction with constraints dictated by details of the surface traversed, it can be seen that the actual task solved by the ant is a relatively simple one. The complexity in this case is in the constraints, not in the information processing system. On the other hand, as can be seen from the description above, the 'simple' task of verbally identifying a duck may require quite a complex cognitive system.

Visual perception

Vision has been of interest to scientists and philosophers since there were scientists and philosophers. Vision is probably the major source of information about the world around us. The ancients may have thought that objects in the world emitted replicas which were directly known by perceivers, but we currently believe that there are complex physical, physiological and computational processes which necessarily occur between the existence of things and their knowledge in the mind.

If we apply the principle of studying the task needed to be done in conjunction with constraints built into the system, i.e. the nature of the visual stimulus and the properties of the human visual apparatus, object and scene perception seems to be a tractable problem. The Gestalt psychologists, Wertheimer, Kohler, and Koffka (Kohler 1947; Koffka 1935) were the first researchers who realized that human vision was constrained by something other than some general purpose learning program operating over the distribution of nerve firings as a function of variations of light energy entering the eyes. They identified organizational principles in the perceptual experience (e.g. common fate, good continuation) which were not directly represented by the punctate stimulation.

James Gibson (1950, 1966) noted that when we physically move through the world, although almost all of the local stimulation changes, there are a great many 'higher order' invariances in the visual field. For example, contours conserve shape over translation, and objects in the direction of motion conserve shape as size expands. Similarly, there are invariances when rigid objects move and there are regularities built into how patterns of ambient light are reflected from different kinds of objects. Gibson thought that all we need to do to perceive the world is to 'pick up' the appropriate invariances in the visual stimuli. Although he greatly underestimated the difficulty in building a perceptual apparatus to respond to these invariances and an information processing system to organize them, he moved a great part of the information processing problem into considering specific mechanisms to account for an identifiable structure in the environment.

Visual perception research now usually starts with constraints based upon regularities found in ambient light reflected off of the surfaces of real objects. No researcher currently believes that the visual system works by simply remembering arbitrary regularities found on the retina. Marr (1982) for example, has a relatively successful theory based on analyzing the computational problem in terms of an analysis of the set of objects we actually perceive in the visual world. He proposed algorithms which could solve the computations, and searched for ways in which the algorithms could be physically realized within the eye and the visual cortex.

Marr's (1982) theory begins with an attempt to identify some of the properties of the visible world which are accessible to the IPS. It tries to identify those visual properties we use to identify the visible properties of objects. It does this instead of attempting to build a visual system that could capture all of the details of the visual stimulus. Visibly, objects consist of surfaces which are seen to be spatially continuous, with discontinuities at their boundaries. An important task of the visual system, then, is to identify the boundaries of surfaces. This had been seen to be a difficult computational task because the surfaces themselves often have different markings which are visually just as distinct, or even more distinct, than the differences between surfaces, and these have to be overridden.

Marr noticed that surface markings are visible phenomena occurring within small localized regions of the visual field. A broader scope receptive field could ignore such local discontinuities. Marr's theory includes a computational system that incorporates a hierarchical analysis of the visible world. This is a major achievement of the theory. Visual processes are identified which can respond to cues leading to smooth contours on a larger scale while ignoring even large local variations in reflectance.

Using these constraints as an important input into his theory, Marr developed a theory of object perception which has become central to much current research. He showed, for example, that different receptors respond to different sized units so that both finer and more global aspects of the visual stimulus can be identified. He suggests that the visual system treats 'objects' of approximately the same size equivalently regardless of the internal visual details, and things of the same size are often grouped together to form larger units. Thus a detailed analysis of our perceptual experience, accompanied by an analysis of the structure of the input into the perceptual system, led to a meaningful informational explanation of how we perceive our visual environment. Without an analysis of the structure of the stimulus input in relation to the perceptual interpretation of that input, understanding the cognitive processes may be impossible.

Problem solving

Many cognitive tasks may be thought of as involving problem solving, perhaps all of them (Anderson 1990). A problem exists when a cognitive system has a goal that it wants to achieve. Examples of problems could include recognizing a duck, solving a calculus problem, making a hand axe, designing a bridge, building a bridge, reading a sentence, writing a novel, removing a brain tumour, etc. If a problem is a complicated or difficult one, it can often be broken down into a set of interrelated smaller problems.

An information processing analysis of problem solving begins with an analysis of the scope of the problem to be solved. What is the knowledge of the organism and what is his situation prior to attempting the problem (the initial state)? What is the knowledge of the organism and what is his situation after the problem has been solved (goal state)? What are the differences between these two conditions? The goal of the analysis is to identify the knowledge and skill required to execute a set of effective procedures that moves the world from the initial state to the goal state.

An analysis of problem solving has at least four components:

(1) Identifying the problem space. The first stage of an analysis of a problem is to identify the initial and goal states (Newell and Simon 1972). These two states define the boundary of the problem space. The larger the 'distance' between the two states the larger the problem space.

(2) Identifying some of the intermediate states between the initial and goal state. Only for trivial problems can the solver go directly from the initial state to the goal state. There are usually going to be relatively stable describable intermediate states which need to be reached. Both the problem solver and the analyst may need to know of these.

(3) Identifying what needs to be done, the 'moves', which enable the problem solver to get from one state to another. In order for a problem to be solved there has to be some procedure by which the situation is transformed from one state to another.

(4) Identifying the resources, e.g. knowledge, skills, material, personnel and time, needed to execute each of the moves. What is needed in order to reach each of the states from the immediately previous state?

Problem solving seems very different depending on whether the problem solver is a novice, an expert, or someone in between. If the problem is a familiar one, and the solver is an expert, problem solution may be relatively automatic. The expert's knowledge and skill greatly enrich the 'initial' state and bring it much closer to the goal state. Because of this, very complicated problems, as viewed from other perspectives, may be simple applications of standard procedures. If the problem solver is a novice, a problem which seems to be trivial to the expert may seem impossible. The initial state is much further from the goal state when the problem solver is a novice who might know neither what intermediate states are needed, nor how to reach them.

Problem solving incorporates the basic components of intelligent behaviour. It is motivated goal-directed behaviour. In order to be able to solve a problem, a person must have a goal in mind, and be able to identify and coordinate a sequence of actions which lead towards that goal. This requires being able to organize and use a data base consisting of representational and procedural knowledge. A successful problem solver who does not have such knowledge or skill must have the ability to attain it from the social and physical environment.

Applications to archaeology

Palaeolithic hand tools

Hand 'chopping tools' seem to have been used by proto-man 2,600,000 years ago. Flint stones which were chipped on one side to give them a sharp edge have been found over varying locations dated over many millennia. The locations and numbers of such objects strongly suggest that they were not naturally formed and located, but rather they were made by intelligent beings (Bordaz 1970). The fact that these objects can be used to split and break bones, among other possible uses, and some of them are found with split and broken bones, suggests that they may have been made for this purpose.

Early man made these 'chopping tools'. Making them requires a sequence of activities that is far too complicated to have been achieved by random activity thousands of times. Thus they were created intentionally. Since one needs a tool to make the chopping tool, there must have been a state of technical knowledge between no tools and the shaped chopping tool. That state most likely is the direct use of naturally found objects as tools. It is highly unlikely that a rock would be first used as a tool to make another tool. The idea of using a tool is a cognitive state prior to the idea of using a tool to make a tool. Thus palaeolithic man undoubtedly used unshaped natural materials as tools for more direct needs before he used them to shape the chopping tools, and this knowledge must have been communicated either directly or indirectly.

Making a tool is a problem which was solved within primitive cultures. What cognition did they have in order to solve it? What is the initial state for a palaeolithic toolmaker? The individuals who made tools had to know what a chopping tool is and what its properties are. This knowledge logically either has to be creatively invented from observing the value of naturally occurring broken stones or it has to be known within the community. It is highly unlikely that these tools were invented more than a very few times. Thus the community had to have the knowledge and had to communicate it to the toolmaker in one way or another.

One intermediate state is the presence of an appropriate stone to shape in the toolmaker's hands. To reach that state the toolmaker needed to know where to find the stone and how to select one of the right size, and how to determine that it is made of the right material. Again, this could logically be done by trial and error, in which case the toolmaker would have to show a great deal of diligence since only a very few of the tools made would be functional.

A second intermediate state consists of bringing the unshaped stone together with a 'hammerstone' (which also had to be selected) to shape it with a plan to make the chopping tool. These tools are made by repeatedly hitting one stone with another. The toolmaker had to learn how to hit them together to produce the cutting edge. This latter is a skill which has to be learned. Whether toolmaking was a common skill learned and practised by many in the community, or a rare one learned only by a few, it is evidence of intelligent behaviour.

Different tools developed over many generations gradually became more regularized and efficient. Some archaeologists have used experimental methods to investigate the difficulty of reaching the different intermediate states in making these tools. One can also do research to find out what these artefacts may be used for. Structural analyses, experiments and finding similar artefacts in current use among some peoples can help understand their role in the society (Bordaz 1959). These efforts, combined with data on the kinds, quantity and distribution of artefacts, may lead to a detailed account of some of the knowledge different prehistoric peoples attained.

The weights at Mohenjo-daro

Colin Renfrew has discussed some objects found in the Mohenjo-daro site. They are described as 'attractive and carefully worked cubes . . . made of coloured stone which had to be imported over some distance' (Renfrew 1982: 16–17). These cubes were found to be of a limited number of different sizes. The weights of the larger cubes were limited whole-number multiples of the weight of the smallest. Each of the smallest cubes weighed about 0.836 grams (= u). The larger cubes weighed 2u, 4u, 8u, 16u, 32u, and other larger sizes (Renfrew mentions 320u and 1600u). From the slides that I saw of these cubes they seem to be quite carefully squared off.

Renfrew makes several assertions from these cubes about cognition of the culture producing them including:

(1) That the society in question had no developed concept equivalent to our own notion of weight or mass.

(3) That there was a system of numeration, involving hierarchical numerical categories (like tens and units), in this case apparently based on the fixed ratio of 16.

(4) That this weight system was used for practical purposes (as the finding of scale pans corroborates), constituting a measuring device for mapping the world quantitatively as well as qualitatively. (Renfrew 1982: 17; his numbers)

We can learn quite a lot about the cognition and culture of these people from careful study of these cubes. They were carefully and intentionally made, so there was a reason to make them. The weights must have had a role in the culture. It is not obvious how to shape cubes to be in small whole-number weight relation to one another. A problem analysis shows the difficulty. If the cubes have the same density, i.e. are made of the same substance, and they are similar in shape, the second smallest (weight = 2u) would be about 1.26 times as large as the smallest on each of its dimensions. The third smallest would be slightly less than 1.59 times as large as the smallest on each of its dimensions. If the cubes were made of different substances, the linear dimensions would vary depending on the density of the stone.

It is unlikely that this culture had the means to measure and cut the different lengths to the second or third decimal point, so the 'weight maker' may have been a skilled and knowledgeable artisan who could cut and size the stones to a high degree of precision from experience. He would need to select stones of the right size for shaping and he would have to be skilful in that process. It would take an expert with many thousands of hours of experience to become skilful enough to recognize the right stones and to shape them the right size without a detailed supporting technology (see Norman 1982; Frake 1985). If the stones all came from the same quarry it is possible that a less skilful person could bring back a large number of stones and the artisan could select from among them. Or the artisan may have gone to the quarry to select the appropriate stones, either to shape them at the quarry or at a 'factory' elsewhere.

There are other possibilities in finding the appropriate stones for shaping. They may have brought a set of weights (standards) to match the stones against so that they were of approximately the right size for shaping and then used the

standards to compare the linear dimensions against. They might have developed a set of rulers marked with the appropriate lengths to mark them off on the stones to be shaped into cubes. Either of these techniques require a high degree of planning and preparation. In any of these cases, including that of the skilled artisan, if the cubes were really accurate to the third decimal, there would probably have to be a final testing and refining of the cubes by balancing them against one another to get them to be exactly the right size.

From an information processing analysis, we can conclude that at least some individuals in the culture had to spend a great deal of time in the manufacture of the cubes. These individuals had to be highly familiar with the relative linear sizes of the cubes needed as well as of their weight. They had to be skilled at judging the relative weight of 'raw' stones. They needed to know what tools to use and how to use them to cut the stones roughly and then to refine the weights by some fine-tuned chipping or sanding process. They had to organize and control the cutting process in order to end up with an object of the right size and shape. Each of the surfaces were close to planar and abutting surfaces were close to being perpendicular to one another. They had to know how to check the weights, probably by balancing one against another on a balance scale, and to refine them when they were not accurate.

The artisans and the community obviously knew that two of one size was equal in weight to one of the next, so they had to be familiar with the concept of doubling. If there were no 3u, 5u, and 7u, etc. weights, we cannot be sure that they understood the process of counting sequentially. Renfrew (1982) suggests that there were 320u and 1600u cubes. Doubling would not give multiples of ten; I do not know the process that would lead to these weights. Without further evidence one probably should not conclude that the larger cubes were derived from the same system.

These people understood that quantity was based on proportional mass rather than proportional linear dimensions, and used that to establish relative value. Processes involving proportional weights imply the concept of a unit of mass. They had to know that two of size u equals one of size 2u, etc., in order to construct the sequence of weights.

It is very likely that these weights played an important role in some exchange system. This exchange system would have to be based on the quantity of substances rather than (or in addition to) the number of items. The system must have been fairly important since the society had to commit significant resources to its production. I do not know what status the weight artisans had, but they had to be highly trained and skilled individuals. They probably attained their degree of mastery by some kind of apprentice program, because they had a lot to learn in order to produce accurate weights. The fine finished form of the weights strongly suggests that accuracy was considered very important. An untrained individual could not simply go out and make the weights.

Conclusion

There is evidence of the mind of man in every archaeological site. Just about every artefact and every edifice was intentionally created. Almost all of them required detailed knowledge accompanied by a modicum of skill. Studying them in detail from the point of view of what was the cognition that underlay the construction and use of these objects informs us about what the peoples of these communities knew, thought and did. To the extent that there is minimal variability in a set of equivalent artefacts, such as tools with very similar shapes and sizes, or temples oriented in exactly the same direction, there is evidence of both planning and skill. Cognitive science has been developing concepts and methods that allow us to identify and specify many of the intentions, and cognitive and behavioural processes that went into the planning, design and construction of these objects. These are part of the conceptual world of the ancient peoples, and they can help us understand some of the cognitions and motivations involved in the use of these objects after they were constructed.

Since intentional actions are motivated actions, to the extent that a project required a great deal of time and effort, there must have been very important reasons to sustain the effort.

References

Anderson, J. A. 1990. *Cognitive psychology and its implications*. New York, W. H. Freeman

Binford, L. R. 1983. *In pursuit of the past: decoding the archaeological record*. New York, Thames and Hudson

Bordaz, J. 1970. *Tools of the Old and New Stone Age*. Garden City, NY, Natural History Press

Brainerd, W. S. and L. H. Landweber 1974. *Theory of computation*. New York, Wiley

Broadbent, D. E. 1958. *Perception and communication*. London, Pergamon Press

Cottrell, L. (ed.) 1960. *The concise encyclopedia of archaeology*. New York, Hawthorn Books

Dretske, F. I. 1981. *Knowledge and the flow of information*. Cambridge, Mass., MIT Press

Fodor, J. A. 1975. *The language of thought*. New York, Cosswell

Frake, C. O. 1985. Cognitive maps of time and tide among medieval seafarers. *Journal of the Royal Anthropological Institute* 20: 254–70

Gibson, J. J. 1950. *The perception of the visual world*. Boston, Houghton Mifflin

1966. *The senses considered as perceptual systems*. Boston, Houghton Mifflin

Koffka, K. 1935. *Principles of gestalt psychology*. New York, Harcourt Brace and World

Kohler, W. 1947. *Gestalt psychology*. New York, Liveright

Marr, D. 1982. *Vision*. San Francisco, W. H. Freeman

Newell, A. 1981. Physical Symbol Systems. In *Perspectives in cognitive science*, ed. D. A. Norman, Norwood, NJ, Ablex

Newell, A. and H. A. Simon 1972. *Human problem solving*. Englewood Cliffs, NJ, Prentice Hall

1976. Computer science as empirical inquiry: symbols and search. *Communications of the ACM* 19: 111–26

Norman, D. A. (ed.) 1981. *Perspectives in cognitive science*. Norwood, NJ, Ablex

1982. *Learning and memory*. San Francisco, W. H. Freeman

Pylyshyn, Z. W. 1984. *Computation and cognition: toward a foundation for cognitive science*. Cambridge, Mass., MIT Press

Rapaport, W. J. 1990. Cognitive Science. In *Encyclopedia of computer science and engineering*, 3rd edn. ed. A. Ralston and E. D. Reilly, pp. 185–9. New York, Van Rostrand Reinhold

Renfrew, C. 1982. *Towards an archaeology of mind*. Cambridge, Cambridge University Press

Shannon, C. E. and W. Weaver 1949. *The mathematical theory of communication*. Urbana, Illinois, University of Illinois Press

Simon, H. A. 1969. *The sciences of the artificial*. Cambridge, Mass., MIT Press

Wiener, N. 1948. *Cybernetics*. New York, Wiley

4

From domain specific to generalized intelligence: a cognitive interpretation of the Middle/Upper Palaeolithic transition

STEVEN MITHEN

Introduction

One of the tasks facing cognitive archaeology is to contribute towards an understanding of the nature and evolution of the human mind. We need to make explicit reference to past cognition when interpreting the archaeological record and to draw inferences from that data concerning *ancient minds*. Did, for instance, *Homo habilis* have language, *Homo erectus* self-awareness or Neanderthals the capacity for analogical reasoning? While fossil endocasts may inform about brain structure, the character of past cognition must be largely inferred from the archaeological record. And to draw such inferences archaeologists need to engage with, or rather become participants in, the cognitive sciences – just as Bloch (1991) has recently argued for anthropology. This is essential since we cannot pretend to understand the ancient mind without entering debates concerning the character of the modern mind.

In this paper I focus on one of these debates, that concerning whether the mind is a general purpose learning mechanism or composed of a series of relatively independent mental modules – psychological mechanisms dedicated to specific tasks or behavioural domains. My review of this debate suggests that a major feature of human cognitive evolution has been increased accessibility between mental modules resulting in a generalized intelligence, though one remaining within a modular architecture. I consider whether the Middle/Upper Palaeolithic transition may have constituted a phase in human evolution during which there was a significant development from domain specific to generalized intelligence.

Mental modularity

A major question facing those concerned with the modern mind is the extent to which it is a general purpose information processor/learning mechanism, as opposed to being a series of mental modules – psychological mechanisms each dedicated to a specific purpose. A trend within cognitive science has been to see the mind as the latter, although several different notions of mental modularity have been proposed. While Fodor (1983) used the term 'mental modules', others have used 'adaptive specializations' (Rozin 1976), 'multiple intelligences' (Gardner 1983), 'Darwinian algorithms' (Cosmides and Tooby 1987) and 'cognitive domains' (Cheney and Seyfarth 1990). Each of these is an alternative perspective on the same basic idea – that the mind (of humans and other animals) is composed of a series of discrete psychological mechanisms, which may be based in their own neurological structures. Also at issue is the degree of accessibility – the flow of information and transference of psychological processes between mental modules.

The existence of some degree of mental modularity is well established for many non-human animal species which display remarkable cognitive feats in some areas, but are unable to apply such information processing to other tasks. For instance, bees are able to navigate over vast distances and salmon 'remember' a specific river in which they spawned; yet neither of these show comparable 'intelligence' in other areas of their lives. In Cosmides and Tooby's terms, they have specific Darwinian algorithms for these tasks.

Chomsky (1972) used a similar argument to propose that human language is a discrete, partly innate, cognitive module. The speed at which children acquire language implies specialized psychological mechanisms for language acquisition, rather than the use of a general purpose learning mechanism. After children have acquired complex grammatical structures and extensive vocabulary, they may still remain limited in other cognitive domains, such as the use and manipulation of numbers.

Fodor (1983) built upon Chomsky's work to argue that not only language, but all processes of perception, should be thought of as modules. He characterized these as computationally elaborate, domain-specific and informationally encapsulated. By the latter term he referred to the limited database of knowledge they have access to. The most compelling example is the persistence of optical illusions when they are 'known' to be false: the visual perception module is encapsulated from such knowledge. Fodor argued that these perceptual modules typically work very quickly and without control (e.g. one cannot stop oneself hearing other than by physical means). He found support for such notions of modularity by drawing on evolutionary theory, and citing examples of cognitive pathologies which impair some mental processes but leave others intact.

Fodor drew a contrast, however, between the modularity of perception and the generalized nature of cognition, or 'central processes'. According to Fodor, these latter are concerned with thought, reasoning, and problem solving – more generally with the fixation of belief. In central processes the information acquired by each module of perception is integrated to create a mental model of the world.

Multiple intelligences

The 'multiple intelligences' theory developed by Gardner (1983) bears both similarities and differences to Fodor's approach. It makes no distinction between perception and cognition but characterizes the mind as composed of six types of intelligence:

Linguistic intelligence – that concerned with phonology, syntax, semantics and pragmatics.

Musical intelligence – the ability of individuals to discern meaning and importance in sets of pitches rhythmically arranged and also to produce such metrically arranged pitch sequences as a means of communicating with individuals.

Logical mathematical intelligence – this concerns understanding the world of objects, actions and the relationships between these.

Spatial intelligence – the capacity to perceive the visual world accurately, to perform transformations and modifications upon one's initial perceptions, and to be able to recreate aspects of one's visual experience even in the absence of relevant physical stimulation.

Bodily-kinesthetic intelligence – the control of one's bodily motions and capacity to handle objects skilfully.

Personal intelligence – this has two aspects. On the one hand it concerns access to one's own thoughts and feelings, while on the other it concerns the ability to notice and make distinctions among other individuals, with particular relation to their moods, temperaments, motivations and intentions.

Gardner argued that these intelligences interact with, and build upon, each other, but at the core of each is a computational capacity or information processing device which is unique to that particular intelligence and upon which are based the more complex realizations and embodiments of that intelligence. Gardner emphasized the significance of the cultural environment as to the manner in which type of intelligence will develop in each person. He noted the stress laid in the Western world on logical-mathematical

intelligence. On this basis, he criticized Piagetian approaches for their almost sole focus on this when building a supposedly general theory of cognitive development.

Social and non-social intelligence

Gardner's notion of 'personal intelligence' is essentially the same as that of 'social intelligence' and 'social knowledge'. This is likely to have arisen early in human evolution (Humphrey 1976) and recent literature concerning non-human primates and cognitive development in children has given the notion of a distinctly 'social intelligence' substantial support (e.g. Byrne and Whiten 1988; Cheney and Seyfarth 1990, 1992). Social intelligence is that which enables one to interact effectively with other group members, particularly with regard to forming social alliances. This requires abilities to know and exploit the character of other individuals and their social relationships, and may involve a high degree of deception (Byrne and Whiten 1992). As such, social intelligence has been characterized as distinctly Machiavellian (Byrne and Whiten 1988). Humphrey argues that for modern humans social intelligence requires 'being sensitive to other people's moods and passions, appreciative of their waywardness and stubbornness, capable of reading signs in their faces and equally the lack of signs, capable of guessing what each person's past holds hidden in the present for the future' (1984: 4–5).

Cheney and Seyfarth (1990, 1992) contrasted social knowledge with non-social knowledge – that concerning other animal species, their interactions and the physical world – i.e. both animate and inanimate objects. Some of these may be relevant to survival and non-social knowledge may be alternatively termed ecological knowledge. As a cognitive domain it appears to combine elements of Gardner's spatial, logical-mathematical and bodily-kinesthetic intelligences. Cheney and Seyfarth conducted a unique series of experiments to evaluate the relative degrees of social and non-social intelligence in vervet monkeys. They found that, as theory predicted, vervet monkeys displayed much greater intelligence when interacting with conspecifics than with the non-social world. Many of the cognitive processes they used, such as the ability to classify conspecifics with regard to abstract categories, appeared inaccessible when interacting with either inanimate objects or members of other species. For instance, although a male may have no difficulty in assessing the relative social ranks of other males, he might be unable to rank the relative amounts of water in a series of containers. In addition, while the monkeys were very able to draw inferences from the behaviour of other individuals, they were very poor at drawing inferences from secondary visual cues, even when these appeared to be of considerable ecological value. For instance, the python is a major predator of the monkeys but they seemed unable to recognize the danger inherent in a recently made python track.

Darwinian algorithms

A more extreme approach to mental modularity has been taken by Cosmides and Tooby (1987, 1989). They embed their approach more firmly in Darwinism, arguing that the study of cognition makes the essential link between evolutionary theory and behaviour. Rather than positing domains or modules, they believe that the mind is composed of a large series of psychological mechanisms each dedicated to a very specific problem, the solution of which was of benefit in the evolutionary environment of modern humans. They coined the term 'Darwinian algorithms' for those innate, domain-specific processes used for tasks such as kin recognition and foraging behaviour. Consequently, they stress the need to understand the character of that evolutionary environment since it provided the selective pressures for the particular psychological mechanisms that evolved and which we possess today. As such, Darwinian algorithms are now used in environments very different from those in which they evolved. As a consequence, it is likely that many forms of modern behaviour will show no adaptive relationship to the modern environment, although they can be effectively studied from a Darwinian perspective.

Accessibility and hierarchization

Accessibility refers to the degree of contact between mental modules. Rozin and Schull (1988) have argued that a critical feature of the human mind as compared with the minds of other primates, is the high degree of accessibility. Much of our own experience suggests that this is indeed the case. As Cheney and Seyfarth (1990) note, we use analogical reasoning not only to classify different types of kinship relations but in a diverse range of activities, such as when arguing about the taxonomic relations of hominid fossils. One of the major features distinguishing the human mind from that of other primates may be our ability to extend knowledge gained in one context to new and different ones. Similarly, we routinely use one psychological mechanism, probably evolved for a specific task, for a diverse array of problems. For instance we may use those evolved for interaction with conspecifics in the interaction with other animal species, as in anthropomorphic thinking. Gardner (1983) has recognized the significance of accessibility for human intelligence. While maintaining the idea that there are core psychological processes restricted to each intelligence, he notes that 'in normal human intercourse, one typically encounters complexes of intelligences functioning together smoothly, even seamlessly in order to execute intricate human activities' (1983: 279). The 'central system' of Fodor (1983) is the ultimate example of accessibility; for here information from all perceptual modules is combined to create a model of the world.

As Rozin and Schull (1988) describe, the theory of accessibility suggests that the principal course of cognitive evolution and development has been from domain-specific cognitive processes to a more generalized intelligence. They suggest that this fits with the developmental phenomenon of *décalage* – the sequenced appearance of the same ability in different domains, and with aspects of the development of number concepts and language. However, Greenfield (1991) has recently described the reverse process with reference to specific neural circuits. She described increasing modularity during development of those cognitive processes which control language and tool use. These become increasingly located in separate neural circuits.

Some resolution of this conflicting evidence may be found in the notion of hierarchization of cognitive processes during development and evolution. Gibson (1983, 1990, 1991a, b) has stressed the significance of hierarchical mental construction skills. That is, the development of new mental structures, each constructed by an integration of those operating at a lower level in a cognitive hierarchy. Such hierarchization appears well established in child development. For instance Case (1985) describes how the transition from one cognitive stage to another involves the hierarchical integration of executive structures that were assembled during the previous stage, but whose form and function were considerably different. Gibson (1983; Parker and Gibson 1979) argues that in this respect human ontogeny does recapitulate its phylogeny, challenging Gould's (1976) arguments to the contrary. The process of hierarchization may be a principal means by which accessibility between mental modules occurs. It helps explain how modularity *and* accessibility may increase with experience during development.

Summary

As described, there are several perspectives on the notion of mental modularity. Some, such as Cosmides and Tooby, take an extreme view, while others such as Fodor, consider that modularity applies to perception alone. The wide range of different views largely arises from the lack of research on domain specific intelligence, leaving it as a vague and little understood area – but nevertheless of critical importance (see Cords 1992; Cheney and Seyfarth 1992; Dugatkin and Clark 1992; Tomasello 1992).

As archaeologists wishing to engage with such work, we

should not feel constrained to commit ourselves to one or other perspective at present. For some issues, the most simple distinctions, such as that between social and non-social intelligence, may be most appropriate. For others, we may wish to refer to a more complex model, such as that of Gardner's 'multiple intelligences'. We may feel that we should define and focus on other forms of intelligences, or make distinctions within those defined by Gardner (1983).

One such development might be a greater concern with 'technical intelligence', in relation to the working of stone. As abilities in this area are likely to have had considerable selective value in human evolution, we may follow Cosmides and Tooby (1987, 1989) in suggesting specific psychological mechanisms or Darwinian algorithms evolved to facilitate the production of stone tools. This would be making an important distinction in the domain of non-social intelligence by distinguishing between interaction with inanimate and animate objects. Similarly, in light of our interest with subsistence, it is appropriate to define a 'natural history' intelligence with respect to the exploitation of animals and plants.

The important point to draw from this brief review is simply the notion of modularity – the idea that certain cognitive abilities may be dedicated to particular behavioural domains. Equally important is the notion of accessibility between mental modules. The argument that this is a particular, and indeed essential, feature of the modern human mind is persuasive. As such, we might ask whether the Middle/Upper Palaeolithic transition – regarded as marking the appearance of modern behaviour and thought – may represent a significant phase of increasing accessibility between mental modules. In this regard, the many behavioural changes associated with the transition would be largely a consequence of this development in human cognition. Consequently, I now turn to the transition and, following a brief synopsis of the major issues, consider the relative degrees of mental modularity possessed by Lower/Middle and Upper Palaeolithic hominids.

The Middle/Upper Palaeolithic transition: a cognitive event?

Changes in the archaeological record that may reflect the first appearance of fully modern cognition appear after *c.* 50,000 BP with the start of the Upper Palaeolithic. Most notably, we see the introduction of bone, antler and ivory technologies, the creation of personal ornaments and art, a greater degree of form imposed onto stone tools, a more rapid turnover of artefact types, greater degrees of hunting specialization and the colonization of arid regions (Mellars

1973, 1989; White 1982; Mellars and Stringer 1989). The extent to which these mark a real break in cultural/cognitive evolution, or rather a change in the manner in which archaeologists describe and interpret their material, is hotly debated (Clark and Lindly 1989; Mellars 1989; Lindly and Clark 1990).

On a global scale, the transition to modern humans and modern patterns of behaviour present a complex spatial and temporal mosaic – the apparent correlation between hominid type and culture in southwestern France is the exception rather than the rule (Mellars 1989; Chase and Dibble 1990). In most parts of the world, including the Levant, art remains a rare phenomenon during the Palaeolithic. But 'modern' behaviour and thought can be inferred from other types of development. In particular, we see at 50,000 BP, or soon afterwards, the colonization of the final parts of the globe, notably Australasia, Siberia and ultimately the New World. As Whallon (1989) has argued, the colonization of such areas with low density, diversity and predictability of resources is likely to have been possible only after fully modern human cognitive capacities had evolved, possibly to allow the required social structures, such as alliance networks to develop.

The appearance of language?

In light of the magnitude of the behavioural changes at the transition, Mellars (1991: 64) has asked whether we can 'identify some kind of major "threshold" in human cognitive development' associated with the transition. He suggests, along with Whallon (1989) and Binford (1989), that the transition marks the first appearance of fully modern language.

This is a very enticing argument. We cannot doubt that hominids with language will behave and leave an archaeological record very different to hominids without language. There are compelling arguments, however, that language arose considerably earlier in human evolution than at the time of the Middle/Upper Palaeolithic transition.

The repeated efforts by *H. erectus* to colonize the temperate zone of Eurasia implies developed food acquisition techniques and social alliances, which in turn imply certain linguistic abilities. Deacon (1989) has argued persuasively, on the basis of neuroanatomy, that brain development relating to language occurred early in human evolution, and no further neurological changes occurred after the appearance of archaic *Homo sapiens*.

In addition, the relationship between language and the particular behavioural changes at the transition remains ill-defined. Many of these changes relate to the performance of complex practical tasks, such as the working of bone and antler. Anthropologists have noted the minimal role that language plays in the transmission of such skills and it is probable that the knowledge to perform them is necessarily non-linguistic in character (Bloch 1991). Indeed, if we follow the modularity arguments described above, the appearance of a linguistic intelligence may not have substantial effects on many realms of behaviour. As Donald (1991) described, people who lack linguistic capacities, whether they be prelinguistic children, the illiterate deaf mutes of history or those suffering paroxysms involving language loss, all remain competent in many cognitive areas, such as episodic memory, manual skills, knowledge of the environment and the ability to cope with complex social situations.

In light of these problems with the 'language thesis' we need to explore alternative possible cognitive developments. One of these is the notion that the transition marks a substantial increase in the degree of accessibility between mental modules and the development of hierarchical cognitive processes. This finds considerable support in the archaeological record.

Mental modularity and the transition

My argument in this section will be that the archaeological record of the Lower and Middle Palaeolithic reflects the behaviour and thought of hominids with relatively high levels of mental modularity as compared to modern humans. Three cognitive domains can be considered: social, technical and natural history intelligence. In each of these we have evidence for cognitive abilities not dissimilar to those of modern humans. But with regard to technical, and especially natural history intelligence, we can also recognize that something is 'missing'. And I suggest that this missing element is access to cognitive abilities in the other domains.

Social intelligence

It is practically impossible to draw any direct inferences from the archaeological record concerning the character of social interaction during the Lower and Middle Palaeolithic and, consequently, the nature of social intelligence. Some broad generalizations can be proposed. For instance, to have survived in glaciated northern latitudes it is likely that hominids would have formed large groups requiring complex social interactions for their maintenance (Gamble 1987; Mithen 1994; see Dunbar 1988). Also, the high levels of morphological similarity between artefacts in many assemblages, such as handaxes (e.g. see Wynn 1989; Roe 1981), imply abilities at imitation which depend upon complex social relationships and social intelligence (Mithen 1994). While the archaeological data relating to social

interaction are ambiguous or absent, we can nevertheless be confident about inferring high levels of social intelligence for Lower and Middle Palaeolithic hominids simply due to its presence among monkeys and apes, as discussed above. Byrne and Whiten (1992) have presented a provocative scenario for the evolutionary trajectory of social intelligence, proposing that by 5–8 ma the last common ancestor of human and chimpanzee had sophisticated abilities in the attribution of intention to others and the imagination of alternative possible worlds. Moreover, they argue that while modern great apes may lack language, they may possess an understanding of the concept of communication. Consequently, we are able to infer at least this level of social intelligence for Lower and Middle Pleistocene hominids; if language had appeared, the complexity of social interaction and degree of social intelligence would no doubt have been substantially greater.

Technical intelligence

As discussed above, the value of stone tools in early hominid subsistence may have provided selective pressures for the evolution of specific Darwinian algorithms concerning the knapping of stone, which we may refer to as a technical intelligence. Even within the very earliest industries considerable sensorimotor skills are evident in the manufacture of tools, implying sophisticated perceptual and cognitive abilities with respect to stone working. Essentially modern cognitive abilities at working stone are evident with the Acheulian, and may be traced in the Oldowan (Gibson 1991b). The manufacture of bifaces involved long procedural templates (Gowlett 1984). Wynn (1989) has argued that the later Acheulian bifaces exhibit the use of complex spatial concepts. These are manifest in procedures such as the removal of a flake which maintains, or creates, three dimensional symmetry for an artefact. This implies the ability to make three dimensional mental rotations. The long procedural templates and use of such advanced spatial thought testify to cognition in stone knapping not substantially different from that of modern humans.

The Levallois technologies of the Mousterian also display levels of technical intelligence no less sophisticated than those of modern humans. It is now well established that the *chaînes opératoires* used by Middle Palaeolithic flint knappers were as long and complex as those used in the Upper Palaeolithic (Boëda 1988; Geneste 1988; Bar-Yosef and Meignen 1992; Mellars 1991). Along with the evidence for the transport of raw materials and tools over as much as 60–80 km (Geneste 1985; Roebroeks *et al.* 1988) this provides substantial grounds for inferring considerable planning depth and anticipation of future needs.

In general, stone industries from the Acheulian onwards

appear to reflect a high level of technical intelligence, notably involving spatial thought and motor co-ordination. While these cognitive abilities were present, they were not applied to the working of bone, antler and ivory. As Dennell (1983) argued, these require a different range of motor movements, such as cutting, grooving, sawing and grinding which may have depended upon additional cognitive processes to those used in knapping stone. But it is nevertheless remarkable that such developed technical intelligence may be present with regard to the working of stone, and to be apparently absent with regard to other materials. This may be one of the strongest indications of high degrees of mental modularity prior to the transition. Moreover, as will be discussed below, the rate of technological change during the Lower and Middle Palaeolithic was minimal, implying that stone tools were playing a very different role in the adaptations of pre-modern hominids.

Natural history intelligence

Here I am referring to the cognitive abilities used in the interaction with animals and plants, and more generally those used to track environmental variability. The detailed monitoring of environmental variability and fine-tuned adjustment of foraging behaviour is one of the most impressive features of modern hunter-gatherers. For this they use a vast array of cues from which substantial amounts of ecological information can be inferred by using a detailed understanding of animal behaviour and ecological relationships (Mithen 1990). The use of technology is critical in such adaptation and significant correlations between technical and environmental variability can be traced (Torrence 1983). Such fine grained environmental adaptation, involving long-term planning, the anticipation and prediction of animal movements, and flexible response to environmental variability can be inferred from the character of Upper Palaeolithic faunal assemblages (Mellars 1989; Mithen 1990). The degree to which this is present among Middle and Lower Palaeolithic hunter-gatherers is debatable.

Even though the interpretation of Lower and Middle Palaeolithic faunal assemblages is fraught with problems, we must nevertheless infer a relatively high level of natural history intelligence for early hominids. A specifically natural history intelligence is likely to have been essential for the colonization of northern latitudes after 1 ma and to account for the diverse range of subsistence activities evident in the archaeological record. In contrast to the vervet monkeys described above, Middle, and probably Lower, Palaeolithic hominids are most likely to have been able to use secondary visual cues, such as animal tracks, in their hunting activity. Indeed, when appropriate methodologies are applied such environmental adaptation can be directly

inferred. For instance, Stiner and Kuhn (1992) have demonstrated that in West Central Italy a detailed analysis of faunal remains and lithic assemblages can monitor behavioural variability during the Middle Palaeolithic that probably relates to environmental change.

The Middle Palaeolithic of southwestern France provides the most detailed and analysed data on early Palaeolithic subsistence. In particular, the faunal assemblages from Combe Grenal have been the subject of considerable discussion. In contrast to Binford's (1985) views, these, and other Middle Palaeolithic assemblages, are likely to reflect a substantial degree of large game hunting, as opposed to scavenging (Chase 1986, 1989). However, as Mellars (1989) concluded when reviewing the faunal and settlement data, such hunting is likely to have been less systematic, less intensive and less logistically organized than that of the Upper Palaeolithic. Middle Palaeolithic hunters appear to have undertaken far less prediction and anticipation of animal movements. This would have limited the degree to which economic practices were able to track environmental change, resulting in the economic 'conservatism' that Chase (1986) recognized at Combe Grenal.

He concluded that animal exploitation practices remained unchanged through all but the major environmental changes. This persistence in the undertaking of the same activities at the site, in spite of environmental change, provides a dramatic contrast to the behaviour of modern humans in which site function and economic activities are very sensitive to even minor environmental variability (e.g. Binford 1982). As Chase (1986) notes, the inferred Middle Palaeolithic behaviour is difficult to explain in terms of economic rationalism. This may indicate that while the natural history intelligence of Middle Palaeolithic hominids was clearly sufficient to allow them to survive in a range of harsh environments, it nevertheless did not allow hominids to attain such fine-tuned adaptation to environmental variability as found among modern humans.

As noted above, this fine grained tuning partly derives from the use of technology. As such, the natural history and technical intelligences of modern humans are intimately intertwined. During the Upper Palaeolithic this results in the constant adaptation of technology to new environmental conditions. For instance, when temperatures in Europe fell to a minimum at *c*. 18,000 BP technology became more complex and tools specialized, forming appropriate tool kits for hunting on tundra-like environments (e.g. see Strauss 1991; Zvelebil 1984). Prior to the Upper Palaeolithic, however, technology does not appear to have played this role, suggesting a separation between technical and natural history intelligence.

The most telling evidence is the stasis in technology

during the early Palaeolithic. We have evidence for *H. erectus* and archaic *H. sapiens* living in a very diverse set of environments stretching from Pontnewydd Cave in North Wales (Green 1984) to the Cape of southern Africa (Keller 1973). Yet the degree of technological variability is limited and does not appear to correlate with fine grained environmental variables (Isaac 1977: 219; Binford 1989). It seems that the technology of early Palaeolithic hominids was not used to adapt to fine grained environmental variability, let alone restructure environments in the manner of modern humans. Binford (1989) makes a perceptive characterization by describing such technology as an 'aid to' rather than 'means of adaptation'. In sum, there appears to be limited connection between technical and natural history intelligence.

Summary: intelligence and mental modularity prior to the transition

To summarize, it is most reasonable to infer relatively high degrees of social, technical and natural history intelligence prior to the transition. In many respects these appear to be similar to those of modern humans, and consequently we find considerable evidence for continuity across the transition. However, there also appear to have been major differences. Natural history intelligence does not appear capable of achieving the same degree of fine grained environmental adaptation as found among modern humans, and to be separate from technical intelligence. Similarly the cognitive processes involved in the working of stone appear to be restricted to that material, although the working of bone or antler appears to require similar skills of manipulation and spatial thought. Overall, we might suggest that while high levels of social, technical and natural history intelligence were present, the cognitive abilities within each were restricted to that specific domain, i.e. Lower and Middle Palaeolithic hominids had high degrees of mental modularity. Their intelligence is most appropriately characterized as 'domain specific'.

The demise of mental modularity

If, as Mellars (1991) suggests, the transition marks a major cognitive threshold, then a dramatic increase in the degree of accessibility between mental modules appears likely. After the transition, the mind appears to possess a higher degree of generalized intelligence – though remaining within a distinctly modular architecture. Cognitive processes evolved for a very specific purpose or use in particular domains, such as stone working or social interaction, became available for other domains of behaviour. The consequences for technology are substantial, as cognitive abilities such as categorization and analogous thinking, previously restricted to social interaction, became available for the manufacture of tools and can account for many of the technological changes at the transition. Other consequences of increased accessibility can be briefly considered by examining two issues: environmental interaction and the origins of visual symbolism.

Environmental interaction after the transition

According to the model of increased accessibility, the intelligence which modern humans use when interacting with the non-social world, and particularly with animal and plant species, partly derives from that evolved with regard to other behavioural domains. The cognitive abilities present in the specialized domain of natural history intelligence became supplemented with those from other domains. The most significant source of these is likely to have been the social sphere and the most important cognitive ability the attribution of mental states – now applied to members of other animal species rather than conspecifics. From the Upper Palaeolithic onwards, the non-social world is explored and exploited partly using thought processes which evolved for social interaction.

Some of the consequences of the use of social intelligence in non-social contexts have been discussed by Humphrey (1976). He suggests that this may account for many types of fallacious reasoning repeatedly engaged in by modern humans. For instance many people have attempted to bargain with nature, such as through prayer, sacrifice or ritual persuasion. Similarly, the use of social intelligence appears to lie at the root of anthropomorphic thinking – the attribution of mental states to animals similar to those possessed by humans. Among hunter-gatherers such anthropomorphic thinking is pervasive, and anthropomorphs in Palaeolithic art indicate it stretches back to the earliest modern societies (e.g. a standing human with a feline face from Aurignacian contexts at Hohlenstein-Stadel: Marshack 1990: fig. 17.17). The predictions of animal behaviour based on anthropomorphic models are invariably correct, or at least as effective as the predictions made by western scientists (Mithen 1990: 76–7, e.g. see Blurton-Jones and Konner 1976; Silberbauer 1981; Gubser 1965). As such, the cognitive abilities derived from social intelligence supplemented those in natural history intelligence to transform the character of human-environment interactions.

The origins of visual symbolism

A further consequence of increased accessibility is that high level cognitive processes arise. Archaeologically, the most significant is visual symbolism, and here I will briefly summarize arguments I have made in detail elsewhere

(Mithen 1992). Visual symbolism first appears at the start of the Upper Palaeolithic with sculptured animals and anthropomorphic figures dating to *c.* 35,000 BP from Vogelherd, Geissenklösterle and Hohlenstein-Stadel in southern Germany (Hahn 1972, 1984). At a similar date, ivory beads carved to represent sea shells are found at La Souquette in southwestern France (White 1989), while a range of enigmatic 'vulva' signs are also found which are likely to have had symbolic status (Delluc and Delluc 1978). While arguments have been made for symbolic images during the Lower and Middle Palaeolithic (Marshack 1990; Bednarik 1992; Duff *et al.* 1992) all of these can be accounted for in other terms (Chase and Dibble 1989; Davidson 1992) – though their presence is important since they indicate that the constituting elements of visual symbolic capacities were present prior to the Upper Palaeolithic.

I have argued elsewhere (Mithen 1992) that the capacity for visual symbolism is constructed from four cognitive and physical processes: (1) the making of visual images; (2) classification, in the sense of recognizing that an image belongs to a certain class of symbols or constitutes the member of a new class; (3) intentional communication; and (4) the attribution of meaning to visual images. All of these are likely to have been present by the Middle Palaeolithic. The first three are found in the behavioural repertoires of many non-human primates. Monkeys, apes and hominids clearly have the physical ability to make marks, while intentional communication and skills at classification are found in social intelligence and arose early in human evolution (Cheney and Seyfarth 1990). The fourth element, the attribution of meaning to visual images, is likely to be restricted to hominids. As discussed above, monkeys (and probably apes) appear unable to attribute meaning to inanimate secondary visual cues, and elsewhere (Mithen 1992) I have argued that this ability evolved with respect to the use of animal tracks in foraging behaviour at least by the time of the later Middle Palaeolithic.

While each of these elements of visual symbolism are likely to have been present for many millennia prior to the Upper Palaeolithic, it was only after the transition that the capacity for visual symbolism arose. The reason is likely to be that these elements were located in different cognitive domains and hence inaccessible to each other. Intentional communication and classification are likely to have evolved as aspects of social intelligence, while mark making and the attribution of meaning, both involving inanimate material objects, were originally located in non-social intelligence. Consequently, these four elements could only have been integrated to form the high level cognitive process of visual symbolism after accessibility between the social and non-social cognitive domains had arisen.

Conclusion

The hypothesis that the behavioural changes associated with the Middle/Upper Palaeolithic transition may be due to increased accessibility between mental modules is not dependent upon a change in hominid species or population replacement. Increased accessibility may have arisen within one species or indeed one society, as people may be able to learn to access domain specific cognitive abilities (Rozin and Schull 1988). The mechanism of increased accessibility (like the notion itself) remains vague; Armstrong (1992) suggests that consciousness has a major role to play. I suspect that the demise of mental modularity was a gradual process involving change both within the cognitive architecture of archaic *H. sapiens* and the appearance of *H. sapiens sapiens* with generally lower degrees of mental modularity. Indeed, we may be dealing with a process that extended after the conventional start of the Upper Palaeolithic.

This hypothesis helps solve one of the major controversies in Palaeolithic studies – the degree of continuity or discontinuity across the transition. It has generally been assumed that when a cognitive ability is present in one behavioural domain, then it must also be present in all others. Consequently, when Binford claims a lack of planning depth in subsistence behaviour (1989), this has been taken (as Binford intended) to imply a lack of planning depth in all behavioural domains. And when planning depth is argued to be present on the basis of technology (Roebroeks *et al.* 1988), this is taken to imply that planning depth must be generally present. From the perspective of mental modularity, however, we should *expect* to find cognitive abilities restricted to particular domains. The question we must ask as archaeologists is not whether an ability is present or absent, but whether it is present or absent in a particular behavioural domain. Hence it is quite possible for early hominids to appear very modern in certain behaviours and for us to find considerable continuity across the transition, but to find difference and discontinuity in others.

As I stressed above, there are several different perspectives on mental modularity and the notion of accessibility remains vague. My discussion of the Middle/Upper Palaeolithic transition has necessarily been brief as I have made a preliminary exploration of the possible significance of the concepts of modularity and accessibility. Irrespective of the specific hypothesis of increased accessibility at the transition that I have proposed, the aim of this paper has been to demonstrate the need for a greater interaction between archaeology and the cognitive sciences. For it will only be from an engagement between these fields that progress will be made on understanding the *ancient mind*.

Acknowledgements

For discussion of the issues in this paper I thank Paola Fillipucci and Mark Lake.

References

Armstrong, D. M. 1992. Monkeys and consciousness (comment on Cheney, D. L. and R. M. Seyfarth, 1992. Précis of How monkeys see the world), *Behavioral and Brain Sciences* 15: 147–8

Bar-Yosef, O. and L. Meignen 1992. Insights into Levantine Middle Paleolithic cultural variability. In *The Middle Paleolithic: adaptation, behavior and variability*, ed. H. L. Dibble and P. Mellars, pp. 163–82. Philadelphia, University of Pennsylvania Press

Bednarik, R. G. 1992. Palaeoart and archaeological myths, *Cambridge Archaeological Journal* 2: 27–57

Binford, L. R. 1982. The archaeology of place. *Journal of Anthropological Archaeology* 1: 5–31

1985. Human ancestors: changing views of their behavior. *Journal of Anthropological Archaeology* 4: 292–327.

1989. Isolating the transition to cultural adaptations: an organizational approach. In *The emergence of modern humans: biocultural adaptations in the later Pleistocene*, ed. E. Trinkaus, pp. 18–41. Cambridge, Cambridge University Press

Bloch, M. 1991. Language, anthropology and cognitive science. *Man* (N.S.) 26: 183–98

Blurton-Jones, H. and M. J. Konner 1976. !Kung knowledge of animal behaviour. In *Kalahari hunter-gatherers*, ed. R. B. Lee and I. DeVore, pp. 326–48. Cambridge, Mass., Harvard University Press

Boëda, E. 1988. *Approche technologique du concept Levallois et évaluation de son champ d'application: Etude de trois gisements saaliens et weichséliens de la France septentionale*. Thèse de doctorat, Université de Paris X

Byrne, R. W. and A. Whiten (eds.) 1988. *Machiavellian intelligence: social expertise and the evolution of intellect in monkeys, apes and humans*. Oxford, Clarendon Press

1992. Cognitive evolution in primates: evidence from tactical deception. *Man* (N.S.) 27: 609–27

Case, R. 1985. *Intellectual development: birth to adulthood*. New York, Basic Books

Chase, P. G. 1986. *The hunters of Combe Grenal: approaches to middle paleolithic subsistence in Europe*. Oxford, British Archaeological Reports (BAR International Series 286)

1989. How different was middle palaeolithic subsistence? A zooarchaeological perspective on the Middle to Upper Palaeolithic transition. In *The human revolution: behavioural and biological perspectives on the origins of modern humans*, ed. P. Mellars and C. Stringer, pp. 321–37. Edinburgh, Edinburgh University Press

Chase, P. G. and H. L. Dibble 1989. Middle palaeolithic symbolism: a review of current evidence and interpretations. *Journal of Anthropological Archaeology* 6: 263–93

1990. On the emergence of modern humans. *Current Anthropology* 31: 58–9

Cheney, D. L. and R. M. Seyfarth 1990. *How monkeys see the world*. Chicago, University of Chicago Press

1992. Précis of How monkeys see the world. *Behavioral and Brain Sciences* 15: 135–82

Chomsky, N. 1972. *Language and mind*. New York, Harcourt Brace, Jovanovich

Clark, G. A. and J. M. Lindly 1989. The case for continuity: observations on the biocultural transition in Europe and Western Asia. In *The human revolution: behavioural and biological perspectives on the origins of modern humans*, ed. P. Mellars and C. Stringer, pp. 626–76. Edinburgh, Edinburgh University Press

Cords, M. 1992. Social versus ecological intelligence (comment on Cheney, D. L. and R. M. Seyfarth, 1992. Précis of How monkeys see the world). *Behavioral and Brain Sciences* 15: 151

Cosmides, L. and J. Tooby 1987. From evolution to behaviour: evolutionary psychology as the missing link. In *The latest on the best: essays on evolution and optimality*, ed. J. Dupré, pp. 277–306. Cambridge, Mass., The MIT Press

1989. Evolutionary psychology and the generation of culture, part I, *Ethology and Sociobiology* 10: 29–49

Davidson, I. 1992. There's no art – to find the mind's construction – in offence (reply to R. Bednarik 1992, Palaeoart and archaeological myths). *Cambridge Archaeological Journal* 2: 52–7

Deacon, T. 1989. The neural circuitry underlying primate cells and human language. *Human Evolution* 4: 367–401

Delluc, B. and G. Delluc 1978. Les manifestations graphiques aurignaciennes sur support rocheux des environs des Eyzies (Dordogne). *Gallia Préhistoire* 21: 213–438

Dennell, R. 1983. *European economic prehistory*. London, Academic Press

Donald, M. 1991. *Origins of the modern mind*. Cambridge, Mass., Harvard University Press

Duff, I. A., G. A. Clark and T. J. Chadderdon 1992. Symbolism in the early Palaeolithic: a conceptual odyssey. *Cambridge Archaeological Journal* 2 (2): 211–19

Dunbar, R. I. M. 1988. *Primate social systems*. London, Croom Helm

Dugatkin, L. A. and A. B. Clark 1992. Of monkeys, mechanisms and the modular mind (comment on Cheney, D. L. and R. M. Seyfarth, 1992. Précis of How monkeys see the world). *Behavioral and Brain Sciences* 15: 153–4

Fodor, J. A. 1983. *The modularity of mind*. Cambridge, Mass., MIT Press

Gamble, C. 1987. Man the shoveler: alternative models for Middle Pleistocene colonization and occupation in northern latitudes. In *The Pleistocene Old World*, ed. O. Soffer, pp. 81–98. New York, Plenum Press

Gardner, H. 1983. *Frames of mind: the theory of multiple intelligences*. New York, Basic Books

Geneste, J.-K. 1985. *Analyse lithique des industries moustériennes du Périgord: une approche techno-logique du comportement des groupes humains au Paléolithique moyen*. Thèse de doctorat, Université de Bordeaux I

1988. Systèmes d'approvisionnement en matières premières au Paléolithique moyen et au Paléolithique supérieur en Aquitaine. In *L'Homme de Néandertal, vol. 8, La mutation*, ed. M. Otte, pp. 61–70. Liège, Etudes et Recherches Archéologiques de l'Université

Gibson, K. R. 1983. Comparative neurobehavioral ontogeny and the constructionist approach to the evolution of the brain, object manipulation and language. In *Glosso-genetics: the origin and evolution of language*, ed. E. de Grolier, pp. 37–61. Harwood Academic Publishers

1990. New perspectives on instincts and intelligence: brain size and the emergence of hierarchical mental construction skills. In *'Language' and intelligence in monkeys and apes*, ed. S. T. Parker and K. R. Gibson, pp. 97–128. Cambridge, Cambridge University Press

1991a. Continuity versus discontinuity theories of the evolution of human and animal minds (comment on P. M. Greenfield, Language, tools and brain: the ontogeny and phylogeny of hierarchically organised sequential behaviour). *Behavioral and Brain Sciences* 14: 560–1

1991b. Tools, language and intelligence: evolutionary implications. *Man* 26: 255–64

Gould, S. J. 1976. *Ontogeny and phylogeny*. Cambridge, Mass., Harvard University Press

Gowlett, J. 1984. Mental abilities of early man: a look at some hard evidence. In *Human evolution and community ecology*, ed. R. Foley, pp. 167–92. London, Academic Press

Green, H. S. 1984. *Pontnewydd Cave: a lower palaeolithic hominid site in Wales*. Cardiff, National Museum of Wales

Greenfield, P. M. 1991. Language, tools and brain: the ontogeny and phylogeny of hierarchically organised sequential behaviour. *Behavioral and Brain Sciences* 14: 531–95

Gubser, N. J. 1965. *The Nunamiut Eskimo: hunters of caribou*. New Haven, Yale University Press

Hahn, J. 1972. Aurignacian signs, pendants, and rare objects in Central and Eastern Europe. *World Archaeology* 3: 252–66

1984. Recherches sur l'art paléolithique depuis 1976. In *Aurignacian et Gravettian en Europe*, ed. J. K. Kozlowski and R. Desbrosses, vol. 3, pp. 79–82. Liège, Etudes et Recherches Archéologiques de l'Université 13

Harrold, F. B. 1989. Mousterian, Châtelperronian and Early Aurignacian in Western Europe: continuity or discontinuity. In *The human revolution: behavioural and biological perspectives on the origins of modern humans*, ed. P. Mellars and C. Stringer, pp. 677–713. Edinburgh, Edinburgh University Press

Humphrey, N. 1976. The social function of intellect. In *Growing points in ethology*, ed. P. P. G. Bateson and R. A. Hinde, pp. 303–17. Cambridge, Cambridge University Press

1984. *Consciousness regained*. Oxford, Oxford University Press

Isaac, G. I. 1977. *Olorgesaille, archaeological studies of a middle pleistocene lake basin in Kenya*. Chicago, Chicago University Press

Keller, C. M. 1973. *Montagu Cave in prehistory*. Berkeley, Anthropological Records No. 28, University of California

Lindly, J. and G. Clark 1990. On the emergence of modern humans. *Current Anthropology* 31: 59–63

Marshack, A. 1990. Early hominid symbol and evolution of the human capacity. In *The emergence of modern humans: an archaeological perspective*, ed. P. Mellars, pp. 457–98. Edinburgh, Edinburgh University Press

Mellars, P. 1973. The character of the Middle–Upper Palaeolithic transition in southwest France. In *The explanation of culture change*, ed. C. Renfrew, pp. 255–76. London, Duckworth

1989. Major issues in the emergence of modern humans. *Current Anthropology* 30: 349–85

1991. Cognitive changes and the emergence of modern humans. *Cambridge Archaeological Journal* 1: 63–76

Mellars, P. and C. Stringer (eds.) 1989. *The human revolution: behavioural and biological perspectives on the origins of modern humans.* Edinburgh, Edinburgh University Press

Mithen, S. J. 1990. *Thoughtful foragers: a study of prehistoric decision making.* Cambridge, Cambridge University Press

1992. The origin of art: mental modularity, ecological intelligence, and the Middle/Upper Palaeolithic transition. Paper prepared for the Second AURA congress, Cairns, Australia, September 1992

1994. Technology and society during the Middle Pleistocene: hominid group size, social learning and industrial variability. *Cambridge Archaeological Journal* 4 (1): 3–32

Parker, S. T. and K. Gibson 1979. A developmental model for the evolution of language and intelligence in early hominids. *Behavioral and Brain Sciences* 2: 367–407

Roe, D. 1981. *The lower and middle palaeolithic periods in Britain.* London, Routledge and Kegan Paul

Roebroeks, W., J. Kolen and E. Rensink 1988. Planning depth, anticipation and the organization of Middle Palaeolithic technology: the 'archaic natives' meet Eve's descendants. *Helinium* 28: 17–34

Rozin, P. 1976. The evolution of intelligence and access to the cognitive unconscious. In *Progress in psychobiology and physiological psychology*, ed. J. M. Sprague and A. N. Epstein, pp. 245–77. New York, Academic Press

Rozin, P. and J. Schull 1988. The adaptive-evolutionary point of view in experimental psychology. In *Stevens' handbook of experimental psychology, Vol. 1: perception and motivation*, ed. R. C. Atkinson, R. J. Herrnstein, G. Lindzey and R. D. Luce, pp. 503–46. New York, John Wiley and Sons

Silberbauer, G. B. 1981. *Hunter and habitat in the Central Kalahari Desert.* Cambridge, Cambridge University Press

Stiner, M. C. and S. L. Kuhn, 1992. Subsistence, technology and adaptive variation in Middle Palaeolithic Italy. *American Anthropologist* 94: 306–39

Straus, L. 1991. Southwestern Europe at the last glacial maximum. *Current Anthropology* 32: 189–99

Tomasello, M. 1992. Cognitive ethology comes of age (comment on Cheney, D. L. and R. M. Seyfarth, 1992. Précis of How monkeys see the world). *Behavioral and Brain Sciences* 15: 168–9

Torrence, R. 1983. Time budgeting and hunter-gatherer technology. In *Hunter-gatherer economy in prehistory*, ed. G. Bailey, pp. 57–66. Cambridge, Cambridge University Press

Whallon, R. 1989. Elements of cultural change in the Later Palaeolithic. In *The human revolution: behavioural and biological perspectives on the origins of modern humans*, ed. P. Mellars and C. Stringer, pp. 433–54. Edinburgh, Edinburgh University Press

White, R. 1982. Rethinking the Middle/Upper Paleolithic transition. *Current Anthropology* 23: 169–92

1989. Production complexity and standardization in early Aurignacian bead and pendant manufacture: evolutionary implications. In *The human revolution: behavioural and biological perspectives on the origins of modern humans*, ed. P. Mellars and C. Stringer, pp. 366–90. Edinburgh, Edinburgh University Press

Wynn, T. G. 1989. *The evolution of spatial competence.* Urbana, University of Illinois Press

Zvelebil, M. 1984. Clues to recent human evolution from specialised technology. *Nature* 307: 314–15

5

Are images animated: the psychology of statues in Ancient Greece

ALAIN SCHNAPP

In the last years of the seventeenth century, the famous astronomer and antiquary of the Vatican, Francesco Bianchini, published *La istoria universale provata con monumenti e figurata con simboli* (Universal history as documented by monuments and illustrated by symbols). In this book, for the first time in the history of archaeology, Bianchini (1747: 10) assumed:

> le figure dei fatti ricoverate dei monumenti d'antichità oggidi conservate mi sono sembrate simboli insieme e prove dell'istoria.
>
> (the representation of events observed on present-day monuments seem to me on the one hand symbols and on the other documents of history.)

He was, in fact, the first who had reflected on the role of symbols not only as figures of the past, but as a cognitive medium leading to the development of an archaeological theory.

This paper is a reflection on symbolism in Greek society (following the direction proposed by C. Renfrew), an attempt to investigate the way in which symbols were used. I shall be concerned with Greco-Roman society, from the seventh century BC to the third century AD, assuming that during these ten centuries a central body of theory and experience was elaborated about making and using images.[1] I shall consider all symbolic artefacts used in either a cultic or cultural context for the very purpose of representation. This definition can already be read in Plato's work:

> *eidola* – is what is common to the various objects that we call by the name of images. (Plato, *Sophist* 240 a)

The function of images

The Greeks were conscious of their specificity: the lived in a *polis*. The city is not only a social structure but an aesthetic conception of politics. *Paideia*, education, is the keystone of the city and, according to Plato, *paideia* consists of: (*grammata*) learning, (*mousike*) cultural entertainment (not only music and performing arts, but also visual arts), gymnastics (*gumnastike*) in the sense of control and development of physical activities. Clearly *paideia* is not a simple concept but a complex body of notions embedded in a global definition of social ability. The city had to provide a wide range of cultural facilities for the entertainment of the citizen. Meanwhile the great originality of Greek culture was that this kind of highly refined art and social performance (theatre) had to face an astonishing creative freedom; poets, architects, craftsmen were in no way controlled by the state, as they were in the Egyptian or Assyrian kingdoms:

> *Clinias*. How, then, does the law stand in Egypt?
> *Athenian*. It is marvellous, even in the telling. It appears that long ago they determined on the rule of which we are now speaking, that the youth of a State should practise in their rehearsals postures and tunes that are good: these they prescribed in detail and posted up in the temples, and outside this official list it was, and still is, forbidden to painters and all other producers of postures and representations to introduce any innovation or invention, whether in such productions or in any other branch of music, over and above the traditional forms. And if you look there, you will find that the things depicted or graven there 10,000 years ago (I mean what I say, not loosely but literally 10,000) are no whit better or worse than the productions of to-day, but wrought with the same art. (Plato, *Laws* II, 656 d–e)

When Plato describes an Egyptian state, he clearly writes about something more Greek than anything else, but nevertheless he focuses his demonstration on the independence (highly dangerous in his eyes) of the Greek artist. At this point Plato, while developing the idea of an authoritarian Greek state, is tempted to establish a censorship which would be in charge of literature and all kinds of cultural creation.

> It is, then, only the poets that we must supervise and compel to embody in their poems the semblance of the good character or else not write poetry among us, or must we keep watch over the other craftsmen, and forbid them to represent the evil disposition, licentious, the illiberal, the graceless, either in the likeness of living creatures or in buildings or in any other products of their art, on

penalty, if unable to obey, of being forbidden to practise their art among us, that our guardians may not be bred among symbols of evil, as it were in a pasturage of poisonous herbs, lest grazing freely and cropping from many such day by day they little by little and all unawares accumulate and build up a huge mass of evil in their own souls. (Plato, *Republic* II, 401b)

The guardians of the city are handsome young men, not only well trained both intellectually and physically, but also on psychological grounds. To be a good citizen implies having a good training for the artistic senses, mostly sight and hearing.

But we must look for those craftsmen who by the happy gift of nature are capable of following the trail of true beauty and grace, that our young men, dwelling as it were in a salubrious region, may receive benefit from all things about them, whence the influence that emanates from works of beauty may waft itself to eye or ear like a breeze that brings from the wholesome places health, and so from earliest childhood insensibly guide them to likeness, to friendship, to harmony with beautiful reason. (Plato, *Republic* II, 401c)

We cannot read Plato as an historian of the city, as his purpose is the building of an entirely new state instead of simply describing contemporary Athens or Sparta. However, when elaborating the definition of *paideia*, he is providing us with important information about the status of visual and performing arts in Greece.

The origins of visual arts in ancient Greece

The use of images – *eikones, eidola* – is, for the Greeks, a central point in religious practice (Vernant 1979). People who do not use images for the purpose of cult are considered with astonishment:

[The Persians] have no images of the gods, no temples, no altars, and consider the use of them as a sign of folly. This comes, I think, from their not believing the gods to have the same nature with men as the Greeks imagine. (Herodotus, I, 131)

For the Greeks, a world without images is unconceivable and even more unthinkable. Maximus of Tyre, Dio of Prusa and Philostratus have explained this incapacity of the Barbarians to worship the gods in the appropriate way (Madyda 1939: 7–10). Cult, in fact, requires the faculty of representing the divinity, and Barbarian art, according to Dio, is characterized by 'insufficiency' and 'paucity' (Dio, *Or* XII, 61). This insufficiency is not only technical, it is

an inability 'to see correctly or to imagine the gods' (Philostratus, *Life of Apollonius* VI.19).

The medium of figuration

In order to worship a god you have to figure that god. But we are soon confronted with a first difficulty: the Greek language does not possess a word for 'statue'. Instead of this, the Greeks used a range of very different formulations: *baetylia, bretas, xoanon, agalma, idruma, kolossos, eidolon, eikon*. Each of these words is related to the existence of specific sorts of images operating in a special cultic context. This is due to the fact that Greek polytheism is determined by the variety of divine figures: to worship a god implies first to be able to distinguish a god from another. Figuration is a major part of this process.

The main character of Greek religion is its variety. Cult can also be related, in particular circumstances, to aniconic supports. We do not know for example if the *kolossos* – wood or wax images used in some funerary rituals – were aniconic or not (Vernant 1974). From a simple stone to a stone sculpture (*kouros*), from the wooden *bretas* or *xoanon* to the marble statue of the gods, from the poor wooden figure to the rich bronzes or even golden and ivory representations of divinity, Greek civilization developed a highly refined system of cultic expression. Each stage of this system had to be inserted in a definite meaning, dealing with the use of each cultic artefact. We can try to conjure up a sort of cognitive map of the kind shown in fig. 5.1.

Of course such a definition does not reflect the variety of chronological and regional attitudes in the representation of the invisible but it reveals to us the psychological background of cultural craftsmanship in ancient Greece.

AGALMA		
ICONIC	ANICONIC	
FIGURATIVE	NON FIGURATIVE	MATERIAL THINGS
WOOD CLAY BRONZE SILVER GOLD	STONE WOOD TREE	SPEARHEAD OBELOI TRIPODS

Fig. 5.1. Cognitive map of images and their medium of figuration

The human body and the body of the god

Why are the gods of the Greeks depicted as human figures? This way of figuring gods was already acknowledged by the Presocratics as a specificity of Greek religion:

> But mortals consider that the gods are born and that they have clothes and speech and bodies like their own. The Ethiopians say that their gods are snub-nosed and black, the Thracians that they have blue eyes and red hair . . . But if cattle and horses and lions had hands, or were able to draw with their hands and do works that man can do, horses would draw the forms of a god like horses, and cattle like cattle, they would make their bodies, such as they each had themselves. (Xenophanes, fragment 170, paragraph 172)

Carving a stone, modelling clay for vases or figurines is more than a mere process of imitation, it requires some creative capacity which is expressed in this quotation from Maximus of Tyre: 'the Greek manner of honouring the gods uses what is most beautiful on earth, in purity of raw materials, in human shape and in artistic precision' (Maximus of Tyre, VII, 3).

Making an image or statue requires not only technical skills, but the capacity to depict the god or the hero in a distinctive way. For the images of human beings, the Greeks also used the word *Somata* which means 'bodies'. Making images was seen as a competition, even between the different kinds of arts:

> So, after all, there was not one kind of Strife alone, but all over the earth there are two. As for the one, a man would praise her when he came to understand her; but the other is blameworthy: and they are wholly different in nature. For one fosters evil war and battles, being cruel: her no man loves; but perforce, through the will of the deathless gods, men pay harsh Strife her honour due. But the other is the elder daughter of dark Night, and the son of Cronos who sits above and dwells in the aether, set her in the roots of earth: and she is far kinder to men. She stirs up even the shiftless to toil; for a man grows eager to work when he considers his neighbour, a rich man who hastens to plough and plant and put his house in good order; and neighbour vies with his neighbour as he hurries after wealth. This strife is wholesome for men. And potter is angry with potter, and craftsman with craftsman, and beggar is jealous of beggar, and minstrel of minstrel. (Hesiod, *Works and Days*, 11–26)

The words used by Hesiod in the Archaic period are exactly the same as those written in the Judeo-Greek Book of Wisdom in the first century BC:

> For a potter kneading his clay laboriously moulds every vessel for our use, but out of the self-same clay he fashions without distinction the pots that are to serve for honourable uses and the opposite; and what the purpose of each one is to be, the moulder of the clay decides. And then with ill-directed toil he makes a false god out of the same clay . . . His concern is not that he must one day fall sick or that his span of life is short; but he must vie with goldsmiths, and silversmiths and copy the bronzeworkers, and he thinks it does him credit to make counterfeits. (Wisdom, XV, 7)

There is no word in Greek to match the German *Kunstwollen* but the idea exists, sealed in the Greek conception of plastic and visual creation: *eris*, competition, is the heart of the machine which produces images – *eidolopoietikê* in Plato's terms.

The Judeo-Christian critic of *Eris* – jealousy – in Greek image making is being answered in a Greek aphorism conserved in the Talmudic tradition:

(1) A certain philosopher asked Rabban Gamaliel: It is written in your Law: For I the Lord Thy God am a jealous God. (Ex. 20, 5)[2]
(2) But is there any power in the idol that it should arouse jealousy?
(3) A hero is jealous of another hero, a wise man is jealous of other wise men, a rich man is jealous of another rich man, but has the idol any power that one should be jealous of it? (Mekilta, *Mahesset Bahodesh*, 1–3)

This is a straightforward answer made by a paganist to a monotheist: while jealousy is part of the Jewish theology, it is also part of image making among the Greeks.

Making *eidola*

Statues, *idrumata*, *agalmata*, are necessary for the performance of cult, for the establishment of religious practice, and the making of these *idrumata* is the task of skilled craftsmen. But what is cultic craftsmanship? The statue, except in certain circumstances, is physically inert, it lies in a temple or in a house:

> For Pytheas of Aegina, winner in the boys pancratium, 485 (?) BC.
>   No sculptor am I, that I should carve statues doomed to linger only on the pedestal where they stand. No! I would bid my sweet song speed from Aegina, in every argosy, and in every skiff, spreading abroad the tidings that the stalwart Pytheas, son of Lampon, hath won the crown for the pancratium at the Nemean games, or ever he showed on his cheeks the hue of summer the soft

harbinger of youthful bloom. (Pindar, *5th Nemean Ode* 1–11)

The poet can compete with the sculptor, he is able to deliver his message through the living memory of men; when the statues or images are material, the poem is immaterial:

> Listen! for, in very deed, we are once more ploughing the field of bright-eyed Aphroditê or of the Graces, as we draw nigh unto the shrine that is the centre of the loudly echoing earth; where, for the prosperous Emmenidae and for the Acragas between the rivers and, chiefly for Xenocrates, there hath been built and prepared in Apollo's golden glen a Pythian victor's treasure-house of song which neither wintry rain . . . with its swirl of shingle, shall buffet and sweep away into the recesses of the sea. But the porch, in its pure brightness, shall proclaim a famous victory with the chariot, celebrated by the lips of mortals, and shared by the father Thrasybulus, and by his race, that was won in the dells of Crisa. (Pindar, *6th Pythian Ode*, 1–18)

The poem is built with no stone, but songs (Svenbro 1976: 190–1). Unlike the thesaurus of stones, the thesaurus of songs cannot be destroyed by rain, wind or frost; it is for ever shining in the immortal memory of men. (This competition between artists is in the same way an economic competition since the poet expects also to be paid for his poems.)

Can poetics really compete with visual arts? Painting images and carving *eikones* is a substitute for absence, a medium to insure the presence of a desired person. So Admetus is attempting to get a substitute for his wife:

> Fashioned by the craftsmen's cunning hands, thy form
> Imaged, shall lie as sleeping on a bed,
> Falling whereon, and clasping with mine hands,
> Calling thy name, in fancy shall mine arms,
> Hold my beloved, though I hold her not, . . .
> (Euripides, *Alcestis*, 348–52)

Image is a medium to avoid absence, to make the invisible visible: for the Greeks, representation understood as the double of a dead person is not a mere poetic metaphor. The *kolossos* – a statue made of wood or clay usually found in graves – has materialized the Greek notion of absence-made-presence. The *kolossos* is more than an image, it belongs to the universe of *eidola*, where the *agalmata* have their place. In the broad spectrum of representations set by the Greeks, the *kolossos* is situated at one extremity while the *eikon* lies at the other. Between these two different ways of figuring human and divine truth, *agalmata*, *bretas*, *idrumata*, *baetylia* and *xoana* express a subtle and precise

graduation. We cannot reconstruct the semiotics of Greek sculpture and painting in a very detailed way, but it is still possible to feel the opposition between an iconic and an aniconic pole (fig. 5.2).

Plato clearly stresses this opposition:

> Some of the gods whom we honour we see clearly, but of others we set up statues as images, and we believe that when we worship these, lifeless though they be, the living gods beyond feel great good-will towards us and gratitude. (Plato, *Laws*, 931a)

The statue (*agalma*) is an inanimate (*apsychos*) image (*eikôn*) which makes the living gods present. The efficiency of image is not on the same level as the psychology of the poem. Both painter and sculptor attempt to capture the attention of the man who looks at their creations by increasing the quality of craftsmanship; the art of images is mostly an art of tricks and illusion which requires knowledge and experience. Socrates speaks with the famous sculptor Cleiton:

> Cleiton, that your statues of runners, wrestlers, boxers, and fighters are beautiful I see and know. But how do you produce in them that illusion of life which is their most alluring charm to the beholder?
> As Cleiton was puzzled and did not reply at once, 'Is it, he added, 'by faithfully representing the forms of the living beings that you make your statues look as if they lived?'
> Undoubtedly. (Xenophon, *Memorabilia* III, x.6–7)

The craftsman becomes really a link between visible and invisible and each image, even non-cultic, attempts to grasp the identity of the subject depicted. But can the image convey the essence of the divinity, is the image itself divine? The Socratic answer to this question is another question (as

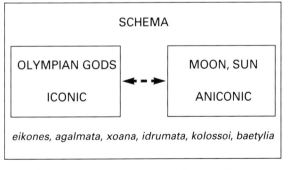

Fig. 5.2. Schematic representation of the opposition between iconic and aniconic images in Greek sculpture and painting

usual): is figuration a living part of the figured? Plato was aware of the dangers residing in the use of precious metals:

As regards votive offerings to the gods, it is proper for a reasonable man to present offerings of reasonable value. The soil and the hearth are in all cases sacred to the gods; wherefore no one shall consecrate afresh what is already sacred. Gold and silver, which in other States are used both privately and in temples, are objects liable to cause envy; and ivory, which comes from a body bereft of soul, is not a pure offering; while iron and bronze are instruments of war; of wood forming a single piece a man may offer in the public temples whatsoever he wishes, and of stone likewise, and of woven stuff an amount not exceeding a month's output by one woman. For woven stuff and other materials, white will be a colour befitting the gods; but dyes they must not employ, save only for military decorations. Birds and statues make most god-like gifts, and they should be no larger than what one sculptor can complete in a single day; and all other votive offerings shall be modelled in similar lines. (Plato, *Laws*, 956a–b).

The religious offerings should not be the expression of wealth. This statement was, of course, often expressed in the great Judeo-Christian polemics (Donohue 1988: 135ff.), even by Greek polytheists: what is more important, the value of metal or the value of artistic craftsmanship? The Christian answer is worse than Plato's:

Say you the stone, or wood, or silver is not as yet a god? When then does he come to the birth? See him cast, moulded, sculptured – not yet is he a god; see him soldered, assembled, and set up – still not a god; see him adorned, consecrated, worshipped, then finally he is a god – by a man's will and act of dedication. (Minucius Felix, *Octavius* XXII, 5).

Good craftsmanship is a means to achieve sculpture and painting, but in a certain sense it is the end of representation. If the image is so similar that it could be taken for a living being, it could enter into competition with the god it is supposed to represent. Image making is a deceiving art, because its first purpose is exactly to deceive. Many voices were raised against the use of images in the city: on theological grounds (Xenophanes), or artistic (Pindar), philosophical (Plato), or even comical (Aristophanes), but

without images the *polis* would have been more a city of ghosts than a city of gods.

Since Winckelmann, classical archaeology had considered the history of Greek images as the evolution from aniconic to iconic representation, and the historians of religion mostly agree. But if we consider the cognitive dimension of Greek image making, we may be sure that this widely accepted statement is wrong.

Notes

This paper is part of a work in progress on the meaning of ancient Greek imagery. A presentation of this project was published in Schnapp 1988.
1 Clerc 1915 and Donohue 1988 have presented the global file.
2 On this problem see Donohue 1988: 130.

References

Bianchini, F. 1747. *La Istoria universale provata con monumenti e figurata con simboli*. Rome, Antonio de Rossi

Clerc, C. 1915. *Les théories relatives au culte des images chez les auteurs grecs du IIème siècle après J.C.* Paris

Donohue, A. A. 1988. *Xoana and the origins of Greek sculpture*. Atlanta, Georgia, Scholars Press

Madyda, L. 1939. *De pulchritudine imaginum deorum quid auctores Greci saec. II. p. Chr. judicaverint*. Cracoviae, Academia Polana Litterarum

Schnapp, A. 1988. Why did the Greeks need images? In *Proceedings of the 3rd symposium, Ancient Greek pottery and related pottery*, ed. J. Christiansen and T. Melander, pp. 569–74. Copenhagen, Carlsberg Glyptothek-Thorvaldsens Museum

Svenbro, J. 1976. *La parole et le marbre, aux origines de la poétique grecque*. Lund, Studentlitteratur

Vernant, J.-P. 1974. Figuration de l'invisible et catégorie psychologique du double: le colossos. In *Mythe et pensée chez les Grecs II*, pp. 65–78. Paris, Maspero

1979. Naissance d'images. In *Religions, histoires, raisons*, pp. 105–37. Paris, Maspero

1991. Psyché: simulacre du corps ou image du divin?, Destins de l'image. *Nouvelle Revue de Psychanalyse*, XLIV: 223–30

PART III

Approaches to cult practice and transcendental belief systems

6
The archaeology of religion

COLIN RENFREW

Any attempt to encompass the archaeology of mind must inevitably consider the archaeological approach towards religion. For if the archaeology of mind, as envisaged in chapter 1, may be considered in terms of a series of functions of the symbol, of various ways in which symbols may operate, the role of symbols in coping with the unknown and with the supernatural is surely one of the more significant (see Renfrew and Bahn 1991: 358–63). But there is the danger here that we may carry to the inquiry our own culturally-encapsulated, and therefore perhaps stereotyped, view of what religion is. Through our acquaintance, in the first instance, with the great religions of the Book (Judaism, Christianity, Islam), all of which proclaim a unitary deity, we undoubtedly begin from a very special viewpoint. Even some acquaintance with other great, contemporary faiths such as the Buddhist, Hindu, Jain and Zoroastrian, serves in some ways to reinforce the impression of coherently codified (and thus literate), authoritative systems of belief, operating often in an urban context. A preliminary knowledge of the religious systems and the pantheons of Ancient Egypt, Greece and Rome might, at first, reinforce this view of text-based, well-delineated and formalized structures of belief. Clearly, however, the studies of cultural anthropologists have much to tell us about the religious systems of non-urban societies and of social groups operating on a basis of band or tribal organisation, so that some of these preconceptions can be counteracted and the effects of literacy discounted.

A more serious difficulty perhaps accompanies our very conceptualization of 'religion' itself, as a distinguishable, and in some senses separable, field of human activity. For we shall soon note that, from the standpoint of the archaeologist, religious activities are potentially open to observation only when they might be identifiable as religions by an observer at the time in question. Places set aside for religious observances and objects used specifically for cult purposes may, in favourable circumstances, be recognized as such. Such identification is much less easy when the locus of religious activity has a whole range of other functions, or when the artefacts used there also have other, secular uses. The problem of the 'embeddedness' of cult activity within the other activities of daily life is thus a very real one. And just as economic anthropologists warn us that the economy in simpler, non-state economies is often inextricably embedded within the matrix of the social organization, so might we anticipate that the same could apply to cult observance. The very term 'religion', conceived as a separate dimension or sub-system of the society, could thus prove to be something of a misconception, even among those communities where the supernatural plays a significant role in shaping the thoughts and actions of its individuals.

These, however, are inescapable constraints: at least we can try to be aware of them. We should therefore concede that in many societies the religious life is more varied and more widespread than we might realize, especially if it has this quality of embeddedness.

In all attempts to investigate the early past there is the risk that we first conceptualize, setting up a whole series of categories of our own construction, and then order our data (our observations bearing upon the past) in terms of such categories. The past is then presented in these terms, and it is easy to assume that our description is telling us about the way the past was and the way it was ordered. In some cases, however, all that we are seeing is a reflection and an exemplification of our own a priori categories. Such criticisms have, for instance, been made of the term 'chiefdom', much used for a while among evolutionary anthropologists, and still useful among archaeologists. But it has been pointed out, with some justice, that it can be a cumbersome exercise to set up elaborate criteria by which a chiefdom may be recognized, and then to spend much time and effort arguing whether this culture or that society is to be regarded as a chiefdom against the standard of those criteria. The ultimate moral must be that such classifications are not useful in themselves. Classifications are of value only if they are put to some use once they are established. These cautionary thoughts are perhaps easier to formulate than they are to apply in practice, but right at the outset of our consideration of the archaeology of religion, it should be acknowledged that the very use of the category 'religion' inevitably influences some aspects of the discussion.

Aspects of religion

Religion is not an easy term to define. But it clearly implies some framework of beliefs. These cannot, however, be restricted to general philosophic beliefs about the world or about the way it works. They must relate to forces which are not merely those of the everyday material world, but which go beyond it and transcend it.

The Shorter Oxford Dictionary offers one convenient definition (Onions 1973: 1978) for religion: 'Action or conduct indicating a belief in, or reverence for, and desire to please, a divine ruling power . . . Recognition on the part of man of some higher unseen power as having control of his destiny and as being entitled to obedience, reverence and worship.' This convenient definition has many merits, but not all its components may be of universal validity. For instance, there are some oriental belief systems (such as that following Confucius) which are generally recognized as religious but which avoid specific divinities and where such powers as are postulated are immanent, not readily to be separated from other aspects of the world with which they are to be associated.

To speak of the 'supernatural' in such a case might be misleading if it were taken to imply a belief in spirits or other separable entities. But the Shorter Oxford Dictionary definition for 'supernatural' is perhaps a broadly acceptable one (Onions 1973: 2193): 'That is above nature; transcending the power of the ordinary course of nature.' Transcendence does not necessarily imply separation.

These are important and basic points. Durkheim, for instance (1965: 47) was able to define religion without reference to the supernatural (although he could not avoid the term 'sacred'). Geertz (1966: 4) offers a definition which indeed avoids the supernatural and the sacred, but which is so lacking in focus that it could apply to secular ritual or even to the system of values which is used to uphold a monetary economy. Such a definition lacks any sense of what must surely be a component of any religion: the individual religious experience.

Religious experience

Central to the notion of religion is that of a personal experience for the individual which seems to him or her not only important, but of a larger significance. This is a feature carefully discussed by Rudolf Otto (1917) in a work which still makes valid points, where he laid emphasis on the sense of the numinous which he viewed as central to religious experience. It cannot be escaped that when we allow ourselves to speak of the religions of early societies we are making something of a cross-cultural assumption, namely that there was indeed some variety of numinous experience enjoyed by the members of those societies, some sense of mystery and of external, non-human power. We do not need to assert that such a power has any real existence – that is a matter for the individual's religious beliefs today. But to talk

of the archaeology of religion presupposes that religious experience was available then as now. This is a point which it would be very difficult to demonstrate, although such an experience is certainly perfectly plausible as a motivating force for some of the symbolic monuments which we may observe from the past. But the existence of such an experience in the past seems to be an assumption which the student of early religion has to make: there is a uniformitarian assumption there which needs to be recognized.

This is a question which I believe was largely avoided by Durkheim, and then less subtly (and less successfully) by Geertz, in the discussions cited above. Both avoided placing such religious experience as a central feature of their definition of religion, preferring instead to see religion rather as a social phenomenon. But it seems to me that when we are speaking of the belief systems of other people, while we do not need, ourselves, to share or even to understand those beliefs very well, we can scarcely avoid the view that they, the participants in the culture, did indeed themselves believe them. While other aspects of the diagram offered by Rappaport (1971a, 1971b) may be open to discussion, the place within it of religious experience seems appropriate.

Mystery and purpose in the human condition

Every religion, by definition, involves a system of beliefs which offers answers to profound existential questions. Indeed most religions provide, at the individual and at the collective level, answers to those basic existential questions posed so effectively by Paul Gaugin in the title to one of his canvasses: 'Where do we come from? Where are we? Where are we going?' Most religious systems offer a coherent view of the nature of the present world, of the origins of the world and of future human destiny. At a personal level also the mysteries of birth, death and of what happens after death, are resolved.

It should be noted here that the answers supplied by religious belief systems to these questions, and in particular those of origin, are often provided in mythological form. The 'answer' takes the form of a history, a kind of historical narrative. But the personnages are not simply historical people. They have a greater significance, indeed for the community or culture in question a universal significance. The answers to general questions are not general propositions, as they have become for us in the aftermath of the scientific revolution, following Descartes and Newton. They are specific, narrative propositions, as Frankfort et al. (1949) have so clearly shown. But they do serve to answer the questions.

Most religions indicate also how we can take steps to harmonize with the world, and often, through this process how we, through our actions (or our prayers) can influence the world in a manner favourable to our own aspirations. Such concerns lead naturally to ethical concerns, towards beliefs about how our actions should be governed. And consequent upon a view of how we should regulate our own actions comes the notion of social sanctions to ensure that they do indeed conform with such precepts and, in some cases, the notion of divine sanctions towards the same end.

Archaeological recovery of these belief systems may, in most cases, be exceedingly difficult. But it is a principal purpose of the present discussion to identify various aspects inherent within most or all religions, which we can expect to accompany those other aspects which may be more readily identifiable in the archaeological record.

As we shall see below, iconographic representation is one of the most promising routes towards the detail of some belief systems. Interpretations may often be difficult but, in some cases, we may be able to detect reference to what may be recurrent (although not, of course, universal) themes across cultures. One such theme, the passage of the 'soul' or 'spirit' after corporeal death, is familiar in Christian iconography through depictions of the judgement day, of which the celebrated 'Last Judgement' by Michelangelo is one of the more recent. Analogous concepts may be found in Mesoamerican depictions, and they are, of course, a recurrent preoccupation in the mural decoration of Egyptian

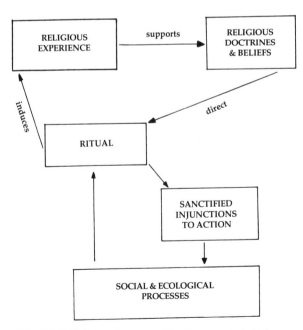

Fig. 6.1. Religion as interpreted by Rappaport: beliefs direct ritual which induces religious experience. (After Renfrew and Bahn 1991: 358.)

tombs and sarcophagi, as well as in papyrus texts of the Book of the Dead.

The social aspect

Central to the notion of religion, although not well brought out in the definition by Onions cited earlier, is the circumstance that it is a *shared* belief system. Religion in this sense implies a community of believers: Durkheim (1965) speaks of 'beliefs and practices which unite into one single moral community called a Church, all those who adhere to them'.

This view of religion as a social and cultural phenomenon is naturally one which preoccupies the cultural anthropologist. It is, of course, important to the archaeologist who, as noted earlier, hopes to define actions, ritual actions, which were carried out at specific places in special ways. The setting apart of the place, and the special distinctive manner of the actions, will always be important for the detection process, the recognition process undertaken by the archaeologist. Of course Durkheim intended the term 'church' purely in the social sense, to indicate a community of persons. But the term 'church' in our language, as in several others, implies also a special place dedicated by those persons for special activities, rituals, undertaken in relationship to the beliefs shared by that community. These activities are, in most religions, formalized. They are carefully prescribed and accompanied also by proscriptions (things which must not be done, forbidden words, taboos). As noted, they often take place in special places, in the manner established by tradition and by doctrine. They are also coherently time-structured: they take place at special times of day, on special days of the week and at special occasions in the year.

These generalizations are of crucial importance to the archaeologist, although there has been very little broad, theoretical discussion of them. For it is usually through the investment of effort into the construction of special places (whose remains may be preserved), through the use of special equipment in rituals at those places (which may also be preserved), in the development of iconic representations for use in such places, and in some cases through the depiction of such rituals, that we have our principal insights into past religions. These matters are further discussed in the next section.

Another important and very interesting social aspect of most religions is that the belief system, as it relates to the supernatural, is inevitably related in some ways to the social reality of the culture. Karl Marx, one of the first thinkers to deal seriously with the sociology of thought (Marx and Engels 1977) saw the religious beliefs of a society as part of the ideological superstructure which he viewed as arising from the relations of production within a given social formation. One does not need to follow all his assumptions to see that there is much in this idea. Whether man is made in the image of God or vice versa, it is certainly the case that the deities of many human societies have been conceived of as anthropomorphic, although animal gods (theriomorphic) are at least as common. The notion of a hierarchy of divinities is one which comes more easily to a society which is itself hierarchically structured, for instance to a state society. It is difficult to imagine such a feature in an egalitarian society organized at band level.

The functions and consequences of religion

Various thinkers have considered religious systems not from the standpoint of the content of their belief structures nor of their communal behaviour, but in terms of their consequences for society as a whole. Within the Marxist view, for instance, with its emphasis upon class antagonisms, religion is viewed as a means, developed by the élite, for the manipulation of the masses. Within most state societies it is indeed the case that the ruler (the 'king') has a special place in relation to the leading religious specialist (the 'chief priest') and in many state societies the two offices converge (the 'priest-king'), sometimes with the deity ruling through this head of state (a theocracy), or at least inspiring and sanctioning his actions (the 'divine right' of kings). Marxist archaeologists have also applied such ideas to societies generally regarded as essentially egalitarian, where, for instance, the elders are seen as using religious beliefs to ensure their own favoured and privileged position in relation to younger members of society (Tilley 1984). A very different view of religion is taken by anthropologists working broadly in the 'functionalist' tradition of Malinowski, for whom religious beliefs and rituals are useful in governing and regulating various aspects of the social system (e.g. Rappaport 1971a). The earlier 'functionalist' view saw religion as useful in ensuring the smooth functioning of society by ensuring some considerable degree of community of belief, some acceptance of the social system and hence some general social solidarity among members of the community. More recent work, notably by Rappaport, would accord religious beliefs a further, more active role, in bringing into play mechanisms of a broadly homeostatic nature whose timing is governed by ritual.

A further, broadly evolutionary, perspective has been proposed by Lachmann (1983) who contrasts the variability in all human behaviour with that among species where quite complicated social behaviour is genetically determined, for instance among bees. In his perspective there are enormous advantages in cultural evolution, precisely in the special human ability to learn, and thus to change the whole behaviour of society in the space of just a couple of generations. But there are penalties too, in terms of lack of

stability of behaviour and in the risk that valuable information, no longer stored in the genome, may become lost between generations. It is here that the devices used by religion for the very long-term storage of information may be particularly useful. For, as Lachmann stresses, it is through religion that 'ancient wisdom' is most effectively stored and transmitted. Much of the repetition associated with religious ritual may be regarded as 'redundant' in the information theory sense, and secure transmission is thereby more adequately assured. It is the case that the oral transmission of religious knowledge has been shown to be enormously effective. The Hymns of the Rigveda, recorded in archaic Vedic Sanskrit, were preserved orally for many centuries before being set down in writing about the fifth century BC at a time when classical Sanskrit was already in use. Much of their vocabulary was by that time not well understood, but later scholarly study has shown the accuracy of transmission to be remarkably high. This gives support to Lachmann's view that a coherent religious system, with its high survival value, confers a selective advantage upon the society which possesses it.

In general, the wider effects of religious beliefs have been little considered by archaeologists. Yet clearly frameworks of religious belief provided strong motivational contexts for many aspects of the behaviour of ancient societies. This has been well documented, for instance, for the case of the ancient Maya (Schele and Miller 1986) and the role of sacred concepts, both in the development of urbanism and in its specific forms, has been emphasized by a number of authors, including Wheatley (1971). For the traditional Marxist historian these may be mere epiphenomena, where the superstructure follows the economic infrastructure, but neo-Marxist thinkers are inclined to give greater causal weight to ideational factors. For the functionalist there is a similar inclination to see symbolic factors as contributing to greater efficiency in the culture system and thus having an adaptive value, but perhaps not much more than this. Such a view seems related to the Binfordian notion that ideational and religious aspects are akin to 'palaeopsychology' (see chapter 1), and that more basic causal factors reside in the ecological relationship between humans and their environment.

Today, however, within the framework of cognitive-processual archaeology, such assessments seem deficient. It is no longer sufficient to see the ideational component of early societies (including their religions) as simply some superstructural reflection of the more substantial infra-structure, albeit one that is readily subverted by the dominant élite in their ceaseless application of the class war. Nor can religion be seen as purely and simply a device for promoting efficiency, or even for lengthening the memory span of society within an evolutionary context. The causes of religious change are not well understood and, indeed, have scarcely been addressed in any coherent way. Even the notion of the evolution (in the sense of gradual, endogenously-produced change) of religious beliefs and practices has scarcely been developed. It is often, in practice, widely assumed that any new religious form has an outside origin; the local factors favouring or resisting change have not yet been analysed in detail. But the religious system of an early society can no longer be considered a secondary factor in the explanation of culture change.

Recognizing religion

Some of the foregoing discussion may seem a shade premature, when it is quite evident that the identification and elucidation of early cult practices from the archaeological record is a challenging task, and the analysis of the belief systems which sustain them an even more difficult problem. The appropriate methodology for these tasks is only now being developed, and the focus of attention has so far been upon the recognition of cult (Renfrew 1985: chapter 1; Renfrew and Bahn 1991) rather than upon any attempted inference towards the belief system underlying it. So far, as we shall see in the next section, this has been examined largely in the context of the analysis of the iconography of depictions in which aspects of the world are figuratively represented.

Constraints of space preclude the detailed analysis here of the problems which face the archaeologist seeking to identify sanctuaries or other places devoted primarily to cult practice and to recognize the equipment of cult. The nub of the matter was touched on above, in the discussion of the social aspect of religion. As noted, it is, in general, only where religious practices involve either the use of special artefacts or special places, or both, that we can hope to discern them archaeologically. The logic of the inquiry must, I believe, start from the general properties of religious belief and of cult practice as discussed in the earlier section. This is not to assert that all the belief systems involved are similar or even comparable, but it does imply that the term 'religion' carries with it certain correlates which are certainly general if not necessarily universal and by which the investigation can be advanced. I have argued (Renfrew 1985) that cult observances employ a range of attention focusing devices. When sacred ritual takes place, it is situated at the boundary between this world and the other, supernatural world: the very act of religious observance ensures that the celebrant is situated within this liminal zone or boundary area which itself possesses certain characteristic features. And the purpose of much religious ritual is to secure the attention (if one may put it that way) of the deity or of the transcendental

forces which are invoked. This, in general, requires the active participation of the celebrants in speech acts (or song acts) and in a range of ritually determined actions, which may also involve the making of offerings, whether of food or drink, or of material goods. Such considerations as these can allow the formulation of a series of indicators, which can reasonably suggest to the archaeologist that religious ritual has taken place. It is not intended that these should be used as a mechanical check list, nor is any particular 'score' to be regarded as conclusive. But any archaeological recognition of ritual and hence of religion, is likely to be based upon such indications, as well as upon information from representational schemes of painting or other depictions, and on information from such texts as may survive.

Archaeological indicators of ritual (from Renfrew and Bahn 1991: 359–60)

Focusing of attention

(1)   Ritual may take place in a spot with special, natural associations (e.g. a cave, a grove of trees, a spring or a mountain-top).
(2)   Alternatively, ritual may take place in a special building set apart for sacred functions (e.g. a temple or church).
(3)   The structure and equipment used for the ritual may employ attention-focusing devices, reflected in the architecture, special fixtures (e.g. altars, benches, hearths) and in movable equipment (e.g. lamps, gongs and bells, ritual vessels, censers, altar cloths, and all the paraphernalia of ritual).
(4)   The sacred zone is likely to be rich in repeated symbols (i.e. 'redundancy').

Boundary zone between this world and the next

(5)   Ritual may involve both conspicuous public display (and expenditure) and hidden exclusive mysteries, whose practice will be reflected in the architecture.
(6)   Concepts of cleanliness and pollution may be reflected in the facilities (e.g. pools or basins of water) and maintenance of the sacred area.

Presence of the deity

(7)   The association with a deity or deities may be reflected in the use of a cult image or a representation of the deity in abstract form (e.g. the Christian Chi-Rho symbol).
(8)   The ritualistic symbols will often relate iconographically to the deities worshipped and to their associated myth. Animal symbolism (of real or mythical animal)

may often be used, with particular animals relating to specific deities or powers.

(9)   The ritualistic symbols may relate to those seen also in funerary ritual and in other rites of passage.

Participation and offering

(10) Worship will involve prayer and special movements – gestures of adoration – and these may be reflected in the art or iconography or decorations or images.

(11) The ritual may employ various devices for inducting religious experience (e.g. dance, music, drugs and the infliction of pain).

(12) The sacrifice of animals or humans may be practised.

(13) Food and drink may be brought and possibly consumed as offerings or burned/poured away.

(14) Other material objects may be brought and offered (votives). The act of offering may entail breaking and hiding or discard.

(15) Great investment of wealth may be reflected both in the equipment used and in the offerings made.

(16) Great investment of wealth and resources may be reflected in the structure itself and its facilities.

These then are some of the categories of information which may be useful to the archaeologist. It is not, however, the presence or absence of specific diagnostic criteria of this kind which are significant, but rather the documentation of repeated actions of a symbolic nature which are directed, it may be inferred, towards non-terrestrial and therefore transcendent forces.

The negative form employed in the term 'non-terrestrial' has a wider implication. For if a given practice, which might otherwise be taken to have a religious function, can be explained in other, 'functional' terms, such an explanation is likely to be the preferred one. I am not confident of the logical strength of that assertion, but it certainly reflects the prevailing process of archaeological inference whereby, if a feature cannot plausibly be explained in rational, 'functional' terms, then it may be ascribed a 'ritual' function. The archaeological category 'ritual' thus often becomes an essentially residual one, defined principally by the absence of something else, namely a good alternative explanation. The purpose of the foregoing list of indications is to counter, in part, this prevailing attitude. But at the last analysis, is that attitude altogether misguided?

The question is complicated further by the important and difficult question of play. For it is the very nature of actions undertaken in play that they are in some sense symbolic. In many cases they mimic other actions, and in that sense represent and thus symbolize them. In other cases the play is

undertaken following well-defined rules. These are rules which generate repetitions (redundancies) of action and often give rise to special modes of behaviour including gestures which may be analogous to those of ritual. Play will certainly use attention-focusing devices and often involves the participation of most of those present. Special equipment is used, very much as for religious rituals, and play often takes place in a special location which, while not precisely a 'liminal zone' in the sense used earlier, may nonetheless partake of some of its qualities. When, for instance, the play is conducted between potentially hostile teams, it may have to take place on neutral ground which is, indeed, in a boundary area of some kind. For all these reasons, the distinction between play and religious ritual is, in practice, a difficult one archaeologically, just as is the distinction between toys and cult images (although the two categories need not be entirely exclusive anyway). At a last analysis it may well be found that in several ways play and religious (and other) ritual are indeed homomorphic: that is to say they share the same forms. Both are symbolic, metaphorical. Perhaps therefore they are not always exclusive. Certainly religious rituals may often have as participants individuals who do not subscribe fully to the belief systems which those rituals are supposed to proclaim. Is such participation so different from play? And while a high seriousness of purpose, and dedication towards a transcendental entity, may well be the key discriminating factor between them play too can be a serious business. In Mexico as in Turkey, lives have been lost in recent years in disputes between supporters of rival football teams.

A further area of human activity also deserves to be brought into the discussion at this point: burial. The disposal of the dead is generally considered, by archaeologists, under a different rubric from that of religion. This may be the case because burials, like death, are of frequent occurrence. But that is hardly a persuasive reason. Nearly every burial, however, constitutes a highly symbolic act. That is to say it has a purpose not simply to get rid of a lifeless and possibly noisome corpse (which can be done in a number of effective and inexpensive ways). Many burials involve a considerable investment of effort and the use of well-defined symbolism. Of course the investment, as has been well argued, may have the twin objectives of enhancing the status of the person undertaking it (the person doing the burying, rather than the one who gets buried) and of securing rights to the property of the deceased. Neither of these need involve religious concepts. But at the same time, where there is a belief in an after-life, it is likely to have an influence upon the details of the practice of burial. Other aspects of the burial may also be symbolic of the world-view of the community since burial is the last of all rites of passage and the most permanent.

So far most of the discussion by archaeologists seeking a theoretical context within which to consider burial has centred upon the social questions touched upon above: questions of prestige, of social persona and of property (Binford 1971; Saxe 1970; Chapman, Kinnes and Randsborg 1981). The emphasis has been very much upon 'tombs for the living' to use Fleming's telling phrase (Fleming 1973). But it is easily forgotten, amongst all this Binfordian talk, that tombs may indeed also be for the dead. Their construction and the other circumstances of burial may reflect (and have a role in developing) a belief system relating as much to eternal values as to the present secular world. Moreover, it may not be unduly naive to bypass the cynicism of Marx and to suggest that many members of society actually did hold the purported beliefs in question – persons of high rank as well as low. The celebrated paper by Ucko on this topic (Ucko 1969), in its presentation of many different circumstances and of varied responses to circumstances, served to give the impression that the relationship between form of burial, form of religious belief and form of society was in general not a coherently patterned one. But while the relationships may certainly differ, that need not imply that patterning is lacking. There is much to learn, I believe, about ancient belief systems, including systems of religious belief, by drawing on the detailed study of ancient burial practices. The relationships remain to be investigated in a systematic way.

The iconography of religion

The most coherent insights into the belief systems of the past must come, if we exclude from the discussion the information available from written texts, from the analysis of symbolic systems. In such systems a coherent, non-verbal language is employed in such a way that someone familiar with the conventions can understand the significance of the symbols (i.e. what they signify). In many cases the propositions which are asserted are not novel: the principle of redundancy in religious ritual extends to representation, and the divine sentences may be repeated just as often and as authoritatively as the calligraphic inscriptions in an Islamic holy place.

Nor need it follow that the symbols which we seek to understand are directly representational in the figurative sense. It is not necessary that we recognize human beings, or deities, or forms which depict entities already known to us from the world of nature. Recently I spent a very interesting afternoon with George Eogan examining the incised schemata visible on the kerbstones which surround the great passage grave of Knowth in the Boyne Valley in Ireland (Eogan 1986). Although the precise significance of these designs is not yet clear – that is to say what, as signs, they signify – there is the strong intuition, not yet made formally explicit, that there is in operation here some coherent system, consistently used.

Much the same can be said for the cup-and-ring markings of the British Bronze Age which have recently been subjected to study by Richard Bradley (this volume). The close study of the contexts of occurrence may, in favourable cases, reveal correlations which give indications of the way these symbols were used. As noted in chapter 1, to seek to attain their meaning in any complete sense (as it would have been understood by their makers) is hardly a feasible undertaking.

More complex figurative systems, although rarer, may offer commensurately greater rewards (in the sense of more complex analyses of 'meaning', when that term is understood in the more restricted sense of limited but coherent interpretation, rather than comprehensive insight). Constraints of space prevent a fuller discussion here of these problems, for which a coherent methodology has not in any case yet been established.

It is already clear, however, that the interpretation of complicated figurative schemes depends crucially upon the successful identification of the successive representations of repeatedly occurring individuals, whether these are humans, deities or mythological persons. In favourable circumstances a clue may be given by specific attributes, such as those which accompany individual saints in Christian iconography (often the instruments of martyrdom, as for St Catherine of Alexandria and her wheel). In the Maya case, the juxtaposition of specific glyphs along with royal representations has now allowed the elucidation of what are, in effect, narrative cycles for the reigns of individual kings (Schele and Miller 1986). The great fresco cycles in Byzantine churches can certainly be read in this way, although it must be admitted that in such cases it certainly helps the viewer to know the basic story first. Indeed, in many cases where depictions are used in a religious context, their role is to reinforce what is already known and perhaps to act as a mnemonic. Partly for this reason they may not always supply sufficient information to make reasonable inferences possible for the uninitiated.

For the archaeologist, for whom such symbolic material is rarely abundant, one crucial question is the extent to which evidence from different sites may justifiably be brought together under simultaneous consideration, to provide a corpus of material sufficient to allow of systematic analysis. The analogy may perhaps be drawn with a number of small archives, each consisting of just a few tablets found at various different sites, and all in what is thought to be a single script. To what extent can this body of material be amalgamated? In the case of written records the answer can be provided internally, as it were, by close study of the script employed on the tablets from the various locations whose unity or diversity can thus be evaluated. In the case of iconic representations, however, the answer is not always so clear. This question is equivalent to asking whether the same system of beliefs, and the same symbolic system for linking the signifier and the thing signified, are in operation at the various sites. A categorical answer is not always possible, but where a considerable range of specific symbols is found in each location, with a good degree of overlap between them, it may be reasonable to infer, in some instances, that a single coherent system is in operation.

These are crucial questions for the archaeological interpretation of data bearing upon early religions. They, and others like them, have not, in general, yet been very clearly addressed. As noted in chapter 1, the methodology of cognitive-processual archaeology is still underdeveloped. But already it is clear that in many cases there is patterning there among the data. This is an inviting field of study.

References

Binford, L. R. 1971. Mortuary practices: their study and potential. In *Approaches to the social dimensions of mortuary practices*, ed. J. A. Brown, pp. 6–29 (Memoirs of the Society for American Archaeology 25)

Chapman, R., I. Kinnes and K. Randsborg (eds.) 1981. *The archaeology of death*. Cambridge, Cambridge University Press

Durkheim, E. 1965. *The elementary forms of religious life* (translated by J. W. Swain). New York, Free Press [first published 1912]

Eogan, G. 1986. *Knowth and the passage-tombs of Ireland*. London, Thames and Hudson

Fleming, A. 1973. Tombs for the living. *Man* 8: 177–93

Frankfort, H., H. A. Frankfort, J. A. Wilson and T. Jacobsen 1949. *Before philosophy*. Harmondsworth, Penguin [first published in 1946 as *The intellectual adventure of ancient man*, Chicago, University of Chicago Press]

Geertz, C. 1966. Religion as a cultural system. In *Anthropological approaches to the study of religion* (ASA Monographs 3), ed. M. Banton, pp. 1–46. London, Tavistock

Lachmann, P. J. 1983. Why religions? An evolutionary view of the behaviour of bees and men. *Cambridge Review*, 28 January 1983: 22–6

Marx, K. and F. Engels 1977. *The German ideology* (edited by C. J. Arthur). London, Lawrence and Wishart

Onions, C. T. (ed.) 1973. *The shorter Oxford dictionary*. Oxford, Clarendon Press

Otto, R. 1959. *The idea of the holy*. Harmondsworth, Penguin (1st edn, 1917)

Rappaport, R. A. 1971a. Ritual, sanctity and cybernetics. *American Anthropologist* 73: 59–76

1971b. The sacred in human evolution. *Annual Review of Ecology and Systematics* 2: 23–44

Renfrew, C. 1985. *The archaeology of cult*. London, Thames and Hudson

Renfrew, C. and P. Bahn 1991. *Archaeology, theories, methods and practice*. London, Thames and Hudson

Saxe, A. A. 1970. Social dimensions of mortuary practices. PhD dissertation, University of Michigan

Schele, L. and M. E. Miller 1986. *The blood of kings, dynasty and ritual in Maya art*. New York, Brazilier

Tilley, C. 1984. Ideology and the legitimation of power in the Middle Neolithic of Sweden. In *Ideology, power and prehistory*, ed. D. Miller and C. Tilley, pp. 111–46. Cambridge, Cambridge University Press

Ucko, P. 1969. Ethnography and archaeological interpretation of funerary remains. *World Archaeology* 1: 262–80

Wheatley, P. 1971. *The pivot of the four quarters*. Edinburgh, Edinburgh University Press

7
Ancient Zapotec ritual and religion: an application of the direct historical approach

JOYCE MARCUS and
KENT V. FLANNERY

This chapter is dedicated to José Luis Lorenzo, whose thoughtful advice in 1979 led to the discovery of the temple sequence below Structure 13 at San José Mogote

We see today a growing interest in cognitive approaches to archaeology, a genuine desire to reach back for the mental templates that underlie human behaviour. While this interest is surely commendable, we should guard against two possible negative outcomes. One such outcome would be the conversion of cognitive archaeology into a fad or a narrow speciality that ignores all other aspects of prehistory. The other would be the delusion that our search for the ancient mind is a recent advance for which our generation is solely responsible.

To avoid the first pitfall, we prefer to speak not of 'cognitive archaeology' but rather of 'holistic archaeology', a discipline in which cognitive variables would be given equal weight with ecological, economic and sociopolitical variables. As far back as 1976 we called for 'a framework for analysis which is neither a mindless ecology nor a glorification of mind divorced from the land' (Flannery and Marcus 1976a: 383).

To avoid the second pitfall, we remind ourselves that many previous generations of archaeologists were just as interested in topics such as ideology, cosmology, iconography and religion (e.g. Caso 1945, 1958; Thompson 1950, 1966, 1970, 1973). Consider, for example, the brilliant writings of Frankfort *et al.* (1946) on the mind of ancient Egypt and Mesopotamia nearly half a century ago. Even the so-called 'processual archaeologists' of the 1960s and 1970s, with their love of subsistence, optimal foraging, human ecology and locational analysis, did not always ignore the roles of ideology and cosmology in shaping

human societies. To be sure, some archaeologists concentrated so hard on the way prehistoric societies provisioned themselves with food and *matériel* that they allowed the realm of the mind to be claimed by humanists.

When processual archaeologists – most of whom are anthropologists – waive their right to include cosmology and ideology in their reconstructions, one gets the kind of dichotomy which we have seen in Mesoamerica: anthropologists writing about settlement and subsistence, while humanists write about religion and cosmology. And the humanists, for the most part, do not have the ecological and evolutionary perspective of the anthropological archaeologists. Thus we have Aztec gods like Tezcatlipoca and Tlaloc projected back onto Formative societies such as the Olmec (e.g. Covarrubias 1942; M. D. Coe 1973), and polytheistic state religions used as models for the early village religions which preceded them by 2000 years (e.g. Joralemon 1971). In this paper, we will try to show that ideological and cosmological principles evolved (and were readapted over time) as Mesoamerican cultures went from egalitarian village societies to ranked societies or chiefdoms, and finally to urban civilizations.

No archaeologist who works for any length of time with the Indians of North, Middle, or South America can fail to see the important roles that religion, cosmology and ideology have played in shaping their societies (Marcus 1978). The problem comes when we try to decide by which *scientific method* we will study those subjects. It is simply not enough to rely on one's intuition and assert what we believe to be true, as some of our humanistic colleagues have done of late. Cognitive archaeology needs a methodology, just as 'settlement and subsistence archaeology' does.

Potentially, there are a number of methodological approaches that could be used. In this chapter, we will combine three which we feel suit the problem of ancient Zapotec ritual and religion. These approaches are (1) the Direct Historical Approach; (2) the analysis of public space and religious architecture; and (3) the contextual analysis of religious paraphernalia.

The Direct Historical Approach

Throughout the late nineteenth and early twentieth centuries, New World archaeologists used ethnographic data from elderly living informants, as well as ethnohistoric records, to interpret the archaeological sites they were excavating. For a long time this approach constituted a traditional method, although it had not been given a formal name.

Classic examples of the method can be found in Arthur C. Parker's *Archaeological history of New York* (1922); William Duncan Strong's *An introduction to Nebraska archaeology* (1935); and William A. Ritchie's two works, 'The Algonkin sequence in New York' (1932) and 'A perspective of Northeastern Archaeology' (1938). Finally, in an article entitled 'The Direct-Historical Approach in Pawnee Archaeology', Waldo R. Wedel (1938) gave the approach its name.

The Direct Historical Approach (DHA) was seen as a way of working back in time from the known to the unknown, using ethnographic and ethnohistoric data to interpret prehistoric remains. For example, both Wedel and Strong used Pawnee ethnographic and ethnohistoric data to enhance their reconstructions of the protohistoric and Upper Republican cultures of Nebraska, which preceded the historic Pawnee. Archaeologists using the approach made it clear that they felt most comfortable with their reconstructions when they could show *continuity from the archaeological record to the ethnographic present* – in other words, when they could plausibly show that the same ethnic and linguistic group had continuously occupied the area from prehistoric to historic times.

It would be a mistake, however, to assume that the DHA only emphasizes continuity while ignoring change, even in such supposedly 'conservative' areas as ideologies, religious beliefs and ritual institutions. The fact is that most American archaeologists, especially since the 1930s, have been concerned with both continuity and change. For example, Strong's (1933) paper on 'The Plains culture area in the light of archaeology' documents the way the introduction of the horse from Europe transformed Plains horticulturalists into mounted nomads. Indeed, one reason the approach was so widely used at that time is because so many archaeologists of Strong's generation were well-rounded anthropologists who knew ethnology and ethnohistory as well as they knew archaeology.

In southern Mexico, both Alfonso Caso (1932, 1966) and Ignacio Bernal (1949, 1958, 1965, 1966) used ethnohistoric data on the Zapotec and Mixtec of Oaxaca to enhance their reconstructions of prehistoric cultures in that region. The Valley of Oaxaca is one of those 'fortunate' areas (from the perspective of archaeology) where there was great continuity from prehistoric to Spanish Colonial times. In 1983, a group of our colleagues joined us in taking advantage of that continuity to trace the Zapotec and Mixtec civilizations out of their common ancestral culture (Flannery and Marcus 1983). In that symposium, we used a kind of DHA to the Oaxaca region, looking for both continuity and change through time.

One reason ritual and religion could be seen as appropriate themes for a DHA in Mesoamerica is that the ethnohistoric and ethnographic data from that region emphasize how conservative and slow to change those aspects of culture

were. Within the realm of the sacred, a high premium was placed on maintaining tradition and preserving anachronisms. Despite long-term continuity, however, one can see adjustments being made over time as the sociopolitical infrastructure of society evolved.

Architecture and the public use of space

A second approach to recovering cognitive information from prehistory lies in the study of changing patterns of public architecture or the use of public space, where many religious and ideological principles are expressed in physical remains (e.g. Flannery and Marcus 1976a, 1976b). For example, the careful excavation of a sequence of superimposed temples at sites such as Kaminaljuyú (Kidder, Jennings and Shook 1946), Uaxactún (Ricketson and Ricketson 1937; Smith 1950) and Tikal (W. R. Coe 1990) has given us data on the evolution of Maya temples and the range of activities that took place on their floors. Later in this chapter we will present a comparable sequence of temples from a secondary administrative centre within the Zapotec state centred at Monte Albán, Oaxaca.

Contextual analysis of ritual paraphernalia

A third approach to the study of ancient ritual and religion is the 'contextual analysis' defined and described by Flannery (1976) for Formative Oaxaca villages. This type of analysis is based on Rappaport's (1979: 176) observation that ritual *must be performed*, and that to be valid it must be performed over and over again in certain prescribed ways. This means that those artefacts used in ritual should exhibit a pattern of use and discard which is non-random and yields insights into the nature of the ritual itself. In other words, although religious beliefs are mental constructs which cannot themselves be directly recovered archaeologically, those beliefs may direct ritual practices which are performed with artefacts that *can* be directly recovered. In this paper we will show that certain artefacts left behind in Zapotec temples reflect rituals of human and animal sacrifice which follow from the religious beliefs recorded in ethnohistoric documents.

Relationships among approaches

Let us now briefly review the three approaches used in this paper and the way in which they are related. First, our DHA begins with descriptions of the ideology, religion and ritual practices of the Zapotec of Oaxaca, Mexico, as they were described by the sixteenth-century Spaniards. This historic information gives us some insight into the cognitive world of the Zapotec, as well as certain expectations about the kinds of public buildings and ritual artefacts we might find in the archaeological record. We can then examine the archaeological record to see if, and when, such buildings and ritual paraphernalia appear, and whether their form and pattern fit our expectations.

It seems to us almost certain that some of our expectations will be met and others will not; it also seems likely that the archaeological record will contain unexpected types of information, for which the Spanish accounts do not prepare us. Resolving the contradictions between our ethnohistoric expectations and our archaeological observations will be one challenge of the method; another will be to decide whether those cases in which our observations and expectations fit are genuine continuities, or only superficial similarities.

Zapotec ethnohistory

Sixteenth- and seventeenth-century documents written by the Spaniards (or by Indian nobles at the Spaniards' request) constitute a very rich body of material for the study of prehispanic philosophy, religion and ideology. Among these documents are (1) Spanish friars' accounts of 'pagan' religious practices such as human and animal sacrifices, incense burning and bloodletting; (2) dictionaries of indigenous languages, containing many religious and philosophical terms; (3) answers to standardized questionnaires (*relaciones*) elicited from indigenous nobles between 1579 and 1581 at the request of the Spanish throne; (4) prehispanic and early Colonial native maps on deer hide or cloth; and (5) prehispanic and early Colonial manuscripts (*codices*) that contain calendric, ritual, genealogical and pilgrimage data.

While these documents are rich in detail, their use requires a careful attempt to 'factor out' Colonial Spanish prejudices. After all, many of the Spaniards were missionaries whose goal it was to eliminate 'heathen' practices which they regarded as barbaric and repugnant. The Spaniards also had Classical Greco-Roman religion as their subconscious paradigm for 'pagan' beliefs, and tended to speak of things such as 'pantheons of gods' when they were more likely seeing lists of deified royal ancestors (Marcus 1978, 1983a, 1983b).

The principal ethnohistoric sources for Zapotec religion date from the sixteenth and seventeenth centuries, and were written by Spanish friars and administrators. First and foremost as a source was Fray Juan de Córdova, who in 1578 published both a dictionary (*Vocabulario en Lengua Zapoteca*) and a grammar (*Arte en Lengua Zapoteca*) which contained important data on religion (Córdova 1578a, 1578b). His work built on that of his superior, Fray Bernardo de Alburquerque, who had arrived in Mexico around 1535.

By 1540, Fray Alburquerque was the vicar of Tehuantepec and the city of Oaxaca. Fray Juan de Córdova joined Alburquerque in 1547 in the convent of Antequera (modern Oaxaca City). Both friars learned Zapotec well, since their conversion of the Indians required them to master the language in all its subtlety. Alburquerque wrote an important manuscript (*Doctrina Cristiana en Lengua Zapoteca*) which was never published, but was used by other friars in their sermons. Ultimately, Córdova was assigned to the convent at Tetícpac (modern San Juan Teitipac), and later was named vicar at Tlacochahuaya in the Valley of Oaxaca (see Fig. 7.1).

A second source on Zapotec religion is the work of Fray Gonzalo de Balsalobre (1656; Berlin 1957; Marcus 1983b) who from 1634 to 1665 was a priest in what is today Sola de Vega, Oaxaca. Balsalobre recorded 'survivals of pagan beliefs', eliciting some of his data from a Zapotec *cacique* or native lord who had been baptized 'Diego Luis'.

A third source are the works of Fray Francisco de Burgoa (1670, 1674), whose two seventeenth-century books supply important data on Zapotec religion. Still a fourth major source are the well-known *Relaciones Geográficas* (Paso y Troncoso 1905, vol. IV), written between 1579 and 1581 by Spanish scribes who were completing questionnaires at the behest of Charles V of Spain.

Zapotec religion

From the ethnohistoric sources given above, it appears that sixteenth-century Zapotec religion had at least four principal features. First, it was an *animatistic* religion, which attributed life to many things we consider inanimate. Second, it emphasized the worship of natural forces, such as lightning and earthquake. Third, one of its fundamental components was reverence for human ancestors, especially royal ancestors. And fourth, man's relationship with great natural forces and supernatural phenomena was governed by reciprocity: each supernatural blessing required an appropriate sacrifice by the recipient.

Ironically, anthropologists have often associated most of these features with 'primitive' societies. Complex societies, such as chiefdoms and states, have often been assumed to have one of two kinds of religions – either monotheism or an elaborate pantheon of gods and goddesses, often in human form. These preconceptions are the result of our Greco-Roman bias and do not fit the religions of most prehispanic civilizations.

Natural and supernatural forces

The Zapotec had a concept of vital force that distinguished 'living' from 'nonliving' matter. They used the word *pèe* or *pi*, a word which can be translated as 'breath', 'spirit' or 'wind', to designate this vital force. Anything lacking *pèe* was considered inanimate and could be manipulated by technology, such as the irrigation systems used for rainwater after it had reached the ground. However, the clouds from which rain came were conceived of as animate, and therefore had to be approached through religious ritual.

Anything with *pèe* – a river in flood, the moon, the foam on top of a cup of hot chocolate, or a bolt of lightning – could move, and thus was considered alive and sacred. All items with *pèe* were deserving of respect and could not simply be manipulated; they had to be addressed respectfully during ritual, and a reciprocal relationship established with them.

The Zapotec addressed items with *pèe* by invoking the life force within them. For example, they used the expression '*Pitào Cociyo*'[1] or 'Great Spirit [within] Lightning' to petition Lightning to pierce the clouds, to send rain down to earth where it could be directly manipulated by humans; as long as the rain stayed up in the clouds, man could not utilize it for his own purposes. They used '*Pitào Xòo*' or 'Great Spirit [within] the Earthquake' when asking Earthquake to stop shaking the earth. In return for the granting of these requests, the Zapotec made appropriate offerings of their own blood, of incense, of food, of sacrificed animals and humans, and of non-perishable exotics such as jade, shell, obsidian and so forth.

Most deserving of respect were great universal forces, such as the lightning and earthquake mentioned above, and also fire, wind, hail and clouds (Fig. 7.2). In fact, clouds were regarded as the beings into which Zapotec ancestors – *penigòlazaa*, 'old people of the clouds' – had metamorphosed after death. Royal ancestors, in particular, were

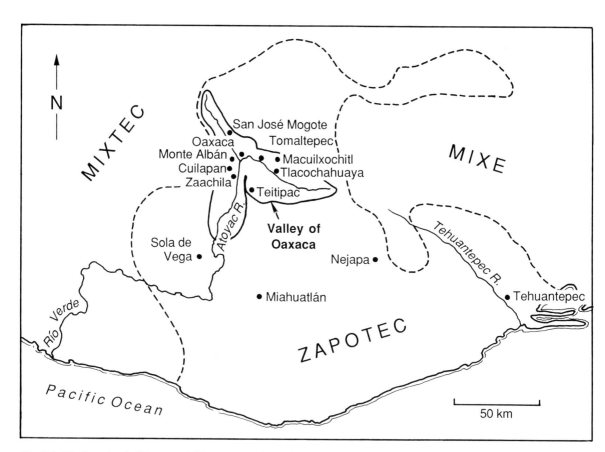

Fig. 7.1. The heartland of Zapotec civilization was the Valley of Oaxaca, Mexico, which lies some 380 km southeast of Mexico City at an elevation of 1500 metres. By the time of the Spanish Conquest, however, Zapotec speakers had spread northeast into rugged mountains, and south and east to the Pacific Coast. On this map, which gives localities mentioned in the text, the irregular dashed line separates the Zapotec from speakers of Mixtec or Mixe languages.

thought to have the power to intercede with powerful super-naturals on behalf of their descendants on earth, but only if those earthly descendants made the appropriate offerings and petitions. Something was offered in anticipation of a request being met, and also in return for a concession. The kinds of offerings ranged from food and drink to one's own blood, a sacrificed quail, a turkey, a child or an adult human, depending on the request, the severity of one's need or the magnitude of one's gratitude. The smoke from burning incense was thought to rise upward until it eventually reached the clouds; so, too, did the smoke from a human heart burned in a charcoal brazier.

Just as the smoke from burning incense was a way of communicating with royal ancestors and supernatural beings, various narcotics were used by the Zapotec to communicate with the spirit world. One of these was *Datura* or *pinijchi-pitào* ('ghost of the great spirit'), with which the Spaniards said the Zapotec 'saw visions' (Marcus and Flannery 1978: 73–4). Others included tobacco (*Nicotiana* sp.) and hallucinogenic mushrooms (*Psilocybe* sp.), the latter generally taken only by very experienced religious specialists because an overdose could be toxic.

As the transformation of deceased royalty into clouds demonstrates, the concept of metamorphosis from one life form to another was an important concept in Zapotec philosophy and religion. Partially metamorphosed figures are frequently seen in Oaxaca art (Fig. 7.3), and an example from our own excavations will be given below.

Finally, some rituals among the Zapotec were calendrically scheduled. Like other Mesoamerican peoples, the Zapotec had two calendars, one secular (365 days) and one ritual (260 days). The 260-day ritual calendar was called the *piye*, a term whose initial phoneme suggests that it had *pèe* or vital force. Thus ritual time was alive, it moved, and its calculations were in the hands of religious specialists. The 260-day calendar was divided into four equal parts called

Fig. 7.2. Zapotec effigy vessel showing an anthropomorphic Cociyo, or Lightning, with 4 containers on his back. Ethnohistoric data suggest that these containers were for rain, wind, hail and clouds, the major elements associated with Lightning. Height of piece, 15 cm. (Drawn from a photo in Caso and Bernal 1952: Fig. 54.)

cociyos or 'lightnings', each 65 days long. Another name used for these 65-day periods was *pitào*, or 'great spirit'.

On a cosmological level, the Zapotec world was divided into four great quarters, each associated with a colour. The main axis of this division was the east–west path of the sun, the result being that many ancient maps have east at the top, and many temples face east or west.

Archaeologically recoverable features of Zapotec religion

Before beginning our search for ritual or religious data in Oaxaca prehistory, let us consider those features of Zapotec religion that might be archaeologically recoverable. One of the most obvious would be the standardized two-room temple known as *yoho pèe*, 'sacred house' or 'house of the vital force'. At the time of the Spanish Conquest, such temples were manned by full-time priests. To the less sacred outer room came persons who wished to make an offering; the actual sacrifice would be performed by full-time specialists in the more sacred inner room. No layman was allowed to enter the inner room, while the priests rarely left it (virtually 'living in it', according to ethnohistoric sources).

The Zapotec priesthood had a hierarchy of high priests (*uija-tào*), ordinary priests (*copa pitào*), lesser religious personnel, and young men educated to enter the priesthood (*bigaña*). One seventeenth-century source (Burgoa 1674) says that the high priest or *uija-tào* had as his chief function the consultation with the supernatural on important matters,

Fig. 7.3. Flying 'cloud person' modelled in stucco on the wall of a late prehistoric tomb from Zaachila, Oaxaca. Sixteenth-century Oaxaca peoples conceived of the clouds from which their ancestors had descended as flying turtles (Marcus 1983d: 195), which explains the turtle carapace on the flying figure.

and then the transmitting of this information to his assistants and to others down the hierarchy. This high priest had the power to place himself into an ecstatic state (possibly with the aid of drugs), and he believed what he saw in his visions. The Zapotec ruler treated the high priest with great respect, principally because the latter had close contact with the supernatural and could see into the future. The ruler often turned to his high priest for advice and followed it diligently (Seler 1904: 248). Some of the high priests were, in fact, brothers or other relatives of the ruler.

Hierarchically below were other priests, also recruited from the nobility. At the lowest level were diviners (*colanij*), who probably were not always drawn from the nobility. These diviners usually interacted directly with the common people, helping them with individual decisions – whom to marry, when to marry, the naming of one's children, when to plant, etc. Such diviners took the decision-making out of the hands of the individual and left the decision up to 'fate' or 'fortune', whose will was determined by casting lots (often with maize kernels or beans) in groups of 2s, 3s, 4s, and so forth.

The ancient Zapotec distinguished between two kinds of blood: flowing blood (*tini*) and dried blood (*rini*). Flowing blood was preferred for a whole range of rituals, and it was collected on papers, feathers and other perishable items for inclusion in caches. While special priests sacrificed humans and animals, almost all Zapotec practised autosacrifice of small amounts of their own blood, using distinctive paraphernalia such as stingray spines, shark's teeth, obsidian lancets and leaf spines of maguey (*Agave* sp.) to perforate veins or skin. Some priests even let their fingernails grow long in order to use them as bloodletting instruments. When the act of bloodletting – removing blood from the fleshy parts of the body, especially the ears and tongue (Burgoa 1674) – was completed, the person would leave his bloodletting paraphernalia in a cache or in the temple itself. Since the blood itself was often caught on grass, feathers, papers placed in a basket, and other perishable materials, such offerings would be difficult to recover archaeologically. However, slips of bark paper similar to those used to catch drops of flowing blood have been found in the deposits of dry ritual caves (Moser 1983).

Many animals, including quail, turkeys, deer and dogs, were offered in sacrifice. Quail were considered especially appropriate for sacrifice because the Zapotec regarded them as 'clean' or 'pure' animals. That is because the Zapotec observed quail drinking from dew drops; even today, Zapotec who observe them doing so comment that quail 'will not drink dirty water'. In Oaxaca, the two quail most frequently encountered are the Montezuma quail (*Cyrtonyx montezumae*), which inhabits pine-oak forests, and the common Bobwhite (*Colinus virginianus*), which inhabits the weedy borders of maize fields (Fig. 7.4).

Evidence for human sacrifice is also clear in the ethnohistoric record. For example, sixteenth-century information indicates that infants, children and adults were sacrificed to Lightning, the most powerful supernatural depicted in Zapotec art. Slaves and captives taken in war were the most common adult sacrifices, with specially-trained priests cutting out their hearts with leaf-shaped flint or obsidian daggers while the victim was still alive. This was done so that the heart would still be beating, i.e. it would still possess *pèe* when offered to Lightning.

The Zapotec accompanied their rituals with the burning of incense (*yàla*), believing that the aromatic smoke rose to join with the clouds in the sky above – an effective way to address one's ancestors so that they could intercede on one's behalf. The resin of the copal tree (*Bursera* sp.), which is native to the Valley of Oaxaca and much of southern Mexico, was a preferred incense.

Given this brief discussion, it should be clear what some of the archaeologically preserved evidence for ancient Zapotec religious ritual might be. First, we might expect to find two-room temples, often oriented to the east–west axis of the sun. Second, we should look for the braziers in which offerings of incense (and sometimes human hearts) were burned. Third, we should look for flint or obsidian daggers of the type used in human sacrifice, and for the kinds of smaller tools used in ritual bloodletting – stingray spines, shark teeth, obsidian lancets and so on. Fourth, we should look for the skeletal remains of those animals regarded as appropriate for sacrifice, such as quail, dogs, turkeys, deer and others. Fifth, we should look for the use of ritual drugs such as *Datura*, *Psilocybe*, or even *Nicotiana*, which might

*Fig. 7.4. The two species of quail most often sacrificed in Zapotec temples. Left, the Montezuma quail (*Cyrtonyx montezumae*). Right, the common Bobwhite (*Colinus virginianus*). Both birds are 20–25 cm in total length.*

appear among the archaeological plant remains. Sixth, we should look for evidence of the 260-day *piye* or ritual calendar. Seventh, we should look for depictions of Lightning, Earthquake, and other supernatural beings in the art of the ancient Zapotec. Finally, we should look for evidence of ancestor worship and the metamorphosis of ancestors into *penigòlazaa* or 'cloud people'. If any or all of these features are present, it may be possible to reconstruct parts of ancient Zapotec religion by use of the Direct Historical Approach.

Obviously, some of the elements on this list are likely to be harder to find than others. There are also major unanswered questions about their relationships. When the Spaniards arrived, all these features were part of an impressive complex of religious practices engaged in by hundreds of thousands of Indians sharing a common language and political system. Did all the features of this complex appear at once, or did they appear one by one during the long archaeological record in Oaxaca? If the latter were the case, in what order did the features appear, and does that order tell us something about the course of Zapotec cultural evolution? Finally, does the archaeological record give us any additional information, not mentioned by the Spanish chroniclers of the sixteenth century? In the remainder of this paper, we look back over three millennia of Oaxaca prehistory in an attempt to answer those questions.

Early evidence of Zapotec ritual

As we look back over Oaxaca's archaeological record, we can see that the various elements of Zapotec religion did *not* all appear simultaneously. Some were in evidence almost as soon as permanent village life began, while others did not appear until after the state had formed. Moreover, even those elements which appeared early did not remain static over time; they were reworked and reinterpreted as ideologies changed with each stage of cultural evolution.

One of the first practices for which we have indirect evidence is the ritual use of narcotics. At least one of Oaxaca's early villages has a stratigraphic sequence of small public buildings which may be analogous to the 'men's houses' used by egalitarian village societies elsewhere (Flannery and Marcus 1990: 23–9). A significant feature of such buildings was a small, centrally placed circular pit filled with finely powdered lime (Flannery and Marcus 1990: fig. 2.3). This lime might have been stored for ritual purposes, such as mixing with narcotics like tobacco. The use of tobacco was widespread among the Zapotec, and is mentioned in sixteenth-century *relaciones* from Macuilxochitl, Miahuatlán, Nejapa and other places in Oaxaca (Paso y Troncoso 1905). Unfortunately, actual macrofossils of *Nicotiana* have not yet been found in archaeological contexts.

Prismatic obsidian blades of the type used for ritual bloodletting appear in the archaeological record by 1150 BC, but owing to the many purposes to which these tools could be put, they cannot be used as proof of bloodletting. A better case can be made for the stingray spines which appear between 1000 and 850 BC (Fig. 7.5a). In a previous contextual analysis of ritual paraphernalia, Flannery (1976) showed that during this period, autosacrifice had begun to reflect emerging hereditary inequality: relatively high status individuals used genuine stingray spines, lower status individuals used imitation stingray spines whittled from deer bone, and very high status elites of the Mexican Gulf Coast used imitation stingray spines carved from jade (Flannery 1976: fig. 11.7). Now we can add the fact that between 700 and 500 BC, high status individuals in both Oaxaca and the Valley of Morelos used imitation stingray spines chipped from large obsidian blades (see Fig. 7.5b and Parry 1987: 125–31).

It is also during the period 1150–850 BC that lightning first appeared in Oaxaca art. Marcus (1989) has suggested that certain designs on the pottery of this period reflect a dichotomy between sky and earth, with sky represented by

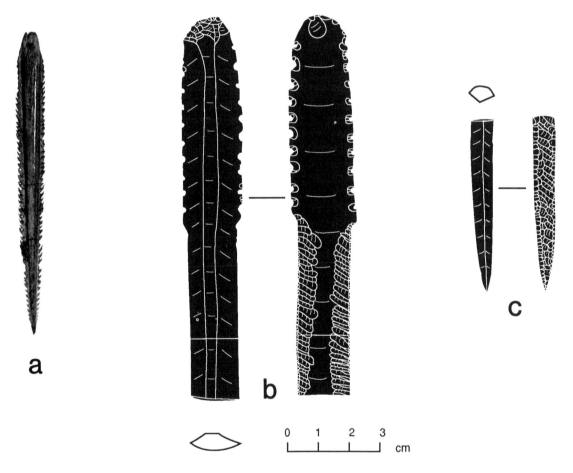

Fig. 7.5. Artefacts used in ritual bloodletting (autosacrifice). a, *spine from the tail of a stingray (family Dasyatidae), House 17, San José Mogote (900–850 BC). An attempt has been made to drill a hole in the base, presumably so that it could be worn around the owner's neck.* b, *basal half of a large, broken, imitation stingray spine made from an obsidian blade, Structure 28 patio, San José Mogote (600–500 BC).* c, *tip of an obsidian bloodletting lancet (600–500 BC). (b, c redrawn from Parry 1987: fig. 52).*

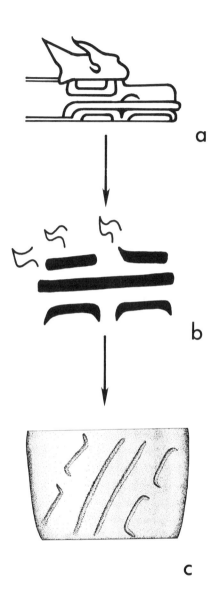

Fig. 7.6. Representations of the 'fire-serpent' or 'sky-dragon' in the art of 1150–850 BC. a shows a naturalistic representation found on pottery at sites near Mexico City. b shows an abstract version carved on pottery vessels in Oaxaca, where the serpent's gums become inverted Us and his eyebrow flames become simple curving lines. c shows a burial vessel from Oaxaca with an even more abstract version of b.

lightning (the 'fire serpent' or 'sky dragon') and earth represented by the 'were jaguar' or 'earth monster'. As shown in Fig. 7.6, lightning could be represented as a realistic serpent with flames rising from his eyebrows, or by a stylized design where U-elements represent the serpent's gums and sine curves represent his eyebrow flames. While certain artistic representations of this supernatural force were specific to Oaxaca, they were apparently only local versions of what seems to have been a pan-Mesoamerican motif (Marcus 1989). It would therefore not be accurate to refer to these early motifs as representing a specifically 'Zapotec' deity.

Another ritual behaviour of this period was the use of small, handmade pottery figurines to create ritual scenes. Because some of these figurines were posed in the most common burial position of the period, we have argued elsewhere that they may depict deceased ancestors (Flannery and Marcus 1976a). Even today, when such figurines are found by the Zapotec of Tehuantepec, they are referred to as *penigòlazaa*, 'old people of the clouds' (Marcus and Flannery 1978: 55; Marcus 1983b: 347). Assuming that we have interpreted those figurines correctly, they would constitute our first evidence for the important role played by the ancestors in Zapotec religion.

Several new elements appeared between 700 and 500 BC, when the archaeological site of San José Mogote had become the largest settlement in the Valley of Oaxaca. By that time, San José Mogote was the ceremonial centre for a network of some 18–20 villages in the northern part of the valley, serving an estimated 1,300–1,400 persons. A carved stone monument located between two public buildings on the site's most prominent pyramidal mound gives us our oldest depiction of a human sacrificial victim, possibly a captive taken in raiding (Fig. 7.7). The victim is shown naked but with a complex scroll covering his chest, possibly depicting blood issuing from an open wound like that made for removal of the heart during sacrifice. Between his feet are two hieroglyphs which give the day '1 Earthquake' in the Zapotec *piye* or 260-day ritual calendar (Marcus 1976). While this may be the personal name of the victim (taken from the date of his birth), its significance here is that it shows that by this period the ritual calendar was already in existence.

The rise of the Zapotec state

A major turning point in Zapotec prehistory was the founding of Monte Albán, the fortified mountain-top city which, for roughly a millennium, was the capital of the Zapotec state (Blanton 1978). While Monte Albán was founded some time around 500 BC, it is not until its second

Fig. 7.7. Top view and eastern edge of Monument 3 at San José Mogote, a carved stone which depicts a sacrificed individual with the date (or personal name) '1 Earthquake' between his feet. A ribbon of blood runs east from the complex scroll design on his chest and ends in two stylized drops which run down the edge of the stone.

archaeological period, Monte Albán II (200 BC–AD 100) that we see overwhelming evidence for the diagnostic characteristics of an archaic state.

During Monte Albán II, Monte Albán was a city of 416 hectares, with an estimated population of 10,650–19,000 persons. Below it was a hierarchy of settlements with at least four tiers: secondary administrative centres of up to 70 hectares, tertiary centres of 2–8 hectares, and more than 400 small farming villages with no apparent administrative functions.

At the top two tiers of this hierarchy were rulers who lived not merely in elite residences, but in actual palaces whose construction required corvée labour. At the top three tiers of the hierarchy there were standardized, two-room temples which fit the description of the Zapotec *yoho pèe*, or 'house of the vital force', seen at the time of the Spanish Conquest. Each consisted of a more sacred inner room, to which we presume only the priests had access, and a less sacred outer room, to which we presume other worshippers could come. Although both rooms had doorways flanked by columns (Fig. 7.8), the inner room had a narrower doorway and was reached only after a step up of 20–30 centimetres above the level of the outer room. At its peak, Monte Albán's Main Plaza may have had twenty such temples; San José Mogote, a secondary centre during Period II, had ten; and Tomaltepec, perhaps a tertiary centre, had a single temple.

Other archaeological manifestations of the Zapotec state were ball courts (more than one at the capital, usually only one at secondary centres); royal tombs with ceramic effigies of apotheosized royal ancestors at both the capital and secondary centres; and monuments at the capital com-memorating military conquests. These monuments included a list of more than forty places evidently conquered by Monte Albán between 200 BC and AD 100 (Marcus 1980, 1983c: 106–8; 1988). Monte Albán – only one of several communities located on defensible hilltops during this period – had 3 kilometres of defensive walls built along the gentler and more easily climbed slopes of the mountain. In other words, by *c.* 200 BC we are dealing with an urban, expansionist, militaristic state with royal families living in palaces, priests directing a state religion in standardized temples, and royal ancestor worship. By now the depictions of Lightning in Zapotec art were no longer generalized 'fire-serpents' or 'sky-dragons', but recognizable depictions of the powerful supernatural *Cociyo* (Fig. 7.9).

More temples have been excavated at Monte Albán than at any other Oaxaca site, but much of this excavation was carried out in the 1930s and 1940s and has never been published in detail. There is evidence that some temples had important offerings under their floors or in their foundations, perhaps left during 'rituals of sanctification' (Rappaport

1971, 1979) which converted secular ground into sacred ground. For example, in Mound 'g' – the pyramidal platform for a temple of such limited accessibility that it may have been used only by the Zapotec royal family – archaeologists found two skeletons, probably both female, associated with a mother-of-pearl mosaic, two necklaces of greenstone and

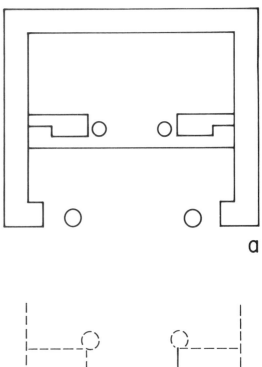

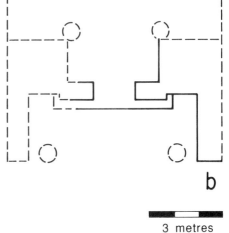

3 metres

Fig. 7.8. Ground plans of Zapotec temples, with circles representing columns. a, *temple found in Mound X, Monte Albán (Caso 1935).* b, *temple found in Mound I-bis at Cuilapan (Bernal 1958). (Redrawn from Marcus 1978: fig. 2.)*

shell, and six pottery vessels. At a depth of 9.5 metres inside Building I – the platform for a more accessible temple in the Main Plaza – was a Monte Albán II offering inside a stone masonry 'offering box' typical of Zapotec temples. This

|_____|
5 cm

Fig. 7.9. By Period I of Monte Albán, according to Caso and Bernal (1952: 24), there were representations of Lightning which are recognizable as the supernatural Cociyo of Zapotec ethnohistory. This battered fragment of a larger vessel from the Valley of Oaxaca shows an anthropomorphic figure with the typical buccal mask, serpent tongue, flat nose and gaping mouth of Cociyo; note also the heavy, serrated eyebrows, which probably evolved from the flame eyebrows of the earlier 'fire serpent'. At this early date (perhaps 300 BC), depictions of Cociyo did not yet have the protruding fangs of later versions like those shown in fig. 7.16. (Drawn by John Klausmeyer, from an illustration by Abel Mendoza (Caso and Bernal 1952: fig. 26).)

offering included a necklace of marine shell, flower-shaped jade ear ornaments, two mosaic masks (one of jade and turquoise, the other of iron pyrite and shell), and a bone carved in the shape of a chess pawn (Flannery 1983: 103–4). Below and around the offering box were the remains of sacrificed birds, unfortunately never identified. It would be interesting to know if they included quail, doves, macaws or turkeys.

Even the temples at secondary centres, such as Cuilapan (Bernal 1958) and San José Mogote (see below) had important subfloor offerings. For example, a temple in Mound I-bis at Cuilapan (Fig. 7.8b), excavated by Saville in 1902, had a dedicatory offering which included an apparent sacrificed child covered with hematite pigment and accompanied by 17 jade figurines, 400 jade beads, 35 marine shells, 2 pottery ear ornaments, and disintegrated mosaics of shell, obsidian and hematite (Bernal 1958: 25). Interestingly enough, such offerings are not described by the sixteenth-century Spaniards, who saw the final temple at each community but were not present when the foundations were laid and the dedicatory offerings deposited.

Temples at San José Mogote

Some of the details of Zapotec ritual can be inferred from a sequence of Monte Albán II temples on Mound 1 at San José Mogote. This series of three stratigraphically superimposed buildings – Structures 36, 35, and 13 – was excavated by Marcus during two field seasons, 1974 and 1980.

The sequence of temples appears in Fig. 7.10. Structure 36, the oldest, dates to the very beginnings of Monte Albán II (200 BC–150 BC?). It measured roughly 11 m × 11 m and was slightly T-shaped, the inner room being smaller than the outer. Interestingly enough, both columns flanking the inner doorway and all four columns flanking the outer doorway were tree trunks of baldcypress (*Taxodium* sp.), covered first with a layer of small stones and then white stucco. So hardy is this wood that much of it was still preserved in identifiable form in the column bases below the floor. (Unfortunately *Taxodium* is not much help for radiocarbon dating, since individual trees can live 1000 years.)

Other details of Structure 36 included a niche in the south wall of the outer room, in which the priests may have stored an incense burner – or one of those Zapotec effigy vessels the Spaniards (drawing on their European background) called 'idols' or 'demons'. The floor of the temple was burned or stained grey with smoke wherever incense burners had been allowed to sit for any length of time, and the circular stains from this activity allowed us to see which areas had been favoured locations for burning copal. Especially common were sooty circles in the centres of the inner and outer rooms, signs of burning along the back wall of the inner room, and stains atop the step between the outer and inner rooms. The white-plastered interior walls of the temple bore geometric designs in polychrome paint like those seen on certain stuccoed ceramics of Monte Albán II (see Caso, Bernal and Acosta 1967: Lám. III–IV).

Structure 35, built over the deliberately razed and levelled remains of Structure 36, dated to the middle of Monte Albán II (*c.* 50 BC?). It was larger than Structure 36 (measuring roughly 12 m × 13.5 m) and also slightly T-shaped like its predecessor. In the rubble layer between the two buildings we recovered occasional bird bones, including the remains of a Montezuma quail which might have been sacrificed in the earlier temple. Structure 35 was the best preserved of the temples on this spot and will be described in detail below. Its columns – one on either side of the inner and outer doorways – were made from large stones stacked one above the other and surrounded by small, stony rubble covered over with white stucco. Evidently these rubble columns, also characteristic of later Zapotec temples, had now replaced tree trunks.

Finally, above the deliberately razed and levelled remains of Structure 35, sat Structure 13. This temple dated to the end of Monte Albán II (AD 100–200?). Though poorly preserved, it seems to have measured about 15 m × 8 m and to have been rectangular rather than T-shaped. Its columns – two flanking the inner doorway and four flanking the outer doorway – were of rubble with a core of larger stones, like those of Structure 35. One of the building's most distinctive features was a basin 75 cm in diameter and 22 cm deep, built into the floor near the southeast corner of the inner room. There were no signs of burning in this basin; on the basis of ethnohistoric analogy, it may have served either (1) to hold water for washing the artefacts of sacrifice, or (2) to receive blood from some type of sacrifice.

Structure 35

Like Structure 36 below it, Structure 35 had circular stains on its floor in certain places where incense burners had been fuelled with charcoal. Fig. 7.11 shows an artist's conception of the temple, with incense burners set in the most frequently burned or stained areas. (The artist's placement of those *incensarios* is only designed to indicate the most favoured locations, since we doubt that so many burners would all be in use at one time. Indeed, it is possible that certain locations were appropriate for some rituals and not for others.)

While most Zapotec temples that we have excavated appear to have been swept periodically (with the debris dumped in extraordinarily large cylindrical or bottle-shaped trash pits in the talus slope behind them), in the case of Structure 35 we were lucky enough to find some artefacts still on the floor. All those artefacts, as shown in Fig. 7.12, were in the extreme southern part of the smoky, windowless inner room, and especially its southwest corner – perhaps an area where the shadows were deepest, and the final sweeping was less thorough. The artefacts – all of obsidian – included two broken, leaf-shaped bifacial daggers of the type usually called 'sacrificial knives', the tip of a bifacial lancet, forty-two prismatic blades and five flakes (Fig. 7.13). While the lancet and prismatic blades are artefacts usually associated with autosacrifice (ritual bloodletting) by priests, the bifacial daggers are of the type shown in scenes of human sacrifice. This collection of tools, evidently overlooked when the floor was swept for the last time, probably represents only a tiny fraction of what was used during the lifetime of the temple.

The most spectacular artefacts of Structure 35, however, were not found on the floor or in nearby trash pits. They lay

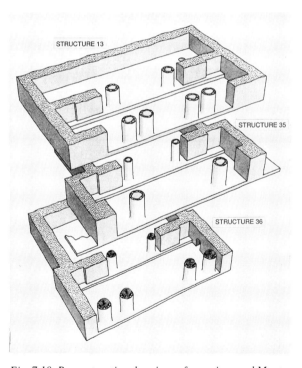

Fig. 7.10. Reconstruction drawings of superimposed Monte Albán II temples on Mound 1, San José Mogote. All temples face west. The artist has preserved the actual position of each building above or below the others, while exaggerating the vertical separation slightly so that the layout of the lower temples can be seen clearly. (Drawing by D. West Reynolds.)

in the offering boxes beneath the floor, where they had been left following 'rituals of sanctification' at the dedication of the temple.

There were five offering boxes below Structure 35. Two of these – Features 92 and 93 – lay below the northern and southern halves of the outer room. No artefacts were discovered in either, but this may only mean that their contents were perishable. Feature 93 contained two bones of quail, including *Cyrtonyx montezumae*.

Under the northern half of the inner room were two stone masonry offering boxes, Features 94 and 95, arranged in the form of a T (Fig. 7.14). Feature 95, the larger, contained no artefacts. Feature 94, the smaller, contained two jade statues, two jade beads and several small fragments which could have been by-products of jade-working.[2] All objects lay in a dense vermilion powder which appeared to be hematite or

ochre. The larger of the two statues was 49 cm tall, while the smaller measured around 15 cm (Fig. 7.15).

The larger statue stands stiffly erect, arms held rigidly at his sides, his feet ending in flat soles with no delineation of toes. He has the typical slab-shaped ears common in Monte Albán II and the lobes are pierced, perhaps for perishable ornaments which have since disintegrated. The top of his head has a drilled hollow which could have held the base of a perishable headdress. This allowance for ear and head ornaments, combined with the fact that the figure is clearly a nude male, raises the possibility that he represents a sacrificed noble carved in jade.

The smaller figure also stands erect and has its earlobes drilled to receive ornaments; its neck is drilled through from side to side, possibly so that the figure could be worn as a pendant. Its hairdo, which features two isolated locks on

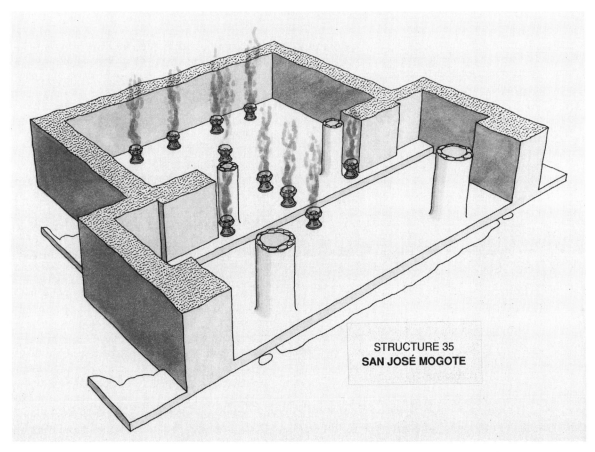

STRUCTURE 35
SAN JOSÉ MOGOTE

Fig. 7.11. Artist's reconstruction of Structure 35 at San José Mogote, a Monte Albán II temple. Incense burners are shown on those parts of the floor which displayed the highest frequency of repeated burning and soot-staining. (Drawing by D. West Reynolds.)

each side of the head, resembles that of the sexually-mutilated prisoner called 'Danzante 12', a carved stone monument from Monte Albán (Caso 1965: fig. 3). Although no sex organs are depicted on the smaller statue, the figure appears to be a male. We cannot claim to understand the full meaning of the Feature 94 offering, but it certainly involved many hours of invested craftsmanship. Perhaps these two figures were intended to 'stand in' for a pair of sacrificed élite males. If so, their semiprecious raw material gave them one advantage over human victims: they would never decay in the ground.

Under the south half of the inner room of Structure 35 was Feature 96, an offering box made of adobes rather than stone. This more complex offering consisted of seven ceramic pieces arranged in the form of a scene, with each piece held in place by the earthen fill of the box. An artist's reconstruction of the scene is shown in Fig. 7.16.

At the centre of the scene was a miniature tomb whose walls were made of adobes set on edge, and whose roof was a slab of volcanic tuff. Inside this miniature tomb was an open bowl, and inside the bowl was an effigy vessel of the type known colloquially to Oaxaca specialists as an *acompañante* because of its frequent occurrence in tombs.[3]

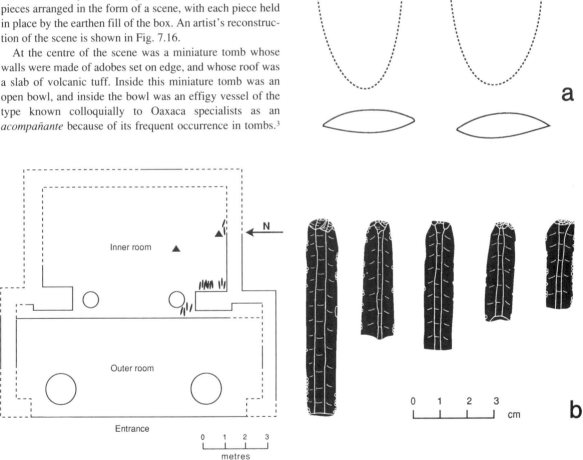

Fig. 7.12. Plan of Structure 35 temple, with the locations of obsidian artefacts on the floor shown by symbols. The black triangles are broken bifacial daggers, while the short black dashes schematically represent concentrations of obsidian blades. (Redrawn from Parry 1987: fig. 49.)

Fig. 7.13. A sample of obsidian artefacts found on the floor of Structure 35 (see fig. 7.12). a, fragments of broken bifacial daggers. b, examples of prismatic obsidian blades. The dagger blades in a would originally have been hafted. (Redrawn from Parry 1987: figs. 50, 51.)

Resting against the north side of the open bowl was the complete skeleton of a sacrificed Bobwhite quail (*Colinus virginianus*). Immediately to the south of the volcanic tuff slab was a pair of deer antlers, like those used by the Zapotec to play the indigenous turtle shell drum.

The *acompañante* is a human figure, identified as a member of the hereditary nobility by his large, spool-shaped ear ornaments and a necklace which probably represents jade beads. He kneels with his arms folded across his chest – an arm position seen in Oaxaca burials for thousands of years – and has dry red pigment on his face and arms. Both the red pigment and the arm position suggest that he may represent a buried noble of some kind, with the bowl serving as the floor of his tomb and the stone slab as its roof.

Lying full length on the roof slab of the miniature tomb is a flying human figure with a long cape flowing behind him. He wears a facial mask depicting *Cociyo* or Lightning, his feet are in sandals, and his anklets bear 'dog-collar' spikes of the type frequently seen on Zapotec incense burners. In his right hand he holds a wooden stick, and in his left he holds a bifid serpent tongue whose base is so long that it wraps around his wrist. There are several reasons why these objects may symbolize the relationship between lightning, rain and agriculture. First of all, the Zapotec words for 'young maize' and 'serpent' are homonyms (*zee* or *ziy*), with one frequently standing in for the other. What we may see here is a figure masked as Lightning, carrying an agricultural dibble stick in one hand and the tongue of a serpent (metaphoric of newly-sprouted maize) in the other.

The symbolism of Cociyo is reinforced by the four ceramic effigies who sit in a row behind the flying figure, witnessing the scene. Each figure is shown as a kneeling woman with a grotesque Cociyo mask and a set of ear ornaments which vary from figure to figure. Almost

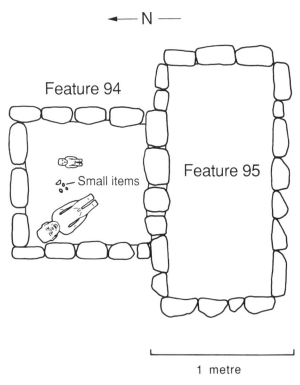

Figure 7.14. Features 94 and 95, two stone masonry offering boxes found below the floor of the Structure 35 temple. Feature 94 contained the two jade statues shown in fig. 7.15.

Figure 7.15. Two jade statues from Feature 94, San José Mogote. Height of larger figure, 49 cm.

certainly these women – each of whose heads is a hollow receptacle – represent clouds, rain, hail and wind, the four elements which we already saw accompanying Cociyo in Fig. 7.2.

What this scene may depict is the metamorphosis of a deceased Zapotec lord into a 'cloud person' or flying figure who is now in contact with Lightning. The flying figure could be a royal ancestor of the kneeling man in the miniature tomb or, just as likely, he may represent the partial metamorphosis of that very same buried noble, caught by the sculptor at a stage where his body is still that of a human, but his face is Cociyo's and he now can fly. It is frustrating indeed to look at this scene and realize that there must be much more information contained in it, even more than the ethnohistoric documents can help us decipher.

Before leaving Feature 96, we should point out that scenes of this type were evidently not rare at other Zapotec archaeological sites. We have seen numerous pieces, which also appear to have been part of arranged scenes, in museums and

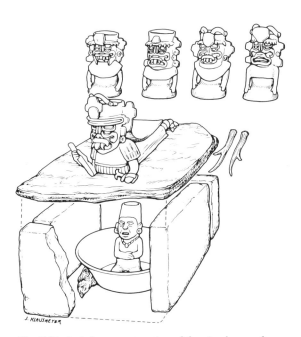

Fig. 7.16. Artist's reconstruction of the ritual scene from Feature 96, an offering box below the floor of the Structure 35 temple. The scene consisted of a miniature adobe tomb with a stone roof, containing a pottery bowl, a ceramic effigy, and a sacrificed quail; a flying figure on the tomb roof, with a pair of deer antlers nearby; and four grotesque effigy figures in the background (see text). (Drawing by John Klausmeyer.)

private collections of Zapotec art. Unfortunately, because they were found by looters rather than professional archaeologists, the pieces have been divided among different collections and their relationship destroyed, so that one can only guess what the original scene looked like.

Summary and conclusions

Many of the ethnographically known elements of Zapotec ritual and religion can be found in the archaeological record, some as far back as the origins of village life. At this early stage, however, many of those elements appear as generalized features or ritual artefacts shared with several other Mesoamerican ethnic groups. Not until Monte Albán II (200 BC–AD 100), when the state had formed, do we finally see all those elements come together as a 'package' that resembles sixteenth-century Spanish descriptions of Zapotec religion. Clearly, therefore, what the Spaniards were describing was *Zapotec state religion*; we know much less about the household ritual conducted by commoners.

As early as 1350 BC, public buildings had storage pits for powdered lime that may have been used with narcotics or hallucinogens. By 1000 BC we see possible depictions in art of lightning and earthquake, and ritual scenes composed of small solid figurines that may represent ancestors. Stingray spines for ritual bloodletting were also present by that time, and between 700 and 500 BC, élite individuals were using obsidian artefacts chipped to resemble such spines. By 500 BC, we also have evidence for human sacrifice and the 260 day ritual calendar, two additional elements of Zapotec ritual.

A new plateau was reached by 200 BC, when standardized two-room temples became widespread at major sites. Those buildings match our sixteenth-century descriptions of temples in whose inner rooms the *bigaña*, or Zapotec priests, actually resided. The *bigaña* are described as letting their own blood with prismatic obsidian blades, and using flint or obsidian daggers to sacrifice slaves and war captives. They are also said to have sacrificed quail and turkeys, and to have burned great quantities of incense. Evidence for all these activities has been archaeologically recovered at temples like Structure 35 at San José Mogote. It is accompanied by the disappearance of many of the elements of pre-state religion, such as small solid figurines and depictions of the 'fire-serpent' and 'were-jaguar'.

What the Spaniards did not tell us – presumably because it took place before their arrival – is that the Zapotec had turned secular ground into sacred ground by placing valuable, labour-intensive offerings in the foundations of their temples. It remained for archaeologists to discover this. The DHA therefore, lies at the interface between archaeology and history. First, ethnohistory tells us what a temple should look like and accurately predicts that we should discover obsidian blades, sacrificial knives, incense burners and quail. Archaeology then reveals unpredicted offerings beneath the temples, but ethnohistory gives us some clues for interpreting them. In the case of Feature 96 at San José Mogote, it suggests that we are seeing metamorphosis, a major career transition of deceased royalty. Ethnohistory makes us less surprised that metamorphosed 'cloud people' wear the grotesque mask of Cociyo – the most powerful supernatural seen in Zapotec art, the version of Lightning preferred by the Classic Zapotec state.

The longer we work with the Zapotec, the more indebted we feel to the earlier generation of anthropological archaeologists who pioneered the DHA. Of course, our debt also extends to the sixteenth- and seventeenth-century Spaniards, without whose accounts it would be impossible to interpret meaning, symbolism, ideology and context in Zapotec archaeological remains. 'Cognitive archaeology' is not easy under any circumstances, but it is made easier when there is so much continuity between prehistoric and historic cultures.

Notes

1 Córdova (1578a) spelled Lightning *Cocijo*, which has for years been the standard spelling. However, he also made it clear that he was using the Latin *j* in his dictionary, reflecting the pronunciation *co-ci-yo*.

2 'Jade' is used colloquially here for jadeite, nephrite, and related metamorphics, since there is no true jade in Mexico.

3 In some Zapotec tombs, *acompañante* figures are so numerous as to seem almost analogous to the *ushabtis*, or servant figures, seen in Egyptian tombs. However, their earspools and necklaces make it clear that they are not depictions of commoners and therefore do not represent servants.

Acknowledgements

We would like to thank Jeremy Sabloff for his very useful comments on this paper.

References

Balsalobre, G. de 1656. Relación auténtica de las idolatrías, supersticiones, vanas observaciones de los indios del Obispado de Oaxaca. [Reprinted 1892 in *Anales del Museo Nacional de México*, Primera Época 6: 225–60]

Berlin, H. 1957. Las antiguas creencias en San Miguel Sola, Oaxaca, México. In Beiträge zur mittelamerikanischen Völkerkunde, Herausgegeben von Hamburgischen Museum für Völkerkunde und Vorgeschichte, No. 4

Bernal, I. 1949. Exploraciones en Coixtlahuaca, Oaxaca. *Revista Mexicana de Estudios Antropológicos* 10: 5–76

1958. Exploraciones en Cuilapan de Guerrero, 1902–1954. *Informes* 7, Dirección de Monumentos Prehispánicos. México, D.F., Instituto Nacional de Antropología e Historia

1965. Archaeological synthesis of Oaxaca. In *Handbook of Middle American indians, vol. III: Archaeology of Southern Mesoamerica*, part 2, ed. R. Wauchope and G. R. Willey, pp. 788–813. Austin, University of Texas Press

1966. The Mixtecs in the archaeology of the valley of Oaxaca. In *Ancient Oaxaca: discoveries in Mexican archeology and history*, ed. J. Paddock, pp. 345–66. Stanford, Stanford University Press

Blanton, R. E. 1978. *Monte Albán: settlement patterns at the ancient Zapotec capital*. New York, Academic Press

Burgoa, F. de 1670. Palestra historial de virtudes y exemplares apostólicos . . . (Reprinted in 1934 in *Publicaciones del Archivo General de la Nación*, vol. 24. México, Talleres Gráficos de la Nación)

1674. Geográfica descripción. (Reprinted in 1934 in *Publicaciones del Archivo General de la Nación*, vols. 25–6. México, Talleres Gráficos de la Nación)

Caso, A. 1932. La tumba 7 de Monte Albán es mixteca. *Universidad de México* 4 (20): 117–50.

1945. *La religión de los aztecas*. México, Secretaría de Educación Pública

1958. *The Aztecs: people of the sun*. Translated by Lowell Dunham. Norman, University of Oklahoma Press

1965. Sculpture and mural painting of Oaxaca. In *Handbook of Middle American indians, vol. III: archaeology of Southern Mesoamerica*, Part 2, ed. R. Wauchope and G. R. Willey, pp. 849–70. Austin, University of Texas Press

1966. The lords of Yanhuitlán. In *Ancient Oaxaca: discoveries in Mexican archeology and history*, ed. J. Paddock, pp. 313–35. Stanford, Stanford University Press

Caso, A. and I. Bernal 1952. Urnas de Oaxaca. *Memorias del Instituto Nacional de Antropología e Historia*, No. 2. México

Caso, A., I. Bernal and J. R. Acosta 1967. La cerámica de Monte Albán. *Memorias del Instituto Nacional de Antropología e Historia*, 13. México

Coe, M. D. 1973. The iconology of Olmec art. In *The*

iconography of Middle American sculpture, pp. 1–12. New York, The Metropolitan Museum of Art

Coe, W. R. 1990. *Tikal report 14. Excavations in the Great Plaza, North Terrace and North Acropolis of Tikal.* University Museum Monograph No. 61. Philadelphia, University of Pennsylvania

Córdova, Fray J. de 1578a. *Vocabulario en lengua zapoteca.* Mexico, Pedro Charte y Antonio Ricardo (reprinted 1942)

    1578b. *Arte en lengua zapoteca.* Mexico, Pedro Balli (reprinted 1886)

Covarrubias, M. 1942. Origen y desarrollo del estilo artístico 'Olmeca'. *Mayas y Olmecas*, pp. 46–9. Mexico

Flannery, K. V. 1976. Contextual analysis of ritual paraphernalia from formative Oaxaca. In *The early Mesoamerican village*, ed. K. V. Flannery, pp. 333–45. New York, Academic Press

    1983. The development of Monte Albán's main plaza in period II. In *The Cloud People: divergent evolution of the Zapotec and Mixtec civilizations*, ed. K. V. Flannery and J. Marcus, pp. 102–4. New York, Academic Press

Flannery, K. V. and J. Marcus 1976a. Formative Oaxaca and the Zapotec cosmos. *American Scientist* 64 (4): 374–83

    1976b. Evolution of the public building in formative Oaxaca. In *Cultural change and continuity: essays in honor of James Bennett Griffin*, ed. C. E. Cleland, pp. 205–21. New York, Academic Press

    1990. Borrón, y Cuenta Nueva: setting Oaxaca's archaeological record straight. In *Debating Oaxaca archaeology*, ed. J. Marcus, pp. 17–69. Museum of Anthropology, University of Michigan, Anthropological Papers, No. 84. Ann Arbor

Flannery, K. V. and J. Marcus (eds.) 1983. *The Cloud People: divergent evolution of the Zapotec and Mixtec civilizations.* New York, Academic Press

Frankfort, H., H. A. Frankfort, J. A. Wilson and T. Jacobsen 1946. *The intellectual adventure of ancient man.* Chicago, University of Chicago Press. [Reprinted in 1949 as *Before philosophy*. Baltimore, Penguin Books]

Joralemon, P. D. 1971. A study of Olmec iconography. *Studies in Pre-Columbian art and archaeology*, No. 7. Washington, DC, Dumbarton Oaks

Kidder, A. V., J. D. Jennings and E. M. Shook 1946. Excavations at Kaminaljuyu, Guatemala. *Carnegie Institution of Washington, Publication 561.* Washington, DC

Marcus, J. 1976. The origins of Mesoamerican writing. *Annual Review of Anthropology* 5: 35–67

    1978. Archaeology and religion: a comparison of the Zapotec and Maya. *World Archaeology* 10 (2): 172–91

    1980. Zapotec writing. *Scientific American* 242: 50–64

    1983a. Rethinking the Zapotec urn. In *The Cloud People: divergent evolution of the Zapotec and Mixtec civilizations*, ed. K. V. Flannery and J. Marcus, pp. 144–8. New York, Academic Press

    1983b. Zapotec Religion. In *The Cloud People: divergent evolution of the Zapotec and Mixtec civilizations*, ed. K. V. Flannery and J. Marcus, pp. 345–51. New York, Academic Press

    1983c. The conquest slabs of Building J, Monte Albán. In *The Cloud People: divergent evolution of the Zapotec and Mixtec civilizations*, ed. K. V. Flannery and J. Marcus, pp. 106–8. New York, Academic Press

    1983d. Changing patterns of stone monuments after the fall of Monte Albán, AD 600–900. In *The Cloud People: divergent evolution of the Zapotec and Mixtec civilizations*, ed. K. V. Flannery and J. Marcus, pp. 191–7. New York, Academic Press

    1988. Comments on 'Ecological theory and cultural evolution in the Valley of Oaxaca' by William T. Sanders and Deborah L. Nichols. *Current Anthropology* 29 (1): 60–1

    1989. Zapotec chiefdoms and the nature of formative religions. In *Regional perspectives on the Olmec*, ed. R. J. Sharer and D. C. Grove, pp. 148–97. Cambridge, Cambridge University Press

Marcus, J. and K. V. Flannery 1978. Ethnoscience of the sixteenth-century valley Zapotec. In *The nature and status of ethnobotany*, ed. R. I. Ford, pp. 51–79. Museum of Anthropology, University of Michigan, Anthropological Papers, No. 67. Ann Arbor

Moser, C. L. 1983. A Postclassic burial cave in the Southern Cañada. In *The Cloud People: divergent evolution of the Zapotec and Mixtec civilizations*, ed. K. V. Flannery and J. Marcus, pp. 270–2. New York, Academic Press

Parker, A. C. 1922. Archaeological history of New York. *New York State Museum Bulletin*, 235–8. Albany, New York.

Parry, W. J. 1987. Chipped stone tools in Formative Oaxaca, Mexico: their procurement, production and use. In *Prehistory and human ecology of the valley of Oaxaca*, vol. 8, ed. K. V. Flannery. *Memoirs of the University of Michigan Museum of Anthropology*, No. 20. Ann Arbor

Paso y Troncoso, F. del 1905–6. *Papeles de Nueva España: segunda serie, geografía y estadística*, 7 volumes. Madrid, Est. Tipográfico 'Sucesores de Rivadeneyra'

Rappaport, R. A. 1971. Ritual, sanctity and cybernetics. *American Anthropologist* 73: 59–76

Rappaport, R. A. (ed.) 1979. *Ecology, meaning, and religion*. Richmond, California, North Atlantic Books

Ricketson, O. G. and E. B. Ricketson 1937. Uaxactún,

Guatemala, Group E, 1926–1931. *Carnegie Institution of Washington, Publication 477.* Washington, DC

Ritchie, W. A. 1932. The Algonkin sequence in New York. *American Anthropologist* 34: 406–14

– 1938. A perspective of northeastern archaeology. *American Antiquity* 4 (2): 94–112

Seler, E. 1904. The wall paintings of Mitla, a Mexican picture writing in fresco. In Mexican and Central American antiquities, calendar systems, and history (24 papers by Seler, Förstemann, Schellhas, Sapper, Dieseldorff, translated from the German by Charles P. Bowditch). *Bureau of American Ethnology Bulletin* 28: 247–324. Washington, DC, US Government Printing Office

Smith, A. L. 1950. Uaxactun, Guatemala: excavations of 1931–1937. *Carnegie Institution of Washington, Publication 588.* Washington, DC

Strong, W. D. 1933. The Plains culture area in the light of archaeology. *American Anthropologist* 35 (2): 271–87

1935. An introduction to Nebraska archaeology. *Smithsonian Miscellaneous Collections*, vol. 93, No. 10. Washington, DC, Smithsonian Institution

Thompson, J. E. S. 1950. *Maya hieroglyphic writing: an introduction.* Carnegie Institution of Washington Publication 589. Washington, DC

– 1966. *The rise and fall of Maya civilization.* Norman, University of Oklahoma Press

– 1970. *Maya history and religion.* Norman, University of Oklahoma Press

– 1973. Maya rulers of the Classic Period and the Divine Right of Kings. In *The iconography of Middle American sculpture*, pp. 52–71. New York, The Metropolitan Museum of Art

Wedel, W. R. 1938. The Direct-Historical Approach in Pawnee archaeology. *Smithsonian Miscellaneous Collections*, vol. 97, No. 7. Washington, DC, Smithsonian Institution

8

The meaning of death: funerary beliefs and the prehistorian

CHRIS SCARRE

In recent years a number of important studies have endeavoured to address the question of the symbolism embedded in prehistoric funerary structures and practices (Shanks and Tilley 1982; Tilley 1984; Hodder 1984; Morris 1988). This reflects an optimism which is prepared to ignore Ucko's warning, illustrated by a wide range of ethnographic parallels, of the difficulty of interpreting beliefs from burial practices, even at a fairly general level (Ucko 1969). It may indeed be fair to dismiss some of Ucko's reservations as rare exceptions to the general run of human beliefs, but the methodological question remains. How far is it possible to investigate past ideologies and beliefs in the absence of written records?

The answer will, to some extent, depend on the precise meaning we attach to terms such as 'ideology' and 'belief', since some aspects of past human behaviour are naturally much more accessible to us than others. We may indeed think in terms of a Hawkesian 'ladder of inference' (Hawkes 1954), where it is relatively easy to infer the form of treatment given to the dead, but clearly impossible, in the absence of written records, to know the names of deities or the details of myths. Hawkes, however, took a gloomy view:

> You can use ethnological data obtained from modern primitives to stimulate your imagination by suggesting the sort of religious institutions and spiritual life your prehistoric peoples may or could have had, but you cannot in this way demonstrate what they did have, and you cannot even hope to unless you can show some real connection between *this* modern and *that* prehistoric. (Hawkes 1954; quoted in Ucko 1969)

Such a view must be considered unduly pessimistic by archaeologists who are possessed today of increasingly sophisticated methods of data collection and analysis and an increasing concern to include the often abundant evidence for past symbolic and cognitive behaviour in their interpretations. It is after all these areas of behaviour which make us distinctively human and separate us most clearly from the animals.

Monumental chambered tombs are among the most conspicuous and impressive ritual constructions of western Europe in the neolithic period, and together with stone circles the most eloquent testimony to the importance of symbolic and ritual practices to these early farming communities. A number of recent studies have endeavoured to interpret the tombs in the light of past ideologies, but the emphasis in these studies has been on the social significance of the burial practices. One of the leading exponents of this kind of approach considers tomb architecture as a socio-political device: 'We can see this architectural complexity as an attempt to "stage manage" or orchestrate the encounter with the ancestral remains. Thus the intention was to influence the way in which these deposits, of symbolic importance to the reproduction of authority within a community, were perceived and interpreted' (Thomas 1990). Others have considered megalithic tombs as economic indicators (e.g. Jarman, Bailey and Jarman 1982). These kinds of approaches may, to some degree, represent a reaction against the speculations concerning the existence and nature of megalithic religion which were prevalent in the 1950s, and which found their most notable expression in Crawford's *The eye goddess* (1957). Yet recent approaches which shy away from the 'difficult' subject of religion and belief run the risk of expending all their energies on what are really only secondary features of the tombs and their significance.

European megaliths are really the starting point for this article, and I shall return to them below. My main purpose here, however, is to probe the limitations of what the prehistorian may realistically hope to discover about the symbolism behind these monuments. To assess how far archaeology alone and unaided can provide knowledge about this, I have chosen to consider a historical, or perhaps more accurately a protohistorical case, from a prehistorian's perspective. The case in question is perhaps the most famous and obvious of all: ancient Egypt. It is with some trepidation that an outsider trained principally in European prehistory enters upon such a well-established sub-discipline of archaeology as Egyptology. Egyptian tombs, however, have been a focus of archaeological interest and research since at least the Napoleonic conquest of 1798 (Clayton 1982), and such is the richness of the Egyptian material that we have here probably more evidence for the nature of society than for any other people at such a distance in time. It therefore provides an excellent instance for considering the interplay between archaeological and historical evidence in our reconstruction of ancient burial practices and beliefs, an example which can throw light on the procedures and limitations of cognitive archaeology in a prehistoric context. This is not to say, however, that our understanding of ancient Egyptian funerary beliefs is comprehensive and complete, and it is indeed the case that much of what we know is reconstruction based on conjecture and interpretation. As one recent authority writes 'Our knowledge of the Egyptian concept of the next world is derived almost entirely from inscriptional evidence and consequently we understand very little about Egyptian beliefs in this sphere from the earliest period' (Spencer 1982: 139). The Egyptian case may nonetheless serve, by way of contrast, to highlight some of the problems we face in endeavouring to understand the remains of the near-contemporary, but much less well documented, societies of prehistoric Europe.

The objective of this discussion is to assess how far a purely archaeological approach could detect and interpret Egyptian royal funerary beliefs if there were no documentary sources to guide us. We will concentrate principally on the evidence of the earliest Egyptian dynasties, from the formation of the unified state *c*. 3100 BC to the fall of the Old Kingdom seven centuries later. For convenience, the discussion will be divided into two parts: the morphological development of the Egyptian pyramid; and, secondly, the significance for archaeological interpretation of the co-existence of parallel or discordant traditions.

Egyptian tombs: mastaba to pyramid

A series of large Egyptian tombs belonging to courtiers of the First Dynasty are located at Saqqara, on the west bank of the Nile facing modern Cairo and a little to the north of the ancient capital of Memphis. These early tombs were an expression of secular symbolism based on the house; since courtiers lived in palaces, the tombs were modelled so as to resemble, externally, the appearance of a palace. The tombs took the form of flat-topped rectangular structures of sun-dried mud-brick, measuring 40 to 60 metres long, 15 to 25 metres wide and standing some 7 or 8 metres high (Watson 1987). Internally, these so-called mastaba or bench tombs housed a number of magazines – sometimes as many as 45 – capable of holding vast quantities of food and other produce which the dead person might require in the afterlife (Spencer 1982). The mud-brick mastaba was, however, only the superstructure of the tomb, and the burial itself was placed in a rock-cut chamber deep beneath the desert surface.

The mastaba form is clearly an expression of the tomb as a house of the dead. We know from later texts that Egyptian beliefs held that the tomb would become the house of the dead person for all eternity, and even if we did not have the benefit of this written evidence the domestic symbolism of the tomb form makes this clear. By the early dynastic period mud-brick architecture was well established in ancient Egypt and was used for town walls and houses as well as tombs (Kemp 1989: 92). Furthermore, the outer faces of these élite tombs were decorated in a particular way, with a succession of recessed niches, to create what has become known as the 'palace façade'. Emery (1961: 131), who excavated many of the early mastabas at Saqqara, expresses this clearly: 'The whole of the panelled exterior of the mastaba was painted in gay colours in designs which imitated the matwork which adorned the outside of the dwelling places of the living; for of course the tomb was a copy of the house or palace of the owner in life.' Whether or not the 'palace façade' was originally adopted from Mesopotamia (Kemp 1989: 92), to the Egyptians of the early dynastic period it clearly symbolized status and power. As such it appears on royal stelae and sealings (Emery 1961).

The archaeologist seeking to interpret the outward form of the mastaba tombs has relatively little need to call on documentary sources, which in any case are extremely rare at this period. It is more difficult to explain the subsequent course of developments. For it is at Saqqara that we can trace the transition from palace-façade mastaba tomb to the earliest royal pyramid, the Step Pyramid of King Zoser. And although it is now known that the kings of the First and most of the Second dynasty were buried at Abydos in the south of Egypt, it is nonetheless clear that the élite symbolism manifest in the princely mastaba tombs at Saqqara is reflected in massively enlarged and enhanced form in the early royal pyramids. These are works in stone, immensely larger and immensely more labour demanding to build. They reflect the increasing power of the king and the increasing wealth of the Egyptian state in its first period of greatness. That much is clear enough, as is the subsequent decrease in pyramid size as royal power diminished and then collapsed at the end of the Old Kingdom (Fig. 8.1). The idea of the pyramid, however, marks a distinct and novel development, without obvious antecedents at either Saqqara or Abydos. How would the prehistorian cope with the symbolic meaning of the pyramid form?

Clearly, if the written sources were removed, much would be lost. At the same time, however, it would be wrong to underestimate the potential of archaeological analysis. We may summarize the position as follows.

First, on the debit side, the true significance of the pyramid shape would be inaccessible in a prehistoric context. As Edwards explains, it is the Pyramid Texts, magical spells inscribed on the walls of the later Old Kingdom pyramids, which provide the most probable explanation; for instance Spell 508 'I have trodden those thy rays as a ramp under my feet whereupon I mount up to that my mother, the living Uraeus on the brow of Re'. Edwards (1961: 291) concludes 'The temptation to regard the true Pyramid as a material representation of the sun's rays and consequently as a means whereby the dead king could ascend to heaven seems irresistible.' Reliefs of the Amarna period – though admittedly much later in date – depict the sun's rays radiating from the heavens in just this way. Furthermore, he proposes a similar symbolism for the earlier Step Pyramid which preceded the first of the true pyramids, citing Spell 619 'A staircase to heaven is laid for him so that he may mount to heaven thereby' (Edwards 1961: 288). The significance of the pyramid as a solar image is backed up by other passages in the Pyramid Texts which express the belief that the king was to join the sun-god Re in the after-life, as a rower helping to propel the god in his solar bark across the heavens each day.

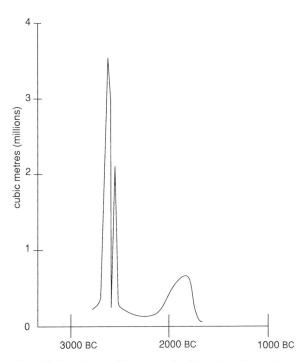

Fig. 8.1. Royal pyramid construction in ancient Egypt, in terms of estimated pyramid volume. Note the sharp decline in the later Old Kingdom (c. 2400–2200 BC), and the more modest scale of the royal pyramids constructed during the Middle Kingdom (c. 2050–1750 BC). (After Lehner 1985.)

The prehistorian would be deprived of the details of this imagery. On the credit side, however, the material *forms* of the royal tombs would still be apparent, even if their *content* was beyond reach. We have seen how the early Egyptian tombs were conceived of as homes for the dead; this is demonstrated not only by the external treatment but also by internal features of the tomb chamber itself: one of those at Saqqara had wooden pilasters decorated with strips of embossed sheet gold from floor to ceiling, and others were hung with coloured reed mats (Emery 1961: 190, 228). At the same time, the palace façades of the early mastabas symbolized temporal power. Here again the tomb is symbolically associated with a dwelling, only in this case it is the highest status dwelling – the royal palace. Thus the palace façade mastabas consciously proclaim the power of the deceased in secular terms.

With the development of the pyramid tomb, all this changes. The contrast with the previous symbolic language of mastaba tomb and palace façade is dramatic. The shape, mass and height of the pyramid was associated with the symbolism of the sun, and proclaimed for all to see the absorption of the king into the mystic solar cult. Thus we have, in these monuments, a confident material statement of divine kingship. The pyramid does not represent a house or building, but an abstract concept. This much would be clear even if we did not know what the concept was. At the same time, the enormous increase in scale which the pyramids represent, as compared with the earlier royal tombs at Abydos, reflects the growth of concentrated, centralized power.

The three stages of development – from tomb as house, to tomb as status indicator (palace façade mastaba), to tomb as religious statement (pyramid) – are all accessible to archaeological analysis, without the need for written statements of Egyptian thoughts or attitudes. Without the Pyramid Texts we would miss the details, but not the substance. Furthermore, the Pyramid Texts were magical spells, hidden inside the royal pyramids and only known to a fraction even of that tiny proportion of ancient Egyptians who could read and write. Many ordinary Egyptians may have been entirely ignorant of their precise content and meaning. But the pyramids would have carried a broader message – of power both royal and divine – a message which I believe would remain accessible to archaeological analysis even without the benefit of written texts.

Discordant beliefs: the meaning of pyramids

The difficulty of extracting any information about ideology from ancient remains has, not unnaturally, discouraged archaeologists from considering the likelihood of parallel or discordant ideologies. Yet it is clear that within each society, both ancient and modern, there are classes or groups of people with differing beliefs and differing interpretations of the events around them. The co-existence of several religions in a single society is perhaps the most obvious example and one which is often readily documented in the archaeological record, for instance through remains of churches, mosques and other places of worship. Hodder (1986: 63–5) has emphasized the importance of considering these discordant traditions if we are to understand the nature of ancient societies. He takes as an example Leone's study of the garden created by the 18th century landowner William Paca at Annapolis, Maryland (Leone 1984). Leone interprets the ordered symmetry of garden and house as an attempt to naturalize the contradiction between liberal values and slave ownership in 18th-century North American society but, as Hodder points out, there is no evidence that the orderly garden layout would have carried the same message for all members of that society, least of all for the slave underclass (Hodder 1986: 65).

It may often be possible for the historical archaeologist, with the benefit of written records, to come to grips with the diversity of beliefs represented in the material remains of the society he is studying. The prehistorian, however, faced with the mute evidence of monuments and artefacts, here finds himself at a considerable disadvantage. Once again, an example from Old Kingdom Egypt may serve to illuminate the problem.

It has long been accepted that the true pyramid is primarily to be seen as a solar symbol, representing the slanting rays of the sun in massive material form. It is possible, however, to trace a very different ancestry for the pyramid, beginning from the small tumuli found within certain mastabas. In archaeological terms this makes a convincing case. In one mastaba at Saqqara, Emery found a rectangular earthen tumulus faced with brickwork above the burial chamber (Fig. 8.2a). Thus, within the palace façade exterior, there was hidden another monument of different and more primitive form. Another mastaba contained a similar internal structure, this time in the form of a stepped platform (Fig. 8.2b). Had it continued upwards, this stepped platform would have provided an excellent antecedent for the Step Pyramid of King Zoser, with the palace façade of the royal mastaba becoming the recessed rectangular enclosure wall of the Step Pyramid complex (Emery 1961: 82–4, 144–6).

This much we follow from the archaeological record without reference to written sources. But where written sources become essential is in understanding the meaning of the mastaba tumulus. We can, of course, seek to explain it simply as a translation into mud brick of the original pile of sand which had been placed over simple pit-graves (Edwards

1961: 43). But later texts suggest it had a more specific religious significance, as a representation of the primeval mound, the first piece of land to appear above the waters of the ocean in Egyptian creation mythology. 'Placing a burial either upon or beneath a symbolic copy of this mound was considered of great importance for the resurrection of the body, owing to the spontaneous appearance of life upon the original mound of the creation myths' (Spencer 1982: 151). The Step Pyramid may be considered the lineal descendant of the mastaba mounds, and the true pyramid the lineal successor of the Step Pyramid; an interpretation which is

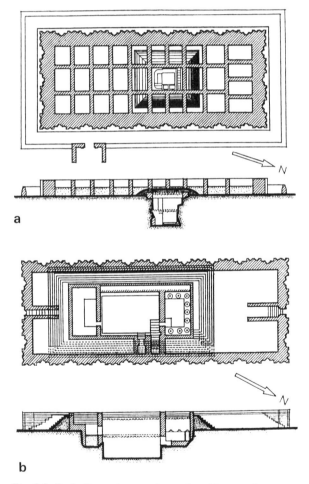

Fig. 8.2. Early Dynastic mastaba tombs with central mounds at Saqqara, Egypt. (After Edwards 1985, reproduced from The pyramids of Egypt *by I. E. S. Edwards (revised edition, Harmondsworth 1985) by permission of Penguin Books Ltd.*

confirmed by the discovery of references in the Pyramid Texts which suggest that the pyramid could be regarded as a representation of the primeval mound (Spencer 1982: 150).

Thus we find ourselves faced with two conflicting interpretations of the pyramid form: as a material representation of the sun's rays – a symbol intimately linked to the royal sun-cult – and as a representation of the primeval mound, essential for rebirth. Here we are clearly beyond the limits of purely archaeological interpretation, yet the analysis which links the pyramid to the internal mound found encased in the Saqqara mastabas is in itself an archaeological exercise, based on the results of excavation. Once again, we are left with the conclusion that careful archaeological analysis can go far to establish the development of the symbolic forms, but cannot ordinarily establish the meaning or content of these symbols.

We have seen, from these two examples, how much our knowledge of funerary symbolism in Old Kingdom Egypt is dependent on archaeological data and interpretation. We have also seen how, in the absence of relevant contemporary written records, our understanding may nonetheless be confirmed and amplified by reference to later texts which fall within the same religious and ideological tradition. In a fully prehistoric context, however, relevant written records are entirely lacking, and our interpretations of funerary symbols and practices must be based on parallels drawn from cultural traditions more distantly removed in space and time.

Back to prehistory

The prehistoric chambered tombs of western Europe are comparable in their monumentality to the burial monuments of ancient Egypt. Lacking written records, however, the symbolic significance of the tomb form, and the nature and purpose of the funerary practices must be established by other means. In the Egyptian cases we have examined, the symbolic forms could be studied by archaeology alone, but meaning was only accessible through knowledge of Egyptian mythology and belief recorded in later texts. The European case is similar: the patterns and linkages between tombs, artefacts and interred remains can be established by careful study of the archaeological record, but for insight into the meaning and significance of those patterns and linkages we have to look to better documented cases. It is here that the problem lies. In the Egyptian case, we were referring to documentary evidence from the same culture as the monuments which we were endeavouring to interpret. In the case of European chambered tombs, there are no comparable examples from later literate European societies to which we can look for insights. Instead, we are obliged to

look beyond Europe, to societies much further afield, where the link is not shared cultural background but a type of funerary monument and burial practice closely similar to those of prehistoric Europe.

The society which provides the best documented and closest parallel for the European chambered tombs is that of the Merina of Madagascar. The argument that sees Merina tombs as a source of insights into chambered tombs is, therefore, basically a case of ethnographic analogy. The Merina tombs represent one of the few living ethnographic traditions, indeed perhaps the only one to have survived to the present day. As such, they have been used as an obvious ethnographic parallel by several archaeologists over the last decade or so (e.g. Chapman 1981; Sharples 1985; Thomas 1988). One major benefit provided by this and similar ethnographic analogies is that they can make the archaeological data less mysterious and alien, a particularly useful consideration where ritual behaviour is concerned (Hodder 1982: 166). In this general respect, the Merina parallel has performed a most useful service. It is, however, worth considering in more detail just how far the assumed similarity between the Madagascan and European cases can throw light on the beliefs and practices associated with the latter.

The two primary similarities between the two cases are the use of monumental architecture and the practice of communal burial. Merina tombs are basically burial vaults, in which an individual's entitlement to burial depends on membership of a *deme*, a kin and village-based association (Bloch 1971). In the present day examples described by Bloch, Merina tombs are of stone and cement, and the roof is a large stone capstone covered by concrete. His account explains that this type of tomb originated in the nineteenth century, when European artisans introduced features such as arcading in the elaborate tombs they built for Merina monarchs and their principal ministers. Prior to this, the tombs had been of megalithic construction, consisting of massive stone slabs and buried up to the capstone in a mound of stones and earth, thus providing a striking parallel to the megalithic tombs of prehistoric Europe, constructed some five or six thousand years earlier (Joussaume 1985; Joussaume and Raharijoana 1985).

Merina burial practices are multi-stage, beginning with the burial of the deceased shortly after death. The second stage of the burial follows two or more years later, and is known as *famadihana*. In this ceremony the body is disinterred, re-wrapped in silken shrouds, and then placed (or replaced) in the tomb. In the course of the famadihana a number of the older skeletons are also removed from the tomb and re-wrapped, in much the same way as the principal interment. During the course of the day, before the tomb is resealed, all the remaining skeletons are re-wrapped in a more hurried way inside the tomb. This is the procedure as recorded by Bloch (1971). Joussaume adds the further detail that in re-wrapping the skeletons of people who had been dead for some time, the bones of three or four individuals would often be wrapped together in the same shroud. The emphasis in this ceremony is on corporate membership of the deme, and on the ancestors who are buried in the deme tomb, since it is through the deme and the ancestors that rights to land are transmitted from generation to generation.

Does the Merina case provide insight into the meaning and beliefs associated with European prehistoric chambered tombs? The question can only be answered by considering how closely the two cases resemble each other at a detailed level.

Two of the most striking features of Merina burial practices are the practice of ancestor worship and the stress on communal solidarity and cohesion which the rituals are designed to strengthen. Bloch (1986: 35) writes 'The tombs stand for the permanent unity of people and land; they place the ancestors in the land.' The ritual of famadihana, when the bodies in the tomb are re-wrapped, may be considered to incorporate elements of ancestor worship. Many of the chambered tombs of western Europe were equipped with passages and portals which would have allowed them to be re-opened from time to time, and it is possible that bodies or bones were brought from the tomb for periodic ceremonies of ancestor-veneration. There is, of course, no way we can be sure of this. However, the segregation and sorting of body-parts found in certain Orkney tombs (twenty-seven skulls in one of the side chambers at Isbister (Hedges 1983); seventeen skulls in the terminal stall at Knowe of Yarso (Callander and Grant 1935)) could well be the result of some such practice. But sorting of body-parts is foreign to the Merina tradition; and indeed segregation of skulls recalls rather the 'skull-festivals' of West African peoples such as the Dowayo of Cameroun (Barley 1983: 99–103).

Community solidarity and cohesion has also been a frequent assertion in recent studies of European neolithic chambered tombs. Shanks and Tilley reach this conclusion in their study of mortuary practices in British and Scandinavian megalithic tombs: 'An assertion of the collective, a denial of the individual and of differences between individuals. The regrouping of the disarticulated remains may represent an assertion of resonance between essentially discrete individuals, and thus a denial of asymmetrical relationships existing in life' (Shanks and Tilley 1982: 150). But what Shanks and Tilley are discussing goes far beyond the accidental mixing of bones; they are discussing the intentional placing and manipulation of male and female

bones from the left and right sides of the body. At Ascott-under-Wychwood, a long barrow in southern Britain, one skeleton had been 'reconstituted' from the remains of two separate individuals, one male, the other female (Chesterman 1977). Other European chambered tombs show a different pattern again. At La Chaussée-Tirancourt, the distribution of non-metrical genetic features indicates that different parts of the tomb were reserved for separate families or kin-groups. In this case, the corporate solidarity of the kin-group (separate areas within the tomb) seems to have been maintained almost in spite of the communality of the collective burial concept (everyone buried in the same chamber) (Scarre 1984).

Thus this specific ethnographic parallel presents us with a paradox. It does indeed suggest two elements of ideology – the reverence of ancestors and the importance of communal solidarity – which fit well with the evidence from the European prehistoric tombs. Yet at the detailed level there are sufficient differences to show that funerary beliefs of west European neolithic tomb-builders probably differed significantly from those of Madagascan societies of the nineteenth century. There is no Madagascan parallel for the art found within the European passage graves. One recent writer (Bradley 1989) has suggested that this contains entopic imagery, and we may perhaps connect this with shamanistic beliefs and practices of which we are otherwise wholly ignorant. There is furthermore no reason to believe that European tomb-builders retained a single fixed belief throughout the whole period and wide geographical region in which tombs were built and used; quite the contrary. The art found on megalithic tombs here provides a vital clue. It is clear that this art can be divided into two stages or periods. The first, itself varying from region to region, consists essentially of abstract images; these, as we have noted, may be associated with shamanistic practices, but give no hint of the worship of a deity or deities. The art of the second phase, in contrast, consists of representations of a schematic female figure with necklace and breasts, sometimes indeed reduced to a row of breasts alone. The representations, which have often – inevitably – been interpreted as a female deity or mother goddess (Fleming 1969), are found only in two areas: Brittany and the Paris basin. They nonetheless suggest that in these parts of France, in what we may call the late megalithic period (late fourth/early third millennium BC), a system of beliefs incorporating specific spirits or deities of human or semi-human form had developed. It is difficult to be sure, but we may have here, in the two stages of megalithic art, a progression in funerary belief associated with the increasing importance of a particular female deity.

We are left with the conclusion that even a close ethnographic parallel leaves much of the European funerary symbolism unexplained, and that attempts to understand such symbolic behaviour in terms of what we may perhaps call 'symbolic universals' (e.g. in the use of body-parts to symbolize social relations: Shanks and Tilley 1982) may contain a degree of truth but must inevitably miss much of the original meaning. This is not a counsel of despair, however, since, as these cases have shown, careful excavation and analysis does allow us to detect symbolic behaviour and to follow its development, even in a purely prehistoric context. This is a valuable, nay vital, aspect of archaeological enquiry, but it remains an enquiry into the externals of what is essentially an internal phenomenon: human thought and belief. Only with the benefit of written sources or oral traditions, or at the very least a rich iconography, can we get within the symbolism and understand its content and meaning.

References

Barley, N. 1983. *Symbolic structures. An exploration of the culture of the Dowayos*. Cambridge, Cambridge University Press

Bloch, M. 1971. *Placing the dead. Tombs, ancestral villages and kinship organization in Madagascar*. London and New York, Seminar Press

1986. *From blessing to violence. History and ideology in the circumcision ritual of the Merina of Madagascar*. Cambridge, Cambridge University Press

Bradley, R. 1989. Deaths and entrances: a contextual analysis of megalithic art. *Current Anthropology* 30: 68–75

Callander, J. G. and W. G. Grant 1935. A long, stalled cairn. The Knowe of Yarso in Rousay, Orkney. *Proceedings of the Society of Antiquaries of Scotland* 69: 325–51

Chapman, R. 1981. The emergence of formal disposal areas and the 'problem' of megalithic tombs in prehistoric Europe. In *The archaeology of death*, ed. R. Chapman, I. Kinnes and K. Randsborg, pp. 71–81. Cambridge, Cambridge University Press

Chesterman, J. T. 1977. Burial rites in a Cotswold long barrow. *Man* 12: 22–32

Clayton, P. A. 1982. *The rediscovery of Ancient Egypt*. London, Thames and Hudson

Crawford, O. G. S. 1957. *The eye goddess*. London, Phoenix House

Edwards, I. E. S. 1961. *The pyramids of Egypt*. Harmondsworth, Penguin

Emery, W. B. 1961. *Archaic Egypt*. Harmondsworth, Penguin

Fleming, A. 1969. The myth of the mother-goddess. *World Archaeology* 1: 247–61

Hawkes, C. 1954. Archaeological theory and method: some suggestions from the Old World. *American Anthropologist* 56: 155–68

Hedges, J. W. 1983. *Isbister. A chambered tomb in Orkney*. Oxford, British Archaeological Reports British Series 115

Hodder, I. 1982. *The present past. An introduction to anthropology for archaeologists*. London, Batsford

1984. Burials, houses, women and men in the European Neolithic. In *Ideology, power and prehistory*, ed. D. Miller and C. Tilley, pp. 51–68. Cambridge, Cambridge University Press

1986. *Reading the past*. Cambridge, Cambridge University Press

Jarman, M. R., G. N. Bailey and H. N. Jarman 1982. *Early European agriculture*. Cambridge, Cambridge University Press

Joussaume, R. 1985. *Des dolmens pour les morts*. Paris, Hachette

Joussaume, R. and V. Raharijoana 1975. Sépultures mégalithiques à Madagascar. *Bulletin de la Société Préhistorique Française* 82: 534–51

Kemp, B. J. 1989. *Ancient Egypt: anatomy of a civilization*. London, Routledge

Lehner, M. 1985. The development of the Giza necropolis: the Khufu project. *Mitteilungen des Deutschen Archäologischen Instituts, Abteilung Kairo* 41: 109–43

Leone, M. 1984. Interpreting ideology in historical archaeology: using the rules of perspective in the William Paca Garden in Annapolis, Maryland. In *Ideology, power and prehistory*, ed. D. Miller and C. Tilley, pp. 25–35. Cambridge, Cambridge University Press

Morris, I. 1988. *Burial in ancient society*. Cambridge, Cambridge University Press

Scarre, C. J. 1984. Kin-groups in megalithic burials. *Nature* 311: 512–23

Shanks, M. and C. Tilley 1982. Ideology, symbolic power and ritual communication: a reinterpretation of neolithic mortuary practices. In *Symbolic and structural archaeology*, ed. I. Hodder, pp. 129–54. Cambridge, Cambridge University Press

Sharples, N. 1985. Individual and community: the changing role of megaliths in the Orcadian neolithic. *Proceedings of the Prehistoric Society* 51: 59–74

Spencer, A. 1982. *Death in Ancient Egypt*. Harmondsworth, Penguin

Thomas, J. 1988. The social significance of Cotswold–Severn burial practices. *Man* 23: 540–59

1990. Monuments from the inside: the case of the Irish megalithic tombs. *World Archaeology* 22: 168–78

Tilley, C. 1984. Ideology and the legitimation of power in the Middle Neolithic of Southern Sweden. In *Ideology, power and prehistory*, ed. D. Miller and C. Tilley, pp. 111–46. Cambridge, Cambridge University Press

Ucko, P. J. 1969. Ethnography and archaeological interpretation of funerary remains. *World Archaeology* 1: 262–80

Watson, P. 1987. *Egyptian pyramids and mastaba tombs.* Aylesbury, Shire

9

Prehistoric cognition and the science of archaeology

JAMES N. HILL

... different kinds of phenomena are never remote; they are either accessible or they are not. 'Nonmaterial' aspects of culture are accessible in direct measure with the testability of propositions being advanced about them.

(Binford 1968: 22)

Introduction

Given that there has been increasing interest among archaeologists in reconstructing what might be called pre-historic 'mental things' (e.g. cognition, perception, ideology, symbolism, values, beliefs etc.), and given that it would be interesting to do so, it behoves us, as scientists, to explore whether, or to what degree, it can be done within the framework of the general method of science. Thus, the question I am asking in this chapter is: 'To what degree are prehistoric thoughts knowable within the context of hypothesis testing?' Can we actually *test* ideas which we may have about such things?

I have long maintained that it is not possible to learn about what was in the minds of prehistoric people – these minds are gone, and their mental contents are not recoverable. While we can examine many aspects of what they *did*, we can understand nothing about what they *thought* about what they did. But is this really true?

Although I continue to maintain that we cannot actually *know* what prehistoric people thought, I now think that it is sometimes possible to make plausible inferences about what they must almost certainly have thought, given very strong circumstantial and analogical evidence. Moreover, I think that some such inferences are testable. I shall present argumentation, and some data, in support of this view, but shall, in the last analysis, argue that testing inferences about

prehistoric mental culture is probably rather limited in its potential for contributing a great deal to our understanding of prehistory.

In this paper, I offer two substantive examples which I think illustrate two different methods that may be useful to a cognitive archaeology. The first draws upon the data and conclusions presented by Howard Winters (1968), in which he used data from the Late Archaic in the US Midwest to infer that conch shells and copper were considered to be materials of value by the prehistoric peoples involved. Winters' study illustrates what I will call, for better or worse, the 'Established Generalization Testing method' (or EGT method).

The second example draws on data and inference by Alexander von Gernet and Peter Timmins (1987), wherein they infer the existence and *meaning* of a very specific prehistoric shamanistic ideology and symbol system in southeastern Canada and the northeastern United States. Their study illustrates what I call the 'Tight Local Analogy method' (or TLA method).

I have no intention of implying that these two methods are the only ones that may be useful to a cognitive archaeology; they are simply the only methods of which I am currently aware.

Example 1: a matter of value

Winters' analysis

Winters' (1968) analyses relate to the Indian Knoll Culture in the Green River area of western Kentucky, which existed from approximately 2500 to 2000 BC. His data were derived from original published excavation reports on eight sites: Indian Knoll (Webb 1946), Carlson Annis (Webb 1950a), Read (Webb 1950b), Ward and Kirkland (Webb and Haag 1940), Chiggerville (Webb and Haag 1939), and Barrett and Butterfield (Webb and Haag 1947). I draw only selectively from his several different kinds of analyses.

Winters classified several thousand artefacts (from all of his sites) into approximately sixty different functional classes, which he, in turn, classified into three major functional domains: (1) 'general utility implements', (2) 'ceremonial equipment', and (3) 'ornaments' (his Table 1). He then examined the contextual association of each artefact class at each site, focusing on the degree to which each class was associated with burials as opposed to trash middens. He discovered that, for most of his sites, 98–99 per cent of the 'general utility implements' were found in the middens, while 75 per cent (or more) of the 'ceremonial equipment' items were found in burial association. The items in the 'ornaments' domain were more evenly split between burial and midden association (1968: 175–84).

Most notable, however, was Winters' discovery that regardless of artefact domain, virtually all of the artefacts manufactured from *imported* materials (conch shell and copper) were found in burial association and *not* in the middens (1968: 181–2). Moreover, given that both conch shell and copper had been imported from distant sources (central Florida and the Great Lakes region respectively), Winters suggests that the reason these materials were deposited only with burials, and not 'casually' in the middens, was that they must have been considered valuable by the Indian Knoll people (1968: 181–2). As he points out, with respect to copper specifically, we would not expect highly valued materials to be found in middens very frequently: '. . . if raw copper is a valued and rare import, it is not particularly surprising that it is missing as an element of the Kentucky middens. The quantity of raw diamonds in the New York City dumps probably does not warrant the screening of these cultural residues' (1968: 201).

In further support of the 'valuableness' inference, he points out that conch shell and copper were only very rarely used by the Indian Knoll people in the manufacture of utilitarian implements, while the peoples in the respective *source* areas commonly used these materials for such implements (1968: 183, 199). The implication, of course, is that people rarely use costly imported materials in the manufacture of their everyday tools; since the Indian Knoll people did not use copper or conch shell in this way, the materials must have been considered valuable.

Additional evidence adduced to bolster this view is that conch shell and copper were not only found almost exclusively in burials, but only with a small minority of the Indian Knoll burials. In fact, even leaving conch shell and copper items aside, very few of the burials had *any* artefacts associated with them at all. In the eight sites from which Winters drew his data, the mean percentage of burials associated with *any* grave goods was 23.9, with a range of 5.7 per cent to 44.6 per cent (see his Table 9). This evidence suggests to Winters that those individuals associated with artefacts were probably members of a 'high-status' or 'élite' group within the society. This suggests that only an 'élite' had access to conch shell and copper materials, and this further suggests that these materials must have been considered valuable (1968: 208–9, 215).

To add further fuel to his argument, Winters points to the fact that these suggested wealth/status differentials were increasing over time in this area:

there seems to have been a noticeable decrease through time in the number of burials associated with [imported] disc-shell beads, primarily necklaces, as the proportional quantities of the beads themselves rose. In other words,

fewer and fewer people seem to have controlled more and more of the shell beads through time. Control of this form of wealth may well have been increasingly concentrated in the hands of a smaller segment of the population. (Winters 1968: 215)

After concluding, on the basis of his archaeological evidence, that the Indian Knoll people had considered conch shell and copper to be valuable, Winters appeals to other studies to lend further support. For example, he cites Slotkin and Schmitt's (1949) analysis of *wampum* in eastern North America, and points to their demonstration of the fact that the continuity of wampum (which consisted of shell beads of special value used as 'money' for exchange purposes) can be traced from the Late Archaic on through the historic contact period (Winters 1968: 185–6). He suggests that the conch shell beads of the Indian Knoll Culture may have served a function similar to wampum, and that the later wampum might also have been deposited in similar kinds of 'élite' contexts (1968: 185–6). This idea is strengthened by Slotkin and Schmitt's demonstration that marine shell, copper and brass, in the historic Fort Ancient Culture, are found precisely in such contexts (1968: 191), and by the fact that historic records report marine shell as being of 'considerable value' (1968: 191).

As a further 'test', Winters turns to data from an historic Fort Ancient Culture site, the Hardin Site (Hanson 1966), which is believed to have been a Shawnee village. It is located on the Ohio River in Kentucky, and was occupied from *c.* AD 1500 to 1675. The data are from midden and burial association, and are presented in Winters' Table 2 (1968: 187–9). His analysis of these 4,526 artefacts demonstrates that 'the parallels between the historic site and the prehistoric sites [Indian Knoll] are remarkable' (1968: 187). The artefacts that were manufactured of locally available materials almost always occurred in the general midden, and almost never in burial context, while the artefacts made from imported materials rarely occurred outside of the burial context. In fact, most of the imported classes of items occurred with burials 100 per cent of the time, while for a few the figure was *c.* 80 to 98 per cent. These were items made of marine shell, copper and brass (1968: 186–90). In comparing these findings with the Indian Knoll results, Winters concludes that:

the parallels between the proveniences of artifacts manufactured from local raw materials and from exotic, imported raw materials are such that they suggest similar *attitudes* towards these commodities on the part of the late Archaic Indian Knoll Culture and the proto-historic and historic Fort Ancient Culture, although we cannot infer any direct continuity in such attitudes during the intervening centuries of Woodland occupations in the Kentucky area of the Ohio Valley. (1968: 190–1; emphasis mine)

Analysis and proposed method

I agree with Winters' conclusion – the conch shell and copper artefacts were almost certainly considered by the Indian Knoll people to have been more valuable than were the other kinds of artefacts that were recovered archaeologically. Moreover, given Winters' demonstration of a similar value system in the much later Fort Ancient Culture, I strongly suspect that this phenomenon was widespread in the eastern half of the United States and that it had very great time depth.

But how do we really *know* that the prehistoric people were cognizant of such a value system? The answer is that we do *not* know this, and can never know it with certainty, short of literally extracting it from the minds of the prehistoric people themselves. At the same time, however, it is well known that we rarely ever find proof of anything in science, outside formal logic and mathematics, so we should not *expect* certainty. We gain and lose confidence in our propositions, and sometimes can *dis*prove them, but we do not gain complete confirmation.

It seems to me that the primary reasons for which Winters' conclusion is so very compelling is that he has (implicitly) employed what I have above called the Established Generalization Testing method (or EGT). This method involves testing the applicability of an established generalization against the structure of the archaeological record. Given that we know that a particular generalization is correct (universally or nearly so among humans), does the evidence in the archaeological record conform in nature and distribution to what one would expect if the *processes* stated in the generalization had been operative in the past? In other words, given these processes, we deduce the test implications implied by them, and then examine the archaeological record in an effort to find them.

In Winters' case, the processes that were tested were those specified in the well-established principle of supply and demand. It must be noted, however, that Winters may not actually have used the EGT method, or the deductive reasoning implied by it; my guess is that he observed his data first and then interpreted them in light of his knowledge of the principle of supply and demand. One could, however, proceed the other way around, beginning with a generalization and then deducing its test implications in the archaeological record. This is the methodological procedure I am suggesting here, and I will therefore recast Winters' reasoning and procedure in that light. Thus, his reasoning and procedure could have been as follows.

After asking the question of whether or not the conch shell and copper had been considered valuable by the Indian Knoll people, he could have recognized that value is determined by the well-established generalization we call the principle of supply and demand. It is well established that the lower the supply of any good or service, and the higher the demand for it, the more valuable or costly it is; conversely, the higher the supply, and the lower the demand, the less valuable or costly it is. This generalization is applicable to all human societies, and is the underpinning for Winters' entire analysis.

Given this, and his hypothesis that conch shell and copper had been considered valuable, his task could then have been to self-consciously test for these materials having been in shorter supply relative to demand than were the other materials in his artefact assemblages. (Note that the demand side of this equation was satisfied by the simple fact that conch shell and copper were indeed found in the Indian Knoll sites; his more difficult task would have been to demonstrate (test for) relative short supply.) In testing for short supply relative to demand, he could have employed the 'if . . . then' reasoning of the hypothesis-testing method: *if* conch shell and copper had been in (relatively) short supply, *then* we would expect to find evidence that these materials were difficult or costly to obtain relative to the other resources (given equal demand). He could then have listed the specific kinds of evidence that one might expect to find in the archaeological record if conch shell and copper had been difficult or costly to obtain.

One such expectation could be that he might find that the sources for these materials were more greatly distant from his sites than were the sources of the other materials.[1] This could clearly be one implication of 'costly or difficult to obtain', and it is precisely what Winters demonstrated. It is easy to think of other test implications as well (see below).

A second test implication for 'short supply' (and thus valuable) might be the expectation that conch shell and copper would be found to have been used only in relatively *restricted contexts* in the Indian Knoll society. That is, these materials might have been reserved for rather special uses rather than for general or widespread usage.[2] This is reasonable because things that are both in demand and in short supply are usually put to relatively special uses (e.g. one does not ordinarily frame windows with gold).

Winters made use of this test implication, of course, in demonstrating that the conch shell and copper were found almost exclusively in burials and were almost never found in the trash middens. He also adduced the comparative evidence that in the *source* areas these materials were used very commonly for general, rather than special, purposes (i.e. tools), and were dumped into the middens. Additional test implications for 'restricted context', for which he might have found evidence, are presented below.

A third test implication (also employed by Winters) is that one might expect to find that very few individuals in Indian Knoll society had access to conch shell and copper.[3] This was demonstrated by showing that these materials were found associated only with *high status* burials (and that the relative proportion of high status individuals decreased over time).

The degree to which one accepts Winters' conclusion regarding the relative value of the conch shell and copper will, I think, be rather closely proportional to the degree to which one accepts the principle of supply and demand (and, of course, the degree to which one believes that he has actually demonstrated short supply relative to demand). It would appear that the principle of supply and demand is no longer in need of testing; it is now so universally accepted that it may simply be 'applied' to our interpretations of the archaeological record. It remains only to demonstrate that in the prehistoric case, the structure of the archaeological data is what one would expect given this principle, and that alternative interpretations of the data structure are unlikely to be correct.

While Winters does not discuss possible alternative interpretations, he does demonstrate convincingly that his data structure is what one would expect if conch shell and copper had been regarded as valuable. Moreover, I cannot think of any viable alternative interpretation of the same data structure.

As suggested above, however, there are additional test implications that Winters might have looked for in the archaeological record if he had had appropriate data available. For example, if a raw material was difficult or costly to obtain (and thus valuable), we might expect it to be rare relative to easily obtained (e.g. local) materials. It might also have been difficult to extract from the environment, such as if its source was located in such a way as to be difficult of access, or the technology needed to extract it was sophisticated or difficult to manufacture or use. Or, perhaps the material was difficult to transport from its source to its destination. Another factor affecting the cost of a material might be competition with others for access to the material. We might also expect that when artefacts were made with costly materials, they would often be reworked or repaired when broken, rather than being dumped into trash middens.

In addition, if a material or artefact were valuable, we might expect to find it in a wide variety of *restricted contexts* other than high status burials. It might be found, for example, primarily in élite residential areas or structures, in

ceremonial structures or caches, in the centres of central-place hierarchies, and so forth. The material might also be expected to have been 'safeguarded' by being placed in high security contexts, such as in features or structures that would have been difficult of access, or hidden locations away from general or easy view. Obviously, we would expect materials of value to be found associated with *other* kinds of valuable materials. We would, on the other hand *not* expect valuable materials to be found in general middens, non-élite houses, structures or activity areas, or with non-élite burials. They should also not be found in areas of easy access or visibility.

Moreover, we would expect to find, as Winters did, that in the source areas of the material, it would probably *not* have been very valuable, and therefore we might expect to find it in contexts quite opposite to those mentioned above. It should be apparent that this list of test implications could go on and on, and that in doing this we are limited primarily by our imaginations.

I argue that when the archaeological record is structured in the manner demonstrated by Winters (1968), or in the more detailed manner I have just suggested, we have a situation in which we can, with little doubt, infer a prehistoric economic value system. This would be a *cognitive* value system, in the sense that the prehistoric people would have been very much aware of it. After all, it was the prehistoric people themselves who created this kind of structure in the record – they *did* the structuring. The idea that they could do this without being cognizant of it is very doubtful. Artefacts were placed with high-status burials, not dumped into middens etc., precisely because the people were aware of their value.

I must emphasize, however, that we are, here, talking about a structured archaeological record that conforms to what one would expect given an already demonstrated established generalization. We already *know* what 'valuable' is and what it looks like. If something is in high demand relative to its supply, it is *by definition* valuable – anywhere at any time. All that is left for the archaeologist to do is to try to find data in the archaeological record that demonstrates low supply relative to demand. This can be done because this kind of situation leaves its physical, material marks in the record. We know what to look for. As long as we are talking about a well-understood concept like 'economic value', we do not have to worry about the possibility that different cultures will understand 'economic value' in fundamentally different ways (different meanings), or that they will behave in fundamentally different ways.

I think I have presented enough here to illustrate the kind of thinking and methodological approach that one can use in testing for the presence of artefacts or materials that prehistoric people thought of as valuable. This general approach may be useful in testing for some other kinds of cognitive things as well. I suspect that there are other established generalizations which involve cognition, and which can be tested against the archaeological record, although I am not currently aware of any beyond the one that I have discussed here (plus the three closely related ones presented in my notes). It would be useful to try to think of more, since I believe that established generalizations of this nature will provide us with the most reliable demonstrations of prehistoric cognition. Moreover, it seems clear that the hypothesis-testing method will be useful in testing the processes involved in such generalizations.

This must be done with care, however, because there are undoubtedly a large number of very well-established generalizations that almost certainly cannot be tested against the archaeological record. For example, while it is probably generally true that people believe in an after-life, it is by no means clear that that belief would leave material evidence in the archaeological record. Are there, for example, any universally acceptable test implications for such a belief? Perhaps there are, but they are unknown to me. And what about the generalization that all people grieve when close relatives or friends die? What evidence would this leave in the record?

The difficulty is that things like grief, and belief in an after-life, are acted out differently in different cultures. And it is this *acting out* that has the potential for leaving evidence in the record, not the grief or the belief in an after-life themselves. Since cultures differ in the ways in which they act out these things, there are no universals that would permit us to generate test implications having universal (or even widespread) validity. For example, in one culture, the belief in an after-life may have been symbolized (and manifest) by the placement of red ochre in the deceased's grave, while in another culture it may have been manifest by placing something else with the deceased, or simply by offering a prayer during the burial rite. We have no way of knowing what to expect in the way of data that might inform us about such universal aspects of mental culture as grief, or the belief in life after death. The symbols associated with these things in different cultures are arbitrarily assigned, as symbols usually are, and we can have little or no chance of understanding their meaning to the prehistoric people.

I think it will only be possible to test for such things in situations wherein we have very 'close' ethnographic analogies, which can be used to generate test implications. If, for example, we have information on the symbolization of a belief in an after-life that is drawn from ethnohistoric information on the immediate cultural descendants of a prehistoric culture, it may allow us to generate reasonable tests against the archaeological record. In other words, we would know what to look for.

My next example (von Gernet and Timmins 1987) presents a situation of this general nature, and illustrates the second of the two methods I am presenting in this paper. Before closing the present discussion, however, I must make two important points regarding the methodological approach just presented. (1) the EGT method does not necessarily require the use of established generalizations that are *universal* in nature; they can be of limited, yet widespread scope, although this would lower the probability of their being applicable to interpreting a given specific prehistoric archaeological record. (2) Generalizations that are agreed upon as being universally applicable (i.e. to *all* societies), such as that all peoples believe in an after-life, probably do not need to be tested against the archaeological record at all. In this kind of situation, we can simply assume that since the generalization applies to all peoples, it most certainly is applicable to any specific prehistoric society we might be studying (assuming, of course, that the inhabitants of our sites were *Homo sapiens sapiens*).

Example 2: a matter of symbolism

Von Gernet and Timmins' analysis

The von Gernet and Timmins (1987) analysis is an attempt to document the existence of a very specific prehistoric shamanistic ideology and symbolism at the Calvert Site, an Early Iroquoian village in southwestern Ontario which had been occupied between *c.* AD 1100 and 1200 (Fox 1982). One of the features in it was a small, circular pit measuring 24.5 cm in diameter and 8.0 cm deep. In the pit were discovered three bones of the now extinct Carolina parakeet (*Conuropis carolinensis*), a stone pipe bowl, a slate tool and an antler artefact, all of which were judged to represent an intentional deposition rather than refuse. The bird bones and pipe bowl were the focus of their analysis (von Gernet and Timmins 1987: 35).

It was discovered that one of the bird bones had come from the head (a premaxilla), another from the wing (the proximal half of the left carpometacarpus), and the third from the tail (a pygostyle). Prevec observed that these bones had come from the extremities of the head, wing and tail, and she concluded that 'since these bones are left in a [bird] skin if it is to resemble the living creature, it is probable that the identified bones formed part of a skin that had ritualistic use' (Prevec 1984: 7). Von Gernet and Timmins concluded that a complete parakeet skin had been placed in the pit alongside, or attached to, the pipe, and they suggest that this association was not accidental, but rather represents 'a well documented association recurring in a diversity of cultural contexts' (1987: 35).

They then proceed to document the historic association

between birds and pipes with a wide variety of ethnographic and ethnohistoric accounts, ranging in date from the seventeenth through the nineteenth centuries. This association is evident and widespread throughout the northeastern United States, southeastern Canada, large portions of the Great Plains, and numerous other places in the New World. They also demonstrate, using *archaeological* evidence, that the association was widespread in central and eastern North America at least as early as the Adena/Hopewell cultures (*c.* 500 BC–AD 500), and that it has been found in prehistoric contexts throughout the New World, including the American Southwest, Mexico, Bolivia and elsewhere (1987: 38). The authors conclude that 'there is evidence that bird/pipe associations are at a level of universality beyond particular cultural peculiarities' (1987: 38); and although they are unable to establish direct historical continuity between any of these early cases and the one at the later Calvert Site in Ontario, they argue that this is unnecessary because the association is so widespread and ancient that it probably represents an ancient 'substratum of beliefs' shared by many Indians over a wide region (1987: 37–8).

Then, using the same wide variety of ethnographic and ethnohistoric sources, the authors demonstrate convincingly that the bird/pipe (and tobacco) association was associated with *shamanism*. The accounts clearly document the fact that there was a very widespread tradition of Indians (usually shamans) smoking pipes adorned with bird feathers and skins, throughout the Great Lakes and Plains regions. In fact, there are numerous accounts of the skins actually being impaled on the pipe stems, including references to 'precisely the same rare species of parakeet found in the prehistoric feature' at the Calvert Site (1987: 36).

They also cite evidence demonstrating that the tobacco used was hallucinogenic, and that the shamans smoked it in order to produce altered states of consciousness to enhance visionary experiences. *Nicotiana rustica*, as well as other species, 'were capable of producing major dissociational states and were consumed in quantities sufficient to reach the pharmacological threshold at which most humans experience the sensation of flight or other out of body phenomena' (1987: 38).

The ethnographic information also reports that these shamans commonly stated that while they were smoking they felt 'light' (and light-headed), and that the bird or feathers on the pipe seemed to come alive and help them 'fly' on their 'soul journeys', or helped them to 'see better into the world of spirits' (1987: 39). The shamans often believed that they themselves, or their souls, were flying like birds. The birds often symbolized the shaman's soul in animal form, or his 'guardian soul' or 'guardian spirit' (1987: 39).

Von Gernet and Timmins conclude, after adducing truly massive amounts of very specific ethnographic, ethnohistoric and archaeological evidence, that the association of the bird bones and pipe bowl at the Early Iroquoian Calvert Site does indeed represent this very widespread shamanistic ideology, symbolism and practice (1987: 40–2).

Analysis and proposed method

The von Gernet/Timmins analysis is quite convincing, largely, I think, because of the strength and ubiquity of their analogies. The reader is left not at all surprised by the presence of the bird/pipe association at the Calvert Site.

The method involved here is, of course, not new; it is simply that of comparing a prehistoric find with an historic phenomenon (the meaning of which we learn from historic records), and then finding such a high degree of formal similarity that we can assign the same meaning to the prehistoric phenomenon as we do to the historic one. In other words, if the unknown (prehistoric phenomenon) looks the same as the known (historic phenomenon), we conclude that their meaning is the same.

I have labelled this method the 'Tight Local Analogy method' (TLA method) because the analogy must be both 'tight' and 'local'. By 'tight', I mean that we should try to find as many specific similarities as we can between the known and unknown phenomenon, and that we should seek as much variety as possible in the specific kinds of similarities. This is important if the discovered identity is to be convincing.

By 'local', I mean that the likelihood that our identity is correct is enhanced if the two sides of the analogy (known and unknown) are close together in both space and time; the enhancement is even greater when the known and unknown are likely to have been related to the same 'culture'. While von Gernet and Timmins claim that closeness in space and time is methodologically irrelevant (1987: 41–2), I think, nonetheless, that confidence in a given analogy is increased when this is the case.

There are some significant limitations to this TLA method, however. One limitation can be illustrated by pointing to the fact that von Gernet and Timmins could not have assigned *meaning* to the bird/pipe association at the Calvert Site in the absence of historic analogies. While it *is* possible, without such analogies, to use archaeological data alone to establish the existence of a prehistoric bird/pipe association (and other kinds of associations), it is not possible to assign prehistoric meaning to the association without such analogies.

This is an important methodological limitation, because those who use the TLA method are necessarily tied to the historic written and/or oral record in order to discover the 'meaning' they seek. Without this record, little or nothing can be said about such 'mental things' as ideological meaning, religious meaning, symbolic meaning, etc. This means, of course, that the TLA method will usually not 'work' when the data are truly prehistoric, and where there are no 'tight' and 'close' analogies upon which to draw.

Two other important problems with the method, pointed out by Binford (1967a, 1967b), are: (1) we cannot logically study the past by studying the present; we must use prehistoric data if we want to understand what went on in prehistory. Therefore, we cannot *know*, even in the von Gernet/Timmins case, that the prehistoric meaning was the same as the historic meaning; (2) using analogy in this way precludes the study of culture change, since it assumes that there has been no change from the prehistoric to historic context. Nonetheless, this kind of use of analogy, if well done, can be plausible and persuasive, and it may be unreasonable to ask for anything more than this, since: (1) *all* of our inferences about the past are based on analogy, and (2) our inferences are rarely more than plausible and persuasive, even when tested rigorously against the archaeological record.

I want to point out that despite the fact that von Gernet and Timmins apparently reject the use of the hypothesis-testing method (von Gernet, personal communication), it is my opinion that their work can be considered scientific, at least in the sense that they have contributed increased knowledge of prehistory. Moreover, in a sense they actually tested their inference, and did so with data independent of those used in the initial formulation of their hypothesis. The main difference I see between what they did and hypothesis-testing is that their wording is different from what hypothesis-testers are prone to use. They *could* have phrased their initial tentative inference as a proposition, and then proceeded to employ the deductive 'if . . . then . . . ' reasoning of hypothesis-testing.

In this manner, the proposition would have been something like 'The bird/pipe association at the Calvert Site represents a shamanistic ideology and practice involving the smoking of tobacco in order to achieve visionary experiences'. Then, they could have reasoned, '*If* this proposition is correct, *then* we would expect to find strong, detailed and widespread evidence of this in the eastern United States and southeastern Canada. We would expect to find this association and its *meaning* in: (1) the ethnographic and ethnohistoric documents, regarding the historic Iroquois themselves, and the historic tribes surrounding the Iroquois; (2) we might also expect this association (minus its cultural meaning) in the archaeological record of the region.' They could then have proceeded to examine the evidence in these

records to discover the degree to which their hypothesis was confirmed or rejected.

They *could* have gone about it this way, and their results would have been absolutely no different. Clearly, this means that one does not need the hypothesis-testing method in this kind of endeavour. In any case, a use of the hypothesis-testing method in this manner would not have permitted them to escape the previously mentioned fact that one cannot properly use ethnographic or ethnohistoric evidence to test ideas about prehistoric situations (Binford 1967a, 1967b).

Conclusions

I conclude that there are at least two methodological approaches that can be employed in elucidating at least some of the 'mental things' of the past. These have been called the 'Established Generalization Testing method' (EGT), and the 'Tight Local Analogy method' (TLA). These methods have been presented above, and their details need not be considered further here. Since these two methods should permit us to accumulate new knowledge of the past (see Hill 1991), they can, at least in this sense, be called 'scientific'.

Unfortunately, I do not know how many well-established generalizations there might be that can be used to address prehistoric cognitive matters, and that are also testable against the archaeological record. While I suspect that not many such generalizations exist, it would certainly be worthwhile to give this some thought.

Also, how often will we be able to find tight local analogies with which to interpret prehistoric finds, and how often will these have anything to do with cognitive matters? I do not know, of course, although I suspect we will find many more of these than we will find well-established generalizations. As a suggestion, one might peruse the culture trait distribution studies of the 1930s and 1940s in this regard. It might be found, for example, that certain religious or ritual traits, with specified cognitive meanings, were rather widespread, and that they have been described thoroughly enough that we can generate test implications for use against the archaeological record. Certainly, whenever we find prehistoric phenomena that we suspect might be amenable to cognitive interpretation, it will be useful to examine the historic literature in search of good analogies. This will carry with it the methodological limitations already discussed, of course.

There is a third methodological 'option' that I have not yet addressed in this chapter, but shall now discuss briefly because some archaeologists have used it (especially some of the 'post-processual' or 'interpretive' scholars; see, for example, Hodder 1984). However, I believe it to be seriously flawed and not useful. This is the use of 'not well-established generalizations'. These are often based on supposed principles of 'human nature' or 'human psychology'. The approach involves speculation about what appears to be common to *most* people in certain kinds of situations; it is akin to saying, 'My prehistoric people were human, and since all or most humans tend to *think* similar things in given specified circumstances, my prehistoric people probably did too'.

As an example, one might propose that the presence of red ochre in graves symbolizes a prehistoric belief in an after-life. This is based on two generalizations, the first one being that all human groups believe in an after-life. This is well established. The second is that the colour red is usually associated with 'life-giving forces' (the generality of which *not* being well established). The problem with this is, of course, that it is not always the case that people use the colour red to represent 'life-giving forces', nor is it always the case that red things placed in graves symbolize 'after-life'. Such burial accompaniments might have *other* meanings instead – such as symbolizing high status or femaleness. They might even symbolize the deceased's occupation – he could have been a shaman, one of his tasks having been to grind red ochre to paint the foreheads of newborn babies!

Another example might be to propose that elevated mounds such as temples, pyramids, etc., have the universal meaning of being symbols of élite power and control over labour, and that they serve to legitimize élite power. This generalization is plausible, but not actually well established. However, if one accepts it as such, it becomes possible to assign any such mound this kind of meaning. I would not want to do this because a given mound might *not* have had this kind of meaning to the prehistoric people involved; they may have viewed it as a structure serving to raise buildings above swampy or flooded land, or as celestial observatories, or as locations appropriate for communicating with the gods.

In any event, and despite my previous belief in the impossibility of recovering 'mind' from the archaeological record, it is now clear to me that it can in some cases be done, at least in the sense of gaining high plausibility. This is not to say that we can really *know* about what prehistoric people thought, but there are certainly situations in which the archaeological record is structured in such a way that we can very plausibly infer what they 'darn well *must* have been thinking'. We can also test some of our inferences in this regard. I think both of the substantive analyses discussed above are good examples of this.

Nonetheless, I want to argue, in closing, that even though we can in some instances 'recover mind', and this may make archaeology more interesting for some people, it is not some-thing that archaeology will ever be very good at, and it is most certainly not where archaeology will make its most significant contributions.

One difficulty is that we must always infer the thoughts of prehistoric people from what they actually *did* (their behaviour), since it is evidence of behaviour that is available for examination. It is often the case, however, that human behaviour does *not* reflect their thoughts. In other words, as anthropologists have long known, people will often say (and think) that they have certain beliefs, ideologies, norms, values, etc., but not actually behave in conformance with these things. Very often these 'thoughts' are among the most important aspects of 'mental culture' that people possess (cf. D'Andrade 1973: 123; Harris 1974: 242–3, 245; Harris 1988: 133, 476–9, 526–7). It follows, then, that in these instances we will not be able to learn anything about very significant aspects of prehistoric mental culture.

A well-known example of this is Marvin Harris' 'myth of the sacred cow'. To make a long story short, Harris shows that even though the Hindus in India have a very strong religious ideology prohibiting the killing of cattle, they do, in fact, systematically kill cattle (Harris 1988: 133, 476–9). We would be able to discover the latter archaeologically, but not the former.

Similarly, in the United States there are very strong ideologies to the effect that 'all men are created equal' and 'equal opportunity is available to everyone', yet our *behaviour* shows that neither is true. We would see evidence of this archaeologically, but not be able to infer the ideologies.

I submit that this kind of incongruity is very common in all cultures, it involves very significant 'ideology', and it is ideology not accessible to the archaeologist. On the other hand, one can argue that there often *are* straightforward congruities between ideology and behaviour, so that my concern here is not terribly important. I do not know how important it is, and certainly no one is suggesting that we ought to be able to make inferences about all aspects of mental culture, but this is food for thought nonetheless.

A second difficulty I have with a 'cognitive archaeology', but one which is highly controversial, and upon which there will be little agreement, is that while it may be an interesting pursuit, it may not be a very important pursuit. I think the primary reason for which prehistoric 'mental things' are often considered important is that they are considered to have significant causal efficacy; that is, cultural rules (and so forth) cause people to behave as they do, so that if we really want to understand a culture or culture change, we must get access to the 'rules'. If this were correct, then of course it would be absolutely essential for us to discover these rules, ideologies, etc.

From my perspective, however, these things are epiphenomenal; they are certainly not as important as are ecological circumstances in determining human behaviour. In this, I agree with Marvin Harris (and some others). One of the primary reasons for this view is that cultural 'rules', ideologies and so forth do not exist in a vacuum; they do not arise *sui generis*. They are developed in response to specific human material conditions that require them (usually so that society can function smoothly). When these environmental conditions change, the 'rules' follow suit. How else can one explain the existence of the rules in the first place, if not in response to something?

As an example, it would be inappropriate to argue that a cultural rule specifying the size and shape of fish-hooks is what causes them to be made in a particular size and shape. Rather, it is the task of trying to catch a particular kind of fish, with a particular kind of mouth, that determines the size and shape of the fish-hook. Similarly, having an ideology that requires worshipping 'fish-gods' does not cause people to fish; it is the other way round. That is, if people fish for a living, it may create a need for fish-gods!

I do not mean to imply that cultural rules have no effect on people; they certainly do, especially in the short-run. But to see them as equal in importance to ecological conditions in causing human behaviour in the long run (which is the time frame of most interest in archaeology) is, I believe, to misunderstand fundamentally.

The third and final reason for not investing heavily in a cognitive archaeology is that it is not archaeology's strong suit – it is not what we can do best. Cognitive studies are much more easily, and better, carried out by social scientists who study living people (who can talk and express their ideas). As archaeologists, we will almost certainly not make any significant contributions to cognitive studies in general, and it is very doubtful that our own cognitive studies will enhance the accumulation of our knowledge of the past to any noteworthy degree. In short, the pay-off, while expectable to a limited degree (see above), is relatively low.

Archaeology's strong suit is presumably the study of long-term cultural change (evolution) in response to major environmental changes. While archaeology is not well equipped to discover many of the fine details of prehistory, it is well equipped to examine the gross, major changes in technology, economy and social organization that have occurred in the past – such things as the evolution of agriculture, the evolution of exchange systems, the evolution of status differentiation, and so on. We can observe the rough outlines of such things in the archaeological record, and we can test many of our hypotheses regarding them. This is where the greatest pay-off is for the science of archaeology.

Note that I am *not* arguing for abstinence with regard to studying prehistoric 'mental things', but simply that I think our data are such that we will usually accumulate more knowledge of human prehistory by emphasizing other pursuits.

Notes

1 This test implication is justified by (and deduced from) another well-established generalization, which is: the more difficult or costly it is to obtain a resource, relative to other resources (given equal demand), the shorter will be its supply relative to these other resources, and thus the more valuable will be the resource in question.

2 This test implication is justified by (and deduced from) another well-established generalization, which is: the more valuable a resource is, the more restricted will be the uses to which it is put in a society (i.e. the more it will be put to 'special' rather than general uses).

3 This test implication is justified by (and deduced from) another well-established generalization, which is: the more valuable a resource is, the fewer will be the number of individuals in a society having access to it.

References

D'Andrade, R. G. 1973. Cultural constructions of reality. In *Cultural illness and health: essays in human adaptation*, ed. L. Nader and T. W. Maretzki, pp. 115–27. American Anthropological Association

Binford, L. R. 1967a. Reply to K. C. Chang. *Current Anthropology* 8: 234–5
  1967b. Smudge pits and hide smoking: the use of analogy in archaeological reasoning. *American Antiquity* 31: 1–12
  1968. Archaeological perspectives. In *New perspectives in archeology*, ed. S. R. Binford and L. R. Binford, pp. 5–32. Chicago, Aldine

Fox, W. A. 1982. The Calvert Village: Glen Meyer community patterns. KEWA, *Newsletter of the Ontario Archaeological Society, London Chapter* 82 (7): 5–9

von Gernet, A. and P. Timmins 1987. Pipes and parakeets: constructing meaning in an early Iroquoian context. In *Archaeology as long-term history*, ed. I. Hodder, pp. 31–42. Cambridge, Cambridge University Press

Hanson, L. H. Jr. 1966. The Hardin Village site. *Studies in anthropology*, no. 4. Lexington, University of Kentucky Press

Harris, M. 1974. Why a perfect knowledge of all the rules one must know to act like a native cannot lead to the knowledge of how natives act. *Journal of Anthropological Research* 30 (4): 242–51.

1988. *Culture, people, nature: an introduction to general anthropology*. New York, Harper and Row

Hill, J. N. 1991. Archaeology and the accumulation of knowledge. In *Processual and postprocessual archaeologies: multiple ways of knowing the past*, ed. R. W. Preucel, pp. 42–53. Center for Archaeological Investigations, Southern Illinois University at Carbondale, *Occasional Paper* No. 10

Hodder, I. 1984. Burials, houses, women and men in the European Neolithic. In *Ideology, power and prehistory*, ed. D. Miller and C. Tilley, pp. 51–68. Cambridge, Cambridge University Press

Prevec, R. 1984. The Carolina Parakeet – its first appearance in southern Ontario. *KEWA, Newsletter of the Ontario Archaeological Society, London Chapter* 84 (7): 4–8

Slotkin, J. S. and K. Schmitt 1949. Studies of wampum. *American Anthropologist* 51 (2): 223–36

Webb, W. S. 1946. Indian Knoll. *Reports in anthropology* 4 (3) part 1. Lexington, University of Kentucky Press

1950a. The Carlson Annis mound. *Reports in anthropology* 7 (4). Lexington, University of Kentucky Press

1950b. The Read shell midden. *Reports in anthropology* 7 (5). Lexington, University of Kentucky Press

Webb, W. S. and W. G. Haag 1939. The Chiggerville site. *Reports in anthropology* 4 (1). Lexington, University of Kentucky Press

1940. Cypress Creek villages. *Reports in anthropology* 4 (2). Lexington, University of Kentucky Press

1947. Archaic sites in McLean County, Kentucky. *Reports in anthropology* 7 (1). Lexington, University of Kentucky Press

Winters, H. D. 1968. Value systems and trade cycles of the Late Archaic in the Midwest. In *New perspectives in archeology*, ed. S. R. Binford and L. R. Binford, pp. 175–221. Chicago, Aldine

PART IV

Prehistoric conceptions of space and time

10
Symbols and signposts – understanding the prehistoric petroglyphs of the British Isles

RICHARD BRADLEY

' . . . Even the noticing beasts are aware
that we don't feel very securely at home
in this interpreted world.'

Rainer Maria Rilke, *First Duino Elegy*
(trans. J. B. Leishman)

Introduction

How did people perceive the landscapes in which they lived? That is an important question for a cognitive archaeology, but one which our source materials may seem poorly equipped to answer. The geographer considers the human experience of place through *written* sources: the 'geographies of the mind' collected by Lowenthal and Bowden consider the 'habits of thought that condition what people learn about environment and environmental processes', but the papers published under that title rely on 'traces of human attitudes left in the form of diaries, letters, textbooks, scholarly articles, novels, poems and prayers' (Lowenthal and Bowden 1976: 6; cf. Tuan 1977, Buttimer and Seamon 1980, Cox and Golledge 1981).

Prehistorians confront additional problems. Their most developed techniques for studying the ancient landscape form only part of an approach whose main concern is with human adaptation to resources. There is much to be learned from studies of food production, but they shed no light on the problems of cognition (Barker and Gamble 1985). The same is true of 'landscape archaeology'. Detailed topographical survey can sometimes show how the landscape was organised, but although it may be possible to recognize changes in its development over time, it is rare for these to be studied alongside the broader changes in perception and practice that they must have entailed. When this does

happen, as in Pred's study of the landscape of southern Sweden, again it is documentary evidence that plays the vital role (Pred 1985).

In any case, studies of landscape history have more limitations than we normally allow, for they are concerned with the organization of *fixed resources* and they presuppose the existence of a network of recognizable boundaries. Such an extensive view of landscape is by no means universal. As Tuan has commented,

> The recognition and differentiation of landscapes does not seem to be an old or common human trait. Among pre- and non-literate peoples, awareness of nature generally takes other forms. Nature is recognised, on the one hand, in local objects – individual animals, plants and rocky prominences. On the other hand, it is perceived as generalised phenomena, as sky, moon, earth, water, light and darkness. (Tuan 1967: 7–8).

Exceptions may occur 'in environments of striking contrasts', but even among literate peoples, 'the reading of significance into arbitrarily selected spatial units of nature is remarkably rare' (Tuan 1967: 8).

To some extent the problem is related to the degree of mobility in the settlement pattern and the extent to which the landscape undergoes physical alteration. Peter Wilson expresses this point succinctly:

> The hunter/gatherer pins ideas and emotions onto the world as it exists . . . A construction is put upon the landscape rather than the landscape undergoing a reconstruction, as is the case among sedentary people, who impose houses, villages and gardens on the landscape, often in the place of natural landmarks. Where nomads read or even find cosmological features in an already existing landscape, villagers tend to represent and model cosmic ideas in the structures they build (1988: 50).

A rather similar idea is found in Ingold's discussion of territorial organization (1986, chapters 6 and 7). Farmers define agricultural territories by enclosing them, but hunter-gatherers perceive their territories in a very different way, by monitoring the paths running between specific *places*. Those places overlook the surrounding land, and hunter-gatherers define their territories by the views seen from them. This has important implications for how they are perceived. For hunter-gatherers, tenure is 'zero-' or 'one-dimensional' because it is based on places and paths respectively. Among agriculturalists it is 'two-dimensional' because it works by delimiting an area of ground (Ingold 1986: 150).

The same contrast underlies the distinction between land

and landscape:

> Regarded as a generalized, creative potential, **land** may just as well be condensed within particular locales, or distributed along particular paths. That is to say, it remains embodied in the properties of the **landscape**. What agriculture achieves through the practical operations of ground clearance and preparation is the *separation* of the **land** from its embodiment in the **landscape**. Hunters and gatherers appropriate the land by holding the objects or features that originally contain it; agriculturalists appropriate the land by disconnecting it from those features so that it may be harnessed in the construction of an artificial, substitute environment. (Ingold 1986: 154; extra emphasis added)

Such contrasts are certainly echoed in parts of prehistoric Europe. In common with many areas of the world, there are few, if any, monuments belonging to the Palaeolithic or Mesolithic periods; they first appear with the adoption of domesticated resources. In some areas, however, there is little evidence for large scale cultivation before the Later Bronze or Iron Ages, long after domestic animals had come into widespread use. There is only slight evidence of sedentary settlement, and land was rarely enclosed. It is a pattern that seems to be found along the Atlantic seaboard, and also across large parts of Northern Europe (Barker 1985, chapters 7–9). In the absence of convincing evidence for the existence of enclosed resources, the distributions of ceremonial monuments are sometimes used to recreate the pattern of land division, or even the extent of an 'agricultural' economy. This process is quite misleading as it confuses *land* with *landscape* when what is really required is a more flexible *archaeology of place*. It seems particularly ironic that such efforts should be made to identify agricultural enclosures in regions where rock art forms an important part of the archaeological record, for its creation placed a cultural mark on the *natural features* of the terrain. Only occasionally has this been considered as a clue to the ways in which that landscape was understood. The best example is provided by the distinctive style of rock art which extends from north west Spain to Scotland and Ireland (De la Peña Santos and Vázquez Varela 1979; García Alén and de la Peña Santos 1980; Morris 1989; Johnston 1989). My essay seeks to redress the balance by considering some ways of studying this material in the British Isles.

Background to the case study

This chapter, then, endeavours to bring together two different fields of archaeological enquiry – studies of prehistoric land use and the analysis of prehistoric art – and does so in an attempt to answer my initial question: how did prehistoric people perceive the landscapes in which they lived? We have already seen how difficult it is to analyse the perception of landscape: it is certainly no easier to interpret a system of petroglyphs in which the imagery is entirely abstract. In each case the challenge is the same, however: to devise explicit analytical procedures that can be replicated by other workers.

The petroglyphs studied in this paper belong to the late neolithic and may have continued in use into the Early Bronze Age, *c.* 3000–1500 BC (Johnston 1989; Burgess 1990). As we have seen, both are periods without much evidence of sedentism in the British Isles. Some of the more fertile lowland areas contain large numbers of stone or earthwork monuments – burial mounds and ceremonial enclosures – but there is little to indicate cereal cultivation, and field systems and land boundaries are extremely rare (Darvill 1987). The same is true of settlements and houses, and the most convincing evidence for the distribution of everyday activities is provided by scatters of flint artefacts (Gardiner 1984; Holgate 1988). Wild plant foods may have been at least as important as cereals (Moffett *et al.* 1989), but lowland sites are dominated by the bones of domesticated animals.

In upland Britain – our main concern in this study – the evidence is basically similar but occurs on a smaller scale. Again, specialized monuments are found rather than settlements, which did not leave a recognizable archaeological signature until the mid second millennium BC (Spratt and Burgess 1985). In many areas these regions were settled on a rather limited scale, and the environmental evidence suggests only a gradual change from woodland to areas of grassland (e.g. Coggins 1986: fig. 8). These regions had played a major part in the Mesolithic pattern of settlement, when they had been exploited by hunter-gatherers. Whereas the archaeological record of the lowlands includes a balanced lithic industry, containing a notable proportion of ground and polished axes, the finds from upland areas include numerous arrowheads, many of them discovered on older Mesolithic sites (Spratt 1982: 125).

The small monuments found in upland areas use the natural topography in a distinctive manner. Frequently they gravitate towards *natural* features such as cliffs, rock outcrops, caves, hilltops and passes, and may incorporate some of these elements directly into their design (Bradley 1991). Thus, prominent rock outcrops can provide the focus for cairns or special-purpose enclosures (Miles 1975: 95–6), lines of upright stones may run up to hilltops or passes (Emmett 1979) and stone settings are sometimes aligned on distant mountaintops (Ruggles and Burl 1985).

It has often been observed how the setting of these monuments owes less to the location of specific resources in the landscape than it does to the existence of well-defined *routes* across the uplands. That may be why so many burial mounds follow prominent watersheds (Spratt 1982: 158–60) or why menhirs and stone alignments are sometimes found in passes (Roese 1980). A number of these monuments assume a linear configuration, and in the case of stone rows the same alignments could be extended and renewed over a long period of time (Emmett 1979). Another feature shared by many of these monuments is the way in which they occupy local vantage points. Much effort has been devoted to assessing their visual impact in relation to lower-lying areas more suitable for year-round settlement (see Roese 1982), but the results have been equivocal and by no means all the monuments can be recognized from a distance. It seems just as likely that these positions were selected because they afforded exceptional views across the surrounding country (Roese 1982: 585–6; cf. Ward 1988 and Johnston 1989: 36–8). These patterns have much in common with the territorial system described by Ingold (1986: 147–58),

although it is unnecessary to suggest that they were the work of hunter-gatherers *per se*: the uplands may have been used for a variety of reasons, and could have sustained both wild and domesticated resources.

Among the archaeological features which characterize some of these locations are natural rocks carved in a distinctive abstract style (Figs. 10.1 and 10.2) (Morris 1989; Johnston 1989). The simplest of the motifs are small circular hollows or 'cup-marks', and these can be enclosed by broken or unbroken rings. Such rings may be single or multiple, and there are cases in which different groups abut one another. Cup-marks or other motifs are sometimes joined by lines, and separate cup-marks can also be grouped together inside an enclosure. Other motifs have a more limited currency, but as a rule most of the design elements are based on circles or arcs, and angular motifs are uncommon. The carvings are usually found on flat or gently sloping surfaces and are rarely superimposed on one another. Differential weathering suggests that identical motifs may have been carved on the same rock at different times (Johnston 1989: 271).

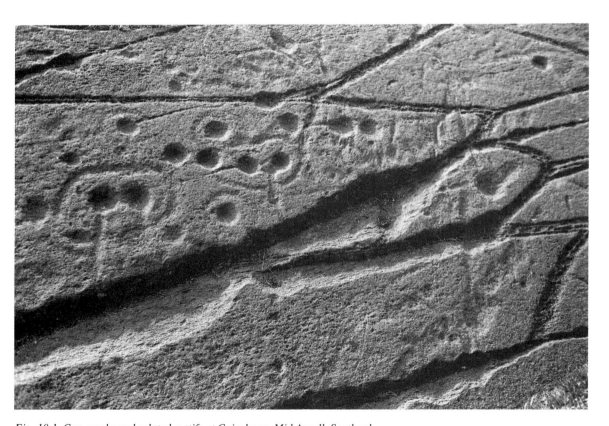

Fig. 10.1. Cup-marks and related motifs at Cairnbaan, Mid Argyll, Scotland.

The origin of this style was probably in the great Irish passage tombs built around 3000 BC, where similar designs occur on the tops and backs of some of the stones in the Boyne Valley (O'Kelly 1982: 146–85; Shee 1972; Shee Twohig 1981: 220–2; Johnston 1989: chapter 6); in certain cases these stones were carved again after the monuments were complete, perhaps eradicating these motifs (O'Sullivan 1986, 1989). Tombs of very similar character are also found in Orkney (Fig. 10.3), but few of these sites were decorated. Some of the same motifs, however, were transferred to other media, and in particular to 'Grooved Ware' ceramics. In Orkney this style of pottery is associated with ceremonial monuments ('henges'), passage tombs and stone-built settlements. In addition, Grooved Ware has a wider distribution, extending as far south as Wessex, where again it is associated with the large henge monuments (Bradley and Chapman 1986). Here the most complex designs are recorded from intentional deposits of artefacts in and around these sites (Richards and Thomas 1984). Similar motifs occur more rarely on other portable artefacts, and all of these are of rather specialized character. Their source in megalithic art suggests that at first they were associated with death and the supernatural.

The open air art has a wide distribution, and sometimes this can be related to the broader patterns described earlier in this paper. In north east England, for instance, there is a tendency for the petroglyphs to be discovered in the border zone between those lowland areas capable of sustaining year-round land use and upland regions more suited to seasonal occupation (Spratt 1982). This pattern is illustrated in Fig. 10.4, which shows how the carved rocks in north Yorkshire are found towards the edge of an essentially lowland distribution of polished axeheads, and how they enclose the higher ground on which neolithic and bronze age arrowheads are found at sites that had already been occupied by mesolithic hunter-gatherers. The same area contains a whole system of burial mounds built along the watersheds, suggesting that the zone with the carved rocks also followed the boundary between two rather different conceptions of territory.

Fig. 10.2. Cup-and-ring marks at Cairnbaan, Mid Argyll, Scotland.

At this point two methods of analysis might be contemplated, both of them cast in the post-processual mould. One possibility is to develop the contextual analysis of the separate motifs, documenting their representation in different media, from their first appearance in passage grave art to their deployment in the Grooved Ware repertoire. Some patterning certainly exists (Bradley 1989), but in the absence of any representational images it seems impossible to work towards the specific *meanings* of these signs, especially when the range of variation is actually so small. The alternative would be to develop this analysis of the location of the art, placing it in its wider setting in relation to the occupation of highland Britain. In order to do this, we would need a better understanding of the nature and sequence of settlement than can be obtained at present. Until then, we are limited to generalizations concerning the placing of some of these motifs in between the settled landscape and areas of more marginal land. Such patterns evoke the familiar distinction between culture and nature, but this style of analysis loses contact with the character of the petroglyphs themselves.

Methodology

A different way of proceeding arises out of this dilemma. Each of the methods outlined above would entail the sacrifice of almost half the available information, whereas a holistic approach would seek to keep them together. At this

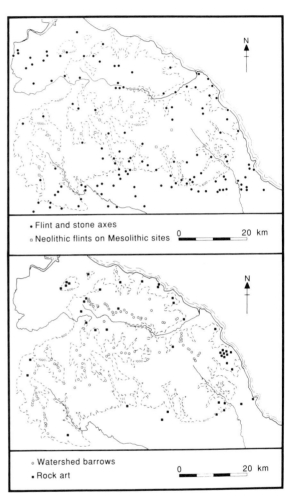

Fig. 10.4. The location of the rock art in the prehistoric landscape of north Yorkshire. The upper map compares the distribution of flint and stone axes with findspots of neolithic arrowheads on sites first occupied during the mesolithic. The lower map depicts the distribution of burial mounds along the watersheds, and shows how the carved rocks are located in a zone between the upland and lowland components of the settlement pattern. (Data from Spratt 1982.)

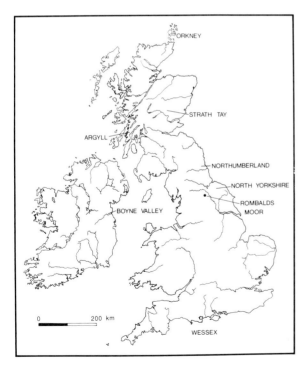

Fig. 10.3. Regions of the British Isles referred to in the text

point it is worth returning to Ingold's account of territorial organization among hunter-gatherers. He stresses the point that normally they do not defend resources; rather, they engage in what he describes as 'advertisement', a process in which the participants may not meet face to face. At such times,

> the communicating parties are not in direct audio-visual contact. During these periods . . . they must perforce communicate by means other than speech, and must indicate territorial limits by resorting to the 'language' of signs. These signs have, as it were, to be 'written down' onto the landscape (or seascape) in the form of durable boundary marks of diverse kinds – notched trees, stone cairns, buoys etc. – whose implicit message can be 'read off' on encounter by others. (1986: 146–7)

This is not to imply that British petroglyphs were necessarily employed as territorial markers, but it could be helpful to think of them, in Ingold's terms, as a 'language of signs'. Although this might have conveyed information of many kinds, it seems unlikely that we can ever arrive at a literal translation. On the other hand, rock art is among the archaeological phenomena that use the natural landscape in a most distinctive way. Although the different signs elude any attempts to read them, we may be able to study the ways in which that language was composed in relation to the landscapes where the petroglyphs occur. Topographical features, such as hills or rock outcrops, can hardly have altered materially, whatever changes happened in the environment. They provide the one fixed point in this analysis (cf. Schaafsma 1985: 261–4).

Rather than embark on an enquiry into the 'meaning' of these signs, it may be wiser to treat the different rock carvings as a source of *information* of greater or lesser complexity. By doing so, we can align this study with other analyses of style and communication, in particular the influential work of Wobst (1977), and Johnson (1982). For our purposes they make two crucially important points. The process of information exchange is one which is extremely sensitive to the number of people involved; beyond a certain threshold, communication becomes more difficult. At the same time, there is an obvious relationship between the complexity of the information needing to be conveyed and the character of the intended audience. Ethnoarchaeological research has shown that it is not necessarily the quantity or frequency of interaction that results in stylistic complexity. Where Wobst stressed the *efficiency* with which information is transmitted, more recent work suggests that the use of complex styles owes more to the *relationships* between the participants, especially where these involve a degree of threat or ambiguity (Braithwaite 1982; Wiesner 1983, 1984).

Is it possible to apply these distinctions to the prehistoric petroglyphs? We can consider several features of the carvings which still command attention today: their size (one of the stylistic features specifically studied by Wobst); the ease with which different design elements can be told apart; the extent to which particular motifs have been elaborated; the range of different devices to be found on the same carved surface; and the extent to which these separate elements are combined. The process is similar to the study of 'design grammars' on pottery (Hardin 1984), but its relevance has to be demonstrated – it cannot simply be assumed.

This was the reason for carrying out a pilot study on the best-recorded series of rock carvings in Britain, the petroglyphs of Mid Argyll on the west coast of Scotland. This was based on detailed measurements of all the motifs (the data were taken from the inventory published by the Royal Commission on the Ancient and Historical Monuments of Scotland in 1988). These were investigated in order to find out whether the different attributes were related to one another in a systematic manner. The work focused on the following features:

(1) the proportion of isolated cup-marks (apparently the simplest of the signs) in relation to the representation of other, more arresting motifs;
(2) the size of the circular motifs (whether or not they enclosed cup-marks) and the number of concentric rings; and
(3) the amount of space left between the separate circular motifs, and the proportion of the available rock surface covered by the petroglyphs.

Each of these features ought to have been immediately apparent to any observer; for example, the greater the spacing between the circular motifs, the easier it would have been to tell them apart. The figures for all the carved rocks with seventy or more design elements were studied by regression analysis. The results of this work are summarized in Table 10.1. They indicate that all of these elements covaried in a consistent fashion, suggesting that visual effects were of genuine importance. Two results of these analyses are particularly revealing. It seems as if the proportion of simple cup-marks was inversely related to the percentage of complex circular motifs, suggesting that these were at opposite extremes of the range of variation. At the same time, there was a close relationship between the size of these circular motifs and the percentage of the rock surface actually occupied by petroglyphs (in this case the analysis includes material from the inventory published by the Royal Commission on the Ancient and Historical Monuments of Scotland in 1971). Since no more than 45 per cent of the rock was occupied by carvings, it is clear that the size and

Table 10.1. *The relationship between selected attributes of the prehistoric rock art of Mid Argyll*

Relationship	Correlation coefficient
Mean number of rings per site: percentage of design elements other than cup-marks	0.822
Mean ring diameter per site: percentage of design elements other than cup-marks	0.754
Mean ring spacing per site: mean ring diameter	0.734
Mean ring diameter per site: percentage of the rock surface carved	0.804

The first three analyses comprise those carved rocks with more than seventy design elements; the fourth uses all examples where the full extent of the rock has been planned.

spacing of the motifs were *not* restrained by the amount of unused stone available for their creation.

It was harder to estimate the number of separate design elements represented at any one site, simply because these are by no means standardized. Even so, there was an obvious tendency for the widest range of motifs to be found on those rock surfaces with the largest circular devices. It was also apparent that the wider the range of design elements at any one site, the more likely it was that they would be linked together (Table 10.2). Very similar patterns were found in a second area of Britain, north Northumberland (Beckensall 1983). The distinctive evidence from that region will be considered later in this chapter.

The exploratory analysis suggested that there might be ways of assessing the visual complexity of different carved surfaces in the landscape. In the light of our earlier arguments, we would expect to find a regular relationship between variations of this kind and changes in the audience to whom these signs were being addressed. Like other components of the archaeological record, the petroglyphs make distinctive use of the upland landscape: might there be a consistent relationship between the complexity of these rock carvings and the distinctive character of human activity in this setting?

Case studies

These studies explore the relationship between rock art and topography in two different situations. The first is where human activity extends from the lowlands into highland

Table 10.2. *The relationship between the number of separate motifs on sites in Mid Argyll, the diameter of the circular motifs and the percentage of design elements joined by connecting lines*

Number of separate motifs	0–4	5–9	Over 10
Mean ring diameter per site	11.6	17.0	25.6 cm
Percentage of linked design elements per site	—	16	23

The sample comprises all the carved rocks with seventy or more design elements.

areas. In this case the distribution of the petroglyphs may stretch from regions that were capable of sustaining year-round land use to others which were better suited to seasonal occupation, as summer pasture and/or hunting grounds. In either case we would expect the audience for the carvings to have changed: from people who might have come into contact on a day-to-day basis in the lowlands, to those who came into the uplands only occasionally, and from a range of different home areas. If so, the petroglyphs on the higher ground would probably have been addressed to a larger and more varied audience. In such cases the relationships between the participants would have been more problematical.

We can explore such contrasts in two areas of the British Isles: Rombalds Moor in north east England and Strath Tay in the southern highlands of Scotland. The petroglyphs of Rombalds Moor have been studied extremely thoroughly (Ilkley Archaeology Group 1986), with the result that the distribution of carved rocks is known in considerable detail. The motifs and their placing in the landscape seem to vary according to the features of the local topography and even the areas with concentrations of worked flint. More work is needed before we can document these patterns in depth. Strath Tay, on the other hand, was last explored thirty years ago (Stewart 1961). The local topography is simpler, with the result that less subtle patterns can be considered here. Our pilot study provided indications that cup-marks and cup-and-ring marks occupied opposite ends of the range of variation (Table 10.1). For that reason it seemed likely that the more complex motifs would be better represented on the higher ground, including those locations which could command extensive views. Conversely, the carvings might be simpler in the areas used for year-round settlement. The evidence from Strath Tay is summarized in Table 10.3, which plots the percentage of cup-and-ring marks against their height above sea-level. As predicted by the basic model, the results of this analysis show a steady increase in

Table 10.3. *The percentage of cup-and-ring marks among the carved rocks of Strath Tay in relation to their height above sea level*

Elevation (metres)	50–150	151–250	251–350	Over 351
Percentage	23	33	42	50

the proportion of more complex carvings with their height above the valley floor.

In other areas, petroglyphs are found at a roughly even elevation, sometimes, as in north Yorkshire (Fig. 10.4), around the edges of land best suited for sustained occupation. In such cases the uplands were probably used by the inhabitants of those areas, and the size of the audience that could have viewed these carvings would have been related to the carrying capacity of the adjacent lowland. We can explore this relationship best by considering the rock art of north Northumberland, recorded in some detail by Beckensall (1983). These carvings have a wide distribution along the Fell Sandstone, a rock particularly well suited to this activity (Fig. 10.5). Towards the northern end of their distribution, the petroglyphs overlook the Milfield Basin, an extensive glacial plain of quite exceptional fertility. Since that basin is bisected by a major river, it may be possible to calculate the maximum extent of any territories overlooked by these sites; if so, this evidence indicates an upper figure of about 7.5 km (for a different approach to this question see Walker 1989).

For this reason the petroglyphs of north Northumberland have been divided into two groups (Fig. 10.5). Group A comprises those carvings within 7.5 km of the freely drained lowland soils and Group B includes the sites which lie further away. If our line of reasoning is correct, the area around them would have supported fewer inhabitants, and the audience for the art would have been proportionately smaller. As a result, their relationships with one another might have posed fewer problems. To what extent are these basic contrasts reflected in the complexity of the carvings?

We can see from Table 10.4 that the petroglyphs in these two groups contrast in the expected manner: where the audience for the art might have been larger and more varied, the percentage of cup-marks was low and there were more motifs of other kinds. The circular motifs were more prominent and more complex than the examples in other areas. They were found in a wider variety of sizes, and care had been taken to space them across the rock surface so that different design elements could clearly be told apart. It was

Table 10.4. *Contrasts between the two main groups of rock art in north Northumberland*

	Group A	Group B
Mean percentage of design elements per site other than cup-marks	53%	37%
Mean number of rings per site	2.0	1.3
Mean ring diameter per site	25 cm	16 cm
Mean number of modal ring diameters per site	4.4	3.0
Mean ring spacing per site	24 cm	20 cm
Mean number of separate motifs per site	11.3	5.0

The sample consists of all sites with more than fifty design elements.

in the areas with ready access to the most productive soils that the widest range of separate motifs was found.

On the other hand, none of these attributes was directly related to the amount of freely drained soil within 7.5 km. Within Group A, areas with only limited access to these resources scored at least as well as those with more extensive areas of productive land. A further factor may have intervened in this relationship. So far, the argument has proceeded on the basis that the obvious audience for these carvings were the inhabitants of the nearby lowlands. This overlooks another characteristic of the archaeological record in this area, for the Milfield Basin and the immediately adjacent uplands contain an important series of ceremonial monuments, in particular henges and stone circles (Harding 1981). These are likely to have served as aggregation sites for a wider population. This would have had an effect on the number of people who might have viewed the petroglyphs and, also, on the extent of regular contacts between them. Again their relationships with one another would have posed greater problems.

We have already seen how commonly rock art is located at prominent viewpoints. The evidence from north Northumberland is certainly no exception (Walker 1989), and a number of these localities enjoy extensive views towards some or all of the monuments. Moreover these locations generally command major routes by which people would have come into these areas. This provides a basis for subdividing the sites in Group A: Group A1 are those carved rocks from which at least some of the monuments could be seen, whilst they were invisible from those belonging to Group A2. (All the sites which seem to have commanded routes leading into the basin belong to Group A1.)

The figures given in Table 10.5 show that nearly all the variation observed in our earlier analysis is created by the petroglyphs that now fall in Group A1; in most respects Groups A2 and B produce rather similar results. This finding is consistent with a range of other studies which seem to indicate that material culture was used in a far more structured manner in the vicinity of large ceremonial centres (Richards and Thomas 1984). In particular, the artefacts deposited in such environments show a much greater investment of *style* than those in other areas (Brown 1990). In the light of our earlier discussion, this may be related to the number of strangers who were coming into contact.

One independent source of information tends to confirm this outline, for in Northumberland a number of fragments of

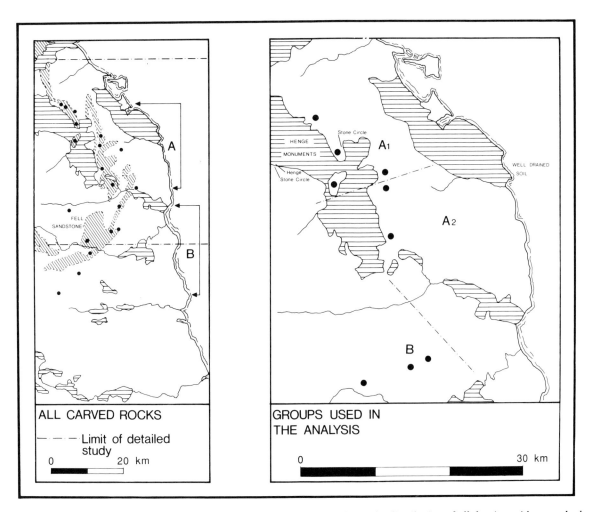

Fig. 10.5. The rock art of north Northumberland. The left hand map shows the distribution of all the sites with petroglyphs in relation to the areas of Fell Sandstone and the extent of the well drained lowlands. It also marks the distinction between the two main groups used in the detailed analysis. The right hand map shows the northern half of this area at a larger scale and distinguishes between sites in Groups A1 and A2. It also includes the positions of the main ceremonial monuments.

Table 10.5. *Contrasts between three groups of rock art in north Northumberland*

	Group A1	Group A2	Group B
Mean percentage of design elements per site other than cup-marks	52%	55%	37%
Mean number of rings per site	2.3	1.6	1.3
Mean ring diameter per site	30 cm	17.5 cm	16 cm
Mean number of modal ring diameters per site	6.0	2.5	3.0
Mean ring spacing per site	29 cm	18.5 cm	20 cm
Mean number of separate motifs per site	14	6	5

The presentation is in the same format as in Table 10.4, but this time Group A has been subdivided. Group A1 consists of those sites more closely related to the ceremonial centres.

carved rock were incorporated in Bronze Age burials; another was deposited in the centre of one of the henge monuments in the Milfield Basin (Harding 1981: fig. 9). Such fragments are sometimes weathered and are usually incomplete, as if they had been detached from larger panels (Beckensall 1983). Some time may have elapsed between their creation and this period of reuse, but when these pieces were incorporated in burials, different motifs were employed in different ways (Table 10.6). The more complex burials were in stone-lined coffins or cists, and here the circular motifs predominate. The simpler burials included cremations covered by one carved stone. Although the sample is smaller, cup-marked pieces were preferred in this context. This distinction mirrors the most obvious contrast seen in the landscape as a whole.

Summing up

The procedure followed in this chapter is rather similar to that described by Layton in a study of Upper Palaeolithic art:

> Looking for specific meanings in Palaeolithic motifs is frustrating and relatively unproductive. Looking for structure is easier, although there are problems in being

Table 10.6. *The associations between specific motifs and burials in Northumberland*

	Rings	Cup-marks only	Other designs
Carved stones in cists	12	1	3
Carved stones covering cremations	1	5	—

(Data from Beckensall 1983.)

> sure that the structures we measure are always the direct reflection of Palaeolithic culture. Given the nature of human cognitive systems, however, it is surely less interesting to know whether, for example, the horse exemplified masculinity or femininity, than to show that Palaeolithic rock art has a structure comparable in its complexity, to that of modern hunter gatherers. (1987, 232)

In this case the detailed analysis differs in two respects. It is possible to demonstrate that the distinction between cup-marks and circular motifs *did* matter to those who created them. They represented the opposite extremes of the range of variation detected in our pilot study, but they also had contrasting associations in the prehistoric funerary record. At the same time, we have not been concerned to compare the structural properties of this evidence with those of rock art in the ethnographic record. Rather, by studying the subtle relationship between topography and the character of the petroglyphs, we have attempted to show how the natural environment may have been perceived. In this respect carved rocks form only part of a range of different phenomena, all of which seem to be related to the properties of *landscape* rather than *land*. It is at this level that they are best compared with the observations made by anthropologists and geographers.

In the opening section of this paper I mentioned that in certain parts of Europe large scale cultivation did not develop until the later prehistoric period. Field systems, land boundaries and occupation sites are difficult to identify, and it seems increasingly likely that archaeologists working in these areas have underestimated the degree of mobility in the settlement pattern. It may be no accident that many of these regions, from the Iberian peninsula to Scandinavia, include distinctive groups of petroglyphs, very few of which seem to predate the adoption of domesticated resources. All is not lost if we are prevented from reading these symbols. Even their organization in the landscape sheds light on the ancient mind.

Acknowledgements

I am most grateful to Frances Raymond for a critical reading of the text and to Colin Burgess for a copy of his paper on Atlantic rock art. I must thank Susan Johnston for kindly sending me a copy of her doctoral thesis on the Irish petroglyphs and Graeme Walker for allowing me to refer to his unpublished dissertation. The participants in the Cambridge seminar were a source of stimulating comment and ideas, and I would especially like to thank Joyce Marcus for her contribution to the discussion. The figure drawings are by Adam Hadley.

References

Barker, G. 1985. *Prehistoric farming in Europe*. Cambridge, Cambridge University Press

Barker, G. and C. Gamble (eds.) 1985. *Beyond domestication in prehistoric Europe*. London, Academic Press

Beckensall, S. 1983. *Northumberland's prehistoric rock carvings*. Rothbury, Pendulum Publications

Bradley, R. 1989. Deaths and entrances: a contextual analysis of megalithic art. *Current Anthropology* 30: 68–76

1991. Monuments and places. In *Sacred and profane*, ed. P. Garwood, D. Jennings, R. Skeates and J. Thoms, pp. 135–40. Oxford, Oxford University Committee for Archaeology

Bradley, R. and R. Chapman 1986. The nature and development of long-distance relations in Later Neolithic Britain and Ireland. In *Peer polity interaction and socio-political change*, ed. C. Renfrew and J. Cherry, pp. 127–36. Cambridge, Cambridge University Press

Braithwaite, M. 1982. Decoration as a ritual symbol: a theoretical proposal and an ethnoarchaeological study in southern Sudan. In *Symbolic and structural archaeology*, ed. I. Hodder, pp. 80–8. Cambridge, Cambridge University Press

Brown, A. 1991. Structured deposition and technological change in the lithic material from Cranborne Chase. In *Papers on the prehistoric archaeology of Cranborne Chase*, ed. J. Barrett, R. Bradley and M. Hall, pp. 101–33. Oxford, Oxbow Books

Burgess, C. 1990. The chronology of cup-marks and cup-and-ring marks in Atlantic Europe. *Revue Archéologique de l'Ouest, Supplément* 2: 157–71

Buttimer, A. and D. Seamon (eds.) 1980. *The human experience of space and place*. London, Croom Helm

Coggins, D. 1986. *Upper Teesdale: the archaeology of a north Pennine valley*. Oxford, British Archaeological Reports (BAR 150)

Cox, K. and R. Golledge (eds.) 1981. *Behavioural problems in geography revisited*. London, Methuen

Darvill, T. 1987. *Prehistoric Britain*. London, Batsford

Emmett, D. 1979. Stone rows: the traditional view reconsidered. In *Prehistoric Dartmoor in its context*, ed. V. Maxfield, pp. 90–104. Exeter, Devon Archaeological Society

García Alén, A. and A. De la Peña Santos 1980. *Grabados rupestres de la provincia de Pontevedra*, La Coruña, Fundación Pedro Barrié de la Maza

Gardiner, J. 1984. Lithic distributions and neolithic settlement patterns in central southern England. In *Neolithic studies*, ed. R. Bradley and J. Gardiner, pp. 15–40. Oxford, British Archaeological Reports (BAR 133)

Hardin, M. 1984. Models of decoration. In *The many dimensions of pottery*, ed. S. van der Leeuw and A. Pritchard, pp. 573–607. Amsterdam, Cingula 7

Harding, A. 1981. Excavations in the prehistoric ritual complex near Milfield, Northumberland. *Proceedings of the Prehistoric Society* 47: 87–135

Holgate, R. 1988. *Neolithic settlement of the Thames Basin*. Oxford, British Archaeological Reports (BAR 194)

Ilkley Archaeology Group 1986. *The carved rocks of Rombalds Moor*. Wakefield, West Yorkshire Archaeology Service

Ingold, T. 1986. *The appropriation of nature*. Manchester, Manchester University Press

Johnson, G. 1982. Organisational structure and scalar stress. In *Theory and explanation in archaeology: the Southampton conference*, ed. C. Renfrew, M. Rowlands and B. A. Segraves, pp. 389–421. London, Academic Press

Johnston, S. 1989. *Prehistoric Irish petroglyphs: their analysis and interpretation in anthropological context*. Ann Arbor, University Microfilms

Layton, R. 1987. The use of ethnographic parallels in interpreting Upper Palaeolithic rock art. In *Comparative anthropology*, ed. L. Holy, pp. 210–39. Oxford, Blackwell

Lowenthal, D. and M. Bowden (eds.) 1976. *Geographies of the mind*. New York, Oxford University Press

Miles, H. 1975. Barrows on the St Austell granite, Cornwall. *Cornish Archaeology* 14: 5–81

Moffett, L., M. Robinson and V. Straker 1989. Cereals, fruits and nuts: charred plant remains from neolithic sites in England and Wales and the neolithic economy. In *The beginnings of agriculture*, ed. A. Milles, D. Williams and N. Gardner, pp. 243–61. Oxford, British Archaeological Reports (BAR International Series 496)

Morris, R. 1989. The prehistoric rock art of Great Britain: a survey of all sites bearing motifs more complex than simple cup-marks. *Proceedings of the Prehistoric Society* 55: 45–88

O'Kelly, M. 1982. *Newgrange: archaeology, art and legend*. London, Thames and Hudson

O'Sullivan, M. 1986. Approaches to passage tomb art. *Journal of the Royal Society of Antiquaries of Ireland* 116: 68–83

1989. A stylistic revolution in the megalithic art of the Boyne Valley. *Archaeology Ireland* 3: 138–42

de la Peña Santos, A. and J. Vázquez Varela 1979. *Los petroglifos Gallegos*. La Coruña, Edicios do Castro

Pred, A. 1985. The social becomes the spatial, the spatial becomes the social: social change and the becoming of places in the Swedish province of Skåne. In *Social relations and spatial structures*, ed. D. Gregory and J. Urry, pp. 337–65. London, Macmillan

Richards, C. and J. Thomas 1984. Ritual activity and structured deposition in later neolithic Wessex. In *Neolithic studies*, ed. R. Bradley and J. Gardiner, pp. 189–218. Oxford, British Archaeological Reports (BAR 133)

Roese, H. 1980. Some aspects of topographical location of neolithic and bronze age monuments in Wales, 1: menhirs. *Bulletin of the Board of Celtic Studies* 28: 645–55

1982. Some aspects of topographic location of neolithic and bronze age monuments in Wales, 3: round cairns and round barrows. *Bulletin of the Board of Celtic Studies* 29: 575–87

Royal Commission on the Ancient and Historical Monuments of Scotland 1971. *Argyll, volume 1*. Edinburgh, HMSO

1988. *Argyll, volume 6*. Edinburgh, HMSO

Ruggles, C. and A. Burl 1985. A new study of the Aberdeenshire recumbent stone circles, 2: interpretation. *Archaeoastronomy* 8: 25–60

Schaafsma, P. 1985. Form, content and function: theory and method in North American rock art studies. In *Advances in archaeological method and theory*, volume 8, ed. M. Schiffer, pp. 237–77. New York, Academic Press

Shee, E. 1972. Three decorated stones from Loughcrew, Co Meath. *Journal of the Royal Society of Antiquaries of Ireland* 102: 224–33

Shee Twohig, E. 1981. *The megalithic art of western Europe*. Oxford, Clarendon Press

Spratt, D. 1982. *Prehistoric and roman archaeology of north-east Yorkshire*. Oxford, British Archaeological Reports (BAR 104)

Spratt, D. and C. Burgess (eds.) 1985. *Upland settlement in Britain*. Oxford, British Archaeological Reports (BAR 143)

Stewart, M. 1961. Strath Tay in the second millennium BC: a field survey. *Proceedings of the Society of Antiquaries of Scotland* 92: 71–84

Tuan, Y.-F. 1967. Attitudes toward environment: themes and approaches. In *Environmental perception and behaviour*, ed. D. Lowenthal, pp. 4–17. Chicago, University of Chicago, Department of Geography

1977. *Space and place: the perspective of experience*. London, Edward Arnold

Walker, G. 1989. *The cup-and-ring markings of north Northumberland*, BA dissertation, Reading University

Ward, A. 1988. Aspects of the siting of cairns in south west Wales with particular reference to ring cairns. *Bulletin of the Board of Celtic Studies* 35: 92–105

Wiesner, P. 1983. Style and social information in Kalahari San projectile points. *American Antiquity* 48: 253–76

1984. Reconsidering the behavioural basis for style: a case study among the Kalahari San. *Journal of Anthropological Archaeology* 3: 190–234

Wilson, P. J. 1988. *The domestication of the human species*. New Haven, Yale University Press

Wobst, H. M. 1977. Stylistic behaviour and information exchange. In *For the director: research essays in honour of J. B. Griffin*, ed. C. Cleland, pp. 317–42. Ann Arbor, University of Michigan, Museum of Anthropology

11

Knowledge representation and archaeology: a cognitive example using GIS

EZRA B. W. ZUBROW

Introduction

There is an apocryphal story about a famous archaeologist who was excavating an Arikara graveyard. Based on previous work, he believed that the Arikara interred the dead in a systematic manner. He suggested that graves were located in a pattern analogous to a checkerboard. Excavating every third square produced nothing for the entire season. The archaeologist was frustrated. During the last day, a crew member suggested they excavate a unit that was not part of this predetermined pattern. Digging one square to the south of their previous excavations they found a grave with a plethora of funeral offerings. The following season, they excavated the same pattern. By lagging the pattern one square to the south they found a grave in each square.

The story illustrates two important aspects of cognitive archaeology. First, the material culture mediates between the archaeologist's cognition and the cognition of the prehistoric native. Second, the material culture reconciles the past to the present.

Originally, the archaeologist believed he knew the organizing principles that the Arikara were using. As the season progressed, he became convinced that he was mistaken. During the second season, he was reassured that he was correct. The archaeological and the native view of spatial organization appeared to correspond although they were separated by cultural differences and five long centuries. Both parties agreed that the inhabitants of the city of the dead had abodes approximately nine metres apart. The archaeologist's initial mistake was a minor problem in knowledge representation. He was able to represent the pattern but not the starting point. In other words, once lagged by fifteen feet, they were the identical perceptions.

The interpretation or reconstruction of previous cognition is not a simple process. The prehistoric native is partially responsible for the creation of information. On the other hand, what the archaeologist knows about the particular prehistoric culture partially determines how material culture expresses cognition. It is also dependent upon the abilities of the archaeologist, the commonalities of the profession and most importantly the universality of aspects of human cognition.

Knowledge is cognitively processed information, and is both represented and the basis of action. Prehistoric natives represent knowledge according to a set of cultural norms. They process this information according to a set of cultural rules when making material objects. Similarly, archaeologists represent knowledge according to a set of modern cultural norms and process the information according to another set of cultural rules when they interpret the material objects.

Fig. 11.1 illustrates this viewpoint pictorially. Material objects carry the information across temporal and spatial discontinuities in the form of artefacts. Justeson (1973) suggested a related concept when he described the earth as a channel for prehistoric information.

This process is not static. The apocryphal story portrays how the archaeologist's views change. The archaeologist's cultural rules, knowledge and even knowledge representation develop as new information about the prehistoric subject is gained, new achievements are made in the field, and innovations amplify the archaeologist's technical and cultural milieu.

Goals

The author believes that cognitive archaeology must be synthetically scientific and interpretative. He follows Maki who claims that although 'observation is theory-laden; interpretation is ever-present; . . . [These] are not, singly or jointly, sufficient for anti-realism' (Maki 1992).

'Realist' and 'anti-realist' causation, 'realist' and 'anti-realist' phenomena and 'realist' and 'anti-realist' explanation may be applied simultaneously to aspects of the prehistoric world.

This paper presents a theoretical framework, a research design, a methodology and a case-study. Concepts of knowledge representation, categorization schemes and cognitive universals determine a theoretical framework. They are combined into the 'figure ground concept' that transforms 'ideals' into 'testable' hypotheses. The methodology makes possible the examination of three different types of 'ideals' against three different types of 'reals' in a single culture area. It uses a 'set of rules' and an 'abstract tool kit'. Theoretical and methodological diatribes are inadequate without application to the field data. Thus, this study includes a case-study based upon an extensive archaeological survey of a classic ethnographic area of the United States – the western part of New York State where the predecessors of the Iroquois lived.

One goal is to show that people had preferences independent of economic necessity. Furthermore, some decisions are independent of utility. A second goal is to demonstrate how ideals may be altered or transformed by reality into an amalgam.

Settlement and housing location are the result of a series of personal and cultural decisions. The ideal pattern of settlement, in the minds of the natives, may be tempered, adjusted and transformed by topographic reality. These ideal forms are grounded in such economic realities as trade and transport, or established upon such cultural realities as heritage, aesthetic norms, or social and religious rules. As archaeologists, one of our ultimate goals is to extract the cultural ideals from the complicated reality in the complex patterns of prehistoric material remains. The prehistoric landscape is the result of numerous compromises between ideal and real.

Theoretical framework

The cognitive war: a brief history

The most vitriolic and controversial current debate among archaeologists concerns the form and reality of cognitive archaeology. It has divided the profession between young and old, created fortified walls separating humanists from scientists, and separated the European heartland from Anglo-American archaeology. Essentially there are two schools of thought. Commanding the humanist bastions are Ian Hodder and his disciples (Hodder 1987, 1989). They believe past cognition only may be understood using interpretative techniques. Replication and testing in a positivist mien is impossible. Non-positivist and interpretative, it was based upon hermeneutics and the philosophical works of Foucault (1972) and was archaeologically espoused by Hodder, and also Shanks and Tilley (1987; Tilley 1990; Binford 1989) and Conkey and Hastorf (1990). It was directed at the ideological and cognitive aspects of prehistoric individuals, and its methodologies have been interpretative and literary, whether one is considering space or object.

The other school is martially garrisoned in the processual camps. This processual archaeology developed in the middle

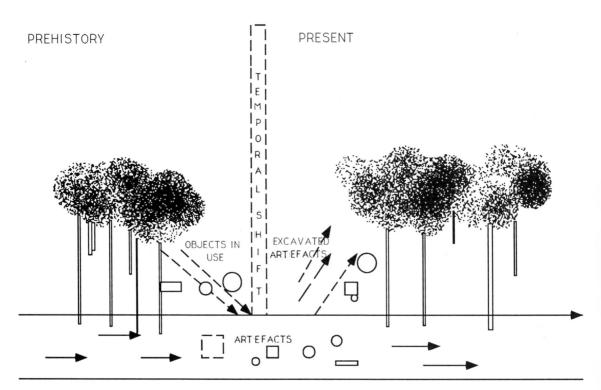

Fig. 11.1. The Earth as a medium of information exchange

1960s. Based on the work of Taylor (1967), Spaulding (1962), Binford and Binford (1968), Clarke (1968), Watson *et al.* (1971), it espoused a positivist archaeology. The processualists stressed the operational reality of both artefacts and spatial phenomena and the explicit and empirical scientism of Popper and Braithwaite. The new dating and archaeometric techniques, the increased availability of remote sensing, and augmented computing power made for a new type of 'social scientific' archaeology. Most of the work emphasized the materialistic and economic aspects of prehistoric societies. The artefactual and spatial analytical methodologies were marked by similar interests. Flying the flags of Binford and Renfrew (Renfrew and Bahn 1991) these forces claim that ideology is a sub-system which can be approached with the same methodology as social and economic subsystems. If these methodologies fail, then ideology and motivation cannot be determined from archaeological remains because motivation cannot be derived from material objects (Dunnell 1971).

A new synthesis

Very recently there have been attempts to bypass the negative aspects of each of these views and develop a new synthesis. The original impetus was Peebles and Gardin's *Representations in Archaeology*. They saw that there were two underlying archaeological conceptions of objects and space:

> (1) the natural or artificial languages used in the representation of archaeological materials in databases and (2) the operations carried out on the symbols that make up these languages in order to create or support the interpretative hypotheses relevant to these archaeological materials. (Peebles and Gardin 1991: 1–2)

Michael Herzfeld explicitly examined archaeological space as a field of decipherable signs. Similarly, some archaeologists, following Hintakka, have asked how the cognition of the archaeologist affects archaeology. How may one guarantee the communication of common knowledge by archaeologists to each other? When one archaeologist describes a site as a 'neolithic camp site' to a second archaeologist, does the second archaeologist actually receive the same information as that transmitted? Is it understood? Do the two scholars denote the same meaning by 'neolithic' by 'camp' or by 'site'? (Zubrow 1989).

This paper suggests the entire processual/post-processual argument is largely irrelevant to understanding prehistoric cognition. The fundamental issues are not how archaeologists interpret prehistoric behaviour nor how archaeologists scientifically test hypotheses. Rather, if one wishes to understand cognition, the primary issues are how

do humans represent knowledge and what do they do with that representation. Given a powerful and productive theory of knowledge representation, the methodology of demonstration hopefully should follow. Another concern is whether humankind uses the same or similar cognitive processes regardless of the culture. Ultimately archaeology's contribution will be to show when and how human cognition took its present form, and how stable knowledge representation has been through the millennia.

Knowledge representation

One function of creating a cognitive archaeology is to understand how knowledge is represented by humans. The phrase 'knowledge representation', as used in the literature, is generally associated with 'natural languages'. Recently, this association has been relaxed in order to consider how knowledge is represented in both human beings and machines. In fact, the major discoveries of the last few years in 'cognitive studies' derive from 'artificial intelligence'. They are the result of attempting to understand the best ways to represent knowledge in the 'artificial language' of computing and robotic machinery, rather than in the 'natural languages' of the human species. Even more, knowledge representation is the encoding of information independent of the medium.

Universal code of meaning

A universal code of meaning is not yet well understood in natural language. Its form is fuzzy when viewed across culture, space and languages. However, lack of clarity is not equivalent to lack of existence. There are other indications of tangibility. The history of science and technology lends credence. Frequently technology is understood across culture, time, and space, even when language creates barriers. Today's teenage child knows what a radio is and how to turn it on. This appears to be almost universal irrespective of culture and wherewithal. Similarly, the use of stone tools has been universal across cultures and times for most of human existence. The plough, the pot and the basket have remarkable ubiquity, and their subtleties are appreciated widely. Measurement, standardization and some form of mathematics is pervasive among cultures. All require related forms of encoding of information.

How humans encode information transcends culture and time. Some argue it is a function of the biological legacy which is shared by all human beings. However, this is an argument for a different forum. What archaeologists must do is decode the information in order to understand what knowledge is represented. Archaeologists stand before the material and symbolic realms of human cognition in much the same way their intellectual forebears stood a century or more ago before the biological and genetic realms of their day. One needs scholars who will find the general underlying principles and the common structures. These archaeological 'Darwins' and 'Mendels' are faced by the overwhelming variety and profusion of examples.

Natural language and archaeology

For some aspects of archaeology, examples of natural language exist in the written documents that survive. On stone, papyrus, wood, metal and other media, examples of language survive in some areas and for some temporal periods. These include the wealth of Classical, Middle Eastern, Biblical and Historical archaeology which are supplemented by verbal description. Noah Kramer's (1967) translation of the correspondence between a Sumerian son at school and his father rings so true with 'admonitions to study', 'requests for money', and warnings about 'ne'er do well colleagues' that five millennia disappear.

Ethnoarchaeologists presently record and describe how modern peoples use their material culture, but they should design research to examine how these people *regard* their material culture. What are the cognitive similarities and differences in classification, not only of material culture among human societies but in how they think about it?

The elements and frameworks of knowledge representation

The standard archaeological categories of object, space and 'time' are well suited for decoding information and representing the knowledge that prehistoric natives use. These are the three traditional elements of archaeology which are at the disposal of archaeologists who are interested in how knowledge is represented. They are independent of the prehistoric culture, area and date in the sense that they are applicable to all. On the other hand, their form varies.

The traditional use of artefacts, location and date are for the archaeologist to discover, categorize and exhibit objects. The function is to answer the questions of 'what, where, when'. In other words, they may locate cultures and sites in the world as viewed by the archaeologist and date these phenomena from the point of view of the present. These same three categories are used in a different manner when examined from the perspective of the archaeologist attempting to determine how knowledge is represented. Artefacts are not only remnants of prehistoric cultures but they are the material objects which carry the information concerning how they were produced and categorized by the native. Location is not the archaeological context but the prehistoric natives' locus which has spatial and cultural referents. Time is not only a mechanism for dating the past from the present, it also exists prehistorically and is a

referent by which the prehistoric native viewed stability and change within their culture, and is thus a temporal referent.

Similarly, there are several frameworks for organizing the testing of hypotheses about cognitive subjects. One may consider reconstruction of prehistoric categorization schemes – an ethnoscience of archaeology. Or one may consider generative rules, referent structures or depictive representations. In other words, these could be a prehistoric grammar of prehistoric phenomena.

Cognitive universals

If there are cognitive universals which apply to all people then it will be considerably easier to do cognitive archaeology. These universals could be the building blocks for understanding cognition and the base line for making comparisons.

This paper suggests that there exist some very simple cognitive universals. By 'cognitive universals' is meant universal to all members of the culture – at least adult members. In addition, the term is meant to imply that cognitive universals are universal across cultures.

The cognitive universals are seen as common to the species. On the other hand, there is no reason to presuppose that these cognitive universals either apply or do not apply across species to *Homo erectus* or *Homo habilis* or across generic lines to *Australopithecus robustus* or *Australopithecus africanus*. These very difficult questions are being asked by Mellars (1991).

What are some of these cognitive universals? It is suggested that there are a series of 'connectors' or 'relationships' which are universal. Among them are

inclusion which is defined as when an object <includes> an object;

bisection or *sub-division* which is defined as when an object is <bisected> into two objects, or a space is <bisected> into two spaces;

contiguity which exhibits forms such as the object <is contiguous> to the object or the space <is contiguous> to the space;

contingency in the sense of 'if a then b' which has a dependency and temporal connotation which exhibits such forms as the object <is contingent> upon the object or the space <is contingent> upon the space;

equality or *equivalence* which exhibits the form object <is equivalent to> object or space <is equivalent to> space;

temporality which exhibits the form object <is before> object; this is closely related to temporal contingency (above) but may not include the connotation of dependence.

orientation by which objects or spaces are oriented in relationship to their spatial referent and takes the form object <oriented> spatial referent.

Any of these universals may be used in a set of rules which are similar to the relational statements that are used in generative grammars. The suggestion is that these rules will be used to develop a calculus of sorts for the recapitulation of the knowledge which results in prehistoric behaviour. These could be used to recreate the rules by which people thought about their prehistoric culture.

This does have real applications. The careful examination of the long sequence of temple development by Flannery and Marcus, in this volume, could be restated in such a set of rules. Other examples are Bradley's rules for settlement organization, and van der Leeuw's paper which reflects the rules for creating ceramic phenomena.

The figure ground relationship

Bennet (1975), Lakoff (1987), Talmy (1978) and others developed the 'figure ground' concept. Originally, it was recognized visually, linguistically and geographically. Yet, it is significantly broader than linguistic or spatial categorization. Languages mark geometric and dimensional distinctions and one may recognize the patterns that these form. Often, these basic geometric and dimensional distinctions are 'cognitive universals' or are 'made up' of the same.

Both the verbal and visual notions of 'figure ground' have commonalities. They are both schema, meaning that one selects part of the referent scene to represent the whole, while disregarding the remaining aspects. For example, in painting, a few lines may represent trees. In language, only certain spatial categories or concepts are marked. For example, in English a person can simply go or one may go 'somewhere'. In Russian one cannot simply go and it is difficult to go 'somewhere'. One can only walk to, or ride to, the edge of somewhere or something, go inside a place, around a place, etc. One cannot just go without specifying how and where.

In general, people orient themselves in space and time. When one orients oneself in space, one expresses the relationship of oneself to a figure and a ground. For example 'Meet me near the St John's College bicycle shed in Cambridge' includes a figure and a ground. I am being oriented and related to the figure (bicycle shed) within the ground referent (Cambridge).

Often, these phrases express a relationship between concrete real world entities (extensional objects) such as the bicycle shed and Cambridge. However, they may communicate a relationship between conceptual abstractions. These conceptional abstractions are labelled 'intensional objects'. 'Meet me near the bicycle shed' is not the same as 'She met him at various pubs'. Both involve meeting but the meeting at pubs is very different from meeting near the bicycle shed. Pubs are a conceptual abstraction. There are many of them and they have certain commonalities in their 'pub character' and in their frequent neighbourhood locations. An extensional 'real world' mapping, as in the case of the bicycle shed, requires a one-to-one representation system. An intensional knowledge representation, as in the case of the pubs, does not require such a one-to-one representation.

What this paper does is show how multiple representations, which make up an archaeological prehistoric region, indicate the figure and ground as well as the cognitive categories and priorities which are being used by the prehistoric native.

Research design

In order to understand the transformation from the ideal to the real, one must define what one means by ideal and then apply it to the domain under consideration – namely settlement pattern. Underlying the ideal are a variety of theories. For example, the Platonic ideal is that all phenomena are imperfect reflections of an ideal, true object (Plato, *Republic*). Thus, an Iroquois village site such as Howlett Hill is just a poor reflection of the more ideal ethnohistoric Iroquois settlement at Brompton Hill which in turn is a reflection of what Iroquois have considered an 'ideal type'.

Ideals can be generalizations from experience (Hempel 1965). Thus, it appears that although there is considerable variation in the length of Iroquois longhouses (20–220 feet), there appears to be an ideal width of about 25 feet. (The range is usually between 20 and 30 feet.)

Another form of the ideal is a proposition whose truth can be established a priori. A device, often used in the natural sciences, is to formulate a rule for a 'supposed' ideal case so that relationships of dependence hold only under certain conditions which are limiting. Nevertheless, these conditions may be rarely realized. These ideal cases and ideal types are not equivalent to an observation. However, the fact that nothing in the real world corresponds to the ideal does not rob it of scientific utility. In short the ideal type is a construct which can be meaningfully compared to reality. For example, other things being equal, unused Iroquois land was held in common.

The second element of the transformation is the 'real'. One element of the 'real' is topographic reality. By topographic reality one means the spatial relationships of the surface features, one to another; it is the surface configuration of both land and water in relationship to each other. This paper will be concerned with a topographic reality far from the European experience. It is based upon a topographic domain which is conditioned by the huge freshwater lakes of Lake Ontario and Lake Erie as well as by the rapidly moving Niagara River that is best known for catapulting over Niagara Falls (Fig. 11.2). Historically this area has been known as the Niagara Frontier and has been the western extremity of the Iroquois cultural area (White 1961).

The third element of the comparison is the cultural reality. The author is limiting himself to a restricted definition. It is suggested that the ideal patterns are not based solely upon environmental or topographic features such as drainage basins but also upon such cultural features as trade routes or traditional homelands. Settlements are frequently located one upon each other. This may be the factual basis of a traditional homeland. It is the site from which the ancestors came, to which one hopes the descendants will return, and it is the spiritual home where one continues to look for secular and religious leadership. One might consider the case of Martin Site along the Niagara river as an example. There is continuous occupation at a single location from a fishing settlement in 3000 BC to the present State Park (Zubrow and Buerger, forthcoming; Buerger 1992).

Societies may adjust the ideal to the real through numerous scenarios. One recognizes that the processes by which knowledge is aggregated are essentially fuzzy. These processes include the transformation of known experience to

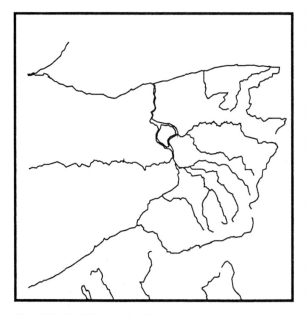

Fig. 11.2. The Niagara frontier

new contexts, the application of hypothesized generalities, and the endurance of simple trial and error.

Methodology

The methodology consisted of four distinct concepts that were combined in a set of steps. In summary these concepts were:

(1) The development of ideal models of settlement patterns which may exist in the mind of the prehistoric native.
(2) The development of databases containing real settlement patterns as determined by archaeological survey and excavation.
(3) The use of Geographic Information Systems to store large amounts of data and create representations that have visual forms.
(4) The application of geographic algorithms for relating and adjusting the ideal to the real.

The methodology consisted of several procedures. First, the database was constructed, consisting of two large sectors – the ideal patterns and the actual databases from the Niagara Frontier. Second, there was the transformation from the ideal to the real.

There are several ideal patterns which could be used. For example, one set of patterns which were used in a preliminary test were idealized geometric patterns. One began with such patterns as simple grids, circles and linear patterns. It is a limited test of cognitive characteristics of pattern and organization (at least in the Western sense). A second set of ideal patterns were developed based upon the chronological character and potentially evolutionary character of the society. One may use the earlier patterns of settlement as ideals for later patterns of settlement. This addresses the concept of 'homeland' and 'heritage'. For example, pre-contact Iroquois settlement patterns could be compared to post-Iroquois settlement patterns on the Niagara Frontier (Zubrow and Olsen 1991). A third set of ideal patterns could be based upon economic patterns. Issues of value, cost, efficiency, supply and demand must be examined from a cross-cultural perspective. For example, there are documents which reflect the actual trade routes and relationships in these areas. For example, the Jesuit Relations provides a historical basis for the contact which came to the Niagara Frontier. A fourth set of ideals are examined as the analysis develops, and one may move to patterns which have deeper semantic meaning to the native. They are based upon ethnographic, ethnohistorical or archaeological depictions, or some combination of these, to begin to reach toward the meaning developed by the prehistoric native. These could be from ethnographic interviews, historical documents or design elements in archaeological phenomena. Two examples will be developed. The first uses the design elements of Iroquois wampum belts; the second uses the Iroquois longhouse (Thwaites 1954).

These patterns are held in an arc-coverage which is designed to be compared with the actual topographic features and the real settlement patterns which are also held in an arc-coverage. The Western New York database is a compendium of site information and collections based upon the Buffalo Archaeological Survey. The survey has been systematically collecting, excavating and surveying all the archaeological sites in Western New York for the last twenty years. It has been directed by Marian White, Neal Trubowitz, Ezra Zubrow, Howard Pomerantz and Ben Nelson, and is presently directed by Elaine Herald. Today there are approximately 4,800 sites known. For each site, the location is plotted on a map and a file of all known archaeological information is kept. Collections are catalogued and curated. The author and his students have been digitizing and building the database – USGS quadrangle by quadrangle for the last five years. In this study, the database consists of 224 sites including camps, cemeteries, fishing sites, as well as village sites which date to the Late Woodland – AD 850 to 1300. A small proportion of these are shown in Fig. 11.3.

The third and fourth concepts mentioned above were the use of the GIS and application of geographic algorithms. The development of a computerized GIS was the creation of a relational database (Date 1986), and required formulating a representation of knowledge. It should be understood that despite its complex appearance, a GIS represents a simplification. In this case, it is standardization of the settlement to territory relationship made possible by the completely artificial environment. Among the processes necessary are structural generalization in the understanding of shape, and structural reduction in creation of visual depiction. It is a type of computerized 'figure ground' analysis and makes use of the 'cognitive universals'. There is numerical generalization and reduction in the use of filters and gradient masks to bring out particular forms of data patterns which may not be evident. There are numerous decisions regarding categorical generalization and categorical reduction. For example, there are the merging of categories, the aggregation or disaggregation of spatial and numerical information, the defining of particular attributes as indicators of categories, and the creation and dissolving of features based upon suppression of attributes or categories. Thematic data needs to be represented as well as symbolic and temporal information. This information may take the form of punctiform, linear, areal or volumetric data. Furthermore, some of the information will be static but other information will

represent dynamic phenomena as in the case of flows or wayfinding. The data may be numerical, textual, image or even analogic or metaphoric (Joao 1991).

A 'rubber sheeting' algorithm was applied to the ideal and real patterns. In some cases, the ideal patterns were shifted to the real data. In others, the shift was in the opposite direction from real to ideal. These patterns could be spatial or numerical, symbolic or thematic. What is rubber sheeting? It is a method to stretch or distort either the cultural or topographic phenomena in a controlled manner. More accurately, it is a 'piecewise transformation' which preserves chosen categories whether they be symbolic categories or spatial categories such as straight lines. It is accomplished through the creation of a set of deformation vectors. A given set of co-ordinates are stretched along the vector 'from the old unstretched location' to the 'new stretched location'. Then the rest of the geometry is adjusted to conform. It is easiest to think of it in terms of simple physical realities. It is similar to what happens to individual spatial locations on the surface of a balloon as it is blown up and as it loses air. Next, imagine what happens as a child pulls and stretches part of the balloon. The algorithm does these operations. Finally,

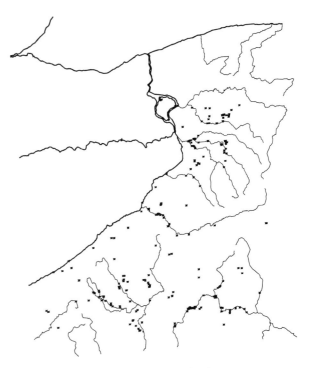

Fig. 11.3. Part of the archaeological database

instead of imagining a simple physical space, imagine a space which is categorically defined. There are locations and spaces inside or outside of the building or, more culturally specific, 'inside or outside of the longhouse'. The definitions of inside and outside may be quite sophisticated. What this case-study does is to set the child to work stretching the categorical, thematic and spatial balloon of prehistoric New York.

Results

The results from the 'simple geometric' and the 'homeland' analyses are reported elsewhere (Zubrow and Olsen 1991). It is sufficient to state that neither was explanatory for prehistoric Iroquoian circumstances along the Niagara Frontier.

Fig. 11.4 shows the rubber sheeting of the archaeological sites to the prehistoric trade routes in Western New York. The trade routes are based upon canoe travel and a series of well-known portages which make an interconnected network. These are documented by sites, historical accounts, and the modern usage (Stites 1905). One may begin to define an ideal trade system based upon preliminary concepts of value, supply and demand, difficulty of travel, utility, and other issues, such as the strategic importance of portages. These are drawn from the Jesuit Relations and other historical sources. Having defined this complex 'economic space', it is possible to ask how much spatial adjustment would be necessary to the real location of archaeological sites in order to create this economic space. The rubber sheeting shows very little movement or distortion toward the trade routes. The implication is that the settlements are 'well positioned' in relation to the factors of trade. In this case, the visual depiction of the movement is the small link lines which show the necessary movement from the real location of archaeological sites to their ideal locations if trade was a paramount concern for the predecessors of the Iroquois. The 'figure' in this case is the site locations, while the trade routes are part of the 'ground' to which they are being referenced. The analysis makes critical use of rules of contingency for supply and demand, inclusion for amounts of goods and distribution of demand, as well as several other rules in lesser roles.

The next two analyses represent a very different approach to the same issue. Let us assume that there are particular thematic patterns which are central to pre-Iroquoian and, for that matter, Iroquoian culture. We know that the quadrilateral patterns of the roman legions are found recapitulated in the settlement patterns of their military camps throughout the Roman Empire. Eventually they were incorporated into the street patterns of many European cities.

In Iroquoian culture one might look to ceramics or a variety of valuables, and to aspects of material character, for themes to be recapitulated in settlement patterns. There was an Iroquoian custom that all important statements should be accompanied by a gift which was indicative of its value. One of these indices of value was the giving of wampum (Speck 1945; Tooker 1978a). The Onondaga tribe, central to the Confederacy, became the 'Keeper of the Wampum' as well as 'Keepers of the Fire' (Tooker 1978a; Blau *et al.* 1978; Bradley 1987). Wampum was made from a group of marine shells which included numerous varieties. There was white wampum made from whelk, as well as the more valuable black wampum from quahog clam. Wampum was given with treaties, as wergild (ten belts for the death of a man, twenty for a woman) and was even used as a form of currency in trade with the Europeans; even the name Hiawatha (Ayonhwathah) has been derived from 'seeker of the Wampum" (Tooker 1978a). Generalizing various specific patterns from numerous belts, one may ask whether it is recapitulated in settlement patterns. Fig. 11.5 shows that this is not the case.

Having created a thematic space based upon a generalized set of patterns found in wampum-belts, and then having asked the question to what extent does the underlying structure of the settlement pattern correspond, the answer is

Fig. 11.4. The application of the 'ideal' trade pattern based upon economic considerations to the 'real' settlement pattern

there is little correspondence in the database. The 'figure' is the geometric pattern and the 'ground' is the distribution of settlements across the landscape. The rules used were *inclusion, bisection, contiguity, orientation* and *equality*, but not *contingency* nor *temporality*.

The graphic depiction is presented in a different form from the economic trade routes. If there was perfect correspondence and no adjustments of the sites were necessary, there would be a flat fishnet surface. Instead, one sees a considerably folded surface. This represents a lack of congruence between ideal theme and reality. The greater the number of folds, the less the congruence. The results are not surprising, for a careful archaeological analysis shows few wampum-belts prior to European settlement. In fact, most are found in historic archaeological sites. Only occasionally do they date as early as the sixteenth century. Therefore, the wampum thematic pattern may not predate the earliest contact.

Next, one examines the thematic character of the longhouse. Longhouses are central to Iroquoian culture. Even today various Iroquois groups call themselves the 'People of the Longhouse'.[1] They are found frequently in pre-contact sites dating back to the Woodland period (Tuck 1971). Longhouses were typically 'multi-family' and 'extended family' homes. They had secular, religious and symbolic status. Although described by Lalemant as a miniature picture of

hell, they did signify status. There were longhouses for principal civil and war chiefs.

Historically, the longhouse has been geographically recreated in tribal geography (Tooker 1978a) and conversely, tribal geography has been recreated in the longhouse (Tooker 1978b). Taking the tribal geography first, one imagines a longhouse oriented east to west through New York State. In this great longhouse, the Seneca are the Keepers of the Western Door (Abler 1978), the Onondaga the Keepers of the Central Fire (Blau *et al.* 1978), and the Mohawk the Keepers of the Eastern Door (Fenton and Tooker 1978). These are the names by which they were known historically and amongst themselves.

Even recently, the Code of Handsome Lake was being practised through the 'Six Nations Meetings'. The Tonawanda longhouse sends announcements to the other tribal longhouses, and when the chiefs gather at the 'Six Nations Meetings' they sit in the longhouse according to rules of tribal location, clan and gender. The longhouse seating thus recreates tribal geographic location. The code is recited and then the ceremony is repeated with variation through a biennial circuit of longhouses which are themselves located in the shape of a longhouse. Thus, the Code of Handsome Lake is insured to be repeated throughout the six nations, in each longhouse every two years (Tooker 1978b).

Fig. 11.6 shows the same analytical approach, as was used in the wampum belt study, to a thematic use of the longhouse pattern in prehistoric Western New York. It shows the pattern as being determinate of the settlement pattern of Western New York. The ideal is the 'western part of a large longhouse' with the settlements being the analogues of post-holes or storage pits.

The longhouse pattern is the figure, the marked category both spatially and artefactually. The ground is again the spatial distribution of sites. The rules used were *contiguity, orientation* and *equality*, but not *inclusion, bisection, contingency* or *temporality*.

The second analysis is shown in Fig. 11.7. It uses the entire longhouse as a thematic template for the settlement pattern. Both of these are far better than geometric patterns of the wampum belt. This is visually indicated by the larger 'flat' non-distorted spaces around the sites.

Conclusions

This paper has attempted to meet several goals. First, it demonstrates how cognitive archaeology may be both realist and non-realist. The concepts of knowledge representation and the methodology of Geographic Information Systems may be applied to the cognitive 'wars'. It allows for the

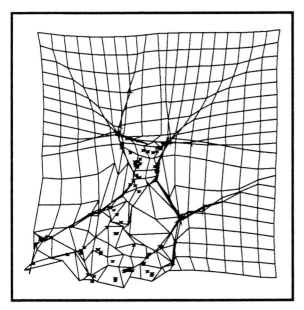

Fig. 11.5. The application of the 'ideal' wampum pattern to the 'real' settlement pattern

formal use of both 'ideals' and 'reals' in a single, analytical structure. Both ideals and reals can be complex data structures which present a model of the knowledge representation of the 'native'. One of its strengths is that one may apply the same algorithms to both the ideal and real, and compare the results as expressed in geographic patterns.

Second, it has provided a standard methodology to handle large amounts of complex data with both spatial and temporal parameters. Although only one example is included here, two more have been completed – one in Mesoamerica and one in Scandinavia (Zubrow and Olsen).

Third, it has provided us with substantive results which are both heuristically useful and can be more accurately refined. In the Northeast, trade patterns were determining site location at the expense of the ideal of regular spacing. Thematically, the geometric designs of the wampum belt are not recapitulated spatially, while the longhouse is recapitulated both in terms of tribal geography, historic and, as now demonstrated, prehistoric site distribution.

Fourth, unlike simply interpretative analyses, there are

better and worse answers. One may demonstrate the lack of fit. There are critical tests. There are negative results.

In short, settlement patterns are complex results of numerous cultural ideals, economic experience and topographic reality. In order to develop a robust understanding, the archaeologist needs robust tools such as knowledge representation and geographic information analysis. 'As *Homo*'s peculiar cognitive capacities are surely the genus' distinguishing characteristic, so it would seem proper to focus upon the cognitive basis of human life.' (Kehoe and Kehoe 1973: 150)

Acknowledgement

Some of the data for this paper were collected by Eleazar Hunt who is gratefully acknowledged for his contribution.

Note

1 Akwesasne notes. Mohawk Nation at Akwesasne near Hogansburg, NY Bimonthly Official publication of the Mohawk Nation at Akwesasne (People of the Longhouse) and contains (from time to time) Longhouse news, the official publication of the Mohawk Nation at Kanawake.

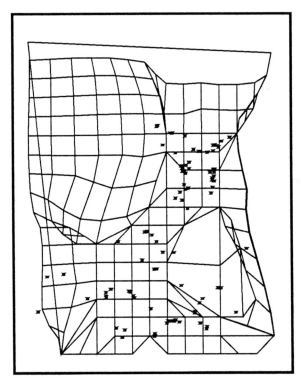

Fig. 11.6. The application of the 'ideal' partial longhouse pattern to the 'real' settlement pattern

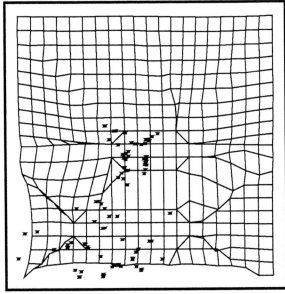

Fig. 11.7. The application of the 'ideal' complete longhouse pattern to the 'real' settlement pattern

References

Abler, T. S. 1978. The Seneca. In *Handbook of North American indians*, vol. XV, ed. B. G. Trigger, pp. 505–17. Washington, Smithsonian Institution

Allen, K. 1990. Modelling early historic trade in the eastern Great Lakes using Geographic Information Systems. In *Interpreting space: GIS and archaeology*, ed. K. Allen, S. Green and E. Zubrow, pp. 319–29. London, Taylor and Francis

Bennett, D. C. 1975. *Spatial and temporal uses of English prepositions: an essay in stratificational semantics.* London, Longman

Binford, L. 1989. *Debating archaeology.* San Diego, Academic Press

Binford, S. R. and L. R. Binford (eds.) 1968. *New perspectives in archaeology.* Chicago, Aldine

Blau, H., J. Campisi and E. Tooker 1978. Onondaga. In *Handbook of North American indians*, vol. XV: Northeast, ed. B. G. Trigger, pp. 418–41. Washington, Smithsonian Institution

Bradley, J. W. 1987. *Evolution of the Onondaga Iroquois.* New York, Syracuse University Press

Buerger, P. 1992. Iroquois prehistory on the Niagara Frontier: the Martin site. Unpublished MA thesis, University at Buffalo

Clarke, D. L. 1968. *Analytical archaeology.* London, Methuen

Conkey, M. W. and C. A. Hastorf 1990. *The uses of style in archaeology.* Cambridge, Cambridge University Press

Date, C. J. 1986. *An introduction to database systems*, vol. I (4th edn). Reading, MA, Addison-Wesley

Dunnell, R. C. 1971. *Systematics in prehistory.* New York, Free Press

Fenton, W. and E. Tooker 1978. The Mohawk. In *Handbook of North American indians*, vol. XV: Northeast, ed. B. G. Trigger, pp. 466–80. Washington, Smithsonian Institution

Foucault, M. 1972. *The archaeology of knowledge.* London, Tavistock

Hempel, C. G. 1965. *Aspects of scientific explanation, and other essays in the philosophy of science.* New York, Free Press

Hodder, I. (ed.) 1987. *The archaeology of contextual meanings.* Cambridge, Cambridge University Press
1989. *The meaning of things: material culture and symbolic expression.* One World Archaeology, vol. 6. London, Unwin Hyman

Joao, E. M. 1991. The role of the user in generalization within Geographic Information Systems. In *Cognitive and linguistic aspects of geographic space*, ed. D. M. Mark and A. U. Frank. Nato Asi Series D. Behavioural and Social Sciences, vol. 63. Dordrecht, Netherlands, Kluwer Academic Publishers

Justeson, J. 1973. Limitations of archaeological inference: an information-theoretic approach with applications in methodology. *American Antiquity* 38 (2): 131–50

Kehoe, A. B. and T. F. Kehoe 1973. Cognitive models for archaeological interpretation. *American Antiquity* 38 (2): 150-4

Kramer, S. N. 1967. *The Sumerians: their history, culture and character.* Chicago, University of Chicago Press

Lakoff, G. 1987. *Women, fire and dangerous things: what categories reveal about the mind.* Chicago, University of Chicago Press

Maki, U. 1992. Truth and reality in the postmodern age. 4th Nordic TAG Conference, 4–7 September 1992, Helsinki, Finland

Mellars, P. 1991. Cognitive changes and the emergence of modern humans. *Cambridge Archaeological Journal* 1: 63–76

Peebles, C. S. and J.-C. Gardin (eds.) 1992. *Representations in archaeology.* Bloomington and Indianapolis, Indiana University Press

Renfrew, C. and P. Bahn 1991. *Archaeology: theories, methods and practice.* London, Thames and Hudson

Shanks, M. 1992. *Experiencing the past: on the character of archaeology.* London, Routledge

Shanks, M. and C. Tilley 1987. *Re-constructing archaeology: theory and practice.* Cambridge, Cambridge University Press

Spaulding, A. C. 1962. *Archaeological investigations on Agattu, Aleutian Islands.* Museum of Anthropology, University of Michigan. Anthropological papers no. 18. Ann Arbor, University of Michigan

Speck, F. C. 1945. *The Iroquois: a study in cultural evolution.* Bloomfield Hills, Mich, Cranbrook Institute of Science

Stites, S. H. 1905. *Economics of the Iroquois.* Lancaster, PA, New Era Print Co.

Talmy, L. 1978. Figure and ground in complex sentences. In *Universals of human language: syntax*, vol. IV, ed. J. H. Greenberg, pp. 625–49. Stanford, Stanford University Press

Taylor, W. W. 1967. *A study of archeology.* Carbondale, Southern Illinois University Press

Tilley, C. (ed.) 1990. *Reading material culture: structuralism, hermeneutics and post-structuralism.* Oxford, Blackwell

Thwaites, R. G. (ed.) 1954. *The Jesuit Relations and allied documents: travels and explorations of the Jesuit missionaries in North America 1610–1791*. New York, Vanguard Press

Tooker, E. 1978a. The League of the Iroquois: its history, politics, and ritual. In *Handbook of North American Indians*, vol. XV: Northeast, ed. B. G. Trigger, pp. 418–41. Washington, Smithsonian Institution
   1978b. Iroquois since 1820. In *Handbook of North American Indians*, vol. XV: Northeast, ed. B. G. Trigger, pp. 453–9. Washington, Smithsonian Institution

Tuck, J. A. 1971. *Onondaga Iroquois prehistory*. New York, Syracuse University Press

Watson, P. J., S. A. LeBlanc and C. L. Redman 1971. *Explanation in archeology: an explicitly scientific approach*. New York, Columbia University Press

White, M. E. 1961. *Iroquois culture history in the Niagara Frontier area of New York State*. Ann Arbor, University of Michigan

Zubrow, E. 1989. Commentary: common knowledge and archaeology. In *Critical traditions in contemporary archaeology*, ed. A. Wylie and V. Pinsky, pp. 44–9. Cambridge, Cambridge University Press

Zubrow, E. and P. Buerger, in preparation. *The Martin Site: two millennia of prehistory on the Niagara Frontier*

Zubrow, E. and I.-M. Holm Olsen 1991. Ideal settlement pattern, topographic and cultural reality: cognitive models and GIS. Paper presented at GIS in the Social Sciences Santa Barbara, California 1991

12
Dials: a study in the physical representation of cognitive systems

CHARLES O. FRAKE

Archaeologists, when reading this chapter, will appreciate that I share with them a peculiar fondness for fine detail even though the details, in this case, do not pertain to material that is 'archaeological' in the usual sense. The central issue raised by these details is, however, a critical one that archaeologists share with all students of the activities of our species: how can one use the perceptible human-produced events and objects of the phenomenal world to make inferences about the non-perceptible abilities, meanings, ideas and intentions in the minds of those who produced and used them? Archaeologists typically must face this problem with severely incomplete data, but the problem is, in essence, the same one faced by all other investigators of human culture. It is, in fact, the same problem faced by all human beings in their daily interactions with their fellows. No one has magic access to the mind of others. We do not even have particularly good access to the cognitive processes of our own minds. All anyone – investigator or native – has are artefacts of cognition. Of course there are artefacts of different kinds – a written text is a different kind of artefact from a stone tool; the sound-waves generated by a conversation with a live human being are different again. But none is an open window to the human mind. The trick is to bring as many kinds of data to bear as possible while keeping in mind the weaknesses imposed by the kinds of data that are not available. One must know the nature of one's particular incompleteness. Even in the most favourable of circumstances, the data for reading the minds of others will always remain incomplete. For that reason, instead of simply contrasting, as kinds of data, things like stone tools, pictures, texts and conversations, it is more revealing to differentiate artefacts of human cognition according to how

they reflect or represent the content and workings of the mind.

Anything made or done by a human being reflects the mental processes that lie behind its production and use. Some artefacts not only thus *reflect* cognition but also intentionally *represent* mental content. They have meaning; they are intended to be read. For the archaeologist to uncover the reading may be impossible. Yet simply to understand how representations come to have readings, and how their form relates to cognitive processes, should add to the value of the archaeologist's interpretations. This paper concerns problems that arise in the interpretations of some relatively simple examples of physical representations belonging to a type which, in contrast to verbal *descriptions*, can be called *depictions*.

Dials

Dial [Presumably derivative of L. *dies* a day, through a med. L. adj. *dial-is* daily. Outside Eng., however, *dial* is known only from a single OF. instance in Froissart, in which the *dyal* in clockwork is said to be 'the daily wheel (*roe journal*) which makes a revolution once in a day, even as the sun makes a single turn round the earth in a natural day'. This would answer to a med. L. *rota dialis*; the transition from 'diurnal wheel' to 'diurnal circle' is easy. But more evidence is wanted.] Oxford English Dictionary

Depictions of the type displayed in Fig. 12.1 have had a venerable history in the Western tradition since ancient and early medieval times. They have served as more than decorations or emblems, although they have seen use in those roles as well. Their basic function has been an instrumental one of representing mental schemata, cognitive maps, for orientation and measurement. Circular representations of this type belong to a general class of depictions for which the peculiarly English word *dial* provides a convenient label. Dials are essentially schemes for dividing the circle. The western world has employed three major distinct dial systems. The hand of a clock dial moves around a circle. Time is marked by its position along that circle. The needle of a compass does the same thing, but its position marks direction. The pointer of an astrolabe or quadrant or modern sextant also intersects a circle, this time to mark a distance, the length of an arc corresponding to the angular altitude of an object. But to tell time, label a direction, or read an altitude, requires a way of demarcating and naming those positions. The circle must be segmented and the segments must be linguistically identifiable. Different dials have come to be associated with each of these goals of displaying time, direction, and distance. There is the *degree dial* of 360 primary divisions associated with the measurement of arc and, in medieval times, with the astrolabe. There is the *hour dial* of twelve primary divisions associated with time reckoning and the clock. And, finally, there is the *point dial* of eight primary divisions associated with direction finding and the compass. As various as the way dials are calibrated are the ways in which the resulting units are represented linguistically by numbers and by names. This differentiation of dials by manner of segmentation and mode of nomenclature is more a product of the separation of cultural practices than it is the outcome of different technical objectives. The measure of angular distance, time, or direction, each can be, and, in fact, has been, served by any one of the dial schemes. The calibration of none of the dials has a compelling practical motivation and none is what one might expect from a cultural tradition of decimal numeration.

Of the three dial systems, the degree dial has long had the closest association with the great minds of the scholarly world; yet the rationale and inherent utility of its 360 primary divisions are obscure. The dial's origins go back to the sexagesimal (base 60) mathematics of the ancient Near East. It has survived, as the primary system of dividing the circle, among scientists down to the present, amalgamating with, but never completely yielding to, the decimal mathematics of later scientific eras. The result is the expression of an angle by a modern astronomer as 130° 17' 20.832". The nautical almanac presents this same angle to navigators as 130° 17.35'. My modern scientific calculator refuses to deal with this angle until I convert it into a straight decimal equivalent of 130.28912°.[1] The great scholar of ancient exact sciences, Otto Neugebauer (1969: 17), comments: 'It is interesting to see that it took about 2000 years of migration of astronomical knowledge from Mesopotamia via Greeks, Hindus, and Arabs to arrive at a truly absurd numerical system.' Apart from these absurdities of the numerical system, there are fundamental practical problems with the number 360. It is a rather fine division of units for everyday use, even at sea. Although my own sailing experience has been exclusively with modern degree-marked compasses, I could still, once oriented, point right away to west northwest. I would have to think a while before I could show you the direction of 292°. Even for scientists, who require such fine divisions, the number 360 has presented problems. It is difficult geometrically to divide a circle into 360 equal units. An instrument maker can get down to 45° by bisection, but after that the task becomes troublesome. Even as late as 1758, the giant quadrant set up at the Royal Observatory in Greenwich was inscribed with 96 rather than 90 divisions so that the scale could be constructed more accurately by bisection. A 90° scale was then marked alongside it but, to ensure precision, the user consulted a table of conversion from 96 division to 90 division readings.[2] In the Middle Ages, the task of accurately inscribing instruments with degree scales must have been even more difficult. Yet no alternative appears in any medieval manuscript diagram or on any instrument for astronomical calculation. Regardless of the difficulties, the degree system was firmly entrenched. The unnecessary complexities of the degree system may, paradoxically, have something to do with its popularity among scholars through the millennia. Because of the difficulty for ordinary minds in handling large numbers, here compounded by the mix of different numerical bases, the very numerateness of the system lends to it symbolic value, an expression of extra-ordinary erudition and mental ability. Through the millennia, science has been elaborating its symbols of prestige in society along with adding to its stock of findings about nature. There are few, if any, physical representations of knowledge whose function is purely the instrumental one of aiding in the use of that knowledge. There is always an element of social display in their use. A consideration of the hour and point dials will strongly reinforce this conclusion.

The hour dial and the point dial are simpler in construction. Both dial schemes first divide the circle into equal and equivalent quadrants. Each then subdivides the quadrant differently. The hour dial divides each quadrant of the circle into thirds, yielding twelve primary segments. These, in turn, may be subdivided to yield a dial of twenty-four segments such as Chaucer's Astrolabe dial (which also had a 360° scheme), some medieval 'scratch dials' (crude sundials inscribed on church walls), and some early clock dials. In ancient times, in so far as records can tell us, the twelve-division dial was the primary schema of both time and direction in both the West and the Far East. In Medieval Europe it was the basis for most systems of reckoning time of day, both scholarly and everyday. The twelve-division dial not only represented the twelve hours of day and of night but also the twelve primary 'winds' of the ancient system of directions. This ancient directional system persisted in scholarly writings throughout the medieval period.[3] There is, however, no evidence, in Europe, of the practical use of the twelve direction system for finding one's way either on land or at sea.[4] In the Far East, on the other hand, it seems to be the only system which has been recorded. Chinese and Japanese compasses appear always to have had twelve primary points. A revealing modern use of the hour dial for directions is that of pilots naming directions relative to an aircraft: 'twelve o'clock high', 'three o'clock low'. This usage, of course, employs a purely mental image of the dial. It is not dependent on having a clock face in front of one. The practice, made famous in the spotting of hostile fighters by

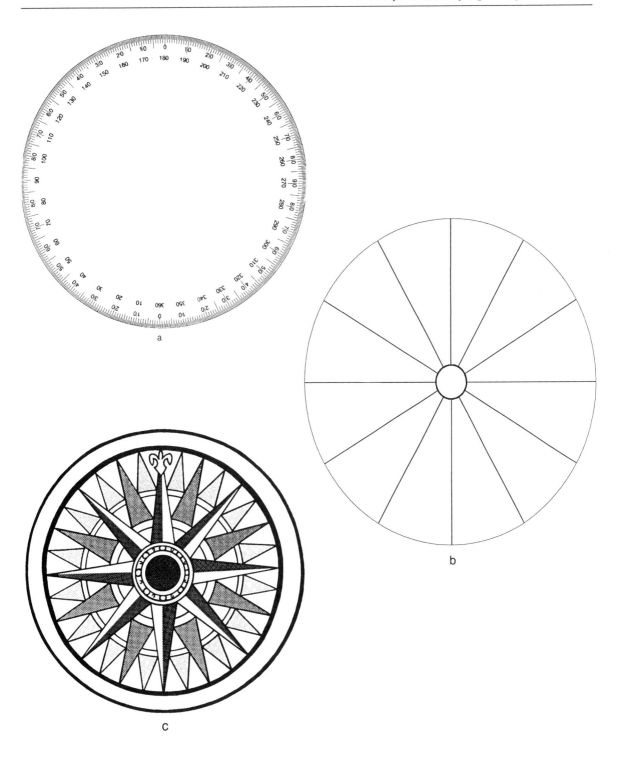

Fig. 12.1. Dials: a. the Degree dial, b. the Hour dial, c. the Point dial

bomber crews in war movies, is one fitted to the need for a quick and easy way to name directions relative to one's own aircraft. These were not situations for a display of calculatory prowess: 'Quick, get that Messerschmidt coming in at 234° 15', 37° below!'

The primary use, since ancient times, of twelve and twenty-four division dials has been to represent the division of the days into hours. A variety of duodecimal schemes for counting the hours all have ancient roots: systems of twelve divisions each of day and night, regardless of the length of each, systems of 24 equal divisions beginning at sunset or sunrise, and systems of 24 equal divisions beginning at a fixed mid-point, either noon or midnight. This last system came to prevail (but did not originate) with the spread of clocks in the fourteenth and fifteenth centuries, but dial representations of time of day on sundials, astrolabes and in manuscripts long precedes clock dials. Early clocks, in fact, typically lacked dials. They were automated bell ringers signalling the day's divisions in an auditory representation. In the Middle Ages, throughout Europe, the latin number words, *prima*, *tertia*, *sexta* and *nona* for the first, third, sixth and ninth bell-rung canonical hours after sunrise had, in ordinary usage, become names for a time of day rather than a count of hours since sunrise. Thus *nona*, literally the ninth hour, had come in many places and situations, to label the sixth hour of midday, hence the English 'noon'.[5] Clocks, the world's first information processing machines, were, like their modern successors, the computers, a force for digitalization. Numbers replaced names as everyday labels for time of day.[6]

The numbering of divisions now associated with the hour dial, while easier for the mind to handle readily than the 360 divisions of the degree dial, shares with the degree dial the awkward notational system of both decimal and sexagesimal units, an awkwardness augmented by the use of the same terms, minutes and seconds, for sexagesimal divisions in each. Keeping the distinctions straight while converting between minutes of time and minutes of arc is one of modern navigation's minor irritations. The tenacity of both the degree and hour dials, in face of these shared irritations, must, in large part, derive from how well they dovetail together numerically. An hour of time is 15° of arc; one degree of arc is four minutes of time. In calculations, such as those performed by the astrolabe, that convert between measures of time and of space, this dovetailing is a critical advantage. Tying in nicely with both dials was the zodiacal reference system of medieval astronomy. This system gave a way of referring to celestial positions that reduced the numerateness of the 360° circle, when mapped on to the path of the sun, by dividing that path into twelve *named* 'signs', each containing 30°. An hour was half a sign. Once one has

an image of the ecliptic as a band of twelve ordered named signs, it is much easier to keep in mind where the sun is when it is 9° in Libra than to visualize its position when it has an ecliptic longitude of 189°. Medieval astronomers, as well as poets like Dante and Chaucer, made much use of this handy system of numbered degrees in a named sign to locate celestial bodies in the sky, sometimes conveying to modern readers a misleading impression of 'astrological' import.

The point dial stands apart from the other Western dial schemes in its complete lack of scholarly credentials. Its origins as a conceptual image are unheralded, and its use is only hinted at through most of medieval history. It provides, however, a reasonable and practical way to cut up a circle. It bisects each quadrant yielding eight points (the 'full' points of the Mediterranean point dial), then bisects these segments to yield eight additional 'half points'. One further bisection produces sixteen additional 'quarter points', to complete the thirty-two point dial. This successive bisection of segments of a circle would seem to be the simplest and most reasonable of the dial schemes. Among seafarers, and others outside the scholarly world, eight, sixteen, and thirty-two point dials have provided the basic directional schema in the western world from, at least, medieval times through the nineteenth century.[7] A thirty-two-division image of directions has also long been used, in a method reminiscent of the airman's '12 o'clock high' system, to name bearings from the perspective of one's ship.[8] Finally, as we shall see, the point dial provided a schema for naming and calculating time.

To illustrate how the form and uses of depictions such as dials can inform their interpretation as representations of cognitive systems, we turn now to some details in the story of the point dial. We begin with the European tradition and then bring in some revealing analogues employed by seafarers in the Pacific and Indian Oceans.

The rose of the winds

> now is thy Horizon departed in twenty-four parts by thy azymutz . . . all be it so that shipmen reckon these parts in 32. Chaucer, *Treatise on the Astrolabe*, 21 (Skeat 1872)

Since ancient times, systems of direction in Europe have been known as 'winds'. 'Rose of the winds' became the label for the, often elaborate, depictions of the point dial on early charts. The divisions of the European point dial, instead of being counted, have always borne names. The names came from the winds, a seemingly ephemeral and shifting phenomenon upon which to base a directional system. There were eight principal or 'full winds'. Their medieval names throughout the Mediterranean, as recorded in pilot books and on charts, were as follows:

N: *tramontana* 'across the mountains'
NE: *greco* '(from) Greece'
E: *levante* 'sunrise'
SE: *scirocco, sciloccho* (Catalan *lexaloch*) 'a southeast wind'
S: *mezzodi, mexjorno* (Catalan *metzodi*) 'midday' or *ostro* from latin *auster* 'south', the only form deriving from a latin direction word
SW: *libeccio* (Catalan *labetzo*) '(from) Libia' (Greek *Libs*) or *garbino* from the Arabic for 'west', i.e. north-western Africa
W: *ponente* 'sunset'
NW: *maestro* (Catalan *magistro*) 'master (wind)', 'mistral'

These eight 'full winds' were divided into 'half winds' and 'quarter winds' giving a total of thirty-two. From the late thirteenth century, charts of the Mediterranean were constructed on a network of bearing lines radiating out from thirty-two point directional roses.[9]

The use of the same words to name directions and winds has been a source of some confusion, not to medieval sailors, but to contemporary commentators. For a sailor to name directions for 'winds' is not at all surprising. For a modern scholar to interpret this naming practice as a discovery procedure used by medieval sailors to determine their direction is an error of misattributed concreteness. It would imply that, if no wind were blowing, the sailor would be completely disoriented. In fact, even if the given wind is blowing, its direction does not determine, at that moment, the direction named after it. If, at a particular time in some location, the mistral were blowing from the Northeast, this would not in any way alter the direction of *maestro*. Far from using the winds to determine direction, in most sailing situations, it is, in fact, the direction of the wind that the sailor is trying to discover. To do so, he must have some means other than the wind for finding direction.

The geographic meanings of the Mediterranean terms would seem to point to a southern Italian or Sicilian origin of the terminology. They thereby suggest an origin independent of, and well prior to, the composition of known early pilot books and charts, which are of northern Italian and Catalan origin. But again, the geographic meanings, whatever they may suggest about origins, had nothing to do with the definitions of the directions. The direction of *greco* remained northeast wherever, throughout the Mediterranean, one was sailing. It remained northeast on Italian galleys navigating the English Channel: '*porlan e las agujas se varda quarta de leuante al greigo*' 'from Portland to the Needles, one heads a quarter from *levante* (east) to *greco* (northeast) (E by N)'

(Kretschmer 1909). 'Wind' was essentially the medieval Mediterranean equivalent of 'direction at sea'.

What marked off Medieval European seafaring from navigation in other parts of the world were not its superior accomplishments, which were matched and even excelled elsewhere, but rather the presence in the Mediterranean of physical representations of the directional scheme, representations in writing in pilot books, in diagrams on charts, and embodied in a navigational instrument, the compass. All of these were present in the Mediterranean by the thirteenth century. Maritime historians have assumed that the division in thirty-two points, already evident in thirteenth-century charts and mentioned, as we have seen, by Chaucer in his treatise on the astrolabe, is evidence for the use of the compass. How could sailors make such fine directional distinctions without a precision instrument to guide them? That is a stock rhetorical question posed by European maritime historians.[10] Yet, if we turn our attention to another seafaring tradition on the other side of the world, the possibility emerges that the question is not after all rhetorical. It requires serious consideration.

The star compass

> The captain recalls his sea lore,
> Remembers the guiding star for Ifaluk;
> When one is down, another rises.
> He remembers those stars
> Deep within him,
> Stars by which he can steer,
> And grows impatient to be on his way.
>
>   A Micronesian song (Brower 1984: 124)

About 4,000 years ago, islanders in Melanesia in the Western Pacific began embarking on longer and longer voyages of exploration and settlement. By 1000 BC they had reached and settled Fiji, Tonga and Samoa in the central South Pacific and were pushing into the Micronesian Islands to the North. Before the beginning of the Christian era, the Polynesian islands of the Marquesas, some 3,000 sailing miles upwind of Samoa, had been reached. By AD 600 each inhabitable island of the south and central Pacific had been discovered and settled – including New Zealand to the South and Hawaii to the North. Keep in mind that the islands of the Hawaiian chain, relatively conspicuous when compared to the atolls of Micronesia, were not discovered by Europeans until Cook's voyage at the end of the eighteenth century. Yet for almost 300 years before that, the Spanish had been voyaging back and forth across the Pacific between Mexico and the Philippines. Magellan traversed the whole Pacific from the tip of South America; he never sighted any land until he reached the Marianas, just east of the Philippines. Not only had Pacific islanders discovered and settled all the suitable islands of the Pacific, but there is solid linguistic, ethnobotanical, and archaeological evidence that they made two-way voyages among them. They sailed, for example, between Tahiti and Hawaii and back again, a distance over three thousand miles of open sea. All this was done by stone age people without writing, charts, or navigational instruments of any kind. In spite of a long series of fanciful theories of lost continents, primitive navigational instincts, and accidental drift voyages, we now know the secret of what made Pacific Island voyaging possible. The secret was knowledge. The navigational abilities of Pacific Islanders depended on a profound general knowledge of the sea, the sky and the wind; on a superb understanding of the principles of boat-building and sailing; and on cognitive devices – all in the head – for recording and processing vast quantities of ever changing information. In most of the Pacific this knowledge was lost during the early periods of European contact, but among the tiny coral islands of Micronesia, long distance voyaging still survives. Studies made by German maritime anthropologists at the turn of the century, as well as more recent investigations, have given us some idea of the shape, extent, and workings of this knowledge.[11]

The question always asked about Pacific voyaging is: how did the navigators find directions on the open sea? The islanders had a variety of ways for finding directions – sea swells, bird flights, winds, and stars – but the directions they found were referenced to a directional system that appealed to the heavens for its rationale and nomenclature. This is the system known in the literature as the 'star compass'.[12] Directions around the circle of the horizon are named for the rising and setting points of selected navigational stars. The resulting schema has thirty-two named directional points. Sailing directions for voyages among the distantly spaced tiny Micronesian islands are expressed as star bearings both between departure and destination islands, and to and from reference islands (*etak*) beyond the line of sight. The trainee navigator must memorize, among many other things, the complete network of star courses to and from all the islands of his universe. He must also learn, by practical experience, how to find directions and keep oriented according to this thirty-two point directional system without the aid, not only of any instruments, but also of any physical depiction of the system. In the Pacific, a thirty-two point directional system was developed and used at sea without a magnetic compass. There is therefore no reason inherent in the nature of the task to assume that the European thirty-two point 'Rose of the Winds' could only have appeared after the development of the mariner's compass.

There would, however, appear to be a critical difference between the Pacific and European directional schemes. The thirty-two points of the Pacific 'star compass', as we conventionally understand it, are not generated by successive bisections of the horizon circle. They are, we are told, marked by the unequally spaced rising and setting positions of navigational stars. This apparent difference suggests that we take another look at the Pacific.

To think of directions as 'winds', as in the European system, is to construe them as straight lines running (or blowing) from where one has come, toward where one is going. Thus a Scirocco wind comes from the southeast and blows toward Maestro, the northwest. If one is sailing on a Maestro course then the direction Scirocco is directly to one's stern. Each direction, each full, half, and quarter wind, has its reciprocal. The representation of the directions as a 'rose' of intersecting lines visually portrays this construal of navigational bearings. There are good practical reasons for sailing directions to be so paired by reciprocals. To follow a direction, whether toward a final destination or on a tack, the vessel, which always remains at the centre of the horizon circle, must lie on a straight line marked by *two* points on the horizon and passing through the centre of the circle. These two points are directional reciprocals. When one sails on a given course, say NNE, it is the reciprocal bearing, in this case SSW, that makes the course a straight line along which the boat is moving. When one turns around to sail home, it is toward the reciprocal bearing that one heads. But Pacific Islanders are reputed to think about directions in another way. The Pacific system, like the Western one, divides the circle of the horizon into thirty-two points, but these are not – at least as the system is currently understood – based on successive segmentations of the circle, but on the intersections of the parallel paths of select navigational stars with the horizon. The segments of the horizon are not equally spaced, there being finer divisions in the east–west axis than in the north–south one. The number of segments seems to be purely arbitrary and only coincidentally the same as the European compass rose. Directions are named as the rising or setting of the star that gives its name to the path. If one were sailing toward the direction named 'Vega Rising', and if one takes that direction to lie where Vega in fact rises at Micronesian latitudes, i.e. 50°, then there is no named direction at the reciprocal bearing of 230°. The closest is Shaula (*lambda Scorpii*) at 238°. Not only do reciprocal courses not have the same name at either end, but, because the segmentation of the horizon is not equal, there will not even be a named compass point in the opposite direction of one's current course. An additional difficulty becomes apparent when one realizes that one can never, at any nighttime moment, use the positions of then visible navigational stars, *or their substitutes*, as a practical instrument to calibrate the horizon precisely at each of the thirty-two points required by the conventional model. A little time playing with a planetary program on a computer will easily demonstrate this difficulty. These conclusions assume we have interpreted the Pacific system correctly. One must keep in mind the possibility that investigators have committed, here, the same error of misplaced concreteness that so often distorts our views of the mental schemes of other peoples.

A hint that this might be so, occurred in a revealing episode recorded in the film of the famous 1976 voyage of *Hokule'a*, the reconstructed Polynesian double canoe, from Hawaii to Tahiti. Piailug, the great Micronesian navigator is trying to point out to a Western investigator the bearings of the distinct swells he is using as directional indicators. One is coming from the direction *mailap* 'Altair Rising'. 'That's East', he explains in English. He is corrected by the Western investigator: 'Yes, well it's really a bit North of East.' 'It's

East', the navigator mumbles and turns again to consider the sea.[13] We should at least consider the possibility that Piailug, who successfully steered the Hokule'a across 3,000 miles of open ocean, in latitudes completely new to him, without the aid of any instruments, charts, or written material of any kind, knew what he was walking about.[14] At local latitudes Altair rises 9° north of east and sets 9° north of west. Yet Micronesian navigators always insist that the direction named for the path Altair is 'East–West', that is, it divides the horizon midway between North and South. Investigators have generally assumed that these simple islanders, who discovered and settled all the inhabitable islands of the entire Pacific well before the period of European long distance voyaging, were just wrong. I have my doubts.

Consider the displays of their directional system used by Micronesian navigators themselves when teaching novices. An eight-rayed octagon is laid out on a mat with sticks. Eight

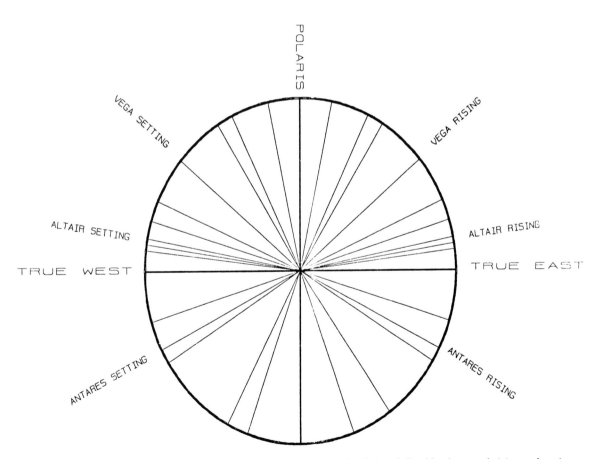

Fig. 12.2. The Micronesian 'Star Compass' with directions interpreted as being defined by the actual rising and setting points of the navigational stars that name them.

large coral stones are placed on the end of each ray, and then equally spaced between each of these are three smaller stones. The mid-stone is placed at each corner of the octagon, the large stones at the centre of each octagon side. This construction not only yields thirty-two equally spaced points, but the eight main points are visually distinguished from the eight subsidiary points and the sixteen final points (Thomas 1987: 83; Low 1983; Goodenough and Thomas 1990). The construction is essentially identical to the European wind rose with its full, half, and quarter winds visually distinguished! In this system Vega rising does have a reciprocal. It is not Shaula, the closest in actual setting position, but the more conspicuous Antares which sets at 240°. As directional names 'Vega Rising' and 'Antares setting' correspond precisely to our NE–SW as bisections of horizon quadrants. These pairs of reciprocals are explicitly taught as part of navigation training: 'Piailug learned his

next two lessons on the mat as well . . . In the second lesson, *aroom*, Raangipi pointed to each star in the circle and asked Piailug to name that star and its reciprocal or "partner" star, thus inculcating the reciprocal relationship between the star points – critical knowledge at sea' (Thomas 1987: 28). Goodenough and Thomas (1990: 3) note that, in Micronesian navigation, 'The diametrically opposite points of this compass are seen as connecting in straight lines through a central point. A navigator thinks of himself or of any place from which he is determining directions as at this central point. Thus, whatever compass point he faces, there is a reciprocal point at his back.' If this is the case, then the actual rising and setting positions of the stars cannot mark the directions which the stars name. My argument is that the stars provide the names, not the positions, for abstract conceptual segmentations of the horizon circle into thirty-two equally spaced points.

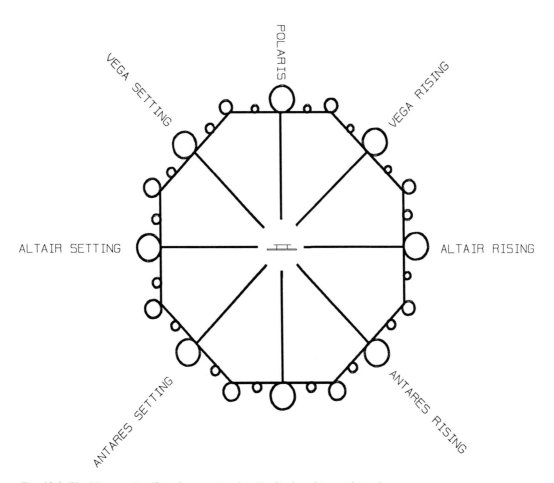

Fig. 12.3. The Micronesian 'Star Compass' as locally displayed in teaching diagrams.

Telling support for this admittedly radical suggestion comes from the sailing tradition of the Indian Ocean where the navigational system of medieval Arab, Persian, and Indian sailors bears striking resemblance to the Pacific system. They too had a 'star compass', a star compass of thirty-two points named for the risings and settings of stars (de Saussure 1928). The same star, Altair, also marked the East-West partition of the Indian Ocean horizon. In the Indian Ocean, there can be no doubt that the star names were names for directions, not literal markers of direction. We know that to be true because a famous fifteenth-century Arab navigator, Ibn Majid, has told us so in his magnificent navigation treatise (composed, unlike medieval European manuals, in poetry): 'Oh my Captain', he says, 'these stars and bearings with the Arabs are only approximate. If you set course exactly on them in a narrow place, then you will have difficulty. *For they are used only for their names and not for their actual position in the heavens*' (emphasis mine) (Tibbets 1971: 74–5).

The standard interpretation of the Pacific 'Star Compass' fails to distinguish the problem of finding one's direction at sea from the problems of conceptualizing, naming, and operating upon the direction found. Just as a wind coming from Greece need not always, or ever, blow from the Mediterranean direction named *greco*, so the star Vega, at a particular Pacific latitude, need not rise in the direction named 'Vega Rising'. Pacific navigators did use stars for finding directions. They used the whole changing visual pattern of the night sky for doing so. They also used the sensory pattern of sea swells passing under the canoe and its outrigger. They used anything they could, such as birds, sea marks, clouds, and even mythical creatures. But when they found their bearings, they referenced them to a conceptual system of abstract named directions that equally segmented the horizon circle into thirty-two points.

If the number of points in the Micronesian 'Star Compass' is not, after all, arbitrary, then why does this number, thirty-two, keep appearing in the directional schemes of seafarers in such widely separated parts of the world? One could, of course, argue for historical connection via the Indian Ocean. A connection between Pacific and Indian Ocean systems is possible,[15] but the differences in rationale and nomenclature of these two systems and that of Europe argues against a link in that direction. Alternatively, there could well be a practical basis for this degree of segmentation. Once one starts with the image of the horizon as a circle and one conceptualizes directions as successive mental bisections of that circle, then thirty-two is about as far as one can go in eyeball determination of navigation. But one can go that far. A thirty-second of a circle subtends 11½ degrees, about a fist's width, along the horizon.[16]

Northern names for a southern rose

Pur north un vent ki surt e vient	For north is a wind which arises and comes
De la u li ciels le char tient.	From there in the sky where the Great Bear lies.
Engleis dient en lur language	The English say in their language
A la guise de lur usage:	In the way they use it:
En north alum, de north venum	To the north we go, from north we come
North fumes nez, en north manum.	North we were born, north we remain.
Autresi dient de est un vent,	Also they say from the east a wind
De suth e de west ensement.	Likewise for the south and the west.

Wace, a twelfth century Norman Poet[17]

There remains yet another revealing wrinkle in our story of the point dial. In discussing European seafaring, we have thus far ignored the sailors of the Atlantic coasts, channels, and seas of Northern Europe. When we venture into these northern waters, we encounter a curious puzzle. It concerns the use of the mariner's compass, an instrument that combines the north-seeking (but never quite finding) properties of a magnetic needle with a physical depiction of the directional schema as a 'compass rose' on a rotating card. There seems little doubt that sailors in the Mediterranean were using the compass by the thirteenth century. There also seems little doubt that the compass, even though it was known, was not regularly used in northern Europe until well into the fifteenth, or even sixteenth, century. What one finds are not records of the use of the compass, but recurrent comments about the neglect of compass and chart among northern seamen. A fifteenth century Italian chart maker, for example, felt compelled to write across his depiction of northern seas: 'In this sea they navigate with neither chart nor compass' (Vogel 1911: 27 (in Köberer 1982: 148)). In a letter, a sixteenth-century German skipper complains about the practice of his colleagues:

Many seamen who sail from Prussia to England and Portugal commonly not only ignore latitude reckoning, but also they heed neither chart nor proper compass . . . *sie tragen die kunst alle im kopf*, 'they carry their art all in their head'. (Vogel 1911, in Köberer 1982: 150)

Many other similar remarks could be cited down through the sixteenth century. It is as though 'sailing with neither compass nor chart' had become a 'remarkable' trait of the northern seafarer's identity.

So the sailors of the foggy and overcast seas of the north ignored a direction-finding instrument that had been long employed by their colleagues in the fair and sunny Mediterranean. But that is not the puzzle. The real mystery is why, in these circumstances, is the system of naming compass directions, and even the names themselves, everywhere of northern origin. The Italian sailor of today does not steer his vessel to the *Sirocco* or the *Maestro* as did his thirteenth-century ancestors throughout the Mediterranean, but rather to the *sud-est* and the *nord-ovest*. 'North', 'South', 'East', and 'West' (and their close formal equivalents in other European languages) are not Romance forms; the practice of combining just these four terms to name all thirty-two points of the compass is not of Mediterranean origin.

By the early fifteenth century the Portuguese were already using the northern system, borrowed, it can be shown, from the English (Baist 1903; Wahlgren 1931). Portuguese sailing directions from that time inform the mariner that 'the Cape of Saint Paul lies *lesnordeste* (ENE) and *oessudoeste* (WSW) with the River of Lagos' (Boxer 1934: 172). Columbus ordered his helmsman to steer, not to the *occidente* or the *poniente*, but '*oeste: nada del noroeste, nada del sudoeste*' (Morison 1942: 174). In France the northern terms, again taken from the English, were used since the twelfth century by seamen of the Atlantic and Channel coast, whereas the southern terms persisted among French sailors in the Mediterranean into the sixteenth century. Eventually the northern names and naming system were rapidly adopted by all European sailors and became the everyday terms for directions in their respective languages (Frahm 1914: Marichal 1956; Rothwell 1955). Why then did the Mediterranean developers of the compass, the chart, and the pilot book replace the directional naming system that lies at the core of all of these with the foreign usage of northern sailors, who were far behind in their gadgetry, their imagery, and their literacy? And why did northern sailors develop a naming system that so elegantly calibrates an instrument for which they initially had little use? That is the puzzle.

One might argue that the northern system is simpler and more logical. One could counter that, even though the Mediterranean terms may have been a bit longer, they were, by the same token, more distinct in pronunciation – an advantage that can be appreciated by any sailboat skipper who has had to shout commands in a howling wind.[18] Certainly the Italians were not bothered by any awkwardness of their terminology. It was they who led in the development of compass, chart, and pilot book; they were the real pioneers in modern navigational technology. In the fourteenth and fifteenth centuries, their galleys regularly sailed into northern waters to England and Flanders. Yet they never felt any need to change their directional terms. They used the Mediterranean system everywhere, for all purposes, through at least the sixteenth century (Mallett 1967).

It was the Portuguese, the founders of scientific, instrument-based, professionally taught, government sponsored navigation, who were responsible for incorporating the northern directional system into the inventory of ocean navigation. This was one element in the new navigator's kit that had no scholarly credentials. It was a mental image of unlettered seamen in northern waters. From the perspective of the Portuguese, the northern nomenclature had only one undeniable advantage over the Mediterranean system. It was different. The Portuguese marked off their 'ocean navigation' from Italian practice by proclaiming a new science, taught in their government school, which was dependent, even more, on manuals, tables and instruments. In early Portuguese and Spanish navigation manuals, a symbol of the new bookish navigation, the northern names of the 'winds' are contrasted with the Mediterranean terms as the 'usages of the navigators of the Ocean Sea' (Nuñes 1537; Medina 1545, 1554; Frampton 1581).

The need to distinguish their system of navigation from that of the Italians and Catalans may, then, have provided the Portuguese and the Spanish with a motive for adopting the northern directional terms. The opportunity was clearly there. Not only did Portuguese traders and fishermen frequently sail north, but, also, their harbours, being outside the Straits of Gibraltar, were much more frequently visited by northern ships than were ports within the Mediterranean. But how could a system associated with the untutored practice of the northern seaman, who shunned chart, manual, and compass, carry sufficient prestige to bolster the symbolic power of Portuguese and Spanish scientific navigation? What did the North have to offer the sophisticated seafarer of the south? What they had was a way of conceptualizing and calculating time, a way that employed the thirty-two point dial.

Time, tide, and the point dial

> Seafarers are so attached to their words of North, South, East, and West that they not only, by means of them, express what is the direction of each place, but also the hours of the day. Fournier, *Hydrographie*, 1643: 441

There was one phenomenon, critical to 'ocean navigation' but largely irrelevant to the Mediterranean navigator, which, for the northern sailor, had long been a part of everyday life: the strong tidal currents and the great range of tidal heights in northern waters. Coping with the tides required not direction finding, but timing. For this timing, the northern sailor employed his directional nomenclature to calibrate a thirty-two point mental image of a dial for telling and calculating the lunar time of the tide and the solar time of day. Table 12.1 shows the correspondence between points and hours.

This cognitive schema for directions thus provided a model for reckoning time – a thirty-two hour day, a segmentation that makes that length of each hour roughly equivalent to the daily difference between solar and lunar time. With this model, sailors could store in their heads the information now provided in bulky tide-tables issued annually for each port. How this was done is depicted in early fifteenth-century tidal charts, which show lines leading from individual ports to compass roses. The point of the rose connected to a line indicates the lunar time of high tide at new or full moon for that port. By counting around the rose, a point per day, to the current age of the moon, a sailor could determine the solar time of high tide on that day (Frake 1985). Mediterranean navigators sailing in northern waters had to learn this system. They were thereby exposed to northern terminology. One Italian who learned was Columbus. In his journal, Columbus used the system to compare the tidal regime of one of his Caribbean anchorages with that of his Spanish port.[19] This practical use in northern waters of the directional scheme perhaps lent sufficient prestige to the northern terminology to support the adoption of that terminology by the Portuguese and Spanish as a symbol of their new scientific navigation of the 'Ocean Sea'. The symbolic power of this usage is demonstrated by the subsequent adoption of the northern, Germanic terminology of N-S-E-W as the everyday terms for directions in the Romance languages. These direction words remain a basic part of our vocabulary, but the directional scheme of the thirty-two point mariner's compass is now obsolete. Depictions of it now survive only in Boy Scout manuals, quilting designs, commercial logos, and other repositories of arcane lore. At sea, even in small sail boats, it has been completely replaced by the 360° dial. Is this use of 360 numbered degrees a technical improvement over thirty-two named points? Or is it equally a display of the scientific credentials of modern navigation?

Physical traces of thinking and knowledge

There are three major lessons to be drawn from this exercise. One is the need to distinguish mental models of directional systems from the physical cues used to find particular directions, a task confounded by the use of names for physical cues, like winds and stars, for abstract directions as well. Another is the need to distinguish mental models from their physical representations in words, diagrams, and instruments. The third is that physical representations and

Table 12.1. *Time of day by points and by hours*

Points		Hours	Points		Hours
32	North	Midnight	16	South	Noon
1	N by E	0:45 AM	17	S by W	12:45 PM
2	NNE	1:30 AM	18	SSW	1:30 PM
3	NE by N	2:15 AM	19	SW by S	2:15 PM
4	NE	3:00 AM	20	SW	3:00 PM
5	NE by E	3:45 AM	21	SW by W	3:45 PM
6	ENE	4:30 AM	22	WSW	4:30 PM
7	E by N	5:15 AM	23	W by S	5:15 PM
8	East	6:00 AM	24	West	6.00 PM
9	E by S	6:45 AM	25	W by N	6:45 PM
10	ESE	7:30 AM	26	WNW	7:30 PM
11	SE by E	8:15 AM	27	NW by W	8.15 PM
12	SE	9:00 AM	28	NW	9:00 PM
13	SE by S	9:45 AM	29	NW by N	9:45 PM
14	SSE	10:30 AM	30	NNW	10:30 PM
15	S by E	11:15 AM	31	N by W	11:15 PM

instruments are not only operational aids to the mind, but are, perhaps equally, public displays. Humans are not simply maximally (or minimally) efficient ecological adapters. Nor are they simply rational (or irrational) calculating machines. They are social animals with social aspirations of being accorded recognition and respect by their fellows, and social fears being confronted with rejection and humiliation. These social motivations shape the design and use of even the most obviously 'practical' of behaviours and artefacts. Because of this, the complexity of a representation does not necessarily mirror the complexity of the system of knowledge that underlies the performance of the task to which the representation pertains. The navigation by Pacific islanders provides a telling demonstration that very complex systems of knowledge and thinking can have very meagre physical manifestations in technology. Where depictions of the system come into play is not, in the Pacific, in the practice of navigation at sea, but in the teaching of it on land. Teaching is an occasion for the public display of knowledge. In that display, as well as in the display provided by old Italian charts, Portuguese navigation manuals, and Breton almanacs, not only was knowledge being imparted but social status and cultural identity were also being established. As a navigator, one must not only be able to find one's way at sea, one must also show the world that one is a navigator.

Archaeologists can make useful inferences about ancient mental worlds from the material manifestations and representations of those worlds. To do so, however, they must keep in their own minds an understanding of these complex kinds of interrelationships among mind, tasks, culture, and society.

Acknowledgements

Support for this research came from the National Science Foundation and the Samuel P. Capen Chair of Anthropology, University at Buffalo. Conduct of the research has been greatly assisted by the staffs of the National Maritime Museum, Greenwich, the British Library, London, the Bodleian Library, Oxford, the Bibliothèque Nationale, Paris, the Beinecke Library, Yale University, and the Huntington Library, San Marino, California. For very useful comments on the paper the author is grateful to participants in the Conference on Cognitive Archaeology, Cambridge University, 1990, which led to this book, as well as to audiences at presentations of portions of this material to cognitive scientists and geographers at the University at Buffalo, Lehigh University, and the University of California, Santa Barbara, and to anthropologists at two meetings of the Association of Social Anthropology of Oceania in Kauai, Hawaii and Victoria, British Columbia. Especially helpful critiques of earlier drafts of this and related papers were provided by Gene Ammarell, Harold Conklin, Richard Feinberg, and Ward Goodenough.

Notes

1 If the degree dial ever dies, it will do so as a victim of a system even more obscure to ordinary minds: one that yields the 2.27401 radians into which those 130.28912 decimalized degrees demanded by my calculator must be converted before my computer will attend to them.

2 This information comes from the exhibit of Bradley's quadrant at the Old Royal Observatory, Greenwich.

3 A notable example is a construction, labelled *De Ventis*, by the thirteenth-century English scholar Matthew Paris found in British Library MS Cotton Nero DD5. It is described by the maritime historian, E. G. R. Taylor (1937).

4 But underground we find an exception! German miners, through at least the late nineteenth century, used compasses whose dials named directions in a twice-twelve hour system (Breusing 1869 in Köberer 1982: 84).

5 The classic work on medieval systems of time of day is Bilfinger (1892). Rothwell (1959) provides a fascinating study of the migration of the names of the hours in medieval France.

6 The relationship between the development of clockwork and the use of numbered hours of equal length, day and night, throughout the year is much less straightforward than commonly presented. An interpretation of this complicated story is being prepared for publication under the title 'The achievement of equality by the medieval hour'. See Landes (1983) and, for a different view, Price (1976).

7 The eight-sided 'tower of winds' of Athens is often cited as evidence of the use of the point dial in ancient times (Taylor 1956: 55). The first-century Latin writer Pliny (Natural History, Book II, XLVI) describes an eight wind system, which he says was formed by subtracting four winds from the 'too subtle and meticulous' twelve division system (Rackham 1979: 260–3).

8 Fifteenth-century Arab sailors in the Indian Ocean also segmented their ship by the thirty-two named divisions of their star compass. (Tibbets 1971: 121, 294).

9 Kretschmer (1909) edited and published texts of medieval Italian pilot books. Other pertinent references are Campbell (1987), Kelley (1982), Motzo (1947), Stevenson (1911), and Taylor (1956).

10 Taylor 1951; Lane 1963; Thompson 1913; Köberer 1982; La Roncière 1897; Schück 1911, 1915, 1918; Wagner 1895.

11 Classical references are Finey (1976); Goodenough (1953), Gladwin (1970), Lewis (1972, 1977), Riesenberg (1976).

12 There have been a number of excellent recent studies of Pacific navigation; yet the 'star compass' that has been presented in all of them is invariably taken unmodified from Goodenough's (1953) analysis, based largely on the results of pre-World War I German investigations. The actual use of the scheme at sea still needs careful checking. Determining, with confidence, the conceptual structure of directional systems that have no physical representation and which may vary considerably with context of use has proven exceedingly difficult, witness several recent investigations in the Pacific and Island Southeast Asia (Feinberg 1988; Conklin 1988; Ammarell 1989).

13 From an exchange between Mau Piailug and David Lewis recorded in the film *The navigators*, produced and written by Sam Low, Watertown, Massachusetts, 1983.

14 Richard Feinberg (personal communication) has suggested that Piailug was here using 'East' in a loose sense of 'somewhere around the place where Altair rises'. But the difference between true east and the rising point of Altair, in low northern latitudes is 9°, a difference that could be very significant in long distance voyages. If differences of this magnitude are not considered important, then why have a 32 point system?

I submit that if Piailug had meant 'a bit north of east', he would have called the direction *paiifung* after the navigational star that names east by north, the next point north of east in a thirty-two point system (Thomas 1987: 83).

15 At the same time that islanders of Oceania were voyaging eastward, their linguistic kin in Island Southeast Asia were making trading voyages westward across the Indian Ocean where, about the time of Christ, they discovered and settled Madagascar. Halpern (1986) presents a case for contact.

16 The popular writer Kenneth Brower (1984: 123) makes the same suggestion in his *A song for Satawal*, a charming account of contemporary Micronesian life.

17 These lines are from the *Roman de Rou*, II, verses 51–8. Wahlgren (1931: 107) gives the text with an etymological commentary. The awkward translation here is my own. For the meaning of Wace's *char*, see Rothwell (1955: 53).

18 French sailors altered the pronunciation of combinations with *est* and *oest* for this reason (Jal 1848; Delbos 1914).

19 The entry reads 'the tide is the reverse of ours, because there when the moon is southwest by south it is low tide in that harbor' (Dunn and Kelley 1989: 159–61). See also Morison (1942: 265), who calls this 'a remarkable lunitidal observation'.

References

Ammarell, G. 1989. Spatial orientation among the Bugis seafarers of South Sulawesi: a research design. Manuscript. Department of Anthropology, Yale University

Baist, G. 1903. Germanische Seemannsworte in der französischen Sprache. *Zeitschrift für Deutsche Wortforschung* 4: 257–76

Bilfinger, G. 1892. *Die mittelalterlichen Hören und die modernen Stunden: Ein Beitrag zur Kulturgeschichte*. Stuttgart. (Reprinted 1969, Wiesbaden, Dr Martin Sändig oHG.)

Boxer, C. R. 1934. Portuguese roteiros, 1500–1700. *The Mariners Mirror* 20.2: 171–85

Breusing, A. 1869. Flavio Gioja und der Schiffskompass. *Zeitschrift der Gesellschaft für Erdkunde* 4: 31–51 (Reprinted in Köberer 1982: 79–95)

Brower, K. 1984. *A song for Satawal*. Harmondsworth, Penguin

Campbell, T. 1987. Portolan charts from the late thirteenth century to 1500. In *The history of cartography*, Vol. I, ed. J. B. Harley and D. Woodward, pp. 371–463. Chicago, University of Chicago Press

Conklin, H. C. 1988. Des orientements, des vents, des riz . . . pour une étude lexicologique des savoirs traditionnels. *Journal d'Agriculture Traditionnelle et de Botanique Appliquée* 33: 3–10

Delbos, L. 1914. *Nautical terms in English and French*. London, Williams and Norgate

Dunn, O. and J. E. Kelley, Jr (eds.) 1989. *The* Diario *of Christopher Columbus's first voyage to America, 1492–1493*. Norman, OK, University of Oklahoma Press

Feinberg, R. 1988. *Polynesian seafaring and navigation: ocean travel in Anutan culture and society*. Kent, Ohio, Kent State University Press

Finey, B. R. (ed.) 1976. *Pacific navigation and voyaging*. Wellington, The Polynesian Society

Fournier, P. G. 1643, 1667. *Hydrographie contenant la théorie et la pratique de toutes les parties de la navigation, précédée d'un inventaire des mots et façons de parler dont on use sur mer*. Paris (fasc. ed. Boudriot 1973)

Frahm, W. 1914. *Das Meer und die Seefahrt in der altfranzösischen Literatur*. Göttingen, Friedrich Hänsch

Frake, C. O. 1985. Cognitive maps of time and tide among medieval seafarers. *Man* 20: 254–70

Frampton, J. (tr.) 1581. *The Arte of navigation of Pedro Medina*. London, Thomas Davis

Gladwin, T. 1970. *East is a big bird: navigation and logic on Pulawat Atoll*. Cambridge, MA, Harvard University Press

Goodenough, W. 1953. *Native astronomy in the Central Carolines*. Philadelphia, University Museum, University of Pennsylvania

Goodenough, W. and S. Thomas 1990. Traditional navigation in the Western Pacific: a search for pattern. *Expedition* 30: 1–16. Philadelphia, PA, University Museum

Halpern, M. 1986. Sidereal compasses: a case for Carolinian-Arab links. *The Journal of the Polynesian Society* 95 (4): 441–4

Jal, A. 1848. *Glossaire nautique: répertoire polyglotte de termes marines anciens et modernes*. Paris, Firmin Didot Frères

Kelley, J. E. Jr 1982. Summary of the south European method of navigation in the late fifteenth century. Unpublished manuscript

Köberer, W. (ed.) 1982. *Das rechte Fundament der Seefahrt. Deutsche Beiträge zur Geschichte der Navigation*. Hamburg, Hoffmann und Campe

Kretschmer, K. 1909. *Die italienischen Portolane des Mittelalters*. Berlin, Instituts für Meereskunde

La Roncière, C. de 1897. Un inventaire de bord en 1294 et les origines de la navigation hauturière. Bibliothèque de l'Ecole des Chartes LVIII: 394–409. Paris

Landes, D. S. 1983. *Revolution in time: clocks and the making of the modern world*. Cambridge, MA, Harvard University Press

Lane, F. C. 1963. The economic meaning of the invention of the compass. *The American Historical Review* 68 (3): 605–17

Lewis, D. H. 1972. *We the navigators*. Honolulu, University of Hawaii Press

1977. Mau Piailung's navigation of Hokule'a from Hawaii to Tahiri. In *Topics in cultural learning*, vol. V, ed. R. W. Brislin and M. Hamnett pp. 1–23. Honolulu, University of Hawaii Press

Low, S. 1983. *The navigators*. A film produced and directed by Sam Low. Watertown, MA, DER

Mallett, M. E. 1967. *The Florentine galleys in the fifteenth century* with *The diary of Luca di Maso degli Albizzi, captain of the galleys, 1429–1430*. Oxford, Clarendon

Marichal, R. 1956. Le noms de vents chez Rabelais. *Travaux d'Humanisme et Renaissance* 24 (8): 7–28

Medina, P. de 1545. *Arte de Navegar*. Valladolid

1554. *L'Arte de Navegar . . . tradotta de lingua spagnola in volgar Italia*

Morison, S. E. 1942. *Admiral of the Ocean Sea*. Boston, Little, Brown

Motzo, B. R. (ed.) 1947. *Il Compasso de Navigare*. Cagliari, Facolti di Lettere e Filosofia della Università di Cagliari, 8

Neugebauer, O. 1969. *The exact sciences in antiquity*. New York, Dover

Nuñes, P. 1537. *Tratado da Sphera*. Lixboa. Photocopy Massachusetts Historical Society, No. 21, 1920

Price, D. J. de S. 1976. Clockwork before the clock and time-keepers before timekeeping. *Bulletin of the National Association of Watch and Clock Collectors, Inc.* 18: 399

Rackham, H. (ed.) 1979. *Pliny, Natural History*. vol. I. (Latin text and English translation). Loeb Classical Library, Cambridge, MA, Harvard University Press

Riesenberg, S. H. 1976. The organization of navigational knowledge on Pulawat. In *Pacific navigation and*

voyaging, ed. B. Finney. Wellington, The Polynesian Society

Rothwell, W. 1955. Winds and cardinal points in French. *Archivum Linguisticum* 7, fasc. I: 29–56

1959. The hours of the day in medieval French. *French Studies* 13: 240–51

Saussure, L. de 1928. L'Origine de la Rose des Vents et l'invention de la Boussole. In *Introduction à l'astronomie nautique arab*, ed. G. Ferrand, pp. 31–128. Paris, Paul Geuthner

Schück, A. 1911, 1915, 1918. *Der Kompass*. 3 vols. Hamburg, Emil Korff, Kruse and Freihen

Skeat, W. W. (ed.) 1872. *A treatise on the Astrolabe by Geoffrey Chaucer AD 1391*, Oxford, Oxford University Press (reprinted 1968)

Stevenson, E. L. 1911. *Portolan charts: their origin and characteristics with a descriptive list of those belonging to the Hispanic Society of America*. New York, Hispanic Society of America

Taylor, E. G. R. 1937. The 'De Ventis' of Matthew Paris. *Imago Mundi* II: 23–6

1951. Early charts and the origin of the compass rose. *Journal of the Institute of Navigation* 4:351–6

1956. *The haven-finding art: a history of navigation from Odysseus to Captain Cook*. London, Hollis and Carter

Thomas, S. D. 1987. *The last navigator*. New York, Henry Holt and Co.

Thompson, S. 1913. *The rose of the winds: the origin and development of the compass card*. Proceedings of the British Academy 6. London, Humphrey Milford

Tibbets, G. R. 1971. *Arab navigation in the Indian Ocean before the coming of the Portuguese*. Royal Asiatic Society of Great Britain, Oriental Translation Fund New Series, vol. 42. London

Vogel, W. 1911. Die Entfürung des Kompasses in die Nord-westeuropaïsche Nautik. *Hansische Geschichtsblätter* 38: 1–32

Wagner, H. 1895. Das Rätsel der Kompasskarten im Lichte der Gesamtentwicklung der Seekarten. *Verhandlungen des XI. Deutschen Geographentages in Bremen*: 65–87 (Reprinted in Köberer 1982: 18–34)

Wahlgren, E. G. 1931. Franç. *surouest, suroît*, Esp. *sur*, Port. *sul*. *Studier i Modern Språkventenskap*. 11: 105–45

PART V

The material basis of cognitive inference: technology

13
Cognitive aspects of 'technique'

S. E. VAN DER LEEUW

Introduction[1]

In trying to isolate reasons for the fact that archaeology has, for so long, ignored the cognitive aspects of material culture studies, one can point to the following – not necessarily in order of appearance or importance:

– The once dominant determinist streak in archaeology often saw 'us humans' as forever trying to adapt to circumstances beyond our control. This attitude has wilfully ignored the reciprocal nature of the relationship between people and what surrounds them, which is at the core of cognition (see below), and has underrated the impact of long-term human activity on the material and natural world, the degree to which human beings have created their surroundings by direct action or selection.

– The predominant evolutionary perspective underwrites a strong theoretical sense of common origins and has led archaeologists to look for, and stress, human universals, both physical and cultural. At first sight, this conflicts with the importance of observed variations, and this apparent conflict has led to a yes-or-no debate on the existence of such universals, for example in material culture. The debate has precluded a more nuanced position, which would entail investigating whether similar processes might underlie very different results.

– There are many ethnographic and other examples indicating that the *results* of cognitive processes are different for different people. The concomitant impossibility of knowing *what* people in the past thought has usually deflected us from studying *how* people think. We have, however, no good evidence that comparing the processes by which people arrive at these different results does not allow us to gain insight into the cognitive dynam-

ics involved. Nor do we have any evidence that these processes are not at least partially universal for all of Mankind. Indeed, it seems to me that if there are human universals at all, they must be located in the interface between matter and mind, in the way that the brain works, rather than in what it achieves (Delbrück 1988).

– Analytically speaking, we have usually approached matters either from an *etic* or from an *emic* perspective, well aware that the two can lead to very different interpretations; what seems the most interesting from the point of view of cognition is, however, how these two perspectives articulate.

– Finally, problems with establishing a fine-grained chronology made it difficult to observe change as it occurs, often forcing archaeologists to lump time into 'horizons', and thus contributing further to an emphasis on statics ('being': results) over dynamics ('becoming': processes). Thus, in palaeolithic studies, we have convinced ourselves that there is a 'sudden' emergence of cognition, of language, of art, and our data have not allowed us independently to question such suddenness. Yet that is what is required if we are to understand the development of human cognition.

The duality of cognition

Elsewhere (van der Leeuw 1989, 1990), I have developed elements of a perspective on cognition which I can only summarize here with extreme brevity.

Perception and cognition together constitute the universal interface between the realm of ideas which a human being has internalized and the realm of matter and energy which surrounds an individual. They serve to reduce the information overload (apparent chaos) of an un-cognized environment to manageable proportions. The reduction is achieved by searching for apparent symmetries (similarities). Cognition allows us to 'fix' instantly in the memory certain symmetries in real, virtual or conceptual space, which disappear the next moment. Repetition of the process also permits us to find and retain temporal symmetries in complex processes with non-harmonic rhythms. Such symmetries are retained for further reference.

Two different steps can be distinguished in the process: (a) searching for a perspective which includes a sufficient number of symmetries (e.g. defining a problem), and (b) defining the dimensions which capture these symmetries (e.g. finding the solution). Of these, the former takes time and is non-linear because it deals with change, with the uncertainties and risks of the unknown.[2] The latter is instantaneous and linear, fixing a dynamic process into a static perception at the moment at which the future becomes the past (see also Atlan, 1992). That moment is experienced as the intuitive 'jump' or 'click' of understanding. It implies that the dimensions needed to understand phenomena, which were thus far perceived in a problematic fashion (i.e. with less than absolute clarity), have been isolated.

A new conception is thus born. Other phenomena of this particular kind can, from then on, be defined with reference to these dimensions. But as soon as a dimension has been cognized, it can also serve as a (new) 'point of view' from which to make observations, providing a new perspective and thus prompting further searches for symmetries, the solution of further problems. The process by which cognition translates perceptions of the material world into ideas is thus based on a reduction of the number of dimensions of the phenomena concerned: the theory is simpler than the reality, the symbol a *pars-pro-toto*.

Cognition is also of central importance in transforming ideas into substance, in the introduction of new forms which fix the transience of creation and thus imply control over matter and energy, stability. In that process, the two steps are reversed: the defined (abstract) dimensions are translated into sets of approximate symmetries in matter and energy. In this case, therefore, a linear configuration is transformed into a set of non-linearities in the material realm. It follows that realizing ideas implies amplification of the limited number of dimensions on which the idea is predicated to the (in principle unlimited) number of dimensions in which it will manifest itself.

The fact that transformation of phenomena into ideas is a reduction, implies that it reduces noise, error and/or variability, and enhances redundancy: the theory always seems more robust than the initial coherence between the phenomena led us to believe. On the other hand, the difficulty in realizing ideas is that, in the confrontation between the two, the idea has to be watered down: the redundancy is reduced and other, non-coherent, dimensions are introduced, enhancing the level of noise, the potential for error and the range of variability in expression of an idea.

This dual role of cognition in simplifying reality into ideas on the one hand, and 'complexifying' ideas into reality on the other underlies the genesis of all material culture, and requires us to do a comparative study between the etic and emic points of view if we are to understand the dynamics involved.

The substitution of form, the information of substance[3]

Creating objects of material culture is an example of the kind of interaction between kind and matter to which I have just referred. Because the kinds of processes in which I am interested are assumed to operate at the cognitive level, and

thus to be universal rather than culture-specific, my first attempt at approaching them was a cross-cultural analysis of the *chaînes opératoires* of a number of prehistoric, medieval and (sub)recent pottery-making traditions in Europe, Asia, Africa and North America (van der Leeuw 1993).

It revealed that behind the considerable variety in the ceramics and the underlying *chaînes opératoires*, one sees a number of similarities in the way in which, in each of the ceramic traditions involved, the substantiation of form and the simultaneous information of substance take place. In an attempt to systematize observation and discussion, I have divided the interface between the ideal and the material realms involved into the areas of *conceptualization*, *execution* and *raw materials*, thereby identifying two main interfaces, between conceptualizations and the techniques responsible for their substantiation, and between these techniques and the raw materials which they use. I have illustrated the realm of each of these with reference to aspects of shaping technique only, well aware that this is only a selection.

Conceptualizations

It is assumed that each potter, wittingly or unwittingly, has different ideas in making the pottery. These ideas might be technological, functional, social, behavioural, economic or anything else. (Our modern, highly fragmented perception is probably the only one which distinguishes these areas anyway.)

Fundamental to the conceptualizations involved in shaping is the *topology* which the potter brings to bear on his or her dealing with shapes. Is a shape seen as a 'horizontal' one, or a 'vertical' one'; is the shape, for example, viewed as a transformation of a sphere, of a cone or of a cylinder; is the transformation a case of 'stretching' or of 'compressing'; what is the 'inside' of the vessel, and what the 'outside', or are the two not distinguished?

Another part of such a conceptualization is the *partonomy* which the potter applies to the shape (i.e. the way in which the potter divides the pot conceptually into parts), for example, what are considered the *basic entities* out of which the pot is made: a number of coils, two or more pot segments, or the whole pot. We have seen that Balfet's (1984) Kabylian coiling tradition has a *continuous* conception of shapes (the whole pot is seen as one, indivisible, entity), and the urban North African throwing tradition a *discontinuous* one (the shape is viewed as made up of separate parts).

The third major element of any conceptualization is the *sequence* in which the pottery is made: bottom-to-top, top-to-bottom, shoulder-top-bottom, etc. Any manufacturing procedure of the complexity of pottery-making (for example flint-knapping) implies that the artisan has a real-time strategy which integrates a large number of steps in a coherent way. Usually, such a sequence is quite fixed, and developing a different sequence to achieve the same aims is difficult, if not impossible. I have argued elsewhere that the fact that on Negros, in the Philippines, the potters begin the making of any vessel with its rim, works against the introduction of a potter's wheel, although the effective use of rotation has been harnessed by these potters in other ways (van der Leeuw 1984).

Topology, *partonomy* and *sequence*, then, are in my opinion three of the fundamental conceptual 'anchors' of any potter-making tradition. They are the aspects which link pottery-making to other aspects of culture, other techniques (alongside other anchors such as those inherent in the human body and the way a particular culture exploits it, i.e. which movements it considers 'natural' and which it does not). What makes them so resistant to change is the fact that they permeate very large areas of the activity of any group of people, the fact that they are shared and form the basis of all communication between the members of the group, and, last but not least, that those members are largely unaware of their existence (cf. van der Leeuw, Papousek and Coudart 1992), which is only called into question when confronted with fundamentally different topologies, partonomies or sequencing.

Executive functions and tools

Whatever the potter's general conceptualizations, making the pots will pose a number of problems. For example, comparison of manufacture by means of a coiling technique, a hammer-and-anvil technique, manufacturing in a mould and throwing, leads to the conclusion that these techniques share the fact that they all cope – in different ways – with the following problems:

(1) the pull of gravity on the object under construction, which may cause the vessel to sag or even collapse during construction (while the paste is wet);
(2) the access which the potter has to have to various parts of the vessel while it is being shaped;
(3) the composition of the raw materials at the potter's disposal;
(4) the speed with which the vessels may be made;
(5) control over the shape;
(6) the width of the range of shapes which the technique allows the potter.

Most conceptualizations may, in themselves, be realized in a number of conceivable ways, each with certain other constraints of their own, such as the control required over the shapes to be produced (moulding produces much better control than coiling), or the time required (throwing or

moulding costs much less time than coiling). Hence, if time is a constraint, the potter will find a way in which to throw or mould the vessels. If the inclusion of large non-plastic particles is another necessity, moulding will be chosen if there is a choice. If not, (s)he will coil (because throwing a thin-walled vessel with large non-plastic particles is impossible). Only by contrasting different approaches to pottery-making can we hope to approach the 'why?' of choices in ceramic manufacture.

Just as one can elicit 'universal' problems in realizing certain shapes, one can also point to 'universal' sets of actions to be undertaken to make pots. The evident ones are delving clay, drying and firing it. But less obvious ones are of importance with respect to shaping. Indeed, shaping from coils, in moulds, or on rotary supports, tournettes, wheels and their various combinations, can all be seen as extensions (or combinations) of four simple manual functions used in interacting between the conceptualization and the substance in which it is to be reified: (a) *squeezing*, a basic function occurring in all shaping of clay, (b) *supporting* the vessel while it is plastic, (c) *controlling* the shape of the vessel, and (d) *turning* the pot in the hands. We proposed to call such the 'executive functions' of pottery making.

Other executive functions only serve to modify an existing shape, rather than actually shaping the clay. These are (e) *cutting* (use of knife or string), (f) *scraping* (extended through the introduction of the rib or the gourd scraper, etc.) and (g) *smoothing* (with a piece of cloth or leather, or the pebble with which a dry vessel is polished). The tools used are usually either objects already present in the potter's conceptual and material world for reasons which do not have anything to do with pottery making (for example the rag used by most potters) or very simple tools such as pieces of string, wood, bamboo or bone. They are, in a very real sense, accessories which do not relate to the core of the manufacturing process.

Executive functions are open to modification or substitution. They relate to conscious choices, or at least to choices which in particular instances can become conscious and manipulable. They constitute the hypotheses, rather than the axioms of the structure which underlies the potter's work. Aspects of the conceptualizations inherent in a set of particular manufacturing techniques are responsible for the continued use of rotary motion and/or support, for example, but the extent to, and the precise way in which, they are used are, in fact, variable and part of the realm of executive functions, mediating between the conceptualization and the raw materials. In many cases, rotary motion and support are actually combined in different ways in the manufacturing process, and the exact way of combining the two may well be quite characteristic of a pottery-making tradition at any point in time, but is open to change without challenging the basic cognitive structure of the tradition.

Tools are here seen as substantiations of (parts of) executive functions, as they are specifically designed to facilitate these. They are themselves, however, the result of interactions between conceptualizations and (other) materials.

The role of raw materials

If the first interface is the one between conceptualizations and executive functions, the second is between the latter and the raw materials utilized. Raw materials have particular constraints, which are, in their interaction with certain executive functions, responsible for complicating the problems already inherent in the first interface. These demand their own solutions. A very plastic clay, for example, needs to be used for throwing, and can be used with a mould; a moderately plastic clay can be used for coiling, and stiff clays are used with a paddle-and-anvil technique. The state of the clay, however, may be modified by a number of simple expedients, and is not an inherent property. Plastic clays may be made stiffer by the addition of dry ones or tempering materials, while stiff clays may be made more plastic by the addition of water, or by removing part of the non-plastic substances in them. Similarly, if straw gives a short, violent fire and that is desired, fine; if that is not what the potter wants, other combustible materials need only be tested in order to find a more suitable one.

From the perspective chosen here, manipulation of the raw materials is considered 'easier' than modification of either conceptualizations or executive functions. The interface between the latter and raw materials is one where the confrontation is the most directly 'objectifiable', where things most clearly 'work' or 'don't work'. As a result, most changes made at this interface do not call any other aspect of the society's 'problem space' into question.

Cognitive aspects of Michoacán pottery making

To illustrate both the approach and what some of these cognitive aspects of pottery making can look like for a particular tradition, I will highlight some aspects of Tarascan pottery making in the state of Michoacán, Mexico.[4]

The chaîne opératoire

The basic sequence with which we are here concerned can be represented by the following simple *chaîne opératoire*. Between brackets are those actions which are optional:

(1) delving of the two clays needed (one called 'red', the other 'white', although these concepts are but relative)

((2) only in dry season: grinding the clays to a fine powder)[5]

(3) mixing and kneading the clays to prepare the paste

(4) cutting a ball of paste of sufficient size to make the whole pot

(5) hammering the paste with a mushroom-shaped pestle

((6) only if the vessel is to be made in more than one mould: cutting the paste into the required number of lumps)

(7) flattening the lump(s) into (a) 'pizza(s)'

(8) placing each 'pizza' of paste in, or over, a mould

(9) pressing it against the mould, while at the same time smoothing the side which does not come into contact with the latter

((10) only if making the vessel requires more than one mould: placing the moulds against each other and smoothing the join on the inside)

(11) drying the paste for a short time

(12) removing the newly-made shape from the mould

(13) drying the vessel until leather-hard

(14) smoothing the surface which was in contact with the mould

((15) only where applicable: polishing part of the surface with a pebble or other smooth tool)

(16) drying the vessel until bone-dry

((17) only where applicable: paint decoration)

((18) only where applicable: dip in glaze)

(19) firing vessel

((20) only where applicable: dip in glaze)

((21) only where applicable: refire)

The study of variations

The only means at one's disposal to map the cognitive structure which underlies this *chaîne opératoire* is to compare the variations encountered among the Michoacán potters. At the most general level, there are two variants, respectively operating with one – horizontally held – mould and with more than one mould. In the latter case, the moulds usually, but not universally, divide the shape to be made into vertical parts. As argued elsewhere (van der Leeuw, Papousek and Coudart 1992), the choice of approach is closely linked to what are considered to be the 'visible' surfaces of the pot, i.e. what are seen as 'inside' and 'outside'. The immutable rule is that the 'outside' of the vessel should have been pressed against the mould. Hence, the 'open' vessels (plates, cups, bowls, etc.) are made *over* one horizontal mould, whereas the 'closed' vessels (mugs, cooking pots, jars, jugs, teapots) are made *in* two or more moulds. Here, we clearly see the particular topology of the Michoacán potters at work.

Confining ourselves to the closed vessels, a further choice

is to be made between horizontal or vertical moulds. In some villages all potters use vertical moulds for closed vessels (e.g. Huáncito, Patamban) while in another (Capula) everyone uses horizontal moulds. In Tzintzuntzan, closed vessels are usually made with sets of vertical moulds, but one potter occasionally uses horizontal ones in attempts to introduce new (and therefore exclusive and better-priced) products. Clearly, differences such as these reflect differences in the cognitive arena, as there are no technical consequences of the choice involved which cannot be overcome by means existing in the area.

Whichever choice is made (and we assume for the moment that is, to a large extent, due to historical differences between the villages), it has implications for the relationship between the shape which the potter has in mind, and the procedure chosen to make it. Thus, the Capula teapots and coffee-pots made in a set of horizontal moulds have a squat shape which reflects this, whereas the Tzintzuntzan coffee-pots (which are made in vertical moulds) have a tall, rather thinner shape which stresses the vertical elements. And as soon as, in Tzintzuntzan, a potter uses a set of horizontal moulds to create a jar, a shape which in that village is traditionally made in vertical moulds, the shape changes dramatically. But the relationship between the shape and the method of its realization is a reciprocal one, so that it is not correct to either impute the shape to the topology or to the executive technique used.

The choice of executive functions affects the range of shapes made, as well as the choice of new shapes which could be introduced within the local context. It is thus by an analysis of the interface between the shapes and the ways they are made, that we may hope to elicit (parts of) the cognitive structure of the executive functions in the area, as well as *re*discover the conceptualizations themselves.

Analysis of the range of shapes

From our perspective, the next step thus consists of the identification of the 'rules' which define that relationship between spatial conceptions and their implementations. There is not one way to go about this, and the proof is in the pudding: are the rules capable of explaining not only the common, but also the exceptional shapes found?

Let us first consider the open pottery shapes made over a single horizontally-held mould, because in these cases the shape of the mould exactly coincides with that of the vessel. There are no constraints of an implementational nature and we therefore have the most direct access to the spatial conceptualizations themselves. Figure 13.1 shows the horizontal variations in shape among low bowls from Tzintzuntzan, which range from a circular one via an oval and a square bowl to two complex forms, a trapezoid bowl

with a dented upper edge and a leaf-shaped bowl. All these can be seen as the result of variations in the distance between the centre of the object and the rim. The circular vessel has no variation in that distance; the oval shape is defined by continuous increases and decreases between two equal minima and two equal maxima at right angles. The square bowl could be defined in the same manner as the oval one, but with a set of four equal maxima and a set of four equal minima, each set meeting in the middle at right angles. A rectangular bowl also has four maxima and four minima meeting in the middle, but not at right angles. In the case of the trapezoid bowl with the dent, the maximal and minimal dimensions do not cross in the middle, nor is the progression between them a smooth one: there is a local minimum (the dent).

Theoretically, one could either see the circular bowl as the exception because of the absence of any horizontal axes of symmetry, or one could see all other shapes as variations on the circular one, if one considers the fact that in the circle there are an infinite number of identical axes of symmetry. The fact that the moulds over which these vessels are shaped have affixed, to their underside, a centrally placed handle (Figure 13.2), around which the potter rotates the vessel during manufacture, seems to me to point to the second perspective, viewing the different shapes of these bowls occurring as the result of the breaking, in different ways, of the universal horizontal symmetry of the circular bowl. Where and how symmetry is broken is a matter of choice, and therefore reflects the structure of the particular 'cognitive sphere' of the potters involved.

Clearly, other ways to vary the shape of open vessels

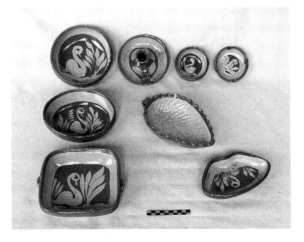

Fig. 13.1. Horizontal variations in shape variation among bowls from Tzintzuntzan

made over horizontally-held moulds could entail changing the vertical cross-section of these moulds, or modifying the surface of the moulds. We find numerous examples of both in the pottery from Tzintzuntzan, and are, at present, inventorying which of the conceivable ones occur, and in which combinations, and which do not.

Other insights are gained by considering the closed vessels from the same perspective, because there are, in this case, a number of constraints imposed by the need to implement such shapes in more than one mould. Most complex closed vessel shapes (Figure 13.3), for example, can conceptually either be seen as a vertical 'stack' of elements, such as the belly, the shoulder and the neck, or as variations in the distance between the wall and the vertical

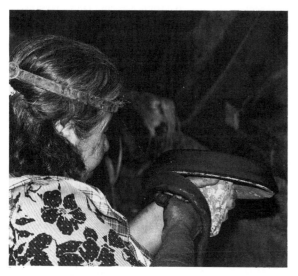

Fig. 13.2. Vessel mould with centrally placed handle

Fig. 13.3. Complex closed vessel shapes

axis in the centre of the vessel. In the former case – which includes most Old-World moulding traditions – the parts are stressed, and where moulding occurs the moulds represent the particular partonomy involved.[6] But in the latter case, the vertical axis which unifies these elements is the more important factor and, as in Michoacán, the moulds cross-cut the vessel parts. In this sense, the horizontal moulding tradition and the vertical one are clearly related: their conception of space is fundamentally identical and equally fundamentally different from any other moulding tradition known. One consequence is the fact that the executive partonomy is defined in dimensions cross-cutting the conceptual parts of the pots. That facilitates the introduction of a wide range of (variations in) shape without changing the executive routines.[7]

Thus, there are, in the area, three ways to break the complete symmetry of a globular vessel: by *truncation* (cutting off part of the globe, at the top, the bottom or the side), by *transformation* (stretching or shrinking one or more axes, and here, more particularly, in either the horizontal or the vertical planes, or in both) and by *combination* (of differently shaped parts) (van der Leeuw and Papousek 1992). In each of these the relationship between the conceptual (etic) and the executive (emic) aspects of the tradition is of interest. In the latter, the same distinction between conceptual partonomy and executive partonomy plays a part: both partonomies have to be coterminous in order to break symmetry by combination. In the case of transformation, we have already seen that the direction of transformation is related to the topological conceptualization of the shape and to the axis or axes of symmetry between the moulds. Truncation turns out to be a less constrained function: ignoring part of a shape can occur in any case. It is clearly only an executive function.

Conclusion

Regrettably, there is no space for a lengthier discussion. This paper has attempted to outline in *pointillé* how the analysis of variation in pottery may permit us to approach some issues concerning the cognitive functions underlying each pottery tradition. Much less has it dealt with the many implications of this approach to pottery-making, which views the material conditions as of secondary importance when compared with the 'mindset' of the potters involved. That will be the subject of another contribution.

Notes

1 The limited space allotted to me unfortunately does not permit me to present all of my argumentation here. This

paper is therefore best seen in relation to four others which have just appeared or are about to appear (van der Leeuw 1991, van der Leeuw, Papousek and Coudart 1992; van der Leeuw and Papousek 1992; van der Leeuw 1993). Together, these papers try to develop a cognitive approach to the concepts of 'tradition' and 'innovation' as used in archaeology. The first of them (van der Leeuw 1991) presents the background for this attempt and sketches the general framework. The second (van der Leeuw, Papousek and Coudart 1992) argues for a cognitive and social redefinition of 'tradition' to replace the usual 'materialist-determinist' one which assumes that an artisan's work is primarily constrained by the nature of the raw materials, tools and economic context in which that work takes place. It is based on ethnographic fieldwork among potters in Michoacán, Mexico. The third paper (van der Leeuw and Papousek 1992) attempts to elicit some of the constraints on innovation which are inherent in the Michoacán tradition of pottery-making. The last (van der Leeuw 1993), which was actually written first, uses the framework in a cross-cultural study of pottery-making. Two other, more distantly related papers, were published in the past few years (van der Leeuw 1989; van der Leeuw 1990).

2   The non-linear nature of the search for a perspective is explained by the fact that in order to cognize change, it is necessary to perceive change in the rate of change.

3   I owe this formulation to Roy Rappaport, who used it in his lectures in 1976 at the University of Michigan.

4   The fieldwork upon which this paper draws concerned itself with the potters of a series of villages in Michoacán, and their products. The villages concerned are Capula (just west of Morelia, the state capital), Tzintzuntzan and the nearby Colonia Lázaro Cardenas on the eastern shore of Lake Patzcuaro, Santa Fé de la Laguna on the northern shore of the same lake, Huáncito in the Cañada east of Zamora, and Patamban and San José de Gracia in the Sierra of Patamban, south of Zamora.

The area is relatively accessible, and hence well-known in the ethnographic and historical literature, among others through the efforts of the Colegio de Michoacán, which has published a large number of monographs and papers on different aspects of the area's history, geography, economy and sociology. The potters of several of the villages are the subject of full-length monographs, notably Tzintzuntzan (Foster and Ospina 1948), San José de Gracia (Hardin 1977), and Patamban (Engelbrecht 1987), and there is a wealth of papers and books concerning the context in which pottery-making occurs (cf. for example Engelbrecht's bibliography).

The fieldwork was undertaken in August–September 1987 (S. E. van der Leeuw and A. Coudart), September 1989 (S. E. van der Leeuw) and July 1991 (S. E. van der Leeuw, D. A. Papousek and A. Coudart). A much more detailed and complete description will follow in due course; the present paper concerns itself only with one small aspect. I wish to acknowledge financial support from the British Academy (1987), the Maison des Sciences de l'Homme (1987, 1991), Cambridge University (1989, 1991) and the Crowther-Beynon Fund (1991). We are most grateful for the support received from the Instituto de Investigaciones Antropologicas of the Universidad Nacional Autonoma de Mexico, and notably from Dr M.-C. Serra Puche and Dr Y. Sugiura who originally suggested the research area, and who have shown continued interest in the development of the work. We would also like to thank the Acting Director of the Ethnographic Museum in Patzcuaro, Don Enrique Luft, and the potter Luis Merigo and his wife Rafaela. Their contacts and their advice made the work easier and their hospitality our stay more pleasant.

The investigations focused on (1) defining the *chaînes opératoires* responsible for each of the products encountered, (2) eliciting the potters' interpretations of these *chaînes opératoires*, (3) contrasting these 'etic' and 'emic' data to determine where choices between alternatives were conscious, and in which cases they were not, and finally (4) mapping parts of the potters' 'problem space' or 'mental map'. The ultimate aim of the fieldwork, which is ongoing, is to investigate the cognitive correlates of tradition and innovation by monitoring closely in which ways potters modify *chaînes opératoires* to introduce new products.

5   Traditionally, this is done by rolling a heavy volcanic stone over it; nowadays, there is increasing use of a pug-mill.

6   It also occurs in some parts of the New World (van der Leeuw 1983). However, it is important to stress that this aspect is independent of the technique used. Wherever in the Old World throwing is the actual technique used, the potter throws the vessel in parts which reflect the same perspective (van der Leeuw 1976).

7   But on the other, it is tied in with a social 'conceptualization', the separation between potters who use ready-made moulds and mould-makers. Potters generally only know the executive partonomy, and therefore are unlikely to be able to conceive of new shapes and make the moulds to implement them. That is the role of the few mould-makers in each group (van der Leeuw and Papousek 1992). The division of labour generally works against the introduction of new variations by individual potters.

References

Atlan, H. 1992. Self-organising networks: weak, strong and intentional – the rôle of their underdetermination. In *La Nuova Critica* NS vol. 19–20 (1/2): 51–70

Balfet, H. 1984. Methods of formation and the shape of pottery. In *The many dimensions of pottery: ceramics in archaeology and anthropology*, ed. S. E. van der Leeuw and A. C. Pritchard, pp. 171–97. Amsterdam, A. E. van Giffen Instituut voor Pre- en Protohistorie (Cingula VII)

Delbrück, M. 1988. *Mind from matter*. San Francisco, W. H. Freeman

Engelbrecht, B. 1987. *Töpferinnen in Mexiko. Entwicklungsethnologische Untersuchungen zur produktion und Vermarktung der Töpferei von Patamban und Tzintzuntzan, Michoacán, West-Mexiko*. Basel, Ethnologischs Seminar der Universität und Museum für Völkerkunde

Foster, G. M. and G. Ospina 1948. *Empire's children: the people of Tzintzuntzan*. Washington, D.C., Smithsonian Institution (Institute of Social Anthropology, Publ. 6)

Hardin, M. A. 1977. Structure and creativity: family style in Tarascan greenware painting. Unpublished Ph.D. Thesis, University of Chicago

van der Leeuw, S. E. 1976. *Studies in the technology of ancient pottery*. Amsterdam, 2 vols.

1983. Analysis of Moundville Phase ceramic technology. In *Prehistoric agricultural communities in West-Central Alabama*, vol. II (Studies of the material remains from the Lubbub Creek Archaeological Locality), ed. C. S. Peebles, pp. 123–32. Ann Arbor

1984. Manufacture, trade and use of pottery on Negros, Philippines. In *Earthenware in Asia and Africa*, ed. J. Picton, pp. 326–44. Colloquies on Art and Archaeology in Asia, 12. London, Percival David Foundation of Chinese Art

1989. Risk, perception, innovation. In *What's new? A closer look at the process of innovation*, ed. S. E. van der Leeuw and R. Torrence, pp. 300–29. London, Unwin Hyman

1990. Rythmes temporels, espaces naturels et espaces vécus. In *Archéologie et espaces*, ed. J. L. Fiches and S. E. van der Leeuw, pp. 299–346. Antibes, APCDA

1991. Variation, variability and explanation in pottery studies. In *Ceramic ethnoarchaeology*, ed. W. A. Longacre, pp. 3–39. Tucson, University of Arizona Press

1993. Giving the potter a choice: conceptual aspects of pottery techniques. In *Technological choices: arbitrariness in technology from the Neolithic to modern high-tech*, ed. P. Lemonnier, pp. 238–88. London, Routledge Kegan Paul

van der Leeuw, S. E., D. A. Papousek and A. Coudart 1992. Technological traditions and unquestioned assumptions. *Techniques et Culture* 17–18 (1991): 145–73

van der Leeuw, S. E. and D. A. Papousek 1992. Tradition and innovation. In *Ethnoarchéologie: justification, problèmes, limites*, ed. F. Audouze, A. Gallay and V. Roux, pp. 135–58. Juan les Pins, APDCA

14
Mindful technology: unleashing the *chaîne opératoire* for an archaeology of mind

NATHAN SCHLANGER

La technologie doit d'abord être vécue, pensée ensuite si le besoin s'en fait encore sentir.

André Leroi-Gourhan (1945: 10)

Introduction

Far from being irremediably incapacitated by the inadequacies of the excavated record, an archaeology of the ancient mind is possible, and quite capable of generating new and interesting knowledge about its subject matter. With their in-depth specialization in the recovery, analysis and interpretation of material culture and of technological remains, archaeologists are, in fact, situated in a unique position from which to make original and consequential contributions to the sciences of the human mind. Let me initiate a discussion of this potential with the following proposition: there are non-trivial relations between the material actions that humans undertake, and their minds in action. It is on the reality or the viability of such a proposition that an archaeology of the mind (the way I see it) will hinge. After all, most of our evidence from the past consists of remains of material actions; if these remains, appropriately studied, cannot somehow inform us on the ancient mind, what other means – short of empathy – will do?

My proposition does not stem solely from an attitude of resigned necessity, whereby we must do with what we have. I contend that even if, transported back in time, we could actually observe a Palaeolithic band *in vivo*, it would be highly informative and rewarding to study their ubiquitous material actions and products in their 'natural' setting. I imply then, in qualifying the relations between mind and technology (material actions) as 'non-trivial', that such

relations cannot be reduced, nor completely understood, through the banal remark that both mind and technology are attributable to the same organism. For us to move beyond this superficial – albeit necessary – level of relationships, and indeed for any positive contribution to the study of the ancient mind to be coherent and meaningful, adequate theoretical and practical conditions need to be constituted.

This present paper is devoted to an exposition, and an assessment, of one practical condition for an archaeology of mind: namely, the judicious use of the *chaîne opératoire* approach to the study of lithic technology.[1] This approach, reinstated in its theoretical milieu and illustrated through archaeological examples, presents one evident attraction: it fosters an explicit concern over the processes, and not merely the states, of material culture. If the becoming of material culture and the succession of material actions can be reconstructed on the basis of static archaeological remains, then the active mind of the past may well be, after all, within reach.

Diagnostic technology

While the *chaîne opératoire* approach may represent a coherent, practical condition for further research, it remains, left to itself, neither self-explanatory nor sufficient. In effect, before venturing further, a wide range of prevalent conceptions, pertinent debates and established knowledge, about both *material actions* and the *mind in action* need be scrutinized. This critical assessment will not be attempted here in any detail, but I nevertheless mention two closely related and in my view essential themes.

First, the state and status of technology. Is it the case, as some would have us believe, that technology is an environmental or external variable, a pre-cultural outpost of civilization to be overcome by evolving hominids? Put succinctly, is technology 'natural'? This question has obvious implication for the ancient mind, at least so far as human origins are concerned. If tools and techniques are little more than a suite of objects, a purely biological extension of the limb, or an asocial mode of adaptation, then indeed it would be a fallacy to assume any relation between mind and material action, except at the most superficial organic level. Without any pretences to originality, I contend that technology, the becoming of material culture, is cultural, and artificial. H. Simon, in *The sciences of the artificial*, highlights the implications of this seemingly banal statement. Engineering, craftsmanship and many things manmade are artificial, in that they 'are not concerned with the necessary, but with the contingent – not how things are, but how things might be – in short, with design' (Simon 1969: xi, *passim*). Thus, anyone who devises courses of action aimed at changing existing situations into preferred ones is a designer. This course of action, being selected for by the actor, is motivated, and, in a cultural sense, arbitrary (Simon 1969; and see Pye 1978; Deforge 1990; Ingold 1986; on the philosophy and nature of design).

In the footsteps of M. Mauss (see below), I would envisage the *chaîne opératoire* in this light: as a practical, operational and coherent means with which to pin-point the part of the artificial, the interplay between fixed and flexible. It is the case that the technical act, dealing as it does with physical entities, is bound by material constraints and regulated by universal propensities and natural laws. A 'material' understanding of techniques is (as I shall show) crucial, but, in itself, cannot satisfactorily explain technical, let alone human, phenomena. The materiality of the technical act (and its outcome) in no way renders it less social, cultural or human – precisely because of its binding arbitrary character.[2]

Techniques may then be 'cultural', but we still need to debate the kind of mind they entail and represent. I am alluding here to a recurrent and influential theme in Western thought which may be conveniently labelled as the *sapiens/faber* split. Succinctly put, this split involves a distinction, a separation, and subsequently an opposition, between two images of mind: the intellectual or conceptual *sapiens* dwelling in the highest realms of pure theory and abstraction, and the practical and perceptual *Faber*, concerned with the ordinary, manual and mundane aspects of everyday life. While this distinction may have undeniable methodological utility on a case by case basis, and while the 'thinking mind' and the 'doing mind' certainly seem to vary in their content, any hierarchically-minded differentiation in their respective structuring or operation are to be viewed with some suspicion. The inherent superiority and interest of the 'thinking mind' has been shown, time and again, to be often a matter of cultural prejudice and academic ethnocentrism.[3] Similarly, the denigration of the 'doing mind' stems not only from the ascribed socio-economic status of those traditionally dealing with material and mundane undertakings, but also from the tacit, non-discursive, and uncodifiable nature of the knowledge brought to bear in ordinary (that is, real) life situations. In recent years, anthropological and psychological analyses of banal and non-academic activities – at work, at home, in the store – indicate that seemingly ordinary problems which need to be solved in daily life are often complicated and non-trivial, that they are in many cases created, reformulated and interpreted in a context of the actors' own making, and that they necessitate original, as well as routine, reflection.

Taking these themes into account and debating them is important. It enables us archaeologists to complement and balance a rather restrictive concentration on language, art and religion, as sole aspects deemed worthy of 'mindful' studies. The practical and material actions that humans undertake, besides being accessible through archaeological studies (via, for example, the *chaîne opératoire*), are related to the mind in action, a 'doing mind' which is not only cultural but also, in several senses, diagnostic.

The *chaîne opératoire* – theoretical foundations

As suggested above, the approach proceeds from the premise that material culture has a relevant history: before being as such, material culture becomes, in a trajectory of induced transformations from natural raw material to cultural matter. The French sociologist and ethnologist Marcel Mauss (1872–1950) was quite clear on this point, and on its implications: '[Man] Creates and at the same time he creates himself. He creates his means of livelihood, purely human things, and his thoughts inscribed in these things. Here is elaborated the veritable practical reason' (1927: 120).

Thus, if the production of matter and the production of meaning are co-incidental (as put by Lemonnier 1990), it is clear that humans are intrinsically implicated in the process of material becoming, from its very initiation. Adopting a holistic attitude, Mauss conceived of humanity as a totality, with all aspects of individual and social reality – including those most material and concrete – forming a synergy, a nexus of physical, psychological and social 'total facts'. While mainly concerned with the latter aspect, Mauss nonetheless convincingly argued in his ground-breaking *Les Techniques du corps* (1936) that even the most corporeal and biological aspects of humanity can be arbitrary in their action, appropriated into the social domain and rendered efficient there. In line with that, he stressed that the technical act is a conscious one, emerging from individually and collectively constituted 'practical reason'. As a methodological consequence, ethnographers, technologists, and, by extension, archaeologists were all urged to pay close attention to all the states and events of any technical action, and to comprehend their *enchaînement organique* and their *moments essentiels* as constituents and reflections of this totality (e.g. Mauss 1941, 1947).

It was André Leroi-Gourhan (1911–1986), with substantially different concerns and preoccupations, who formalized the approach and gave it practical coherence. The intellectual trajectory of this fascinating scholar cannot be detailed here, but his exceptional 'double personality' – as *humaniste* and as *naturaliste* – is crucial to the development of the *chaîne opératoire* approach (whose name he coined). From his archaeological excavations (notably Pincevent) and his ethnographic fieldwork (in the Far East) Leroi-Gourhan obtained a detailed understanding of material culture (1943, 1945), and developed a 'palethnological', behavioural and processual concern over the human past. Profoundly inspired by vertebrate palaeontology (e.g. 1983), Leroi-Gourhan aimed to produce a 'biology of techniques' (1964), approaching them as if they were living and evolving beings. One consequence was a rather deterministic and teleological view of human evolution (of which no more will be said here). The other organic inspiration, however, is of fundamental importance in this context. It involves a structural and functional awareness of techniques: as much as the limb or the organ is structured, serves a purpose and operates in a certain manner, so does the technical element, gesture or procedure. From this vision resulted a formalization of the 'elementary means of action on matter' such as percussion, abrasion, etc. (1943: ch. II; 1965: ch. VIII), and of the inherent properties of raw materials when acted upon. For example, stones are 'solides stables' – their constitution and physical properties are not affected by action, and their shape can be modified only by subtracting some of their substance (1943: 162).

But Leroi-Gourhan aimed for more than systematic componential descriptions. With a 'palaeontology of the gesture', he sought an understanding of the very dynamics of techniques: 'The tool exists only in the operational cycle [and witnesses it] in the same manner that a horse's skeleton bears traces of the rapid herbivore that it once was . . . the tool is real only when within the gestures that render it technically efficient' (1965: 35). The elementary components and constituents of action are in fact integrated in a necessary and logical *enchaînement* of stages and sequences in the process of transformation: 'Techniques are at the same time gestures and tools, organized in a veritable syntax, one which simultaneously grants to operational series their fixity and their flexibility' (1964: 164). For example, the making of a triangular flint point 'necessitates at least six series of operations, rigorously chained, each conditioning the other, and supposing rigorous foresight' (1964: 145). The act of fabrication is then a dialogue between the artisan and the worked material (1965: 132), a dialogue situated at the junction between the external and the internal 'milieu' (1945: 333–5), a dialogue implicating the natural determination of the *tendance* and the cultural idiosyncrasy of the *fait* (1943: 23–43).

Contrasting the technological reflections of Mauss and Leroi-Gourhan, it seems that (while promoting the same practical approach) the former emphasized the cultural *fait* (with its social origins and implications), and the latter attached importance to the overwhelming material and generic *tendance*. Together, these two points of view – propensity and contingent, determined and arbitrary – appear essential for a thorough understanding of techniques and their actors.[4]

Two influential contributions recently made by the anthropologist Pierre Lemonnier clarify the practical potential of this approach. First, Lemonnier envisioned the *chaîne opératoire* as a trajectory, a material enactment leading to a goal. This becoming is intersected by succeeding, simultaneous or overlapping moments. While it has a beginning (as natural raw material), and an end (as accepted product) this trajectory is not necessarily linear (1976: 106). With time, and bound by various constraints and motivations, two kinds of tasks or events can be distinguished: those which are variable and flexible, open to alteration, replacement and idiosyncrasy, and those which are fixed, immutable and 'strategical': they cannot be cancelled, deferred or by-passed without irredeemably compromising the success of the technical endeavour (1980: 9). These 'strategic' moments give the *chaîne opératoire* its rigid frame, and highlight the states and processes through which matter and action pass (cf. also Cresswell 1982 and 1990 on material and social 'focalities'). Besides addressing the *chaîne opératoire* in 'action', Lemonnier outlined its components and structure. The introductory sentence to *Les Salines de l'ouest* is worth quoting in full: 'Defined as socialized action on matter, techniques can be apprehended through three orders of facts: suites of gestures and operations (technical processes), objects (means of action on matter) and specific knowledge (*connaissances*)' (1980: 1).

The approach – current applications

These conceptions are obviously pertinent to a wide array of activities and materials. Besides being my own field of research, I concentrate here on lithic technology for two reasons: the lithic medium – in its durability, its sequential and substractive exploitation, its non-commutative retention of traces of action – is particularly well suited for such studies. As importantly, lithic artefacts have been continuously manufactured for at least 2.5 million years. They are the sole artefactual evidence of our ancestors, to whom we grant, for all intents and purposes, an 'ancient mind'.

As it stands, the *chaîne opératoire* approach to the study of (lithic) technology embodies the convergence of two research traditions: on the one hand, lithic experimentation and replication (following F. Bordes and J. Tixier, among others), and on the other hand, a vision of human behaviour *per se* as the subject and scope of inquiry, advocated in particular by Leroi-Gourhan and his collaborators. The distinction between these traditions is often blurred, but it seems that a certain development can be discerned from empirical practice ('technicians') to theoretical reflections ('technologists'). As the approach is very much current, ongoing research and developments, a critical appraisal may be premature. It appears, however, that this diachronic trend has its synchronic counterpart, entrenched in a long-standing tradition of empirical and inductive research. In that sense, Lemonnier's three 'orders of facts' (see above) do represent a convenient epistemological and methodological hierarchy to address the issue. As adapted to lithic technology (see Audouze 1985 and particularly Pelegrin *et al.* 1988), these 'facts' are rendered as follows: first, the *objects* – more than means of action on matter, they refer both to the tools employed, and to the material outcomes of action: products, debitage or waste; next the series of gestures and *operations* – the technical actions and processes physically undertaken in a sequence of gestures; lastly, the specific *knowledge* brought to bear and put in action in the technical phenomenon.

Before reaching this latter aspect, two examples of innovative archaeological applications of the approach, and the understanding it enables us to obtain, are worth presenting.[5] In his examination of Mousterian assemblages in South-West France, J.-M. Geneste (1985, 1988a, 1988b) conceived of lithic technology as an economic system of production, comprising six phases (Fig. 14.1), further subdivided into some twenty-five diagnostic 'material correlates' (Geneste 1985: 178ff., 249ff.; and see Turq 1989).

Two correspondences were suggested by these studies. One is a relation between the technological and the typological status of the artefact (e.g. notches and denticulates on cortical and undifferentiated products, scrapers on Levallois products). The other is of a spatial and (by extension) economic order: local raw materials were

introduced to the site as complete blocks, whereas distant or exotic materials were first reduced at the extraction site and introduced as more elaborate blanks. Thus, upon the reconstruction of these *chaînes opératoires*, Geneste was able to look anew at the Périgord Mousterian, and to infuse a deadlocked 'tradition vs. function' debate with new dimensions and opportunities (see some implications in Geneste 1988a, b; Roebroeks *et al.* 1988).

The Levallois method – that in which, following F. Bordes' well known definition, the form of the product is predetermined by prior special preparation – has been comprehensively studied by E. Boëda (1986, 1988a, 1988b, 1990). Adopting a practical and experimental stance, and developing a 'diacritique'[6] technological reading of the material remains of knapping actions, Boëda set out to investigate, in depth, this 'special preparation'. In doing so, he has outlined a 'Levallois concept', consisting of the creation and maintenance of a functional, volumetric, and strategic (*sensu* Lemonnier above) distinction between the striking platform (where the blow is delivered), and the striking surface (from which the flake is detached, see Fig. 14.2a). For the detached flake to have a predetermined shape, the striking surface should possess lateral and distal convexities (Fig. 14.2b–c). This functionally necessary configuration may be obtained through various preparatory flakes – that is, flakes whose specific absence from the core is desired. In such a case, a clear-cut distinction may be postulated between preparation and exploitation, and between predetermining and predetermined (i.e. Levallois) removals.

However, the situation may be more complex, both materially and conceptually. If the core is exploited more than once, a specially prepared and predetermined Levallois

Acquisition	----------------Production---------------			Consumption	Discard
Phase 0	**Phase 1**	**Phase 2**	**Phase 3**	**Phase 4**	**Phase 5**
Extraction	Shaping	Production	Retouch	Use	Abandonment
	the core	of blanks	or direct use		
'Entame'	Decortification			Resharpening	Discard
	Striking platform			Recycling	Wear
				Transformation	

Fig. 14.1. Lithic technology as a system of production (After Geneste 1985).

product may, in its turn, contribute to the predetermination of a subsequent and equally desired Levallois product (see Fig. 14.3). This recurrent mode of exploitation, besides being advantageous in productive terms, seems also to indicate a potential for designing, and realizing, an enmeshed and hierarchically interdependent sequence of multiple causalities.

Although presented here in the briefest possible terms, these researches highlight the potential of the *chaîne opératoire* approach to reinsert technical activities in their gestural, spatial and temporal dimensions.[7] These researches indicate that the material actions undertaken by ancient humans may very well, in appropriate circumstances, be apprehended in their logic and their syntax (to use Leroi-Gourhan's words).

Flintknapping – a cognitive activity

Obviously, humans undertake material actions in a range of situations, and for a number of purposes. It can be postulated that, being artificial and intentional, these acts follow certain beliefs, expectations, desires and deliberations. If such is the case, then the intentional (technical) act has, of necessity, some sort of *mental antecedents*. These antecedents could

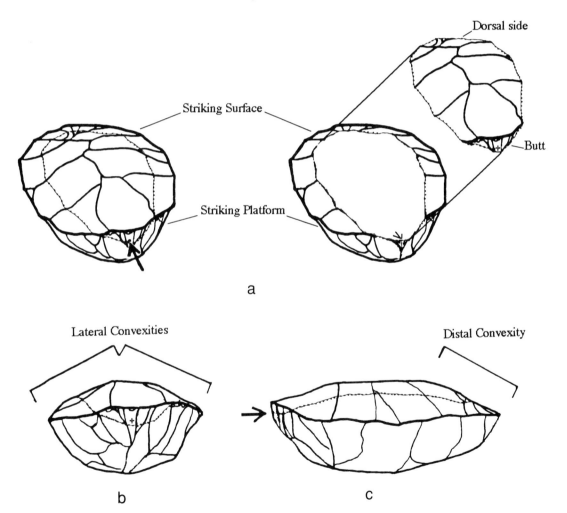

Fig. 14.2. The Levallois concept. a – *Schematic representations of a centripetally prepared Levallois core, showing the distinction between 'striking surface' and 'striking platform'. These distinctions correspond respectively to the dorsal side and the butt of the struck Levallois flake (shown in dotted line).* b *and* c – *proximal and lateral views of the same core, showing the lateral and distal convexities which determine the shape of the Levallois flake (After Boëda 1986, 1988a).*

well be singled out as the focus of substantive research in cognitive archaeology, upon which to forge theoretical and methodological connections with the sciences of the human mind.

Let us then recall some evident 'cognitive' questions: What is known? How is it known? How is this knowledge generated, organized, used, maintained, transformed, transferred, and, indeed, forgotten? To be sure, few of these questions have readily accessible or unambiguous answers in contemporary cognitive psychology, let alone through archaeological research. Nevertheless, the *chaîne opératoire* approach may provide a number of valuable insights and arguments in current debates. For example, both empirical assessments and theoretical reflection may lead to a criticism of two related images of mind, often invoked in palaeolithic and technological studies – the 'black box' and the 'mental template'. The passive mechanistic image provided by the former, and the normative and static nature of the latter appear inadequate and impoverishing. On the contrary, we should be able, with increased technological sensitivity, to consider flintknapping as a cognitive activity, one which involves the mind in action.

To do so, we may adopt, for our own purposes, a well known question in cognitive anthropology: 'What is it that I need to know in order to produce, say, a Levallois flake, or a straight-edged blade?' A distinction could be made between conceptual, abstract knowledge (*connaissances*), and

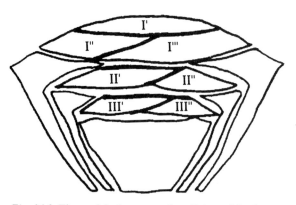

Fig. 14.3. The model of recurrent Levallois exploitation (side view). Surface I produced three Levallois flakes: the first (I') is predetermined by core preparation, and affects the shape of the later two. The second (I'') is in part shaped by the first, and predetermines the shape of the third (I'''). Following phases of preparation, surfaces II and III produced two Levallois flakes each, the first of which (II' and III') is predetermined and redetermining.

practical or procedural know-how (*savoir-faire*). Both of these, argues J. Pelegrin (1990), are present in an 'elaborate flintknapping activity'.[8] As discussed by a number of technologists and anthropologists, know-how also involves, besides instrumental dexterity, evaluations and judgement (Pye 1978: ch. 5). It could then be seen as an overall capacity to succeed in an activity through personal engagement and interpretation, a *heuristic* which enables one to grasp, modify, combine, and (when applicable) transfer and generalize knowledge, in and through practice (see Deforge 1990, and Dougherty and Keller 1982 on the contextual and goal-oriented organization of knowledge in fluid constellations). Besides being informed, the technical act is also formed by intention, purpose and project. Pelegrin (1985, 1986, 1990) suggests, on the basis of experimental and archaeological studies, that the ultimate or governing motivations of the lithic *chaîne opératoire* are often complemented and interlaced by a succession of intermediary and predetermining goals, whose outcome and overall contribution are anticipated. Thus, prior to a sequence of gestures, prior to execution or implementation, there seems to exist, in the mind of the knapper, some sort of 'intentional sequence', organized in a 'conceptual *schéma opératoire*' (Pelegrin 1990, see also Pigeot 1990, and the Levallois method discussed above).

The crucial point about this actual and conceptual sequence is that – as raw material is never standard in shape or composition, and striking actions cannot be undertaken with perfection – it cannot remain an immutable sequence: 'input' and 'output' interact with each other, contingency is all too often necessity. If the blueprint is blurred, and the artefact's template is somehow fluid in its material becoming, so is, in a way, its mental counterpart. In its co-incidentally predictable and random responses, the transformed material creates new problems and generates ever-changing configurations to be perceived and knowledgeably addressed. Techniques are indeed, as Leroi-Gourhan suggested, a dialogue: the lithic medium is, to all intents and purposes, an interlocutor whose physical reactions cannot be ignored, and the human 'partner' needs to monitor permanently, and critically, all undertaken or projected actions, to consider the given results in view of the expected, to assess anew the possibility and desirability of the guiding design, to rectify plans according to imagined future eventualities, and to undertake new material actions in view of the above. In short, to engage in an elaborate knapping activity is to foresee, to continuously choose, assess and decide (Pelegrin 1985, 1990; Pigeot 1990), to apply and thereby, through practice, to generate knowledge.

While the rather simplistic proposition with which this paper was initiated – that material actions and the mind in action are related – is evidently in need of further elaborations and reflections, it is also in my view worthy of them. As archaeologists, we are quite successful at assembling and describing a wealth of artefactual evidence. With such approaches as the *chaîne opératoire*, we may well have means to relate these static remains to human actions – and from there on to address the cognitive issues which concern us. The fact that the material and mental activities in question were undertaken in the remote past, and the fact that they are material, ubiquitous, and, one suspects, utterly ordinary, should not detract from their interest. After all, as Marcel Mauss pointed out long ago (1927) it is in (ordinary) creation that humankind makes itself, its reasoned practices and its practical reason. It may well be that a process of this nature will be unveiled by an archaeology of the modern as well as the ancient mind.

Notes

1 A literal translation – operational chain – seems to do away with the connotations and diversity of the approach. Attempts to study the mind on the basis of stone artefacts have a long history in archaeological research. Leaving aside various searches for 'the pre-historic mentality', important reflections were proposed by Oakley (1952), Holloway (1969) and Alimen and Goustard (1962). In recent years Wynn (1985, 1989) endorsed a Piagetian approach (see also Atran 1982; Graves 1990). Young and Bonnichsen (1984) make explicit use of developments in cognitive anthropology and ethnoscience. Noteworthy also is the work of Gowlett (e.g. 1984, 1990), and that of Kithahara-Frish (1980) and Goren-Inbar (1988).

2 This point has been repeatedly made under various theoretical auspices. E.g. Mauss 1941; Simondon 1958; Haudricourt 1964; Cresswell 1990; Digard 1979; Lemonnier 1986, 1989, 1990; Ingold 1990; Pfaffenberger 1988; etc.

3 'The division between pure reason and practical reason seems scholastic, hardly authentic, hardly psychological, and even less sociological. We know, we see, we feel the profound links that unite them, in their *raison d'être* and their history' (Mauss 1927: 121).

4 The technological reflections of Leroi-Gourhan and Mauss are further discussed in Schlanger 1990, 1991. Leroi-Gourhan's *oeuvre* still awaits a thorough appraisal and dissemination outside of France (see Leroi-Gourhan 1973, 1987, 1988).

5 The *chaîne opératoire* is not, I suggest, a methodological tool in the instrumental and directly applicable sense of the word. The temporal scope (from the earliest

industries to ethnoarchaeology and primate material behaviour) and the geographical scale (France, the Eastern Mediterranean, and Africa) denote a variety of preoccupations and applications. Within these, the works of Geneste, Boëda and Pelegrin mentioned here appear particularly innovative and influential.

6 A *schéma diacritique* is an interpretive drawing of a core or a flake where the recognizable directions of scars (the negatives of previous removals) as well as their sequence of removal are represented (e.g. by means of arrows and numbers).

7 Note as well that these studies pertain to Early (Lower/Middle) Palaeolithic occurrences, involving pre-*Homo sapiens sapiens*.

8 To mention a few – actions-suits and rules to know, pertaining to: the striking implements used; the orientation, location, incidence of the knapping gesture; the need to distinguish functionally between striking platform and striking surface (see Fig. 14.2); the need to create and maintain an angle smaller than 90 degrees between these surfaces; the need to maintain an appropriate convexity of the striking surface and unobstructed access to the striking point; and so on, according to the strategy employed and the products desired (see the works of Boëda and Pelegrin cited above, and Pigeot 1988, 1990).

References

Alimen, M.-H. and M. Goustard 1962. Le développement de l'intelligence et des structures paléo-biopsychologiques. *Bulletin de la Société Préhistorique Française* 59: 389–406

Atran, S. 1982. Constraints on a theory of hominid tool-making behavior. *L'Homme* 22 (2): 35–68

Audouze, F. 1985. L'Apport des sols d'habitat à l'étude de l'outillage lithique. In *La signification culturelle des industries lithiques*, ed. M. Otte, pp. 57–68. British Archaeological Reports, Oxford (BAR International Series 239)

Boëda, E. 1986. *Approche technologique du concept Levallois et evaluation de son champ d'application: étude de trois gisements saaliens et weichséliens de la France septentrionale.* Thèse de Doctorat, Université de Paris X

1988a. Le concept Levallois et évaluation de son champ d'application. In *L'Homme de Néandertal*, vol. IV: *La technique*, ed. L. Binford and J.-P. Rigaud, pp. 13–26. Liège, ERAUL 31

1988b. Le concept laminaire: Rupture et filiation avec le concept Levallois. In *L'Homme de Néandertal*, vol. III:

La mutation, ed. J. K. Kozlowski, pp. 41–59. Liège, ERAUL 35

1990. De la surface au volume: analyse des conceptions des débitages Levallois et laminaire. In *Paléolithique moyen récent et Paléolithique supérieur ancien en Europe*, ed. C. Farizy, pp. 63–8. Mémoires du Musée de Préhistoire d'Ile-de-France 3

Cresswell, R. 1982. Transferts de techniques et chaînes opératoires. *Techniques et Culture* (ns) MSH 2

1990. 'A New Technology' revisited. *Archaeological Review from Cambridge* 9 (1): 39–54

Deforge, Y. 1990. *L'Oeuvre et le produit*. Paris, Champ Vallon

Digard, J.-P. 1979. La technologie en anthropologie: fin de parcours ou nouveau souffle? *L'Homme* 19: 73–104

Doughtery, J. W. D. and C. M. Keller 1982. Taskonomy: a practical approach to knowledge structures. *American Ethnologist* 9: 763–74

Geneste, J.-M. 1985. *Analyse lithique d'industries Moustériennes du Périgord: une approche technologique du comportement des groupes humains au Paléolithique Moyen*. Thèse de Doctorat, Université de Bordeaux I

1988a. Economie des ressources lithiques dans le Moustérien du Sud Ouest de la France. In *L'Homme de Néandertal*, vol. VI: *La subsistance*, ed. M. Patou and L. G. Freeman, pp. 75–97. Liège, ERAUL 33

1988b. Systèmes d'approvisionnement en matières premières au Paléolithique moyen et au Paléolithique supérieur en Aquitaine. In *L'Homme de Néandertal*, vol. VIII: *La mutation*, ed. J. K. Kozlowski, pp. 61–70. Liège, ERAUL 35

Goren-Inbar, N. 1988. Notes on 'decision making' by Lower and Middle Paleolithic hominids. *Paléorient* 14 (2): 99–108

Gowlett, J. A. J. 1984. Mental abilities of early man; a look at some hard evidence. In *Hominid evolution and community ecology*, ed. R. Foley, pp. 167–92. London, Academic Press

1990. Technology, skill and the psychosocial sector in the long term of human evolution. *Archaeological Review from Cambridge* 9 (1): 82–103

Graves, P. 1990. Sermons in stone – an exploration of Thomas Wynn's 'The evolution of spatial competence'. *Archaeological Review from Cambridge* 9 (1): 104–15

Haudricourt, A. 1964. La technologie, science humaine. *La Pensée* 115: 28–35

Holloway, R. L. 1969. Culture: a *human* domain. *Current Anthropology* 10 (4): 395–412

Ingold, T. 1986. Tools and *Homo faber*; construction and authorship of design. In *The appropriation of nature – essays on human ecology and social relations*, ed. T.

Ingold, ch. 3. Manchester, University of Manchester Press

1990. Society, nature and the concept of technology. *Archaeological Review from Cambridge* 9 (1): 5–17

Kithahara-Frish, J. 1980. Symbolising technology as a key to human evolution. In *Symbol as sense: new approaches to the analysis of meaning*, ed. M. L. Foster and S. H. Brandes, pp. 211–24. New York, Academic Press

Lemonnier, P. 1976. La description des chaînes opératoires: contribution a l'analyse des systèmes techniques. *Techniques et Culture* 1 (MSH)

1980. *Les Salines de l'ouest – logique technique, logique sociale*. Paris/Lille, Maison des Sciences de l'Homme/ Presses Universitaires de Lille

1986. The study of material culture today: towards an anthropology of technical systems. *Journal of Anthropological Archaeology* 5: 147–86

1989. Bark capes, arrowheads and concorde: on social representations of technology. In *The meaning of things: material culture and symbolic expression*, ed. I. Hodder, pp. 156–71. London, Unwin Hyman

1990. Topsy turvy techniques. Remarks on the social representation of techniques. *Archaeological Review from Cambridge* 9 (1): 27–37

Leroi-Gourhan, A. 1943. *L'Homme et le matière*. Paris, Albin Michel

1945. *Milieu et techniques*. Paris, Albain Michel

1964. *Le Geste et la parole I – technique et langage*. Paris, Albin Michel

1965. *Le Geste et la parole II – la mémoire et les rythmes*. Paris, Albin Michel

1973. *L'Homme, hier et aujourd'hui, recueil d'études en hommage à André Leroi-Gourhan*. Paris, Cujas

1983. *Mécanique vivante*. Paris, Fayard

1987. Hommage de la SPF à André Leroi-Gourhan. *Bulletin de la Société Préhistorique Française* 84 (10–12)

1988. *Leroi-Gourhan, ou les voies de l'homme*. Actes du colloque du CNRS, mars 1987. Paris, Albin Michel

Mauss, M. 1927. Division et proportions des divisions de la sociologie. *Année sociologique* n.s. 2 [Reprinted in M. Mauss 1969. *Œuvres*, vol. 3, pp. 178–245, Paris, Editions de Minuit]

1936. Les techniques du corps. *Journal de psychologie* 32 [Reprinted in M. Mauss 1950. *Sociologie et anthropologie*, pp. 365–86. Paris, Presses Universitaires de France]

1941. Les techniques et la technologie. *Journal de Psychologie* 41 [Reprinted in M. Mauss 1969. *Œuvres*, Vol. III, pp. 250–6. Paris, Edition de Minuit]

1947. *Manuel d'ethnographie*. Paris, Payot

Oakley, K. 1952. *Man the tool maker*. London, British Museum Publications

Pelegrin, J. 1985. Réflection sur le comportement technique. In *La signification culturelle des industries lithiques*, ed. M. Otte, pp. 72–91. British Archaeological Reports, Oxford (BAR International Series 239)

1986. *Technologie lithique: une méthode appliquée à l'étude de deux séries du Périgordien ancien*. Thèse de Doctorat, Université de Paris X

1990. Prehistoric lithic technology: some aspects of research. *Archaeological Review from Cambridge* 9 (1): 116–25

Pelegrin, J., C. Karlin and P. Bodu 1988. Chaînes opératoires: un outil pour le préhistorien. In *Technologie préhistorique*, ed. J. Tixier, pp. 55–62. Notes et Monographies techniques no. 25, Paris, CNRS

Pfaffenberger, B. 1988. Fetishised objects and humanised nature: towards an anthropology of technology. *Man* (NS) 23: 236–52

Pigeot, N. 1988. Apprendre à débiter des lames: un cas d'education technique chez les Magdaléniens d'Etiolles. In *Technologie Préhistorique*, ed. J. Tixier, pp. 63–72. Notes et monographies techniques no. 25. Paris, CNRS

1990. Technical and social actors: flintknapping specialists and apprentices at Magdalenian Etiolles. *Archaeological Review from Cambridge* 9 (1): 126–41

Pye, D. 1978. *The nature and aesthetics of design*. London, Barrie and Jenkins

Roebroeks, W., J. Kolen and E. Rensink 1988. Planning depth, anticipation and the organization of middle Palaeolithic technology; The 'archaic natives' meet Eve's descendants. *Helinium* 28: 17–34

Schlanger, N. 1990. Techniques as human action – two perspectives. *Archaeological Review from Cambridge* 9 (1): 18-26

1991. Le fait technique total – la raison pratique et les raisons de la pratiques dans l'oeuvre de Marcel Mauss. *Terrain* 16: 114–30

Simon, H. A. 1969. *The sciences of the artificial*. Cambridge, MA, MIT Press

Simondon, G. 1958. *Du mode d'existance des objets techniques*. Paris, Aubier

Turq, A. 1989. Approche technologique et économique du faciès Moustérien de type Quina: étude préliminaire. *Bulletin de la Société Préhistorique Française* 86 (8): 244–56

Wynn, T. 1985. Piaget, stone tools, and the evolution of human intelligence. *World Archaeology* 17 (1): 32–43

1989. *The Evolution of spatial competence*. Illinois Studies in Anthropology, vol. 17, Urbana, University of Illinois Press

Young, D. and R. Bonnichsen 1984. *Understanding stone tools: a cognitive approach*. Peopling of the Americas series, vol. I. Orono, Center for the study of Early Man, University of Maine

15
Prehistoric technology: a cognitive science?

C. KARLIN AND M. JULIEN

It is now well known that the appearance of tools precedes that of man, and furthermore, that tools are not the exclusive attribute of the Hominidae. Recent research in animal behaviour shows that many species, not only our closest 'cousins' the chimpanzees and other great apes, are capable of selecting a branch or a stone to obtain food which is not directly accessible to them and that, in some cases, they may go elsewhere to look for a suitable instrument, or put it aside for later use. Memory, the choice of a suitable instrument, and the medium-term retention of information are the intellectual faculties necessary for the construction of a *chaîne opératoire*.[1] It seems, however, that only some of the great apes are capable of making or reworking a tool (Beyries and Joulian 1990).

The *chaîne opératoire*, however, is not limited to the domain of tools: the building of a nest or a beaver lodge, and the hoarding of food supplies for hibernation, are other examples. The behaviour of certain animal species thus reveals systems of technology which have to be compared with those of humans if we wish to understand what distinguishes innate and learned capabilities. The study of the slow evolution of human intelligence over three million years is clearly one of the research directions which the cognitive sciences must explore in order to understand the dialectical relationship between intellectual activities, which we define as logically-based (analysis of information by induction and deduction), and those which are non-logical (coding of information based on perception and memory, selection, comparison, recoding, etc.).

Greek philosophers were undoubtedly the first to have explained the different categories of human intellectual activity, but the capacity for abstraction, for problem-solving and for the creation of formal systems was already manifest

in material or symbolic form in the great civilizations, either with or without writing, which preceded Greek civilization or which developed in other parts of the world. These elaborate manifestations, however, are only the end-product of a process which had begun, at least for *Homo sapiens*, 100,000 years before and whose origins go back even further. By what methods can we identify the various stages in this process?

Where biological evolution appears more rapid than technological evolution

For the earliest periods of the human adventure, the mastery of intellectual mechanisms can only be approached through the physical evolution of fossil remains. The adoption of bipedalism and the freeing of the hands set in train modifications in cranial architecture and the gradual development of the central nervous system. We may postulate that non-logical forms of intellectual activity, such as perception, memory and the selection of useful information, were acquired at the outset, since these conditions are essential for the survival of higher animals and for their adaptation to the environment. No doubt these faculties were steadily enriched during the process of 'hominization' as a result of the transformation of the east African environment. Around three million years ago, partly contemporary with the bipedal but still tree-dwelling *Australopithecus afarensis* (Johanson *et al.* 1978), the second australopithecine member of the hominid family made its appearance. It was clearly bipedal like its predecessor, but only the fore-limbs show that it retained the ability to move from tree to tree. As time passed, its cranial capacity grew to 600 cm^3, and the blood flow to the brain increased. This hominid, which was not yet *Homo*, was, nevertheless, the first to be associated with an assemblage of knapped stone tools. Some specialists question its ability to make tools, but others consider that he possessed all the physical aptitudes (prehensile hand, upright posture, brain structure) to be a tool-maker. This brings it close to the genus *Homo*, with which he may indeed have had a shared ancestry two or three million years before. According to Coppens, from whom we have taken this rapid synthesis, 'the worked tool though modest in itself, effectively implies knapping towards an idea, a task which is organized and transmitted, a communication which is elaborated' (1989: 14). We can start by trying to find out how this knowledge was transmitted. The simplicity of the *chaînes opératoires* (food-getting, choice of nocturnal sleeping-places, selection and rudimentary working of pebbles or bones), suggests that the 'impregnation' must have been – among others – a fundamental mode of apprenticeship: the observation of simple actions, the copying of behaviour *in situ* without the need for an articulated language.

The first Homo, *Homo habilis* (Leakey *et al.* 1964), was a contemporary of *Australopithecus* for almost two million years. Like the latter, he had to face the drastic climatic change and desiccation of the east African environment around 2.5 million years ago. Fossils of *Homo* are often found at the same sites but they are distinguished generically by their physical evolution. They no longer present any ability for tree-climbing and travel only on the ground, using their feet. Their dentition was that of an omnivore (as was that of the gracile australopithecines), and their larger crania possessed highly developed lateral zones of association. The tools of *Homo* were almost the same as those of *Australopithecus*, though we may note the use of flakes detached from pebbles, suggesting a differentiated usage which varied according to the tasks to be performed. They also seem to have used areas of seasonal settlement, where the remains of a range of animal species, probably acquired by scavenging, hunting or trapping, have been found. Judging by the size of these settlement areas, in particular Melka Kunturé (Ethiopia), and the nature of remains which they contain, we can assume that they lived in small groups of fifteen to twenty individuals. Here then, are the rudiments of a society in which knowledge could be transmitted. There was still nothing exceptional in the development of intellectual abilities, but he had definitely become the dominant hominid species, which reveals the flexibility of its adaptive capabilities and, hence, a more effective brain.

The circumstances which led to his replacement by *Homo erectus* remain little understood, but we may observe that this second *Homo*, despite its slightly better developed brain, continued, at first, to make the same types of stone tool. As Coppens emphasizes, 'during the period from 2,500,000 to 1,500,000 years ago, biological evolution proceeded more quickly in round figures than technological evolution' (1989: 19). This would indicate that physical changes were not accompanied by any clear shifts in socio-technology; that is, unless this technological evolution was characterized by a range of tools made in perishable materials.

The story of *Homo erectus* is associated with the conquest of the Old World. His lifestyle and camp sites were scarcely different from those of its predecessors, but he was responsible, around 1.4 million years ago, for two technical innovations of the greatest importance: the adoption of fire (still questioned by some authorities) and the invention of the biface and hand-axe (Chavaillon 1989). Though the use of fire does not yet seem to have altered the nature of lifestyle and society, this advance in technical mastery indicates intellectual abilities far superior to those we have detected earlier.

Prehistoric technology

The evolution of human intellectual capabilities may be approached by studying the development of technical skills, and by seeking to evaluate the complexity of the concepts underlying them. This technological approach is inspired by a 'conception of techniques as social productions: the "objectification" (in the sense of "put into object") of what are socially elaborated thoughts' (Lemonnier 1990). Even though specialists in prehistoric technology remain fully aware that their search for the 'meaning' of techniques, whose operators no longer exist, will always prevent them from discovering the complete significance of a technical act, their quest is none the less productive.

The concept of the *chaîne opératoire*, first used by ethnologists, has been taken up by prehistorians in order to organize their observations in a logical manner. While various prehistoric activities may be deduced from the nature of the remains discovered at sites, the technical procedures of acquisition, transformation, manufacture and use remain fragmentary, owing to the numerous elements which have disappeared over the course of time. The reconstruction of certain *chaînes opératoires* allows us, however, to arrange the information in a coherent order and, by various analyses, to rediscover the processes involved in techniques of production and, beyond that, the conceptual pattern from which they sprang (Pelegrin *et al.* 1988). Such reconstruction is enhanced by the study of settlement remains. In the best preserved sites, distribution analysis of the different stages of production and utilization of the essentials of daily life can indicate preferred activity zones, discard areas or reserved spaces, and can disclose a structuring of the settlement space which reveals the importance ascribed by people to the different activities.

The study of lithic remains draws advantage from the imperishable character of stone, the abundance of material produced, whether tools or waste flakes, and finally from the nature of the knapping process, intentional and organized, which marks with characteristic scars the elements produced by a succession of technical operations. Through these features, the study of lithic remains stands as one of the principal routes by which to approach the analysis of the development of human intelligence, in so far as capacities for innovation and generalization can be detected in systems of lithic production. Other technical systems, such as hunting and the gathering of plant foods or the activities associated with fire, remain, by contrast, more difficult to understand, since the reconstruction of the operative processes is still too fragmentary. However, new developments in archaeozoology (taphonomic studies, analysis of animal body-parts, etc.) and the physico-chemical investigation of sediments from settlements and hearths, will soon bring a better knowledge of the various elements involved, and help us to understand a little better the stages in the socio-psychological evolution of the human line.

The technical process of knapping hard stone

The morphological classification of lithic assemblages has long led to a simplified division of lithic production into three major stages: the manufacture of bifaces, the production of flakes, and the production of blades. Later classifications were nothing more than variations on this same theme. This typological classification allowed a parallel, cultural classification to be established. The cognitive abilities of those who manufactured these products was considered entirely in 'hypothetico-inductive' terms.

Today, this approach is being replaced by an analysis of production systems. The process of knapping hard stone implies a bodily activity whose strategic moment undoubtedly lies in the 'strike', i.e. a rapid, directed blow, which cannot be modified by eye during its execution. This moment is not purely physical, it relies also on intellectual operations: abstraction, anticipation, the working out of a solution to problems encountered, the construction of models. J. Pelegrin (1991) distinguishes a scale of conceptual knowledge (*connaissances*) acquired through the memorization of concepts – that is, 'mental representations of forms that are considered ideal and also of the materials involved' – and memorization of modes of operation, and of procedural knowledge (*savoir-faire*) that can either be ideational, arising from intelligence and memory, or physical movement, presupposing bodily skills.

Research is developing along two paths that often intersect: on the one hand, technical production, properly speaking (also called the 'techno-psychological' axis (Boëda *et al.* 1990)), together with all it implies of knowledge and know-how, as much at the level of concepts, as of methods and techniques; on the other hand, all the cultural, spatial and economic implications on which this production depends, or which it induces, i.e. technical behaviour, which becomes accessible to us, and social behaviour, in so far as we actually have access to it: which we term here the 'techno-sociological' axis.

The 'techno-psychological' approach to the knapping process

This analysis is made possible not only by the reconstruction of the *chaînes opératoires* through refitting, but also by the experimental practice of knapping, which has now become a method of analysis in its own right. We will retain the term

chaîne opératoire for the reconstructed exploitation of one block.

During the unfolding of a *chaîne opératoire* of knapping, a complex technical knowledge, which, from the beginning of prehistory, has implied a high degree of 'technical awareness', becomes involved in a coherent way. The particular constraints linked to knapping constantly compel the worker to reason: confronted with the laws of cleavage, he must constantly adjust his movements to an evaluation of all the possible methods in a sequence which is predetermined. We have seen that the flint worker bases his technical reasoning on concepts or mental images of ideal geometrical forms, which guide him from step to step. In addition, we know that he constantly evaluates the current situation and chooses, from a range of methods of action at his disposal, 'the one which is preferable according to his motivation but also possible within the boundaries of constraint' (Pelegrin 1991), so that he can progress between each stage. Such a decision implies the construction and the mental assessment of the possible consequences: it therefore partakes of an ideational know-how. The correct outcome of the movements that it induces implies a physical motor skill.

The technical pattern

The act of knapping thus involves intentions, concepts, an evaluation of constraints, preferences within a group of equivalent methods as well as technical decisions. This cognitive order, which organizes the knowledge involved, guiding the worker within a strategy which is adapted to his project and to the raw material which he uses, can be termed a 'conceptual operative schema' (Pelegrin 1986), or a 'conceptual operative strategy' (Karlin 1992). Starting from the observation of a completed *chaîne opératoire*, the prehistorian can deduce this conceptual operative strategy by seeking the intentions and by analysing the methods employed, once the constraints have been defined. The observation of a certain number of *chaînes opératoires* allows the reconstruction of the technical scheme, which defines all the different stages of a particular type of production. Unlike the *chaîne opératoire* which develops in a linear way, the scheme includes, in its construction, all the possible methods, such as missing one stage or going back to a previous one (Fig. 15.1). Its application cannot be mechanical and implies constant evaluation and choice.

Through this approach, we can see, for instance in the pebble tools of the Early Palaeolithic, an algorithmic standardization of repeated, basic movements – with no hierarchical construction (Roche 1980) – rather than shapes. This could be indicative of an instinctive behaviour since it is programmed without aiming at innovation. It also brings to light, as early as the Lower Palaeolithic, the heuristic

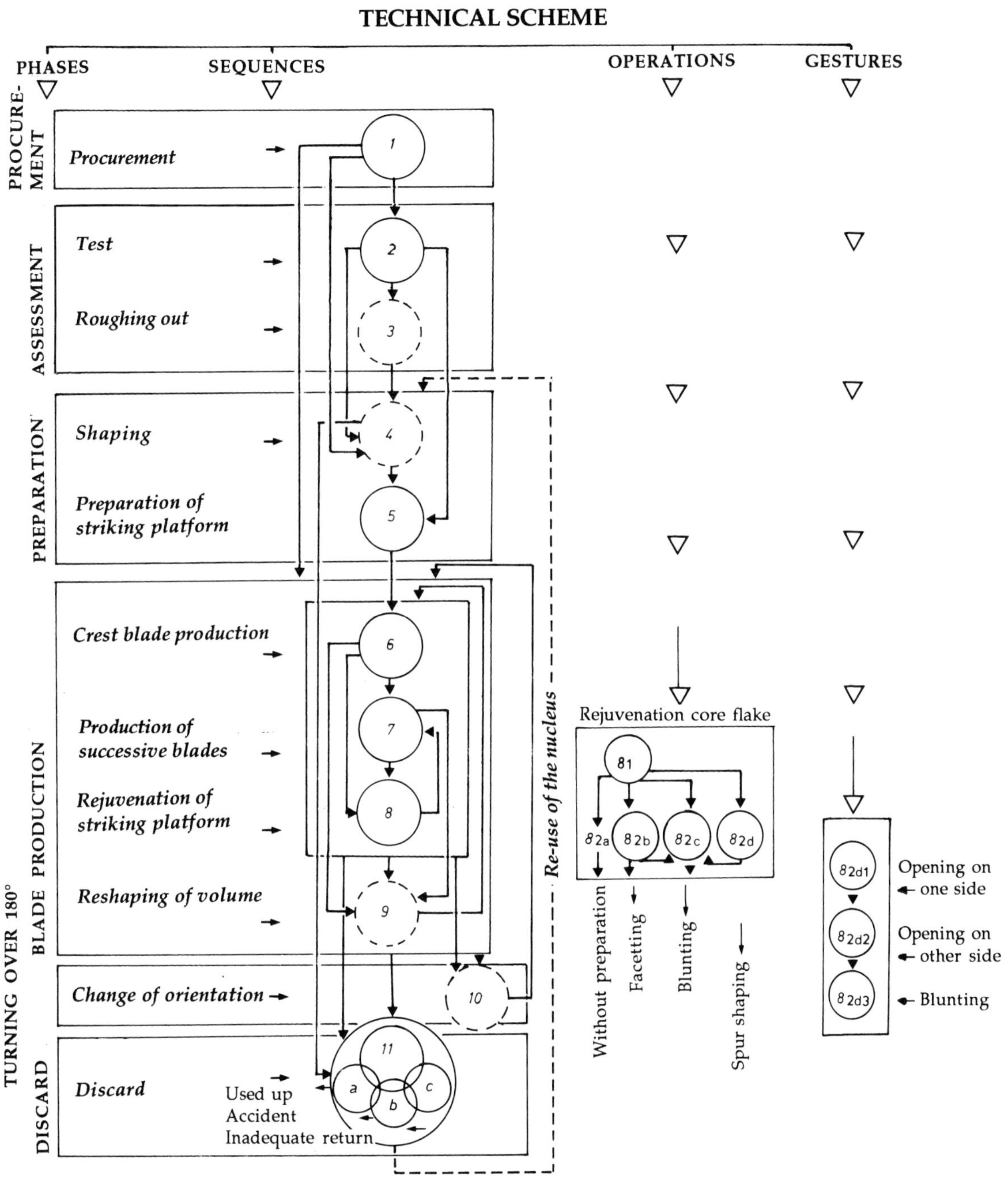

TECHNICAL SCHEME

Fig. 15.1. Organization of the technical scheme defining different stages for Magdalenian blade production

development of imagination, generating a multiplicity of operative patterns that can be grouped according to two major knapping principles: flaking and debitage production, both being either independent or complementary.

Flaking is 'the process of working on a particular piece within a block of raw material, which has, from the start, been determined by the progressive approach of the final shape and volume'. Debitage consists of 'the splintering of a volume of raw material, following a number of specific methods, into units of different shapes and volumes that are obtained in differentiated or standardized series, being either recurring or lineal' (Boëda *et al.* 1990). But the bifacial operational scheme can either have the bifacial piece as its result, or represent only one necessary stage of configuration followed by other stages of work. 'Besides, there is a strong morpho-technical variability of bifacial blanks implying the existence of different methods' (Boëda *et al.* 1990). Boëda thus shows that there is no such thing as a Levallois method, but that there is a Levallois concept based on a volumetric conception of the core: 'the arrangement of two asymmetrical convex surfaces with specific roles that cannot be interchanged. The intersection of those two surfaces defines a unique plane within which all the predetermined removals will be made' (Boëda *et al.* 1990). Several methods of exploitation are therefore possible, which can produce either specifically shaped flakes or blades.

As a result, the element which characterizes the Upper Palaeolithic is not so much its blade production as the way of achieving this production. 'The evolution from a two-dimensional exploitation (surface) to a three-dimensional exploitation (volume) of the core is certainly one of the major factors of leptolithization: the core is conceived as a volume capable of providing an uninterrupted series of blades. The quantity of blades that can be produced is almost equivalent to the core capacity. The maximum exploitation of this volume is linked to the shaping of a specific core, corresponding to a particular option' (Boëda *et al.* 1990). In this it seems that the multiplicity of operational schemes gives way to a certain degree of standardization.

As we can see, the analysis of this evolution is no longer limited to the simple attribution of a diagnostic tool form to a physiognomy, but complex systems of technical thoughts intervene through the analysis of the technical patterns. The work done on the multiplicity of possibilities, on parallelism, on the complementary or intertwined nature of concepts, methods and techniques, demonstrates the complexity of a technical process.

The different levels of know-how

While data for the Middle Palaeolithic only allow global analysis, the rather more complete data available for the Upper Palaeolithic enable us to be more precise about certain characteristics of the knapping process. We will take our examples from the Magdalenian blade production of the Paris basin, as described in the studies of major sites such as Etiolles (Essonne), Marsangy (Yonne), Pincevent (Seine-et-Marne) and Verberie (Oise).

Daily observation shows that the variations in a technical production depend, among other things, on the difference between levels of technical skill, that is to say the degree of proficiency in acquiring both knowledge and a more or less advanced know-how, but also on the personality of the makers. There is no reason to believe that lithic production should escape this rule simply because it is prehistoric.

The division into three groups (good = level 1, average = level 2, bad = level 3) is undoubtedly the simplest division that can be used. At least, it makes it possible to put together comparable lithic units. S. Ploux is currently working on the elaboration of descriptive criteria (Bodu *et al.* 1990) (Fig. 15.2):

– According to her, the first of these criteria seems to be the *complexity of the conceptual scheme*, that is to say the mental construction which guides the execution. The choice of working solution leads the level 1 flintknappers, at Pincevent, to a certain freedom vis-à-vis the morphology of the nodules. Only at Etiolles does the morphology of the flint blocks determine the chosen options, probably because the technical constraints, due to exceptional initial dimensions, limit the possibilities of personal initiative (as well as the desired length of the blades, which may reach as much as 40 cm). By contrast, the level 2 flintknappers choose a simple solution, guided by a relatively stereotyped conceptual pattern, which makes them dependent on the block. Finally, for the level 3 flintknappers, the conceptual pattern is reduced to its minimum or is even completely absent.

– The second criterion is the *degree of preconception of the chaîne opératoire*, that is to say the precision of the forward planning. The level 1 flintknappers, thanks to their strategic approach, can work out a detailed estimate of the whole operative process. At level 2, the flintknappers' attitude is much more tactical. Led by a rather sketchy guideline, they constantly adapt their operations to any new situation, whereas the level 3 flintknappers seem more or less unable to preconceive their work, being able to imitate what they see rather than to assess the block on which they have to work.

– The third criterion is the *discrepancy between a project and its achievement*, which appears to be indicative of the ability to take into consideration all the data concerning the problem which has to be solved. In general, the level 1

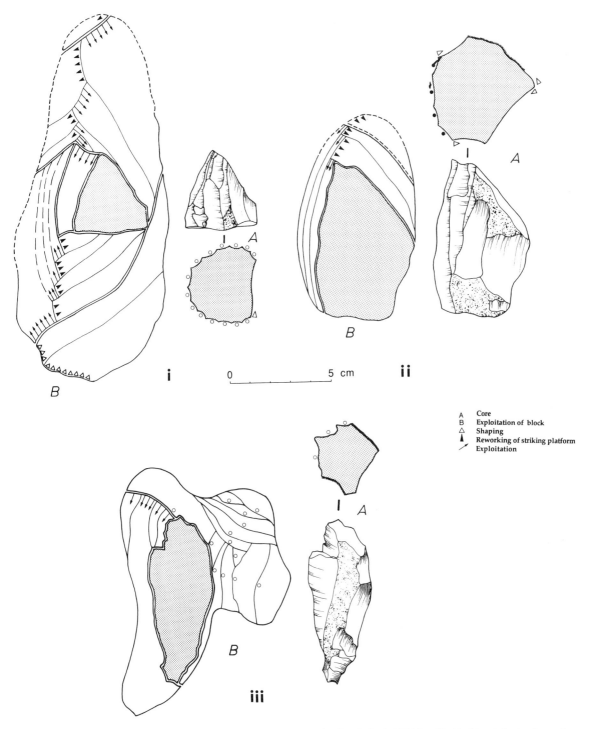

Fig. 15.2. Diagram to show the differences between the three levels of technical skill identified in Magdalenian knapping at Pincevent.
i. Level 1 knappers implement a complex work programme optimizing the primary material. As well as practical experience and knowledge this implies a mastery of concentration and appraisal.
ii. In the debitage of level 2 knappers we find the capacity for neither evaluating all the data nor forward planning. Errors of movement and use of defective material may lead to premature abandonment of the core.
iii. The work of the level 3 knappers (novices) is characterized by lack of knowledge, difficulty with forward planning, and poor control of movement.

flint workers achieve what they had intended. The level 2 flintknappers have some difficulties in making the project and its outcome coincide, whether it is the result of inappropriate material or of incorrect movements. This discrepancy is systematic with the level 3 flintknappers because, in addition to the aforementioned reasons, conception is, for them, a major difficulty.

– The *final state of the core* (nucleus) can have several causes. At level 1, the decision can be imposed by natural constraints, unforeseeable accident, or simply be the result of the exhaustion of the nodule, once a project, which involved a maximum use of the available volume, be it exclusively blade exploitation or successively blades then bladelets, has been carried out. In other cases, it seems that the criterion for abandonment is the 'economic threshold': work stops when the core only allows the manufacture of products of insufficient length. Thus at Etiolles, for instance, the limit is approximately 20 cm, even though it was still possible to make use of what remained of the blocks. This decision may reflect a cultural attitude or correspond to a precise functional need. At both Verberie and Pincevent, this 'economic threshold' is much lower because of the initial size of the blocks, and abandonment occurs when necessary reworking implies a far too drastic reduction of the possible production: there is, in this particular case, a close link between technical constraints, and economic and cultural criteria. If some of the cores of the second level have also been rejected for economic reasons, it is often because a more or less well-mastered operative process, or some negative accidents, have led to premature rejection, which becomes systematic at level 3.

– *Blade production* is one of the aims of the process. It is relatively stable at level 1, with roughly 15 items at Pincevent and Verberie and between 25 and 30 at Etiolles. However, at Etiolles an economic system characterized by a low yield of blades, probably based on the length of the products, is also present at this level of technicality. At level 2, production may vary but never exceeds ten units. It is generally absent at level 3, even though the flint workers were able to manufacture bladelets.

– As for the *quality of blade production*, it is the result of a compromise between technical skills and the planned work. At Pincevent, Verberie or Marsangy, it is good and stable at level 1, linked to an effort towards standardiz-ation of the products. At Etiolles, although it is on the whole good (between 20 and 40 cm long), it is made less stable by the great difficulties posed by the production of such long blades. At level 2, on the contrary, the quality of blade production finds a certain stability as far as size is concerned (between 10 and 15 cm long), whereas at Pincevent the concern for the manufacture of

differentiated blades makes it variable. In any case, it is almost non-existent at level 3. As for the bladelets, those produced at level 3 are more irregular and curved than those produced at the two other levels.

– The last criterion developed by S. Ploux is the notion of *utilitarian productivity*, that is, the capability to adjust production according to need. Criteria of strict selection in the elaborate production of level 1 lead to an average utilitarian productivity. For knapping assemblages involving opportunist flaking, which account for most of level 2, it is higher, as is suggested at Pincevent by the fact that it is more difficult to refit those assemblages and that the useful products have undergone numerous alterations. Finally, at Pincevent, blank production at level 3 does not seem to be influenced by criteria of productivity either for blades or bladelets; whereas at Etiolles, some of the products have been used.

The use of these criteria leads to the composition of three, more homogeneous groups and to the questioning of the sig-nificance of those levels. This particular point, falling under both the techno-psychological and techno-sociological approach, will be addressed later. After having tried to discover the reasons for the differences within a single type of production, we will naturally examine the reasons for the differences within a given level of technical proficiency.

Individual expression

S. Ploux (1989) argues that the entire technical behaviour of an individual is characterized by the phenomena of stability and psycho-motor originality.

The various scars observed on lithic material are the result of the technical process involved, as much as the psycho-motor process underlying it. It follows that each aspect of the technological analysis can be comprehended in terms of psycho-motor operations: reactions, reflection, decisions, execution. Such an analysis can only be made by the investigation of a *chaîne opératoire*, that is to say an assemblage of refitted products. From this correlation, a parallel is drawn between three orders of facts and three lev-els of analysis: movement and the product of the knapping, the succession of movements and the *chaîne opératoire*, and finally the strategy behind their succession and the conceptual pattern (Karlin *et al.* 1992).

A second correlation can be established between these three levels and three aspects of know-how:

– The elaboration of an 'operating conceptual pattern', that is, an intellectual activity, depends on a conceptualized ideational know-how which consists of making a selection among assimilated knowledge with a view to implemen-tation.

– The realization of a *chaîne opératoire*, or psycho-motor activity, depends on an operative ideational know-how which consists of making selected knowledge match a given reality as well as a succession of technical facts. For those two aspects, decision is a crucial factor which may show preferences among the choices made. Moreover, there is a psychological aspect to those choices since a certain investment is required.

– Gesture comes back to a purely motor faculty know-how, including automatic actions that denote habits and motor idiosyncrasy.

Through those various parallels, Sylvie Ploux distinguishes between four, highly independent levels of interpretation: knowledge, know-how, the intention to do and the execution (see Fig. 15.3).

Based on some fifty refitted lithic assemblages from a single settlement unit at Pincevent, this analysis involves a first level of differentiation based on a variable proficiency leading to the identification of three levels of technical skill. The difference between those three groups, the brief duration of occupation and the secondary role played by the knapping activity exclude the hypothesis of a technical progression allowing one group to reach a higher level. However, within groups 2 and 3 some distinctions arose that are still to be interpreted by confronting the purely techno-psychological information with all the other data. At level 2, the homogeneity of the conceptual patterns and the *chaînes opératoires* is contradicted by the variability of the operative mastery. At level 3, a relative stability in the technical behaviour is accompanied by major differences in the final outcome. In both cases it may indicate, within each level, the progression of a single individual or the cohabitation of different individuals, without excluding, for some of those lithic assemblages, the different reactions of a single individual confronted with varying events or changing techno-economic circumstances. Level 1, on the other hand, shows a relative homogeneity between the conceptual patterns and the reconstructed *chaînes opératoires*, together with a personal taste for particular technical methods, which may indicate the production by a single flintknapper.

'Techno-sociological' analysis of an operational scheme

Like the previous section, this approach is illustrated by examples of the Magdalenian population of the Paris basin.

Site function

The sites of Verberie and Pincevent seem to have been chosen for their strategic position along the seasonal migration tracks of the reindeer (Audouze 1987). The main activity was hunting and processing the animals in the autumn. Flint knapping was only regarded as a secondary activity, directly linked to immediate needs. The Magdalenian occupants exploited flint nodules of average to mediocre quality which were available on the river banks.

Beyond this opportunist management of the local lithic resources intended for 'local domestic use', there is also long-term management of a stock of blades, as shown by various products of non-local material brought to the camp site and by the absence of blades in certain, local knapped assemblages. This basic material, which could be described as having a 'territorial usage', is brought from a previous camp, or taken to another place at the end of stay. It was probably intended as a reserve stock for supplying the needs of the group during the nomadic cycle.

The Etiolles site, probably chosen for its outcroppings of flint blocks of an exceptional quality, may have been a place where a basic stock of blades was created for territorial use. The quantity of raw material treated *in situ* is impressive, while animal remains are surprisingly few. Technological study shows a specialization in the knapping activity, aiming at the production of a maximum of large, standardized products to be most probably used in the course of their travels. The management of these stocks shows an ability to plan ahead each stop along the circuit and the repetition of the same circuit over the months or years.

Knapping adapted to different ends

The knapping process may correspond, through different projects, to different purposes. At Pincevent, two types appear to be identifiable.

The first is the manufacture of the aforementioned products for deferred use: the flintknapper makes these for future, still undefined but inevitable requirements. The planning can be long-term – for the duration of the nomadic circuit – or short-term, corresponding in time and space to the temporary camp – as shown by the important circulation of the products – or simply to the dwelling unit to which the flintknapper himself belongs. Those products are standardized, most probably because of their multi-purpose, future use, even though the flintknapper is more or less aware which transformation will optimize the product. Such a standardization implies a *chaîne opératoire* optimal in all its parameters. Only the best nodules are reserved for this purpose and, very often, careful preparation using a hard stone hammer improves the volume by working on the longest axis (keel shape) or across the width (arch shape). Particular care is taken with regard to the forward crest, which will guide the first blade: the rest of the work depends

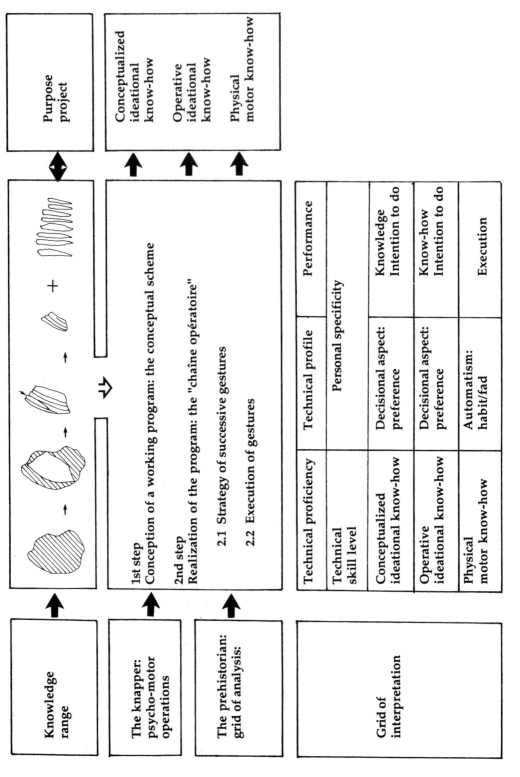

Knowledge range			Purpose project

The knapper: psycho-motor operations

1st step
Conception of a working program: the conceptual scheme

2nd step
Realization of the program: the "chaîne opératoire"

Conceptualized ideational know-how

Operative ideational know-how

Physical motor know-how

The prehistorian: grid of analysis:

2.1 Strategy of successive gestures

2.2 Execution of gestures

Grid of interpretation	Technical proficiency	Technical profile	Performance
	Technical skill level	Personal specificity	
	Conceptualized ideational know-how	Decisional aspect: preference	Knowledge Intention to do
	Operative ideational know-how	Decisional aspect: preference	Know-how Intention to do
	Physical motor know-how	Automatism: habit/fad	Execution

Fig. 15.3. Operative sequence of Magdalenian knapping: the different levels of interpretation (diagram: S. Ploux).

on its successful realization. For each planned blade, the impact is carefully prepared in strict correlation with a mental projection of the end-product. Generally, it has the shape of a blunted spur, that is: a small protuberance visible on the perimeter of the impact surface, indicating a particular point not to be missed by the soft hammer. The technical activity involved in the production of standardized blades is therefore an end in itself.

The second type of project is part of a technical chain, i.e., a systematic series of *chaînes opératoires* (for instance: the preparation of gravers (*becs*) leading to the piercing of perforated batons, which leads, in turn, to the straightening of arrow-shafts (*fûts de sagaie*). There is, apparently, no interruption between the production of the tool and its use for the transformation of other materials. It may be assumed that the need is pre-existent to realization. It is a domestic production which, in contrast to previous productions, is designed for immediate use: the products are shaped for the movement they have to transmit, for the force they have to bear and for the quality of the material on which they have to work. The blocks used are of average quality. Preparation is reduced to a bare minimum, or very often simply absent: execution is guided by the natural volume of the block. Reworking in the course of knapping is slight, except for turning the block to begin from another striking platform.

Correlation between the project and the technical level

The two project types correspond to two types of behaviour. In the first case, it is an anticipating behaviour, whereas in the second case there is a response to a specific need. In the first case, a good level of know-how is required, which implies not only the use of all the knowledge and know-how available, but also the personal concern of the flintknapper, who makes use of his ability to reach his aim, i.e. a standardized production. In the second case, the behaviour is more opportunist and the realization less skilful. The production of tools is a compulsory stage but the attention seems directed towards a subsequent phase of technical activity. The product already bears signs of its future function.

There is thus a relationship between the first level of technical proficiency and the creation of products for territorial use, whereas level 2 seems to correspond to the creation of products for domestic usage. This could indicate a division of tasks between the members of a group sharing a common know-how. It could be argued that the level of proficiency might be obliterated by an opportunist behaviour: it seems possible to identify, in the context of domestic production, opportunist assemblages showing modes of execution partaking undoubtedly of level 1.

However, we have not, so far, detected evidence of level 2 flintknappers in the working assemblages for deferred use. It could be inferred that the skilled workers were in charge of producing the items to be taken away by the group during their migrations. This was an important task since poor forward planning would leave the group ill-equipped. As for domestic production, one can imagine that each member of the group might have provided for his own needs. The relative distinction existing between the two systems might indicate a primitive form of task specialization.

Personal or collective production

The current study leads to the reassessment of the relationship between a flintknapper and his output. Ownership of production may be more collective than has previously been supposed.

Since the notion of a process establishes a continuum with the recognition of sequences ordered into a chronological series, this continuum was further applied to the whole technical process: considerations of space, time and maker. This trend, made necessary, at first, by the need to organize the data into a simple model, was strengthened by the experimental approach, which values the temporal unity of a complete knapping sequence, all the more since knapping is the actual aim and not merely a necessary step towards another activity. Today, this first step is fully mastered and more complex models can be considered.

First, the observation of the circulation of products within a single camp site, as is the case at Pincevent in particular, compels the prehistorian to reflect on the management of the production: the removal of a tool, by the maker, from the production place to the places of use, exchanges, gifts, etc. It also reveals collective activities: those tools, coming from several settlement units, converge into a technical unity. The circulation of the cores and deficiencies in some of the refittings tend to show that the flint worker may not have worked steadily until the nodule was exhausted, and that he was not necessarily the sole user of his own product. Alongside a knapping activity depending on a sole individual, there might also have been a knapping activity fully integrated in the collective activity of the group, which would then give a specific dimension to the technical process. In the first case, an individual masters the whole *chaîne opératoire* which is executed without interruption. In the second case one might assume the existence of a *chaîne opératoire* characterized by both spatial and temporal interruptions. Finally, realization might also depend on the collective needs of the group. These last two cases imply an anticipated planning of labour different from what we had hitherto thought. But research in this area is just beginning.

Transmission and evolution of knowledge

The knowledge and the technical know-how involved in a given process require the acquisition, by each individual, of particular modes of conception and realization. This is what we call 'apprenticeship'.

We assume, on the one hand, that within a population of hunter-gatherers, such an indispensable technique for everyday life as the knapping of hard stones must be acquired at the very beginning of adulthood and, therefore, that apprenticeship occurs during childhood and adolescence. On the other hand, in an open space, where activities seem to have been performed publicly, it can be assumed that flint knapping, like any other activity, was a collective know-how. Everyone knew how to flake stone through having seen it done, though that does not mean to say that everyone could do it. There could be, to paraphrase M.-N. Chamoux (1978), a 'collective technical proficiency', but 'technical performances' only for some individuals.

The stages of apprenticeship

All the lithic assemblages attributed to level 1 and 2 flintknappers at Pincevent have either missing elements or retouched pieces, which indicates that products have been selected for utilization. The blocks attributed to level 3 flintknappers, on the other hand, are characterized by, among other things, the absence of any selection of items for use. Analysis of different criteria of identification in this latter level of competence leads us to the conclusion that this flint knapping was directed more towards the application of concepts still being learned than to the production of usable material. What we can see here is the evidence of apprenticeship.

The child, while still in his mother's care, imitates adults. He strikes blocks of flint, but the conceptual inadequacy and the poor mastery of motor skills leads him to strike in an incoherent manner, and often with a certain degree of strenuousness. Some refitted nodules reveal an 'exploratory' mode of behaviour which corresponds to this early learning phase.

In the next phase, the apprenticeship becomes active. We see the progressive application of concepts of flint knapping, which seems to precede the acquisition of the necessary motor skills. At Etiolles, N. Pigeot (1988) broke down the process of blade production into a series of technical or economic principles which made a gradual appearance during the learning stage: 'The need to work down the long axis of two intersecting planes, an elementary principle in working the core; the concept of the functional pairing of striking platform and blade surface; the facetting of the platform products – the establishment and reworking

of a permanent oblique striking platform, and redirection of the flaking process from a striking platform at the opposite end of the core; the production of blades; spur-shaped impact surfaces – the crest principle – the complex reorientation of the knapping by functional inversion of the faces of the core; improved integration of the preceding principles – economic productivity; last acquisition: knowing when to stop!' This very precise breakdown is made possible by the abundance of the material. Since flint knapping was the principal activity of the group at this site, it is clear that this was a particularly suitable place for learning the necessary processes. At the same time, the special difficulty of working the large cores found at this site required a total mastery of all the parameters of flint knapping, and leads us to suppose a progressive acquisition of the necessary skills, and one which was in large part carefully guided.

At Pincevent, by contrast, knapping is a secondary activity and rarely performed. Apprenticeship is, therefore, opportunist. Nevertheless, a work station dedicated to apprenticeship has been identified. The first exercises show, in a production of bladelets, the integration of basic principles (keel-shaping, arch-shaping and articulation between the striking platform and the surface to be exploited) but also difficulties at every stage. At this particular knapping station, a scattering of the remains can be observed, which may indicate that the bodily technique applied to the knapping activity has not been mastered. There is also, at the same working-station, a small nodule worked out by the production of bladelets which is interpreted as a demonstration piece: the demonstration by a skilled worker of the continual maintenance of surfaces and of the necessary articulation between all the surfaces to be exploited (Ploux 1991). If some relatively 'opportunist' percussions can cast doubt on this identification, a particularly spectacular concentration of the products obtained would appear to confirm the hypothesis of a lesson, whose aim would not have been the striking technique itself, but rather the organization and self-maintenance of the volume, together with the position of the body. The subsequent debitage at the same work station, actually shows that the apprentice has become better at organizing the volume of work, and the concentration of waste, more marked than in the first phase, shows that the body is much better integrated into the technical activity.

As for skilled flint workers at Pincevent, we were able to distinguish between good and average workers. It cannot be excluded that in level 2 we are dealing with an evolving level of competence, when some workers had passed the apprenticeship stage without yet having the experience which would enable them to produce larger blades.

Occupation is too short and the flaking activity has attracted too little attention to enable us to witness the progress of a skilled flintknapper. At level 2, we would then find workers with developing abilities, and workers who had reached the limit of their abilities. The former are designated by the group for a future when everyone expects them to improve their technical abilities: they thus have to invest time and attention, so as to keep up with this technical – and probably social – role. The latter might not be in charge of a high quality lithic production and their abilities could then be directed towards another technical activity. Their knowledge and know-how, as far as knapping is concerned, is restricted to the production of immediately useful tools, especially since they could, and would, call upon the production of the good workers if they needed to. If this hypothesis is correct, it would imply the existence of a system of groups communicating with one another – age sets, for instance -- but also of another system with a division that would prevent exchange – perhaps a sexual division?

Apprenticeship and raw material

Access to raw material seems to follow rules indicating a collective mental representation as well as technical antici- pation. There is first, at Pincevent, a relation between the project and the quality of block: the best blocks are used for the production of standardized blades intended for deferred use, which brings them into the hands of the best flint workers. Ordinary blocks are used for domestic production and are thus handled by any competent flint-worker. Apprentices only practise on nodules of mediocre shape and quality. While access to flint is easy, we have already said that the flint nodules are of varying quality, so that an extravagant use was not possible, especially since the selection of the block, the risks of working on defective material or of errors during the progress of the *chaîne opératoire* are still potentially great. At Etiolles, where raw material is exceptionally good, 'before starting knapping large cores, they had to practise on less valuable cores that had already been in the expert hands of the best technicians' (Pigeot 1988). This behaviour of recovering the blocks that were rejected by the skilled workers, whether the block still had potential or not, can also be found at Pincevent.

To conclude, it appears that the technological approach to lithic industries is mainly based upon a dialectical comparison of the relations existing between knowledge and know-how, becoming themselves the two privileged domains of cognitive investigation. At each technical phase in the evolution of mankind, the reconstruction of the *chaînes opératoires* enables us to question the nature of the concepts that generated lithic production and their modalities of realization. It then becomes possible to sketch- out an assessment of the intellectual and psycho-motor abilities of the men who formulated those concepts.

Even though it is, at first, rudimentary, the conceptual scheme which underlies the manufacture of pebble tools undoubtedly reflects, in material form, the evolution of the cognitive faculties of hominids. Its origins might date back to an even earlier period, since when this technical process becomes perceptible, it is already mastered by *Australo- pithecus*. Later on, the conceptual schemes become more elaborate with *Homo erectus*, who progress from the simple production of pebble tools to the complex production of tools manufactured on blocks or flakes. They invent a type of heuristic approach which offers several solutions to each technical problem, while retaining the algorithmic procedures that enables them to produce pebble tools through a series of repeated, basic movements. From this point, it becomes possible to apprehend, almost tangibly, the faculties of abstraction that led to the elaboration of conceptual patterns, as well as their ability to innovate, to select the best criteria to suit their project, and to anticipate mentally both their needs and their realization. From the intellectual and technical viewpoints at which we have placed ourselves, the continuing evolution of knapping techniques could almost be considered as simply the amplification of these cognitive faculties, even if the passage from the exploitation of 'two-dimensional' blocks (Levallois concept) to the exploitation of 'three-dimensional' blocks (blade concept) constitutes a major step.

Beyond this 'techno-psychological' approach, which considers each type of lithic industry to be the product of a human group in the broad sense, the 'techno-sociological' approach allows us to detect groups of individuals, or even particular individuals, within a given camp site or region. We can also envisage some aspects of their relational system. This approach, better known during the Upper Palaeolithic, is about to be applied to earlier periods. Stock management and waste production indicate an attempt at task specialization together with the adaptation of projects to seasonal activities and a capacity for long-term planning. Similarly, an analysis of the levels of competence within each habitation unit, the assessment of the number of flint workers and of the specificity of their technical behaviour allow us to understand, to some extent, the composition of the group and the relative importance of each individual. It is obvious that an analysis of the social organization of groups of hunter-gatherers will only be made possible thanks to a much more thorough cognitive investigation, but the latter can develop only by retaining a close dialectical relationship with fieldwork data.

Notes

1 In a technical activity, a *chaîne opératoire* takes the form of an ordered train of actions, gestures, instruments or even agents leading the transformation of a given material towards the manufacture of a product, through major steps that are more or less predictable. In the flaking of hard stone, each *chaîne opératoire* translated the exploitation of a flint module – observed in the present thanks to refitting – into a system.

References

Audouze, F. 1987. Des modèles et des faits: les modèles de A. Leroi-Gourhan et de L. Binford confrontés aux résultats récents. *Hommage de la SPF à André Leroi-Gourhan, Bulletin de la Société Préhistorique Française* 84 (10–12): 343–52

Beyries, S. and F. Joulian 1990. L'utilisation d'outils chez les animaux: chaînes opératoires et complexité technique. *Paléo* 2: 17–26

Bodu, P., C. Karlin and S. Ploux 1990. Who's who? The Magdalenian flintknappers of Pincevent, France. In *The big puzzle, international symposium on refitting stone artefacts, Monrepos, Neuwied 1987*, ed. E. Cziesla, S. Eikhoff, N. Arts and D. Winter, pp. 143–63. Studies in Modern Archaeology 1. Bonn

Boëda, E. 1990. De la surface au volume, analyse des conceptions des débitages levallois et laminaire. In *Paléolithique moyen récent et Paléolithique supérieur ancien en Europe*, ed. C. Farizy, pp. 63–8. Mémoires du Musée de Préhistoire d'Ile-de-France 3

Boëda, E., J.-M. Geneste and L. Meignen 1990. Identification de chaînes opératoires lithiques du Paléolithique ancient et moyen. *Paléo* 2: 43–80

Chamoux, M.-N. 1978. La transmission des savoir-faire: un objet pour l'ethnologue des techniques. *Techniques et Culture* 3: 46–83

Chavaillon, J. 1989. Une très longue histoire: l'Acheuléen. In *Le temps de la préhistoire*, vol. 1, ed. J.-P. Mohen, pp. 240–2. Société Préhistorique Française, Editions Archeologia

Coppens, Y. 1989. Hominoidés, Hominidés et Hommes. In *Le temps de la préhistoire*, vol. 2, ed. J.-P. Mohen, pp. 2–21. Société Préhistorique Française, Editions Archeologia

Johanson, D. C., T. D. White and Y. Coppens 1978. A new species of the genus *Australopithecus* (Primates: Hominidae) from the Pleistocene of eastern Africa. *Kirtlandia*, pp. 281–314

Karlin, C. 1992. Connaissance et savoir-faire: comment analyser un procesus technique en Préhistoire. Reunion internacional, *Tecnologia y cadenas operativas liticas*, pp. 99–124. Universitat autonoma, Barcelona

Karlin, C., P. Bodu, N. Pigeot and S. Ploux 1992. Some socio-economic aspects of the process of lithic reduction among groups of hunter-gatherers of the Paris-Basin area. In *The use of tools by humans and non-human primates*, ed. A. Berthelet and J. Chavaillon, pp. 318–40. Oxford, Clarendon Press

Leakey, L. S. B., P. V. Tobias and J. R. Napier 1964. A new species of the genus *Homo* from Olduvai gorge. *Nature* 202: 7–9

Lemonnier, P. 1990. Topsy turvy techniques. Remarks on the social representation of techniques. *Archaeological Review from Cambridge* 9 (1): 27–37

Pelegrin, J. 1986. *Technologie lithique: une méthode appliquée à l'étude de deux séries de Périgordian ancien*. Thesis, Université de Paris X

1991. Les savoir-faire: une très longue histoire. *Terrain* 16: 106–13

Pelegrin, J., C. Karlin and P. Bodu 1988. Chaînes opératoires: un outil pour le préhistorien. In *Technologie lithique*, ed. J. Tixier, pp. 55–62. Notes et Monographies techniques 25. Paris, CNRS

Pigeot, N. 1988. Apprendre à débiter des lames: un cas d'éducation technique chez les Magdaléniens d'Etoilles. In *Technologie lithique*, ed. J. Tixier, pp. 62–70. Notes et Monographies techniques 25. Paris, CNRS

Ploux, S. 1989. *Approche archéologique de la variabilité des comportements techniques individuels: l'exemple de quelques tailleurs magdaléniens de Pincevent*. Thesis, Université de Paris X

1991. Technologie, Technicité, Techniciens: méthodes de détermination d'auteurs et comportement technique individuel. In *25 ans d'études technologiques en préhistoire, bilan et perspectives, XIe rencontres internationales d'archéologie et d'histoire d'Antibes*, pp. 201–14. ADPCA, Juan-les-Pins

Roche, H. 1980. *Premiers outils taillés d'Afrique*. Société d'Ethnographie – Publications du Laboratoire d'Ethnologie et de Sociologie comparative, Université de Paris X, Collection Afrique ancienne 1

PART VI

The material basis of cognitive inference: writing systems

16

Variation and change in symbol systems: case studies in Elamite cuneiform

JOHN S. JUSTESON and
LAURENCE D. STEPHENS

Archaeological study of cognitive systems

'Cognition' refers to the representation of knowledge and to the processes operating on those representations; a 'cognitive archaeology' would investigate aspects of knowledge representation and information processing which are recoverable from the archaeological record. This chapter is part of a workshop on the scientific directions which such investigations might take.

The workshop within which these discussions were pursued was mindful, in particular, of the past quarter century of efforts to improve the scientific grounding of archaeological reconstructions of past lifeways. The classics of this literature are applications of useful theoretical constructs, models of social/cultural processes being investigated, and hypothesis-testing using the empirical data provided by archaeology and often ethnography as well.

Three topical emphases distinguish such archaeological work from ethnography: the study of long-term change; the study of lifeways now extinct or now existing only in unrepresentatively restricted situations; the study of relationships between artefacts and behaviour. The archaeological study of cognitive systems has similar rationales. Each of these emphases is addressed by papers in this volume, and each affects the theoretical and methodological issues whose resolution is crucial to the use of archaeological material in coming to grips with past ways of understanding.

The contribution of this paper to the discussion is based on two premises:

- Cognitive processes and representations are not directly accessible. Because cognition mediates between experiencing an environment and acting in it, we obtain non-

introspective access to cognitive systems through the correspondences between environment and behaviour. This is our only access to it.
- Non-categorial aspects of cognition primarily concern perceptual and motor processes that are presumably universal. What is culturally variable and learned is the categorization of experience and action.

Given these premises, the archaeological study of cognitive systems must chiefly concern correspondences among cultural categories, as well as the material manifestations of the patterns of correspondence. The study of change in these systems depends on the recognition of change in these material manifestations.

Thought-provoking data and examples are needed if we are to come to an understanding of what such investigations may achieve. One of the earliest papers in processual archaeology – Binford's (1962) proposal for a relation between the iconicity of status symbols and the social bases for acquiring status – was such a contribution. Binford was proposing a general theory to account for data specifically from the Old Copper Culture; the theory itself continues to merit cross-cultural investigation.

This paper is concerned specifically with symbol systems. It attempts to show that models of variation and change in symbol systems can be developed and validated on especially advantageous types of data. One body of particularly useful evidence is provided by the development of writing systems. The evidence consists of variation in patterns of sign use, whose changes with respect to language, and sometimes other types of communicative behaviour, virtually define the evolution of the system. Among its advantages:

- Its status as a cognitive system is not in doubt; psychological studies of reading and writing form a substantial proportion of the research in cognitive science.
- Often, enough data is available to permit definitive statistical investigation.
- Developmental evidence survives in culturally and linguistically diverse cases, permitting an adequate base for comparative studies.
- Texts are often datable relative to one another, often in absolute chronologies.

This paper examines variation and change in writing systems in terms of general information-processing issues. We concentrate on an especially revealing set of data, provided by the spellings of *CVC* sequences in cuneiform Elamite. We report here the partial results of a comprehensive analysis, which is still in progress (Justeson and Stephens 1981, 1988).

Repetition, categorization and change

Repetition and categorization are the crucial concepts in the general approach we take to the evolution of symbol systems. Repetition is a pervasive facet of symbolic behaviour, not only in ritual but in everyday language use as well. Repetitions of a word or word sequence can be substantially more likely than the first use of the sequence: having said something once, and having said it in a particular way, the chance of saying it again, and in a similar way, is substantially increased, as is the chance of saying related things in similar ways. This is especially true of *proximate repetition*, the recurrence of a symbol or group of symbols nearby in time or space.

Proximate repetition is rampant in writing systems. In many scripts, several signs or sign sequences are equally viable for expressing a given linguistic form. In Akkadian cuneiform, for example, most *CV* syllables (i.e. syllables consisting of a consonant followed by a vowel) could be rendered by any of several signs; within a single text, however, it was usual for a given *CV* syllable to be rendered always by the same *CV* sign.[1] To a lesser extent, the same abundance of signs for a single value was characteristic of Mayan hieroglyphic writing, and a similar repetition effect can be demonstrated.[2] We pursue, in this paper, a more abstract form of repetition, the tendency toward the use of a spelling convention just recently used in the same or a similar context.

Proximate repetition is not only pervasive in symbolic behaviour, it is also critical to the cognitive organization of the system. It is the basis for learning in classical conditioning, providing unconscious training for associations between repeating elements and recurrent features of their contexts. It provides a mechanism for associative conditioning of a symbol's use upon its contexts, a process that appears to account for unreflective judgements of contingency and causality (Schanks and Dickinson 1987).

Mutual substitution within an otherwise substantially repeated structure is a potent basis for the formation of associations between the substituting elements during the process of interpreting symbolic behaviour. The possible role of this mechanism has been detailed for the case of antonymic adjectives (Justeson and Katz 1991). Given that 'big' and 'little' are good antonyms, while 'large' and 'little' are not, what is it that creates the word-specific associations between these semantically opposed words? The answer appears to be that good antonyms are frequently found in the same sentences, and that they typically occur in phrases that are identical to one another, apart from the substitution of the antonyms: *it was the best of times, it was the worst of times*. Short-term associations form immediately between the

substituting elements, and their inherent associability is heightened: co-processing of repeated structures places repeated elements and, thereby, also substituting elements, into direct correspondence with one another. When the same correspondence is created recurrently, the association and associability of the elements is reinforced and becomes permanent.

As elements with the same structural role in a repeated structure, we expect that substituting elements will tend to be categorized together and processed in comparable ways. In unreflective symbolic behaviour, they should tend to be treated in comparable ways, with the same, or comparable, symbols being selected in both instances. A category of symbol, whose choice is appropriate to one of two corresponding, repeated elements in a given context, is expected to become associated, via classical conditioning, with the other element in the same context.

In practice, the behavioural and linguistic context in which symbols are used is almost always unique, so categorization of contexts and of patterns of symbol use is part of the process of symbol selection. Evidence from controlled experiments concerning human category learning (see Schanks and Dickinson 1987) suggests that weighting is adjusted for features on which unconscious category selection is based when the behavioural results thereof are unsatisfactory. Indeed, categorization may be treated as a process of selecting behaviours based upon their contexts. The adjustment involves an increase in the weight attached to features that have previously proven important and predictive for the domain in which categorization is taking place. Simple computational models of category learning, such as perceptron training, implement this kind of adjustment, and are in substantial, though not complete, agreement with experimental results on classical conditioning (see Hampson 1990, 1991 for discussion, and for a guide to relevant psychological and computational literature).

Symbol systems organize and foster both categorization and the processing of knowledge representations, so some such process of dynamic adjustment must be at work in changing patterns of symbol use. In the case of writing systems, which stand in a direct, if far from isomorphic, correspondence with spoken language, all levels of linguistic structure are potential bases for assessing similarity: semantic, syntactic, morphological, syllabic, phonemic, and phonetic resemblance all provide contextual features relevant to categorization. Some of these structures have mutually reinforcing associations with particular selections of signs or sign sequences, while others are mutually inhibiting; with repeated training on these patterns of association, sign selection is expected to adjust to a stable pattern of statistical correspondence with linguistic structure. It is this kind of adjustment in patterns of sign selection that we find in the evolution of ancient Elamite writing.

Elamite 'broken spellings'

Traditional Elamite orthography

The Elamite script was, in origin, a variety of Akkadian cuneiform, and its traditional spellings followed standard cuneiform conventions. Some C_1VC_2 sequences in Elamite were treated orthographically as containing a C_1V syllable, followed by the initial C_2 of the following syllable; this happens mainly when the next segment is a vowel. For example, *libap* 'servants' syllabifies as *li.bap*; this word is treated as consisting of *li* followed by *bap*, with *li* spelled **li** and the following *b* rendered only in the spelling of the following syllable, *bap*. Such spellings do not enter the discussion below, except when they occur in variation with spellings that do treat the C_1VC_2 sequence orthographically as a single syllable.

Elsewhere – when C_2 closed a word, or preceded another consonant – the C_1VC_2 sequence was treated as a single sequence that was unitary for orthographic purposes; typically, it constituted a syllable in Elamite speech. One option in this case was to use a C_1VC_2 sign: for a minority of *CVC* sequences, one or more signs existed that were specific to the sequence. In *libap* 'servants', for example, the sequence *bap* was sometimes spelled by the sign **bap**; however, because no single sign existed to spell the syllable *lur*, this option was not available for spelling the final syllable of *šalur* 'of the gentleman'.

More generally applicable in this context was *harmonic spelling*, the use of a $C_1V\text{-}VC_2$ sign sequence in which the vowels agree in quality. In *libap*, for example, *bap* was often spelled **ba-ap**, and *lur* in *šalur* was often spelled **lu-ur**. In general, $C_1a\text{-}aC_2$ spelled C_1aC_2, $C_1u\text{-}uC_2$ spelled C_1uC_2, $C_1i\text{-}iC_2$ spelled C_1iC_2. Only two signs, **el** and **en**, existed in either Middle or Late Elamite cuneiform for eC_2. These were used in $C_1e\text{-}eC_2$ spellings for C_1eC_2; for C_2 other than *l* or *n*, C_1eC_2 was spelled $C_1e\text{-}iC_2$, the closest approximation to a harmonic spelling.

During the Middle Elamite period, Elamite scribes reduced the number of signs used, particularly those for *CVC* sequences, and those whose values were rendered by more than one sign. They also reduced the complexity of sign forms, so that fewer strokes were required to render them. Near the very end of the Middle Elamite period, this process began to go so far as to eliminate some complex signs, although no other signs existed to convey the same values, and no traditional convention existed to handle some linguistic sequences for which the previous signs had been used. New means were developed for handling these

situations, and they were extended to situations where the old means sufficed. This extension of the system is the focus of our discussion.

By the Late Elamite period, seven of the most complex *VC* signs had evidently gone out of use; these were **al**, **ar**, **il**, **im**, **up**, **uš** and **uz**. Two others, **it** and **az**, were almost never used for *CVC* sequences.[3] As a result, there was no harmonic spelling available for *Cal, Car, Caz, Cil, Cim, Cit, Cup, Cuš* and *Cuz* sequences. For some of these sequences, **CVC** signs were a traditional alternative, but these cases are comparatively rare. In the majority of cases, no traditional spelling was available. For example, *duš*, 'he receives', was traditionally spelled **du-uš** in Middle Elamite; with the loss of the **uš** sign, this word had to be spelled in some other way.

The new system for spelling words that lacked any traditional means of expression is called *broken spelling*. When no VC_2 existed for a C_1VC_2 sequence, an iC_2 sign was used or, if that did not exist, then an uC_2 sign. Thus, **du-iš** was used to spell *duš*, 'he receives', when the sign **uš** had fallen into disuse. These cases of broken spelling, in which no harmonic alternative was available, we call 'forced broken spellings'.

The new system was also used to spell sequences for which traditional spellings were available; for example, the word *libap*, 'servants', was spelled according to traditional principles as **li-ba-ap** (less often, **li-bap**); but the broken spelling **li-ba-ip** is also found. Cases such as this, in which both harmonic and broken spelling alternatives are available, we refer to as 'optional broken spellings'. The sequences subject to optional broken spelling were *Cak, Cuk, Can, Cun, Cat, Cur, Cap, Caš* and *Cam*.

Hallock (1958) and Reiner (1969: 70–1) proposed that optional broken spelling is an analogical extension of the forced broken spelling pattern, and qualitative evidence supports their proposal. Broken spelling consists of the use of an iC or uC sign for a single postvocalic consonant, since the implied vowel *i* or *u* is, by definition, not that which is being spelled; i.e. in *ša-lu-ip*, *ša-lu* spells *šalu* and **ip** spells only -*p*. Since optional broken spellings entail the use of the same signs – **ip**, **ir**, **iš**, **iz**, **um**, **ul** and **ut** – for postvocalic -*p*, -*r*, -*š*, -*z*, -*m*, -*l* and -*t* that represent these consonants in forced broken spellings, the optional cases are, first and foremost, extensions in the use of these **VC** signs for these consonants. Two other consonants, -*k* and -*n*, are never forcibly spelled broken, because no **Vk** or **Vn** signs were lost. Optional broken spelling of these consonants constitutes an extension of the overall pattern, the use of **iC** signs when available – here **ik** and **in** – to represent postvocalic consonants.

If optional broken spellings are extensions from the use of forced broken spellings, we would expect the contexts most effectively supporting the extension to be those which are most similar to the contexts of the forced spellings. The first set of consonants, which sometimes force broken spelling, should therefore be a more potent source of extension of the system than the second pair, which never force broken spelling. This is indeed the case (see Table 16.1): *every* sometimes-forcing consonant is spelled broken in a higher proportion of instances than *any* never-forcing consonant. We conclude that optional broken spelling is indeed an extension of the forced practice of broken spelling.

As an extension of an orthographic practice, optional broken spelling is amenable to an analysis of its spread in terms of the linguistic and orthographic correlates of forced broken spelling, along the lines suggested above in the section 'Repetition, categorization and change'. To this end, we have conducted preliminary analyses of all optional broken spellings in the published texts from Persepolis (Cameron 1948; Hallock 1969), and additional texts reflected in Hallock's glossary, investigating the features that inhibit or promote the spread of broken spelling from forced to optional contexts. We illustrate the results for broken spelling of *Cat* and of *Cap* sequences. Broken spellings of these sequences are promoted by different specific factors, subsumable, however, under the same set of more basic principles.

Spellings of Cat *sequences*

Orthographic gemination

The extension of broken spelling in part reflects a pattern of 'orthographic gemination' of consonants. A *VCV* sequence may be spelled either . . *VC-CV* . . , with the consonant geminated, or . . *V-CV* . . , with the consonant spelled singly. This orthographic difference appears to reflect a phonetic difference, which was presumably a phonological distinction in Elamite (Reiner 1969: 111–16). This is inferred from Elamite spellings of foreign words and loanwords, e.g. Elamite *ᵐSa-ad-da-ku-iš* for Old Persian *ᶿataguš:* geminated consonants typically spell consonants that were voiceless in the foreign source word, as in Elamite . . *a-ad-da* for Old Persian *ata*; single consonants typically spell foreign voiced consonants, as in Elamite . . *a-ku* for Old Persian *agu*. Nonetheless, this is only a correlation; in some words, there is variation between geminate and voiceless spellings of intervocalic consonants (e.g. *sa-da-bat-ti-iš ~ sa-ad-da-bat-ti-iš* for OP **satapati-*, *ᵐKam-ma-da ~ ˇKam-ma-ad-da* for OP *Guamata*), and sometimes Elamite spellings show the opposite orthographic representation for known Persian and other foreign words (e.g., *Nab-bu-ni-da* for OP *Nabunaita-*, Akk. *Naḫû-na'id* 'Nabonidus').[4] This pattern of variation is consistent with mismatches between

Table 16.1. *Proportions of **CV-VC** spellings that are spelled broken in Achaemenid Elamite CVC sequences*

Sequences whose finals never force broken spelling				Sequences whose finals sometimes force broken spelling				
Can	Cun	Cak	Cuk	Cat	Cur	Cap	Caš	Cam
8%	16%	21%	27%	47%	55%	57%	79%	83%

Proportions are for type frequencies; for token frequency data the differences between the two groups are more pronounced.

the phonetic realizations of different phonological systems; it is more rarely found in spellings of clearly native Elamite words. Because the specific phonetic distinction(s) involved is not known, we refer to it as the 'GEM feature'.

Since orthographic gemination presupposes a following orthographic vowel, it is unavailable for spelling final consonants. Immediately before another consonant, orthographic gemination is found only when *CVC* signs were used for *CC* sequences.[5] Normally, however, spellings of a pre-consonantal consonant C_1 in a *(C)VC_1* sequence had to use *VC_1* or *CVC_1* signs to spell the final consonant; when no *CVC_1* or *VC_1* sign existed for the sequence, broken spellings were forced, whether C_1 called for geminate or single spelling of the consonant.

When some *VC* signs went out of use, there was, in many medial contexts, no traditional means of representing the corresponding consonants as +GEM. This meant that, in medial position, there was often a choice between the use of a 'forced' broken spelling, and the use of a non-geminate spelling of the consonant (e.g. for *hit* in *ᵐHi-ut-ti-ka ~ ᵐHi-ti-ik-ka*, for *nup* in *ʰNu-ip-pi-iš-taš ~ ʰNu-pi-iš-taš*). Geminate spelling is also found preconsonantly, when a *CVC* sign conveys a *CC* sequence (e.g. for *šat* in *ᵐŠa-ut-tar-ri-ud-da ~ ᵐŠa-at-tar-ri-da*). In contrast, when the non-geminated spelling option was phonologically appropriate, i.e. for a –GEM consonant, no *VC* sign was called for; forced broken spelling would not normally arise as an option at all. As a result, the preferred intervocalic context for forced broken spelling is phonologically for +GEM consonants, and orthographically for geminated consonants.

This pattern provides an analogical basis for the extension in the use of *ut* to optional broken spelling of medial, orthographically geminate *-t-*. Only after *a* was there an alternative, *at*, for geminate spelling of *-t-*; after the other three vowels, *ut* was the only spelling available, either as a

Table 16.2. *Intervocalic instances of harmonic (**Ca-at**) and broken (**Ca-ut**) spellings in Achaemenid Elamite according to the consistency of geminate versus non-geminate spellings in the words involved*

	Geminate only	Variably geminate
Ca-at	14	47
Ca-ut	21	32

Words with only geminate spellings have a significantly higher rate of broken spelling than those in which geminate and non-geminate spellings are both found.

Table 16.3. *Intervocalic instances of harmonic (**Ca-at**) and broken (**Ca-ut**) spellings in Achaemenid Elamite according to the consistency of geminate versus non-geminate spellings in the words involved, and according to the presence or absence of **Cat** signs for the sequence involved*

	Cat sign exists		No Cat sign exists	
	Geminate only	Variably geminate	Geminate only	Variably geminate
Ca-at	12	30	2	17
Ca-ut	8	22	13	10

When Cat signs do not exist, the effect shown in Table 16.2 is verified; when such a sign does exist, the effect is absent.

forced broken spelling (e.g. *ti-ud-da* for *ditta-* 'grain storage place', *ᵐŠe-ut-tuk-ka* for the personal name *Šettukka*) or as a forced harmonic spelling (***hu-ut-ta*** for *hutta-* 'to make'). This situation provides a substantial analogical basis for the use of *ut* for geminate *-t-* after *a* (e.g., in *ᵐŠa-ut-tar-ri-ud-da* for *Xšaθrita*) in competition with the traditional but contextually more restricted **at** spelling (e.g. *ᵐŠa-at-tar-ri-da*).

+GEM consonants did, indeed, promote the extension of broken spelling of intervocalic *-t-*. Among words having *CatV* sequences (Table 16.2), those with only geminate spellings have a substantially higher proportion of broken spellings than those that include some geminate and some non-geminate spellings. The difference demonstrates that the effect is specific to the phonological distinction conveyed by orthographic geminations, and not to gemination itself.[6]

The signs ***bat***, ***kat***, and ***rat*** were traditional alternatives to ***Ca-Vt*** spellings of the corresponding phoneme sequences. The use of these signs in geminating contexts would affect the extension of broken spellings by blocking the development of an association between broken spelling and the geminating feature in *bat*, *kat*, and *rat* sequences. This is indeed the case (Table 16.3). Among *Cat* sequences for which ***Cat*** signs were available, the association of broken spelling with the proportion of single *versus* geminate spellings completely disappears; conversely, among sequences for which ***Cat*** signs do not exist, the association becomes much stronger. Furthermore, with the blocking of an effect of orthographic gemination via the spelling +GEM consonants, there is no predictable difference in broken spelling rates between *bat*, *kat* and *rat* sequences on the one hand (whether *-t-* is +GEM or –GEM), and the remaining sequences for –GEM instances of *-t-*.[7]

Along with the blocking of an association of broken spelling with +GEM instances of *-atV-*, the use of ***Cat*** signs should produce an association of these signs with the same

feature, or simply with orthographic gemination. This too is confirmed. Restricting attention to initial *bat* sequences, there are no definite instances and but one unlikely possible instance of geminate in alternation with nongeminate spellings, and in every case the geminate spellings are conveyed by a ***bat-t . .*** sign sequence.

The blocking phenomenon is also a hallmark of classical conditioning, and is demonstrated by the perceptron training model of learning (see Hampson 1990). These results on the structure of the association of optional broken spelling with orthographic gemination support the view that something like classical conditioning is involved in the extension of broken spelling, and, indeed, that the system did evolve by extension from the contexts of forced broken spelling into similar contexts where harmonic spelling was the only traditional alternative spelling. The further contexts of forced broken spelling help to clarify this developmental pattern.

Final and preconsonantal contexts

In spellings of final consonants, there could be no correlation of forced broken spelling with any phonological feature, other than with the occurrence of a word boundary itself. In compound words, the final consonant of a root preceding a vowel-initial root was often spelled syllabically, as in Middle Elamite ***ᵈHu-ban-nu-me-na*** for *Humban-ummena*; however, it was increasingly spelled morphologically, with a ***VC*** or ***CVC*** sign preceding a ***V*** or ***VC*** sign, as in *ᵈHu-ban-um-me-na*. Even the boundary between roots and affixes was sometimes marked in this way. Forced broken and forced harmonic spellings of word- and root-final *-t* as ***ut*** had an analogical basis for extension to those instances that followed *a*, paralleling the case of orthographic geminates.

As bases for analogical extension of broken spelling, orthographic gemination and boundary marking were in conflict. When a –GEM instance of *t* occurred in final position after *a*, *ut* would suggest that it was +GEM while *at* would suggest that it was non-final, if both correlations promoted the use of *ut* in *Cat* sequences. Mutually inhibitory adjustment is expected in such a circumstance. The use of *ut* for +GEM *-t-* extended aggressively, particularly in the absence of *Cat* signs (Tables 16.2–16.3); it is poorly attested in word-final position (Table 16.4a), occurring at a rate comparable to, but perhaps somewhat lower than, that for medial *-t-* uncorrelated with +GEM. Accordingly, medial geminating *-t-* selects for broken spelling, final *-t* of any sort for harmonic spelling. There are too few data to make a case for or against a difference in broken spelling rate depending upon the presence of *Cat* signs; if there is such a difference, the presence of the sign has the same effect of retarding the spread of broken spelling that was seen in the case of intervocalic geminating *t*.

Preconsonantal position similarly provides a basis for the extension of broken spelling (Table 16.4b). After *a*, this context is intermediate in frequency between geminating and word-final contexts, and when *tVC* signs are used for *tC*, it was also a geminating context. The rate of broken spelling in preconsonantal context is not significantly different from that in geminating context, either for sequences having *Cat* signs or for those lacking them, though in the latter case the rate may be somewhat lower.

The major specific conditions on the extension of broken spelling into *Cat* syllables can now be brought together. Final *-t* was preferentially spelled harmonically, intervocalic +GEM and preconsonantal *-t-* was preferentially spelled broken.[8] Note that as a processing issue, the use of broken spelling in preconsonantal context *versus* harmonic spelling in word-final context reinforces the identification of these contexts, which is not explicitly marked (it is implicitly marked by determiners on some nouns, mostly proper names), which in turn provides a basis for interpreting the significance of the broken *versus* harmonic spelling.

Intervocalic –GEM *-t-* favours harmonic spelling, contrasting with broken spelling as a signal for +GEM – but broken spellings amount to 40 per cent of the total. This context is intrinsically difficult for a reader to interpret, since harmonic spelling associates it with word-final, and broken spelling with +GEM contexts. Provided the context is clear, the basic association of intervocalic –GEM instances should be with harmonic spelling, so we expect that broken spellings should be more in use where other cues to non-final position are least compelling; this expectation is testable, but we have not yet completed such a test.[9] In addition, many of the broken spellings categorized with –GEM analytically

Table 16.4. *Word-final and preconsonantal instances of harmonic (**Ca-at**) and broken (**Ca-ut**) spellings in Achaemenid Elamite according to the presence or absence of **Cat** signs for the sequence involved*

	Word-final		Pre-consonantal	
	+ Cat	– Cat	+ Cat	– Cat
Ca-at	9	17	11	8
Ca-ut	0	4	8	24
	a		b	

were probably in fact +GEM, but with some non-geminate spellings used defectively.

These effects can be seen as due to repeated use of the broken, harmonic, and other spelling alternatives, in a variety of contexts. The greater the amount of proximate repetition in which broken spellings, forced or optional, are correlated with contextual features, such as pre-consonantal or geminated +GEM *-t-*, the greater the training on that correlation, and thus the greater the likelihood of broken spelling in the correlated context. Similarly, the greater the training on a correlation of harmonic spelling with word-final context, the greater the accord with that correlation. This effect can be seen in the token frequency data for spellings of *Cat* sequences (Table 16.5). Word-final spellings overwhelmingly favour the harmonic alternative; for words with these sequences only once or twice in final positions, however, broken and harmonic alternatives are about equally likely. Similarly, preconsonantal position strongly favours broken, over harmonic, spelling, and again the preference disappears in the least frequent words. Medial +GEM spellings are too few to draw any conclusions; the least frequent words do have a lower rate of broken spelling than the more frequent, but the difference is not significant and the rates are high in all cases. For medial –GEM spellings, which are significantly, but not strongly, associated with harmonic spelling, there is no significant deviation from a uniform rate of broken spelling with respect to token frequency of the words in which they occur.

Spellings of **Cap** sequences

Although the phonological correlation of forced broken spelling does appear to have been extended in the expected way, *Cat* sequences are the only ones in which such an effect is found. The reason is that every other consonant C_2 that forces broken spelling for some C_1VC_2 sequences is in addition a typically postvocalic grammatical morpheme of high frequency in the existing texts and, in all these cases, it

Table 16.5. *The correlation between broken spelling and phonological context as a function of token frequency*

Lemma frequency	1–2	3–4	5–	1	2	3	4–6	7–	1–2	3–
Ca-at tokens	10	12	2	19	18	17	28	74	4	30
Ca-ut tokens	12	11	20	10	14	13	12	32	4	3
Percent broken	55%	48%	91%	34%	44%	43%	30%	30%	50%	9%
		pre-cons				pre-voc –GEM				final

Table 16.6. *Morphological correlation of broken (**Ca-ip**) spelling with a plural-marking function for **-p** and of harmonic (**Ca-ap**) spelling with no grammatical function*

	tokens		types	
	+ plur	– plur	+ plur	– plur
Ca-ap	37	98	23	60
Ca-ip	224	26	93	14

Table 16.7. *Broken versus harmonic spellings of Cap sequences as a function of the correlation between consonant-specific Cap sequences and the ratio of presence to absence of a plural suffix **-p** in those sequences*

+ plur: – plur ratio		12.1	0.98	0.31
broken	+ plur	168	43	13
harmonic	+ plur	26	6	5
broken	– plur	7	12	8
harmonic	– plur	9	38	51+
broken rate	– plur	.44	.24	<.14
harmonic rate	+ plur	.13	.12	.28

is the grammatical usage that is the basis for the extension of broken spelling to optional contexts. We illustrate the results of these grammatically-based extensions in optional broken spellings of *Cap* sequences, which are primarily extended on the basis of the delocutive animate plural suffix, *-p*.

Because the sign *up* was no longer used in Achaemenid Elamite, the plural of words such as *šalu-*, 'gentleman', were forcibly spelled broken, as in *ša-lu-ip*. Forced harmonic spellings, such as *be-ti-ip* for *beti-p*, 'enemies', and *ᵐSu-ur-te-te-ip* for *Surtete-p*, 'people of Surtete', provided an analogical basis for the spelling of the plural marker as *ip* in the remaining *CVp* sequence type, *Cap*, as in *li-ba-ip* (alongside *li-ba-ap*) for *liba-p*, 'servants'. The correlation of the optional broken spelling with the presence of the plural marker (cf. Cameron 1948: 66) and of harmonic spelling with its absence in *Cap* sequences is illustrated in Table 16.6.

A more refined picture can be obtained by taking into account the initial consonant of a *Cap* sequence. Table 16.7 subcategorizes the data of Table 16.6 according to whether the sequence involved has, overall, a high excess of plural marking to non-plural marking function (average ratio 12.1), approximately equal amounts of both (average ratio 0.98), or relatively few instances of plural relative to non-plural functions (average ratio 0.31).

The results account for most of the deviations from the general correlation between broken spelling and plural marking. *ip* is used in non-plural marking contexts, primarily for shapes in which, overall, *p* most often functions

as a plural marker; *ap* is used in plural marking contexts primarily for shapes in which, overall, *p* least often functions as a plural marker. These deviations are in contexts that are partially reinforced by the plural marker usage, but based upon phonological shape alone.

Positional context has no substantial effect on the correlation of broken spelling with *Cap* sequences. Our presumption is that grammatical usage is far more subject to systematic proximate repetition than is an accidental phonological repetition, and, in itself, tends to agree in rough phonological shape and in syntactic context, as well as in morphological function. There is evidence that proximate repetition is indeed at work in these contexts. We illustrate with the spellings of *liba-p*, 'servants'. The two traditional spellings, *li-ba-ap* and *li-bap*, are found predominantly in types of accounts in which animate plural nouns are not systematically present; in contrast, animate plurals do systematically occur, often together, in the monthly ration texts in which the *li-ba-ip* spellings are concentrated. The latter texts discuss the amounts of rations that various types of people are allotted, with *šalu-p* and *liba-p* prominent among these. For *šalu-p* the only possible spelling is *ša-lu-ip*, a forced broken spelling. The word *liba-p* must often have been written shortly after *šalu-p* by the scribes recording these rations in successive texts, and sometimes within the same text; we quote from PF 1044: 6–12:

30 m.ruh.lg m.ša-lu-ip un-ra d.ITU.lg-na 4 BAR 5 QA.lg du-iš-na
24 m.pu-hu   li-ba-ip un-ra d.ITU.lg-na 3 BAR   du-iš-na
      30 gentlemen each monthly received 4.5 BAR
      24 servant boys each monthly received 3 BAR

Results similar to those for *Cap* are found for the other optional broken spellings whose final consonants sometimes force broken spelling (cf. Table 16.1), all of which involve monoconsonantal grammatical suffixes common in Elamite texts. For optional broken spellings in *CVk* and *CVn* sequences, which never force broken spelling, the broken spelling pattern did make some inroads. However, grammatical correlates in these cases support the *harmonic* rather than the broken alternative. The place name suffix *-an*, found, for example, in *ʰŠu-ša-an* '*Susa*', strongly supports harmonic spelling, and the suffix *-n* for the derived active participle, as in *na-n*, 'saying', is also typically spelled harmonically. However, when this suffix is pronounced *m* by assimilation to a following plural suffix, it is spelled following the broken spelling correlation of *Cam* sequences with suffixed *-m*, so that *nampe*, 'they say', is spelled *na-um-be* alongside the more usual, unassimilated spelling *na-an-be*.

Concluding remarks

The emphases of cognitive studies in archaeology are on systems of meanings – on long term-change of cognitive systems, extinct types of cognitive systems, and the relation between cognition and artefacts. These systems can be studied in considerable detail, without regard to what specific knowledge or meanings they convey.

Symbol systems, in particular, categorize and process knowledge representations. Archaeological study of these systems involves the analysis of patterns of covariation between their material manifestations, and aspects of the archaeological assemblages of which they are a part; these patterns, in turn, reflect variation in symbol selection based upon other aspects of the symbol system, and of the contexts of its use.

We have been concerned, in particular, with evolution in symbolic behaviour. By observing change in patterns of covariation, we hope to make inferences concerning change in the system which it reflects. The Elamite example demonstrates, in some detail, that evolution in a symbol system – i.e. conditioned shifts in symbol selection – follow from reinforcing and inhibitory associations set up by these patterns of covariation, according with processes of classical conditioning via recurrent mutual substitutions in proximate repeated contexts. Once a system is disturbed by a change

introduced into either the set of symbols or their context, adjustment to this change depends initially upon these same types of association, together with those that emerge *de facto* from the contexts in which the novel elements are introduced. We have conducted similar analyses for other writing systems, notably for Mayan hieroglyphic (Justeson and Mathews 1989) and for Norse runic writing.

Proximate repetition of novel and traditional patterns with respect to one another provides a mechanism by which the correlations among facets of the system are redistributed, with weight accruing to predictive features along the lines of associative conditioning models. This provides constraints on analysis and, to some extent, predictive models for evolutionary change in symbol systems. Such constraints provide the theoretical basis on which inference can be made concerning change in past symbolic behaviour.

Notes

1 Throughout this paper, linguistic forms are conveyed in italics and sign transliterations in bold italics.

2 As a display of calligraphic virtuosity in this highly iconic script, scribes occasionally followed a countervailing practice, selecting the largest possible range of signs for a given value. The existence of both patterns can be demonstrated statistically, since they result in fewer than expected instances with an intermediate range of sign variation.

3 Hallock (1958: 259) speculates that *it* was 'reintroduced'; the parallel treatment of *az*, along with *it* the single most complex of the lost signs, was not recognized at the time.

4 Some exceptions are systematic; the initial consonant of a root, when in word-initial position, cannot be spelled geminated, and the same consonant is usually non-geminate even when it occurs medially after a vowel, e.g. the *p* of Old Persian *pati-* is usually spelled non-geminate in compounds, such as **sata-pati-*. In addition, geminate spelling is far more likely when the preceding vowel is long, e.g. the *k* of Old Persian *niyākam* 'grandfather' in *nu-ya-ak-kam-mi versus* the *k* of Old Persian *kasaka* 'stone' in *ka-si-ka*.

5 For example, we presume that *tin* represents *tn* of Elamite *kappa-t-na* in *kap-pa-ut-tin-na* (~ *kap-pa-ut-na*). Such usage is attested relatively often for *CVr* and *CVn* signs. This in turn suggests a basis in language variation, *Cr ~ CVr*. Such variation could result either from deletion of vowels, when the resulting cluster could open syllables, or from the insertion of vowels in consonant + sonorant clusters; both of these processes are well attested in a number of languages, e.g. Latin.

6 In contrast, in spellings of *Cat* and *Cad* in Old Persian words, geminated spellings occur almost exclusively in *Cat* spellings, and broken and harmonic options are about equally often exploited. This shows that the feature GEM is not voicing. Reiner (1969) has suggested tense/lax as an alternative.

7 For Elamite spellings of Old Persian words with *Cat* versus *Cad*, the presence or absence of **Cat** signs has no influence on the rate of broken spelling or even of geminated spellings.

8 This pattern of extension could reflect positional neutralization of the phonological opposition between +GEM and –GEM, with –GEM the usual result in final position, +GEM preconsonantally. We have recognized no independent evidence for such an opposition.

9 This expectation is based on an assumption, for which we have no evidence one way or the other, that the variably geminate spellings do not have a phonetic explanation – e.g. in some further phonetic feature or via some sort of syntactically conditioned neutralization (cf. Reiner 1969: 114).

References

Binford, L. R. 1962. Archaeology as anthropology. *American Antiquity* 22: 17–25

Cameron, G. G. 1948. *Persepolis treasury tablets*. Oriental Institute Publication LXV. Chicago, University of Chicago Press

Hallock, R. T. 1958. Notes on Elamite writing. *Journal of Near Eastern Studies* 17: 256–60

1969. *Persepolis fortification tablets*. Oriental Institute Publication XCII. Chicago, University of Chicago Press

Hampson, S. E. 1990. *Connectionistic problem solving: computational aspects of biological learning*. New York, Birkhauser

1991. Generalization and specialization in artificial neural networks. *Progress in Neurobiology* 37: 383–431

Justeson, J. S. and S. M. Katz 1991. Co-occurrences of antonymous adjectives and their contexts. *Computational Linguistics* 17: 1–19

Justeson, J. S. and P. Mathews 1989. Developmental trends in Mayan hieroglyphic writing. Paper presented at the Symposium on the Language of Mayan Hieroglyphic Writing, Santa Barbara

Justeson, J. S. and L. D. Stephens 1981. Elamite spellings of closed syllables. Paper presented at the annual meeting of the American Oriental Society, Boston

1988. Representational variation and analogical change in Elamite spelling. Paper presented at the annual meeting of the Linguistic Society of America, New Orleans

Reiner, E. 1969. The Elamite language. *Handbuch der Orientalistik*. Abt. 1, Bd. 2, Abschn. 1/2, Lf. 2, pp. 54–118. Leiden/Koln, E. J. Brill

Schanks, D. R. and A. Dickinson 1987. Associative accounts of causality judgment. *The Psychology of Learning and Motivation* 21: 229–61

17

Text and figure in ancient Mesopotamia: match and mismatch[1]

J. N. POSTGATE

It is not necessary to stress that for the archaeologist in search of a society's thought processes, documents from the practice of religion or politics are of prime importance. With the durability of its written output on clay tablets, Mesopotamia offers an excellent opportunity to exploit this avenue, but it has not been followed in recent years. There has been a general reluctance on the part of archaeologists to engage with the written evidence, and those who read the texts have been equally reluctant to cross this barrier. With rare exceptions, when one side decides to make a foray into strange territory, it is just that – a foray, almost a commando raid, which takes some booty, wrenches it from its background and then proceeds to exploit it in their home territory according to their own priorities. This is bound to lead to mistakes: each side must take cognizance of the totality of the other side's data base, and understand how the tempting prizes actually belong in their own context. A totem pole, or a crucifix taken from an altar and nailed to a museum wall, cannot be understood without a knowledge of its provenance. Yet this is the way juicy snippets of information from the other side of the historical/archaeological divide have tended to be treated.

This is therefore, in part, a plea for increased cross-frontier awareness, accompanied by the proviso that one must match the ensemble of each body of data, not just selected items. Every tool at our disposal must be brought in. During the meeting, Kent Flannery emphasised the prime importance of observing and using the entire range of data – more grandly termed a 'holistic' approach – rather than serving up the dainties which suit the palate of a particular model or theory. To illustrate this, and to emphasize the complexity of the procedures, I want to begin with a test-case, that of figurines in Mesopotamia. I hope it will show

how it is only by the combination of textual evidence with close observation of the artefacts and the archaeological context, allowing each to inform the other, that we can move forward rigorously to an advance in the cognitive sphere.

In a deep deposit of successive layers of ashy debris thrown from a large building in the third millennium city of Abu Salabikh we found an unusual concentration of small clay artefacts. They included miniature clay vessels, in some cases very clearly replicas of full-sized pots, and a quantity of human and animal figurines. A few of the animals were well modelled equids or pigs, but the majority are quite crudely formed, as were most of the human figurines.[2]

Any Near Eastern site will yield its share of more or less recognizable clay figurines which the eye of faith or experience will recognize as animals or humans of one kind or another. Usually they turn up in random contexts and the excavators cannot, even if they would, deduce much about their function. As to their purpose, there is a wide variety of choice: are they objects of worship, toys, used in magic, purely decorative, symbols conveying a message, or symbols with a representative function? When an answer is suggested, it is usually intuitive. The fact that the group at Abu Salabikh is concentrated in a single well-defined context in quite large numbers obliges us to seek an explanation for their presence. The figurines and their context alone are not sufficient. Our interpretation needs to draw on parallels from within the cultural environment.

In historical Mesopotamia, animal figurines are not so common. One class is particularly revealing because there is written evidence for their function. These are clay dogs, buried under a house for its protection. Magical manuals give instructions for making them, and prescribe their names, which are to be written on them: 'Don't stop to think, bite', 'Tear out his throat', 'Driver off of demons', 'His bark is loud', and the like. Sure enough, examples have been found by the archaeologists, with just these names written on their backs. So here is one possible explanation: magical images. However, in our third millennium ash-tip we have few if any dogs, and presumably pigs and equids would not be quite so effective in seeing off the forces of evil. *Nil desperandum*, these are not the only inscribed animals. Another class of figurine exists, also dogs, but with inscriptions which make it clear that they have a different function.

Fig. 17.1 is a little clay dog from Sippar (in N. Babylonia) in the first millennium BC. Written on his back are the words 'For the lady Gula, I made a clay dog and presented it to her'. Gula is the goddess of healing, and the dog is her animal. This one is by no means the first in line. A recently excavated clay dog from Gula's home city of Isin, belonging to the later second millennium, has a longer caption: 'To Gula, the lady of the Egalmah temple, lady of life, great physician, giver of the breath of life, his lady – Ili[. .]daya prayed and she heard his prayer. . . . Atanah-ili . . . dedicated the dog'. Although the relationship between the two men named is not known, the general position is quite clear: in gratitude for the goddess' healing intercession, she has a dog dedicated to her. Presumably the little Neo-Babylonian dog performed the same function; we might think that this was a fairly unimpressive gift to the deity, but it need not have been much more significant than lighting a candle in a Catholic church today, and it is noticeable that the donor's name is not mentioned, so that the dog could easily have been bought from a vendor with a range of gift-dogs to suit every pocket.[3]

These two may have been genuine *ex votos* – gifts made to the temple in fulfilment of a vow, once the deity had granted the donor's wish.[4] Others were 'pre-emptive' bribes designed to secure the divine complaisance in advance. The best context for these is the temple excavated at Aqar Quf, the late second millennium capital of the Kassite dynasty, Dur-Kurigalzu. Here, to quote the excavator, there was found 'A pavement of much damaged kiln-baked bricks measuring about 8.00 × 2.00 metres. Over this pavement and in the gaps between the bricks was scattered a collection of some hundreds of broken terracotta figurines in varying states of preservation'. He continues to say 'The subjects of the figurines are broadly of two varieties, namely animals and human-beings, with a considerable preponderance of the

former. The human figures are generally fragmentary but almost all appear to conform to a single convention, in symbolizing the dedicant himself, in a kneeling position to suggest supplication, making some gesture to indicate the character of his request. It will at once be seen, for example from [two examples], where the hands are raised to the eyes, mouth, chest, etc., that the request is obviously concerned with the alleviation of some bodily affliction' (Mustafa 1947).[5]

Here then is another case of human and animal figurines found together in large numbers, albeit about a millennium later than our Abu Salabikh example. What can we deduce of their functions with the advantage of written evidence? Humans and animals, although found together, must be treated separately. The published animal figurines from this find are mostly dogs. One of them has an inscription saying 'To Gula, for the preservation [of the life] of her reverential servant NN' (Fig. 17.2). Others have similar texts. These dogs therefore fall squarely within the same broad category as those from Sippar and Isin: they are gifts to the deity. The same is not true of the human figurines. Mustafa is surely correct in his interpretation of them, as images of worshippers suffering from ailments which it is hoped the deity will cure, something paralleled from many other cultures. Hence they form a special class within a long tradition of three-dimensional images of humans placed in Mesopotamian sanctuaries, one which goes back to the beginning of the third millennium BC, if not earlier. In these early centuries citizens could dedicate statuettes of themselves to stand in the temple, where they would pray unceasingly to the deity. This is explicitly stated on

Fig. 17.1. Neo-Babylonian dog from Sippar (Scheil 1902: 90)

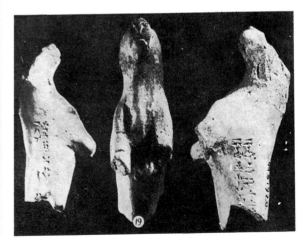

Fig. 17.2. Middle Babylonian dog from Aqar Quf (Mustafa 1947)

occasion. One statue inscription says 'I brought this statue to my Lady's attention, may it speak my prayers' (Sollberger and Kupper 1971: 120 IIC7c). A couple of centuries later (*c.* 1800 BC) a king's daughter, dedicated by her father as a priestess to serve the temple of the Sun-God at Sippar, writes to him 'Am I not your symbol, a suppliant who gives you a favourable report in the Ebabbar temple?' – making it clear that this was indeed the function of the more usual stone representatives which conveyed their dedicators' prayers to the deities in their shrines (Postgate 1992, 131).

At Aqar Quf in the late second millennium it is clear, then, from the inscriptional evidence, that the human and the animal figures have two different functions, and it seems reasonable to guess that the same difference in function should be read back into our third millennium material, despite the absence of inscriptional confirmation.

That there is a significant difference between the two classes may also be gathered from what is, at first sight, a trivial difference in terminology. Whenever the texts talk of dedicating an animal figurine, it is not referred to as 'the figure of a dog', or 'a dog figurine', but merely as 'a dog'. Similarly, in utilitarian inventories ornaments or *ex votos* are simply called 'pig' or 'lion'; or 'lapis lazuli pig', 'copper lion'. It is not that the language does not have a word for an image, but that it is not appropriate in this context. The common Akkadian word for an image is *ṣalmum* (corresponding to the Sumerian **alan/m**): this may refer to figures of any size, and various functions, from an over-life-size divine statue to a metal figure weighing a few shekels, but

they all share one essential characteristic: they are anthropomorphic. That is to say, they may be images of gods, or of humans, or of demons and other supernatural beings, but not of animals. This may seem surprising at first sight to the philologists, and indeed I cannot rule out the possibility that somewhere in the great variety of texts which have come down to us there is not an exception: but no instance of *ṣalmum* referring to an animal is recorded in the Chicago Assyrian Dictionary.

In exploring this difference I would like to use two words: 'effigy' to translate and explain the Akkadian *ṣalmum*, and 'substitute' for the animal figurines.[6] The functions of anthropomorphic effigies can be described graphically by the diagram below (Fig. 17.3). The effigy is the representation of a separate, specific, individual, whether a particular god, person or demon. Some of these individuals may seem more real to us today than others, but the textual evidence makes it clear that even the demons had their own individuality – they were not undifferentiated members of a class. The effigy is not, in itself, that individual, but a projection of it – to use a modern analogy, it is a 'terminal', connected to the individual entity itself in such a way that influences on one are transmitted to the other. This will become clearer if we explain the four types of effigy shown in the diagram:

Type 1 is the god's effigy: this was probably always an anthropomorphic image of a god, usually a statue or statuette. Humans in a temple cella may communicate directly with the effigy, which can mean praying to it, or

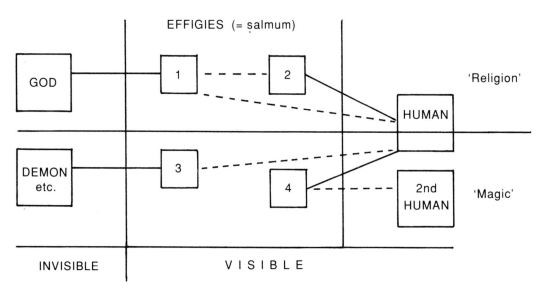

Fig. 17.3. The functions of anthropomorphic effigies

feeding it. As in Egypt we know of rituals called 'opening' or 'washing the mouth' designed to 'activate' such effigies: one text says 'without the mouth-opening ritual this effigy will not smell the incense'.[7] Gods could also be represented by more abstract symbols which may be called *šurinnum* ('symbol') or *kakkum* ('weapon'), terms which overlap with each other and with *ṣalmum*, but these do not receive the same anthropomorphic attentions.

Type 2 is the human worshipper figure: humans may take themselves in person to the temple, and there communicate with the god's effigy, but they cannot be there all the time. If, though, they have an effigy of themselves they can install it in ('bring it into') the cella, where it can perform that role for them permanently. We have already seen a curious incarnation of this idea in the shape of the king's daughter ('Am I not your symbol'), and the Kassite figurines of sufferers holding their affected limbs are merely specialized applications of the same principle. Larger models of feet or legs from the Gula Temple at Isin, of male and female genitalia, best known from the late second millennium Assyrian capital Kar-Tukulti-Ninurta, and the Old Babylonian couples engaged in sexual congress on beds can also be classified here without straining the thought categories involved. Each can be seen, not as a member of a class, but as a particular couple, or the afflicted portion of a specific individual.[8]

Types 1 and 2 have been classed together under the heading of religion, whereas 3 and 4 belong in the milieu of magic. Space does not allow us to pursue the ways in which this important distinction is reflected in texts and archaeology, so I must just ask the reader to believe that most applications of effigies can usefully be divided along these lines.

Type 3 is the figurine of a supernatural being, whether an evil demon or a good spirit. These are, of course, usually encountered in magical contexts, and some are further described below. They are often of clay and other low-value materials, but the principle is still the same. The actions applied to the effigies are transmitted to the demon itself – such as burying it, burning it, or putting it in a boat to be floated away downstream. It is worth stressing that these figures too are called *ṣalmum* – the same term as is used for statues of the king. Note that it is an important part of any magical procedure – just as of a medical diagnosis – to give a name to the malignant force, and so to identify it. So when we read 'You make the effigy of the ghost, ... and you put on it the horn of an ox', we must be careful to translate it so, and not 'an effigy of a ghost'.[9]

Type 4 is the effigy of a human, used in a similar way to be the channel through which magical influences are conveyed to the human individual. This is attested, for instance, in the potency incantations. In one case the practitioner is to 'take clay from both banks of the river and make a figurine (*ṣalmu*) of the woman, write her name on its left hip', then bury it, and recite incantations over it. Then 'that woman will come to you (and) you can make love to her', so that the effigy has acted as a channel of influence to the woman herself. In another case the influence works in the other direction, with the effigy being imbued with an evil influence actually affecting the individual: after a meaningless spell translated aptly by its editor as 'abracadabra', we read 'The ritual: you mix together dough (made of) emmer and potter's clay; you make figurines of the man and the woman, put them one upon the other, and place them at the man's head, ... then put them near a pig. ... If the pig does not approach the figurines, (it means) that man has been affected by sorcery'. The editor correctly translated 'figurine of the' (not 'a') 'man' or 'woman' (Biggs 1967: 46).

Here then is an important distinction made between human and animal figurines. On the one hand, the human figurine falls into a class of effigies, with divine statues, magical images of demons, or statuettes of worshippers. On the other hand, the animal figurine is described as just an animal. It is not, we all know, a real live (or dead) animal, but neither is it the effigy of a specific animal: although of clay, or metal or stone, it is an animal in its own right. When presented to the goddess, the clay dogs are themselves the gift, substituting for a flesh-and-blood dog perhaps, but not representing one. This difference corresponds (happily) with the different function we need to assign to the two classes, and it is even clearly delineated in the case where a magical ritual requires an effigy of a substitute! This is where a substitute entity is needed onto which the evil threatening a person can be diverted. The extreme version of this is the installation of the substitute king on the throne during the period in which life-threatening omens are predicted for the royal person; but the ritual texts tell us of regular procedures by which a substitute (called (*an*)*di*/*unanu* in Akkadian and **níg.sag.íla** in Sumerian) is represented by an effigy (*ṣalmu*): the two concepts are quite discrete.[10]

To sum up, we have seen in the Kassite temple at Aqar Quf a very similar find to that at Abu Salabikh some 1000 years earlier, in which human and animal figurines occur together. The iconographic attributes of and inscriptions on the Kassite examples match, well, other textual evidence for two distinct functions of figurine, the effigy (for specific anthropomorphic entities) and the substitute (constituting an autonomous member of a class). In this light we are entitled to associate the earlier find with the same cognitive system: in other words, we may speculate that the human figurines are effigies of individuals, perhaps placed in a temple context to worship and receive divine influence for their donors, whereas the animals will belong in a class with the miniature vessels, and represent substitutes for real sheep, jars and bowls given to the temple as an offering. Similar substitutes can be found in association with sanctuaries in other times and places, whether bronze age Palestine or modern Buddhist shrines.

The facts may, of course, be open to other interpretations: what I want to stress here is that ours derives its strengths from the combined exploitation of various avenues of approach. Starting from archaeological evidence for their association with one another and with their provenance, we have interpreted an assemblage of figurines by observing their individual characteristics, drawing parallels with similar phenomena at other times within the same Mesopotamian culture, and bringing in the further dimension of written evidence, whether captions on figurines themselves or separate accounts of ritual practice. Finally, we have noted that our reconstruction of the function of the figurines gives a situation which can be paralleled in other cultures. It is hardly a surprise that the process is immensely more productive than treating each class of evidence independently, and it should not be necessary to stress how important it is that we continue along these lines. Now, though, I should like to examine the process itself and direct attention away from the textual or archaeological data themselves, towards the nature of the links between them.

Match and mismatch

Our case-study above is an example of a gratifying congruence between two classes of evidence. At its best, each attribute of the archaeological material can be accounted for directly from the corresponding written evidence: not merely the iconography, which first commands attention itself, but other essential attributes such as the material of which the object is made, the quality of execution, archaeological provenance, etc. This is not always so: there are cases of equally clear mismatch, where there may be an equal range of attributes seeking explanation, but the textual sources may offer no such neat answers. Such a situation is described by Winter in the case of the Stele of the Vultures: ' . . . the correspondence between text and imagery is not exact. Significant elements within the verbal narrative are not depicted on the stele, while certain of the details so carefully depicted in relief are not fully described in the text. Read in conjunction with the imagery, the text does help to identify the specific conflict and interpret certain details of the pictorial narrative. But the visual imagery has its own agenda, not identical to that of the text' (1986: 22). In this second half, I shall argue that these mismatches should not be swept under the carpet, but welcomed in their own right: we should direct our attention quite deliberately to the reasons why the match is good in some and bad in other cases, since this will expose more of the discrete identity of the two classes, starting with a couple of well known instances of good match.

The deified king

Fig. 17.4 shows the design on a cylinder seal of the Ur III Dynasty, from Sumer about 2025 BC. It shows King Ibbi-Sin seated on his throne, receiving the owner of the seal who is ushered (indeed almost dragged) into his presence by his personal goddess. Fig. 17.5, which is contemporary, is at first sight very similar, but there are significant differences in detail. There is still a suppliant, led onto the scene by his personal goddess, but the figure on the throne is not the king

Fig. 17.4. Cylinder seal, Ur III Dynasty (Porada 1948, No. 292)

but a god: there are at least three clear indicators of this. One is the king's rounded hat which is replaced by the horned head-dress characteristic of gods at this date, and worn also by the introducing goddesses. Next is the royal robe which is smooth, with fringes, whereas the god (again like the goddesses) wears the traditional flounced robe of deities. Finally, the king sits on a simple stool covered with a fleece or fleecy cloth, while the god occupies a piece of furniture which we know to be if not actually an altar, at least modelled on one. The comparison of these two scenes would suggest that, at this time, kings might be treated very much like gods, but that some distinctions were maintained.

Now look at the historical sources. There is ample evidence that the kings of the Ur III Dynasty assumed some form of divine status during their lifetimes. Their names were preceded, like those of gods, with the divine determinative. At Eshnunna we even have a temple dedicated to the divine Shu-Sin, and there is a wealth of archival evidence for offerings made to kings and for priests belonging to their cult. Why this deification? An answer to this can be found in the traditional roles of the gods in Mesopotamian religion: like members of the British Parliament they may have a dual role. They usually have a geographical constituency (whether a land, a city or a village), and major deities also have a 'ministerial portfolio'. Thus Shamash is the sun god (with responsibilities *inter alia* for justice), but he is also the local patron deity of the cities of Sippar and (in his Sumerian name Utu) of Larsa. The Ur III state united all the ancient South Mesopotamian city-states under one rule, but in itself it constituted a new territorial entity with no previous communal identity. As such it had no patron deity. Rather than create a new one, or redeploy an old one, King Shulgi resolved this by stepping into the breach himself – an intriguing parallel to the Divus Augustus. His inscriptions

explicitly call him 'the god of his land', and no doubt it was in this role that his sons perpetuated the tradition. And yet the iconography clearly suggests that the divinity of the king was kept firmly separate in contemporary perceptions from that of the established gods. Sufficient explanation for this is surely given by the king's evident humanity and mortality.

Apotropaic figurines

We have long and detailed instructions to Mesopotamian exorcists on the ritual words and actions for protecting a building from malign forces. They often include making figurines and burying them in the foundations or under the floors. The dogs that we mentioned above belong here, but most of the figures are anthropomorphic. The attributes of each figurine are specified precisely: the material of which they are made, their stance, the weapons or other objects they are holding – all are defined. When they are of clay, a short text is often to be inscribed on them, such as 'Go out evil, come in good', 'Come in favourable demon, go out evil demon', or 'Go out death, come in life'. Sure enough, as with the dogs, figurines exactly matching these descriptions have been unearthed on Assyrian sites, complete with captions, so no doubt can persist (Wiggermann 1992).

Good matches of this kind between the iconography and the texts are encouraging. They tell us that we are not wrong to expect some of the attributes of iconographic figures or scenes to have a definite meaning. Most of the attributes of each class of artefact, which we might have expected to have significance, turn out to have significance, and so indeed do some attributes we might not have expected. The ritual texts tell us that some of the figurines are meant to be of different substances from others, and to be holding different weapons. The propagandistic literature of early Mesopotamia tells us that the hat, the throne and the robe were among the formally

Fig. 17.5. Cylinder seal, Ur III Dynasty (Porada 1948, No. 277)

recognized symbols of royalty; if we search the texts, in time we shall surely find the fleecy rug which seems to have been *de rigueur* on the royal stool.[11] In each case the iconographic attributes vary with a consistency which would have led us to guess there was some significance, and in each case this is confirmed by the texts.

Bad matches

However, these neat matches are the exception. To describe cases of bad matches in detail is less easy, but a couple of examples may serve. In Fig. 17.6, we have one example of a cylinder seal design of the Akkad Dynasty. Here, it is generally agreed, we have elements from the myth of Etana, a shepherd who was taken up to heaven on an eagle. This myth exists as a written composition from some 500 years later, and some, but not all, of the elements of the earlier design can be matched in the poem. The curious thing is that there are no cylinder seals contemporary with the written composition which show this design (nor do we have a written text contemporary with the seals, though this could possibly be blamed on the chances of survival). So why did cylinder seal designers use this motif at one date and abandon it later, and why are details of the design not matched with the text as we have it?

We have no easy answer to these questions, and this underlines our ignorance of the motivation behind the choice of iconographic scenes: why was a scene like this suitable to feature on the seals, almost uniquely in its human narrative, and why did this only happen in the Akkad period? In other words, it is the mismatch itself which points out the extent of our ignorance. It is here that we need to tread carefully and place both the text and the iconography in their own context. Then an explanation for the mismatch might be illuminating.

Fig. 17.7 is another example from the cylinder seal

repertoire: a man, in a flat cap, fights with a bull, and two bull-men attack lions. The seal-owner's name occupies a cartouche above a little calf and tree. Animal-combat scenes are the most frequent seal design for several centuries before the Dynasty of Akkad. They change greatly in style and iconographic repertoire throughout this period, and virtually every combination of men, monsters, and wild animals is represented. We have no inkling as to their significance. They agree with nothing that has survived into the written literature of later Mesopotamia, and although we only have very scarce contemporary literary texts, those which we do have do not suggest that we could expect anything radically different from that with which we already are familiar. In other words, whatever the significance of these scenes (and one can hardly adopt the position that they have none), it is not a message that is conveyed in the literary idiom. Unlike the iconography of politics or the ritual instructions for the exorcists, the message of the animal contest scenes belongs in a system which is not represented in the written record.

It is true, of course, that relatively few genres of information were committed to writing at this early date, and this is another reason why there is no match. But the same does not apply to our third example, the 'sacred marriage'. Textual sources are quite unambiguous in telling us that around 2000 BC there was a formal ritual in which the king engaged in sexual intercourse with a priestess representing the goddess Ishtar (= Inana; see Postgate 1992: 265–7; also Klein 1981: 32–6). The ritual is described in literary compositions called royal hymns, and was presumably accorded importance in the ideology of the age. However, this is not something that features on cylinder seals of the time: it is true that in earlier centuries there are scenes of sexual intercourse on cylinder seals; and on contemporary terracotta model beds scenes of domestic bliss are enacted more often than the

Fig. 17.6. Cylinder seal, Akkad Dynasty (Porada 1948, No. 236)

number of published examples might suggest. But scholars are loath to connect either of these with the sacred marriage rite – and probably rightly, because there are no good confirmatory details to sustain the match.

In the past, such a miss would be ignored, or each side would dismiss the irrelevance of the other side and continue to interpret its own material without regard to the other. This is surely a mistake. We need to concentrate on the relationship between the two data sets, because that relationship itself will tell us something. Explaining a mismatch will always be difficult, and inevitably involve speculation. Sometimes there may be a better match than we can see because of gaps in our evidence, or a failure to detect the significant attributes. In the ritual instructions for an exorcist concerned to promote his client's potency, which we quoted above, the figurines were made of 'emmer dough and potter's clay'. Here the text indicates that the substance is significant; but even if, as archaeologists, we succeeded in detecting the difference between such a figurine and one made more prosaically of just clay, we would probably not have guessed the 'emic' quality of the difference. Nevertheless, there will always remain genuine cases of mismatch, and there the existence of the mismatch is a significant attribute in its own right.

This is clear because our two cases of good match are not coincidental. The very consistency and elaboration of the two systems is a reflection of their social context. Textual statements about divine Ur III kings are propaganda from public contexts within the political orbit of the ruling dynasty. They are transmitting a message loud and clear. The figured statements are on the cylinder seals used by officials in the exercise of their public functions. Each is addressing the same audience, conveying the same message, with a coherence of detail which reflects a carefully structured ideology. Both text and figure are effective and belong in the same cultural context: this therefore tells us something positive about both. Similarly, the standardization of the apotropaic figurines is a clear reflection of the concern for ritual correctness which is itself expressed in the care with which the exorcist's instructions are written down, lest an error be made. The good match is there because it was an end in itself.

Notes

1 The text covers the same ground as the spoken contribution to the Cambridge meeting, but includes some thoughts on 'effigies' which were first presented at a meeting of the British Association for Near Eastern Archaeology at Cambridge in December 1991. I am very grateful to Prof. Irene Winter, of the Department of Fine Arts, Harvard University, for helpful and percipient comments on an earlier draft of this paper.

2 Postgate 1982; a final report on the ash-tip and its contents has been edited by Dr A. R. Green, and will appear in 1993 as *Abu Salabikh Excavations*, Vol. 4.

3 No doubt the real dogs which were found buried in a cemetery of their own round the temple of Gula at Isin were *ex votos* in the same way (cf. Hrouda 1977). For the clay dog see Hrouda 1977: 43 and Taf. 8, and Edzard and Wilcke, in the same volume, p. 90.

4 That doubts expressed in the past about the existence of genuine *ex votos* in Mesopotamia were over-cautious is shown in Grayson 1990.

5 A similar discovery was recently made at Nippur by Prof. McG. Gibson (press reports).

Fig. 17.7. Cylinder seal, Early Dynastic period (Porada 1948, No. 144)

6 It is not easy to find a satisfactory terminology agreeing with modern English usage. I have followed Irene Winter's advice in discarding the term 'icon' as a rendering of *ṣalmum*, as being too general. The choice of 'effigy' is my own.

7 See the *Assyrian Dictionary* (Chicago: Oriental Institute, Vol. 16 (Ṣ), 79a.

8 For Isin models see Spycket 1990, with interesting additions by Stol 1991; for Assur Andrae 1935; for Old Babylonian beds see e.g. Postgate 1992: 104.

9 For a recent survey of Mesopotamian magical practices as reflected in the texts see Thomsen 1987.

10 As Irene Winter reminds me, in pre-Ur III Sumerian texts divine statues are not described as **alam** like the humans, but merely with the deity's name, like the animals. This may be seen to imply that in earlier times, to use Winter's words, 'once consecrated, the image IS the god'.

11 Perhaps the fleecy item mentioned in Shulgi Hymn X, 1. 60 (Klein 1981: 138)?

References

Andrae, W. 1935. *Die jüngeren Ischtar-Tempel in Assur.* Wissenschaftliche Veröffentlichungen der Deutschen Orient-Gesellschaft 58. Leipzig

Biggs, R. D. 1967. *ŠÀ.ZI.GA: Ancient Mesopotamian potency incantations.* Texts from Cuneiform Sources II. New York, J. J. Augustin

Grayson, A. K. 1990. Old and Middle Assyrian royal inscriptions – Marginalia. In *Ah, Assyria . . . Studies in Assyrian history and ancient Near Eastern historiography presented to Hayim Tadmor,* ed. M. Cogan and I. Ephal, pp. 264–6. Jerusalem, The Magnes Press

Hrouda, B. (ed.) 1977. *Isin-Išān Baḥriyāt I: Die Ergebnisse der Ausgrabungen 1973–1974.* Munich, Bayerische Akademie der Wissenschaften

Klein, J. 1981. *Three Šulgi hymns.* Ramat Gan, Bar Ilan University Press

Mustafa, M. A. 1947. Kassite figurines: A new group discovered near 'Aqar Quf. *Sumer* 3: 19–22

Porada, E. 1948. *Corpus of ancient Near Eastern seals in North American collections, I. The collection of the Pierpont Morgan Library.* Washington, DC, The Bollingen Foundation

Postgate, J. N. 1982 Abu Salabikh. In *Fifty years of Mesopotamian discovery,* ed. J. E. Curtis, pp. 48–61. London, British School of Archaeology in Iraq

 1992. *Early Mesopotamia: society and economy at the dawn of history.* London, Routledge

Scheil, V. 1902. *Une saison de fouilles a Sippar.* Mémoires publiées par les membres de l'Institut Français d'Archéologie Orientale du Caire I/i. Cairo

Sollberger, E. and J.-R. Kupper 1971. *Inscriptions royales sumériennes et akkadiennes.* Paris, Les Editions du Cerf

Spycket, A. 1990. Ex-voto mesopotamiens du IIe Millénaire av. J.-C. In *De la Babylonie à la Syrie en passant par Mari,* ed. O. Tunca, pp. 79–86. Liège, Université de Liège

Stol, M. 1991. Review of Spycket 1990. *Bibliotheca Orientalis* (Leiden) 48: 553–6

Thomsen, M.-L. 1987. *Zauberdiagnose und Schwarze Magie in Mesopotamien.* Carsten Niebuhr Institute Publications 2. Copenhagen

Wiggermann, F. A. M. 1992. *Mesopotamian protective spirits: the ritual texts.* Groningen, Styx and PP Publications

Winter, I. J. 1986. After the battle is over: The Stele of the Vultures and the beginning of historical narrative in the art of the ancient Near East. In *Pictorial narrative in antiquity and the Middle Ages,* ed. H. L. Kessler and M. S. Simpson, pp. 11–32. Studies in the history of art, vol. 16. Washington, DC

PART VII

Conclusion

18
Cognitive archaeology reconsidered

EZRA B. W. ZUBROW

What is cognitive archaeology?

There are two major aspects to cognitive archaeology. First, cognitive archaeology is a rather loosely-defined area including the evolution of the whole complex system of human mental abilities and their material representations. Second, there is a facet which considers how cognitive processes impact the archaeologists who do archaeology.

The first aspect focuses on what can be learned about perception, attention, learning, memory and reasoning from the study of past cultures. It is concerned with 'when', 'where' and 'how', in hominid and cultural evolution, cognition became such an important part of the human experience. Cognitive archaeology embraces aspects of behaviour, language and imagery. It frequently has been noted that archaeologists believe that patterns of material culture reflect the patterns of human behaviour. Yet, what has not been emphasized is that human behaviour has been goal directed as long as it has been observed. It thus reflects many cognitive issues. Archaeologists in the 1990s believe that the patterns of material culture reflect not only the patterns of social behaviour but, as importantly, the patterns of human cognition. Since language is fundamental to cognition, the archaeologists concerned with cognitive questions have tended to emphasize the development of the linguistic record.

The second aspect of cognitive archaeology focuses on what could be described as 'reflexive' archaeology. How do the cognitive processes of the archaeologist limit how archaeology is practised? Archaeologists are, to some extent, a product of their time and culture. In addition, they are a product of their individual field and excavation experience, as well as their idiosyncratic personalities and histories.

Consequently, archaeological interpretation may be a personal creation, and the construction of archaeological narratives may be fulfilling and intellectually profitable for the individual.

Yet, there is an archaeological 'common knowledge' that is not interpretative. It is neither idiosyncratic nor culturally specific – it exists beyond the individual and is cross-cultural. Far more than social or cultural anthropology, archaeological fieldwork is, and has been, a joint and cumulative endeavour. Excavations and surveys are labour intensive and require the efforts of many individuals over many years. The nature of the research requires the ability to communicate information between researchers across space and time.

Frequently, information from the beginning of the excavation needs to be incorporated into studies done decades later. On large sites there are regularly inter-disciplinary teams of researchers working concurrently, and sometimes expeditions from different institutions will share the workload. The history of archaeology is replete with examples of different archaeological expeditions, even from different nations relocating and returning to sites partially excavated by their predecessors. Re-examining notes, reports, and the field work of the earlier expeditions, they incorporate the earlier work into their attempts to move forward knowledge of the particular prehistoric event, site or society. Furthermore, the analysis of archaeological remains is replicable and laboratory results are interdisciplinary. There is not only a 'commonality' of information but a 'common knowledge' within archaeology that is shared by the majority of archaeologists around the world. It is the basis of what is generally known as archaeological practice or science. This may be as simple as the common definition of what is meant by a radiocarbon dating or dendro-chronology, or as complicated as the definition of a particular culture. It may be indirect as in the determination of the dietary preferences of prehistoric hominids by abrasive patterns on occlusal surfaces of teeth, or the direct recognition of a particular style of ceramics such as Mesa Verde Black on White. In short, there are substantive, methodological and theoretical commonalities.

The schizophrenic character of cognitive archaeology

This book has emphasized the first aspect of cognitive archaeology. Traditionally, archaeologists have been quite schizophrenic regarding this element. For some it was relatively easy to study; for others it was difficult to explore; and for some scholars impossible to know.

Historically, for those who found it relatively easy, it was sufficient simply to ascribe their own motivations, their concepts, and their belief structures to peoples vastly separated by space, time and culture. Some justified this on principles of the 'psychic unity' of human kind; most, however, simply made the assumption without justification. For example the beliefs of the economic 'rational man' or the goals of the 'proto-scientist' were ascribed to societies as far distant as Upper Palaeolithic hunters and gatherers and the Maya. V. Gordon Childe, describing his writing of *Man makes himself*, noted:

> the archaeological record is interpreted as documenting a directional process wherein men by applications of science steadily increased their control over non-human nature so that their species might multiply and incidentally secrete laws and political institutions, religions and art. (In Daniel and Chippindale n.d.: 16)

For him, the past was the playing out of the goals of a western industrialized scientific society at various points throughout a developmental trajectory.

In contrast, a sizeable group claimed that prehistoric cognition was difficult to study, as exemplified by Gordon Willey's words in the same forum.

> I would recommend approaching causality with caution . . . There is an unavoidable tension in archaeological research, a tension between the material remains we study and our attempts to grasp the ideas which once created, shaped and arranged these remains. This is a tension the archaeologist must learn to live with as he goes about trying to resolve it. (In Daniel and Chippindale n.d.: 112)

For some archaeologists such as Dunnell (1971) the solution was simply to stop studying cognition. It was a subject forever closed to the present, for one could never determine such phenomena as motivation from the material record. Since it was closed – even the effort was futile.

For others, the key was to give up the scientific aspects of archaeology and to focus upon interpretation. Non-positivistic, hermeneutic, and interested in narrative and post-modernist discourse, the philosophical works of Foucault (1972) and others were archaeologically reinterpreted by Hodder (1987, 1989), Tilley (1990) and Shanks (1992). Interpretation, although insightful, could not be replicated, substantiated, nor built upon by itself.

However, as this book has shown, it was not necessary to reinvent the intellectual wheel. Much is known regarding human cognition. Much is known about the general path human evolution, prehistory and history have taken. It is not what is written large which is unknown, but what is written small. The details of the development of prehistoric cognition are what are unclear. Simply put, many of the

ideas, techniques and concepts of 'processual archaeology' may be applied to problems of cognition.

What are some important questions for the future of cognitive archaeology?

What does one want to know about the prehistory and development of human cognition, and what should be the role of archaeology in the future understanding of cognition? One knows that all humans process a variety of environmental, sensory, and other stimuli. For modern humans a stimulus proceeds through a sequence of processing stages until it either drops out of the neuro-cognitive system or is deposited in long-term memory. Sensory memory is relatively unselective in its contents and has a large capacity. Anthropologists, linguists, ethno-scientists and archaeologists have used the Sapir-Whorf hypothesis to suggest that cultures focus sensory memory and classify its contents in a variety of ways. These classifications depend on the relevant importance of the elements to a particular culture.

Archaeologists should be able to reconstruct these processes, to determine when different classifications, different types of classifications, and different types of organizing principles for classification appear in human and cultural evolution, and to show how they change over time. For example, although equally unselective, the sensory memory of a palaeolithic hunter-gatherer along the edge of the Würm ice may well use quite different organizing principles from that of a neolithic peasant on the edge of Greece. There is a critical role for ethnoarchaeology in this endeavour. One needs to determine commonalities across cultures of the elements, the classifications and the organizing principles that are focused by sensory memory.

In addition, there appear to be certain cognitive universals. For example, one knows that all people maintain information about personal experiences, personal location, and their general world, regardless of culture. The exact information, the language, the definitions and the forms vary but the need to maintain this information is presently universal. When did it become universal? When did each of these domains become important? Are they characteristic only of modern humans? Are they characteristic also of *Homo sapiens neanderthalensis*? If one examines the late neanderthal sites in France or the early *Homo sapiens sapiens* sites in Europe or the Middle East, would the same domains be apparent? Is conscious recognition of these domains universal? Does it cross the species barrier to *Homo erectus* or *Homo habilis*? Does it occur in other genera such as the Australopithicines over a million years ago?

Consider personal and social location. One locates oneself in relationship to known physical (such as mountains) and social (such as home) landmarks. One chooses the vocabulary and grammar of description. It clearly varies by task and social status. Numerous studies of spatial languages have been completed. The greater the specificity needed, the more restricted the allowed vocabulary and the more limited the terms of spatial reference must be. For example, contemporary air controllers are limited to a very circumscribed and highly defined spatial vocabulary. What are the material and behavioural correlates of such task-limited spatial languages? Today they are highly significant; there is no reason to assume that they would not have been equally important prehistorically in such tasks as hunting, travelling, trading or other forms of subsistence, as well as many others.

Psychologists have argued that short-term memory, unlike sensory memory, has a very small capacity. New items quickly displace the old ones. One function of the development of art, counting, measurement and writing, as well as other symbolic systems, is to increase the length of time that information may be maintained in short term memory, and to increase the length of time that it can be accessed and brought from long-term into short-term memory. Therefore, as well as the traditional archaeological questions regarding the size of the artefacts, their number, and their distribution, there are questions about their symbolic aspects, and the consideration of artefacts as material correlates of knowledge representations which are incorporated into their production. For such studies the questions of symbolic meaning need to be supplemented with questions regarding symbolic duration, symbolic penetration and symbolic efficiency. For example, are some symbols more effective than others in increasing the length of time that the knowledge may be accessed? If so, is there a selection process by which less effective symbols are replaced by more effective symbols? What are their material and archaeological concomitants? Or turning to the knowledge represented in artefact production, consider briefly the vast range of artefact material 'sourcing studies'. What may be inferred about the concepts of personal or social location from the reconstruction of flint sources, clay pits or the vast range of studies of prehistoric trade routes?

Archaeologists should ask similar questions about long-term memory, the permanent memory store. If its capacity is virtually unlimited, and forgetting from long-term memory is not so much a loss of information as retrieval failure, then the development of human culture is the development of mechanisms to reduce this 'retrieval failure'. Yet, archaeologists find over and over again that long-term memory does not last very long – even with the reinforcement of language, story telling, art, symbol systems etc. Protohistoric events, peoples and sites are as frequently forgotten as remembered. The fact that one is not sure who one's ancestors are, or where they lived, is far more than a trivial personal question. It is indicative of an important archaeological question. One fundamental rationale for archaeology is to determine where the species, and its cultures, came from in the broad sense which includes 'how' and through what 'processes' and what does it 'mean'. Today, it is a standard question to ask how sites are created. Most archaeologists study site formation processes as well as their converse, the study of the mechanisms of site destruction. Both sets of processes have important cognitive correlates. There is a correlation among 'creating', 'recognition' and the symbolic processes of 'naming' cultural entities that is conversely reflected in 'destruction', 'denial' and 'forgetting' of the same cultural entity. A general question is how and why do individuals or cultures forget such cultural entities as villages?

Archaeologists need to study the reinforcing mechanisms of memory. Some general rules are known but when they first occur, how they diffuse and through what mechanisms are important archaeological questions. For modern humans it has been shown that patterns of symbols are easier to remember if they form comprehensible patterns or are in some kind of holistic context. This rule appears to hold, whether one is considering pictorial, verbal, or written symbols, and it holds across languages and cross-culturally. Incomplete partial strings are easier to remember than random strings; words are easier to learn than letters. One does not need to hear every word to understand a sentence nor every sentence to understand a paragraph. Realistic pictures are easier to remember than abstractions, and complete pictures are easier to understand and remember than pieces of pictures. There is, of course, a great deal of informational redundancy in human symbol systems. Such questions as 'when and what are the earliest pictures' have a new relevance to archaeologists and psychologists in this context. For example, the expectations are that early pictures are holistic, realistic and contextually complete. They should not be fragmentary designs. Does the prehistoric record suggest this contention? Is redundancy increasing or decreasing through time, and in which symbolic systems? Does symbolic redundancy make any difference in adaptation or other aspects of prehistoric society?

Imagery is an important component of the information stored in memory. When do people think in images and when in words? How are the two related? Under what conditions is an image representation more appropriate than a word or propositional one? Both systems, image and word, appear to exist simultaneously, for modern people do use both words for narratives, mental imagery for visualization. Visualization includes such problems as estimating the distance between two points or mentally rotating a geometric figure in order to compare it with another figure, or transforming it to fit a preconceived shape. Both may be used together or at least interactively. For example, when one tries to describe the face of a person in another location to a third person, the process is to use words to distinguish relevant aspects of the mental image one maintains. The development of village life, agricultural landscapes, architecture and settlement systems are material correlates of these systems – visual imagery systems which are shared and communicated verbally or through written symbols. Archaeologists have studied them in other contexts. They need to be explored in a cognitive context.

Conclusions

The critical issues in cognitive archaeological research deal with such questions as: what is the nature of the memory representation and knowledge representation, and when and where did it first occur? What are the information encoding mechanisms and processing constraints of humans and why? How are they related to adaptation, to the development of imagery, and language? How is long-term memory organized, and does it vary across the hominid genera and species? How does the development of society affect the acquisition of knowledge? What is the nature of human meaning, and how does it relate to the ideological and social aspects of human evolution? These are not easy questions and no single book will solve them.

The author believes that archaeology in the 1970s and 1980s was divided. Mainstream archaeology, whether declaring itself processual or not, was concerned with a general set of processual problems including trade, adaptation, social status, economic production and material behaviour to name a few in addition to chronology, culture definition, and event and process reconstruction. Generally, there was, and continues to be, a consensus about the type of data, types of techniques, and types of analyses which are needed to substantiate the conclusions which most of these archaeologists accepted. There was a *commonality* to this

archaeological exercise, the archaeological methodology, and even archaeological theory and problems that transcended individual interpretation. This type of archaeology does not concern itself with ideas of cognition, ideology or meaning. The post-processual archaeologist took up the latter, and showed how important and intellectually profitable these areas are. If nothing else, they taught that cognitive archaeology was important. This book was a conscious attempt to suggest that mainstream archaeology, using the application of the scientific method to prehistoric data, has important contributions to make regarding such topics as cognition, symbols and meaning. Whether or not the individual articles or the book itself are successful is less important than that the attempt was made. Cognition should not be the sole preserve of the post-processualists. Hopefully, this will be a harbinger of other studies.

Archaeology is about to leave one millennium and enter another. There is a need to continue asking fundamental questions. Among them is what does it *mean* to be human, and how and when did this condition emerge?

References

Daniel, G. and C. Chippindale (eds.) n.d. *The pastmasters: eleven modern pioneers of archaeology.* Antiquity Publications. London, Thames and Hudson

Dunnell, R. C. 1971. *Systematics in prehistory.* New York, Free Press

Foucault, M. 1972. *The archaeology of knowledge.* London, Tavistock

Hodder, I. (ed.) 1987. *The archaeology of contextual meanings.* Cambridge, Cambridge University Press
    1989. *The meaning of things: material culture and symbolic expression.* One World Archaeology, vol. 6. London, Unwin Hyman

Shanks, M. 1992. *Experiencing the past: on the character of archaeology.* London, Routledge

Tilley, C. (ed.) 1990. *Reading material culture: structuralism, hermeneutics and post-structuralism.* Oxford, Blackwell

Index